INTRODUCTION

These wills were abstracted under the auspices of the Genealogical Society of Pennsylvania in the early 1900s. Copies of these abstracts were made available to various libraries in Pennsylvania and microfilm copies made by the Genealogical Society of Utah (LDS). Recently bound photostat copies of the abstracts were offered for sale by the Genealogical Society of Pennsylvania.

We extend our appreciation to the Genealogical Society of Pennsylvania and encourage membership in the Society (1305 Locust Street, Philadelphia, PA 19107-5699), whose collections are mainly housed at the Library of the Historical Society of Pennsylvania (1300 Locust Street, Philadelphia, PA 19107). We encourage use of its holdings and facilities which are available at a modest fee.

> F. Edward Wright
> Westminster, Maryland
> 1998

ASTON, GEORGE. Phila. Merchant.
Mar. 25, 1813. Jan. 3, 1815. 5.391
To niece Ann Warder, Jr. (wife of Jeremiah Warder, Jr. and daughter of late brother Peter Aston). To nephew George Aston, Jr. (son of said late brother Peter). To children of sister Mary Madeira. Trustees and Execs.: Zaccheus Collins, Eliston Perot, Thomas Savery, all of Phila. Property in Hawkins Co., North Carolina. To nieces Esther, Maria, Sarah, Hannah and Catharine Madeira (daughters of John Madeira and my sister, Mary, his wife). To nephews George A., Charles, Jacob, Peter and William Jones Madeira (sons of said John and Mary Madeira). To cousin Hannah Evans (widow of John Evans and mother-in-law to Samuel Williamson, silver smith). To Esther Phipps (wife of Joshua Phipps and daughter of uncle, George Aston). To John Lownes, Edward Lownes and George Lownes (sons of Caleb Lownes and his late wife, Margaret). To Sarah Robeson and Elizabth Robeson (daughters of Jonathan Robeson, deceased and Sarah, his wife). To George Aston Milnor (son of Isaac Milnor of Phila). To Isabella Collins, a coloured woman (wife of Cato Collins). Guardians of the estates of minor children of said sister Mary Madeira, friends Jacob Parke and James Pemberton Parke of Phila.
Witnesses: Anne Biddle, Jacob Parke, Peter Thomson.
Codicil: July 8, 1813. To cousin Hannah Way (widow of Joshua Way and daughter of uncle, Thomas Green, deceased). To Mathilde Way and Phebe (daughters of cousin, Hannah Way).
Witnesses: Jacob Parke, Peter Thomson.
Codicil: Feb. 26, 1814. To cousin Mary Marache (wife of Solomon Marache). To Isabella Duncan and Rebecca Miles (daughters of said Mary Marache). To my gardener, Robert Braziere and to his wife, Catharine Braziere. Said nephew, Charles Madeira, lately deceased.
Witnesses: Benjamin Ferris, Peter Thomson.

OSTAIN, FRANCIS. Township of Passyunk. Co. of Phila. Farmer.
Dec. 26, 1814. Jan. 7, 1815. 5.409.
To wife, Mary Ostain. To children, Maria, Catharine, Eliza, John and Samuel Ostain.
Execs: Said wife, Mary, and friend Andrew Hannis of the Township of Moyamensing, farmer.
Witnesses: Philip Peltz, Henry Crumley.

BOYER, DOLLY. Phila. Now residing in Northern Liberties. Phila. Co.
Nov. 9, 1814. Jan. 13, 1815. 5.409.
To my three nephews William H. Reinolds, Charles Reynolds and Simon Reynolds, sons of sister Mary Reynolds, deceased. To children of brother James Boyer and sister Sarah Millard.

Execs.: Brother James Boyer, brother-in-law Thomas Millard and friend Isaac Heylin, all of Phila. Co.
Witnesses: Clement Miller, William Millard.

ROBINSON, WILLIAM. Township of Lower Dublin. Phila. Co. Taylor.
Nov. 9, 1814. Jan. 14, 1815. 5.411.
To niece Martha Austin. To niece Ann Robinson and to Mary, daughter of my niece Martha Austin, above named. To brother Jonathan Robinson. To friend John Robinson. All residue to children: John, William Tennent and Elizabeth Robinson. Friends Thomas Webster and Samuel Leech, Jr. guardians of the persons and estate of said children. Said sons to be placed with Zerech Fox of Lower Dublin, farmer, and said Samuel Leech, Jr. of Chelbenham Township, to be brought up in habits of industry.
Execs: Thomas Webster and Samuel Leech, Jr.
Witnesses: John Trunk, Isaac Dorland, Miers Fisher.

HOZEY, ISAAC. District of Southwark. Co. of Phila. Lumber Merchant.
May 24, 1811. Jan. 16, 1815. 5.414.
To wife Mary Hozey, otherwise Mary Shortall. To children by present or late wife: Jane, James, Charles, Margaret, Thomas S. and Mary Hozey. To Margaret Jones (mother to my late wife Jane Jones). To James Shortall.
Execs: Margaret Jones, Joseph Snyder, David Ware, Charles Penrose.
Witnesses: Jesse Williamson, Barnet Quinn.
Letters granted to Margart Jones.

TATEM, JEREMIAH. Phila.
Dec. 21, 1814. Jan. 24, 1815. 5.425.
To wife Mary, rents, profits, etc. of all estate. After her death, to my children.
Execs: Friend Anthony Cuthbert of Phila., mast maker, and son-in-law Daniel Smith, Jr.
Witnesses: Thomas Mitchell, James Twaddell.

HANCKEL, JOHN MICHAEL. Northern Liberties, Phila. Practitioner of Physic.
June 21, 1811. Jan. 26, 1815. 5.427.
To be buried in Friends burying ground. To wife Anna Dorethy Maria Hanckel, and at her death, to my daughter Anna Dorethy Henrietta Hanckel. After death of said wife and daughter, to my other children.
Execs: Son Christian Hanckel and friends Jacob Meyer of Phila., printer, and John Conrad of Germantown, Phila. Co.
Witnesses: Elijah Conrad, Richard Pryor.

Codicil: Jan. 2, 1815: Executors in will all absent. Appoint wife Ann
Dorothea Maria Hanckel, John Landy, Charles L. Smith.
Witnesses: Reuben Jureman, John Smith.
Letters granted to said wife.

RITTENHOUSE, ABRAHAM. Roxborough Township. Co. of Phila.
Miller.
Nov. 5, 1814. Jan. 28, 1815. 5.428.
Legacy to my housekeeper, Susan Fasoon. All residue to three sons:
Enoch, Samuel and Jacob Rittenhouse.
Execs: Said three sons.
Witnesses: John Huston, Peter Rittenhouse.

DUFFIELD, JACOB. Lower Dublin. Co. of Phila.
Jan. 12, 1815. Feb. 2, 1815. 5.430.
Provides for wife Elizabeth Duffield. To son Jacob Duffield. To
daughter Elizabeth Snyder. To daughter Mary Lukens. To daughter
Hannah Eckert, wife of Philip Eckert. To daughter Tacy Wilkenson. To
grandchildren: Jacob, Esther, William, Charles and Phebe Wilkenson,
and granddaughter Sarah Tillyer. To sons John, Amos and Jesse
Duffield.
Execs: Sons John, Amos and Jesse.
Witnesses: Jacob Sommer, James Paul, Jr.

FRESHWATER, ARGYLE. Phila. Hairdresser.
Jan. 20, 1815. Feb. 3, 1815. 5.432.
To my housekeeper, Eleanor Asborn, all my property, appointing her
my Executrix.
Witnesses: I. Lenington, Abner Avery, Henry Meyer.

HEYL, GEORGE. Township of Germantown. Co. of Phila.
June 10, 1812. Feb. 6, 1815. 5.432.
Wife Dorothy to have all estate, and after her death, to my children:
George and William Heyl, Mary Clapier, Elizabeth Johnson and
Susanna Harman.
Execs: Said wife Dorothy, sons George and William Heyl.
Witnesses: Abraham G. Claypoole, John Romeis.

FYE, ANDREW. Township of Springfield. Montgomery Co.
Wheelwright.
Jan. 20, 1806. Feb. 7, 1815. 5.434.
To grandchildren Sophy Fye, Andrew Fye and Elizabeth Fye. To son
Philip Fye. To daughter Catharine White.
Exec: Said son Philip Fye.
Witnesses: George Peirce, Jacob Bisbing.

TAYLOR, ELIZABETH. Township of Lower Dublin. Phila. Co.
Jan. 2, 1815. Feb. 11, 1815. 5.435.
To children Tacey, Mercy, Amos, Hannah, Phany and Sarah Taylor.
Execs: Brother Robert Hilborn, daughter Tacey Taylor.
Witnesses: John Robinson, Amos Hillborn.
Letters granted to Robert Hillborn.

WILLARD, JOSEPH. Byberry Township. Phila. Co.
Sept. 27, 1814. Feb. 13, 1815. 5.436.
Wife Martha Willard to have all estate during life. Four children: Thomas Willard, Benjamin Willard, Rachel Marjoram and James Willard.
Execs: Son Thomas Willard and my friend Ezra Townsend.
Witnesses: Griffith Street, Joseph Croasdale.
Letters granted to Thomas Willard.

SMYTH, FREDERICK. Roxborough. Phila. Co. Esquire.
Jan. 2, 1812. Feb. 14, 1815. 5.437.
Legacy to my domestic John Chandler and his son John Chandler. To friend's wife Elizabeth Bordley. To George Keel, my assistant on the farm at Roxborough. To Catharine, wife of said George Keel, and to their son Elias Keel. To Mrs. Deborah Logan, wife of neighbour Dr. Logan. To friend Edward Shippen Burd, Esquire. To friend James Gibson, Esquire. To friend Dr. John Redman Cone. To friend William Hamilton, Esquire.
Execs: Friends James Gibson, Esquire, Dr. John Redman Cone.
Witnesses: Archibald McCall, William Bead.
Codicil: Dec. 10, 1813. To Mrs. Owen, my housekeeper. To Mrs. Maguire.
Witnesses: Arch'd. McCall, John C. McCall.
Codicil: July 5, 1813. To William Manning, Esquire. To Mr. and Mrs. Needham. To Mr. and Mrs. Fellows. To Robert Stone, Esquire and to Mrs. Stone. To Rev. Mr. Cooper and Mrs. Cooper. To Rev. John Smith and Mrs. Smith. To Miss Smyth, daughter of late brother Affley Smith. To son of Mr. Needham to whom his parents have given my name.

TRIMBLE, MARY. Northern Liberties. Phila. Co. Singlewoman.
Feb. 4, 1815. Feb. 15, 1815. 5.441.
All my estate unto George Donnaker, late of same place (my nephew) now an officer in the Army of United States.
Execs: Brother[s] James Trimble of Harrisburgh, George Trimble of Phila.
Witnesses: Jane Sweager, Samuel Williamson.

5

SHUTE, MARY. Widow. City of Phila.
Feb. 3, 1815. Feb. 29, 1815. 5.442.
To three younger daughters of William Stevenson and to said William's youngest son, Peter Stevenson. To Ann Brady. To cousin Catherine Poltney, if she is not living, to her daughter. To son John Shute, if heard from.
Execs: Friends Nathan Sellers and William Stevenson.
Witnesses: Maryanne Wetherill, Hannah Stevenson, daughter of William Stevenson, William McFarland, affirmed.

REDWOOD, WILLIAM, the Elder, formerly of Rhode Island, now of Burlington, New Jersey.
Nov. 27, 1813. Jan. 23, 1815. 5.445.
To sister-in-law Rachel Crukshank, wife of Joseph Crukshank, of Phila. All estate in Rhode Island unto my daughter, Sarah Redwood Fisher, wife of Miers Fisher. All residue of estate to son, William Redwood, Jr.
Execs: Brother-in-law Joseph Crukshank, my grandson William Wharton.
Witnesses: Nathaniel Coleman, William Allinson, Stephen Pike.
Codicil: May 27, 1814.
Witnesses: William Andrews, Isaac Elliott, Joseph Walton, affirmed.
Letters granted to William Wharton.

HIGGINS, FANNY. Phila.
Jan. 9, 1815. Feb. 24, 1815. 5.447.
To Plim Clover of Phila., blacksmith, and his wife Hager Clover, all estate.
Execs: Jeames Johnson, painter, Plim Clover.
Witnesses: William Topham, Charles Gragin.

SMITH, WILLIAM. Phila. Tavern Keeper.
Feb. 9, 1815. Feb. 27, 1815. 5.447.
To wife Elizabeth Smith. To daughter Catharine Smith, son William Smith and child with which wife is now pregnant.
Execs: Said wife Elizabeth, friends John P. Harper, Michael Doran.
Witnesses: John Cooke, Math'w. Redmond.
Letters to Elizabeth Smith.

ELLIOTT, JOHN MADES. Phila. Waiter.
July 20, 1811. Feb. 28, 1815. 5.449.
Provides for wife Dianah.
Execs: Absolom Jones, Cyrus Porter, Peter Richmond, John Bowers, Cato Corrin.
Witnesses: Anthony Cain, Solomon Clarkson, Peter Richmond.
Letters granted to John Bowers and Cato Corrin.

CASTER, JACOB. Oxford Township. Phila. Co. Yeoman.
Feb. 11, 1815. Feb. 28, 1815. 5.450.
To wife Catharine. To children of son Henry. To son Jacob. To children of son John. To sons Isaac and George. To youngest daughter Catharine. To daughter Elizabeth. To daughter Sarah, now wife of Henry Shoch; Elizabeth, now wife of Jonathan Magargill; Hannah, now wife of John Deckart; Mary, now wife of Jacob Lutz; Christiana, now wife of William Gray.
Execs: Son Jacob, sons-in-law Jonathan Magargill, John Deckart.
Witnesses: John Deprefontaine, George Fox, William Kelly.
Letters to Jonathan Magargell, John Deckart.

JOHNSON, FRANCIS. Township of Blockley. Phila. Co.
May 3, 1805. March 1, 1815. 5.452.
To wife Alice Johnson. To daughter Mary Erwin Renshaw. To son Alexander Washington Johnson.
Sole Exec: Said wife Alice.
Said wife and friend, Joseph Reed of Phila., Trustees for portion bequeathed to daughter Mary Erwin Renshaw.
Witnesses: Josiah Randall, Eliza B. Brown.

LEVY, AARON. Phila. Gentleman.
June 28, 1802. March 1, 1815. 5.453.
To friend Charles Hall. To wife Rachel, and after her death, to adopted son Simon Gratz of Phila., merchant. To his brother Hyman Gratz. To Fanny Etting. To Joseph Gratz. To Benjamin Gratz. To Sarah Gratz. To Rebecca Gratz. To Rachel Gratz. To Rickey Hay.
Exec: Friend Frederick Beates.
Witnesses: Andrew Leinau, Abraham Stein, Philip I. Dunn.

ROUSH, JOHN. Phila.
Feb. 6, 1815. March 2, 1815. 5.455.
To nephew Jacob Carver. To niece Charlotte Seitz and Franklin Carver and John R. Carver, sons of above-named Jacob Carver. To brother Matthias Roush, and after decease of said brother, to niece Charlotte, wife of Christian C. Burklee, after her decease, to her children: Mary, Mark, Richard and Frederick Burklee. To niece Mary, sister of said Charlotte Burklee. To niece Elizabeth Weckerly, and to her son John Fisher and her daughter Hetty Armstrong, children by her first husband. To friend Robert Whitehead.
Execs: Said brother Matthias Roush, Christian C. Burklee.
Witnesses: Abraham Will, Joseph Cake.

CARTER, JASPER. Phila. Late Painter and Glazier and since, Livery Stable Keeper.

Feb. 23, 1815. March 2, 1815. 5.456.
To Ann Hughes, alias Ann Carter, who has lived with me for many years. To Jane Dwarf, bound by Indenture to me. After death of said Ann Hughes, alias Carter, all real estate to be sold, monies to my brothers and sisters: John Carter of Phila., Stable Keeper; Joseph Carter of same place, painter and glazier; Mary, wife of Edward Trimmer, now or late of London, fruiterer; Elizabeth, wife of Tilberry of London.
Execs: Friend Robert Pullen of Phila., silver plater, said Ann Hughes, alias Carter.
Witnesses: Nicholas Chevalier, Thomas Mitchell.

BROWN, JACOB. Phila. Iron Merchant.
Sept, 1809. March 3, 1815. 5.458.
To wife Esther Brown. To daughters Susanna, Charlotte and Mary Brown. Share for son George, if he is not heard from in ten years, to be divided amongst my other children. To sons Joseph and Benneville Brown. Wife, Esther, to be guardian of said daughter Susanna. After decease of said wife, daughter Catharina to be guardian. To said daughter Catharina.
Execs: Said wife Esther, son Joseph Brown.
Witnesses: Michael Steinauer, William Steinauer, R. Whitehead.
Codicil: Feb. 7, 1815. Son Benneville Brown, also to be Exec.
Witnesses: George D. B. Keim.
Letters to Joseph D. Brown, Benneville Brown.

WHEELER, JOHN. Northern Liberties. Phila. Co. Windsor Chair Maker.
Feb. 14, 1815. March 4, 1815. 5.460.
To mother Mary Knous. To brother Samuel Wheeler of county aforesaid, chair maker.
Execs: Said Mary Knous, Sam'l. Wheeler.
Witnesses: John Schlatterer, Edward D. Corfield.
Letters to Samuel Wheeler.

SMITH, JOHN. District of Southwark. Mariner.
Aug. 28, 1812. March 8, 1815. 5.461.
Estate to wife Ann Smith, appointing her Exec.
Witnesses: T. T. Lacroze, George Wine, Richard Renshaw, affirmed.

GERHARD, CONRAD. Phila. Gentleman.
July 6, 1813. March 9, 1815. 5.462.
Annuity, etc. to wife Elizabeth Gerhard. All residue to son William Gerhard.
Execs: Said son William, friend John Jordan.

Witnesses: Robert Whitehead, Jesse Oat.
John Jordan renounced.

TROTTER, WILLIAM. Phila. Merchant.
Feb. 21, 1815. March 8, 1815. 6.1.
Estate to wife Mary Trotter and my seven children: Rebecca, Daniel, Ann, Margretta C., Emmeline, Sansom William and William Trotter.
Execs: Brother Joseph, wife Mary.
Witnesses: Ann Douglass, Joseph Trotter.

SPRUNCE, PRINCE. Formerly of Duck Creek Hundred, Delaware, late of the City of Phila.
Jan. 3, 1800. March 9, 1815. 6.2.
Trustees: Friends Thomas Wistar, Abraham Garrigues, Caspar W. Haines. To mother Mary Stout (formerly a slave to John Spruney). To cousins George Miller and Prince Miller, children of my sister Rachel Miller. To friend Jonathan Trusty. To African Bethel Church of which I am a member.
Execs: Friends Jonathan Trusty, Robert Green, Richard Allen.
Witnesses: Chas. Macknet, Daniel Pastorius.

RUMMEL, GEORGE. Phila.
Feb. 21, 1815. March 13, 1815. 6.3
Estate to wife Mary Rummel, dawter Cathrine Rummel.
Execs: Said wife and daughter.
Witnesses: Rudolph Neff, Jacob Ford. Letters to Mary Rummel.

HAILER, FREDERICK. Phila. Gentleman.
Jan. 19, 1815. March 13, 1815. 6.4.
Estate to wife Christiana. Late brother-in-law Michael Shubart. To widow Shubart, wife of late brother-in-law Michael Shubart. To George Frederick Hailer, son of nephew David Hailer, deceased, and Mary, his sister. Also, Christiana Schyder and Sarah Schyder, my step-daughters.
Execs: Said wife Christiana, friends Adam Eckfeldt, Andrew Leineau.
Witnesses: Henry Kammerer, John Christian Blummer.
Codicil revokes appointment of Adam Eckfeldt and Andrew Leinau as Executors. Appoints wife Christiana Hailer, sole Executrix.
Witnesses: Same as to will.

RIDDLE, WILLIAM. District of Southwark. Baker.
Dec. 19, 1814. March 13, 1815. 6.7.
To wife Johanna Riddle. To sons John, William, Edward and James.
Execs: Friends Andrew Montgomery of said District, teacher, John C. Kelsey of Phila, accountant.
Witnesses: Richard Renshaw, Nicholas Bunting.

ROBINSON, JOHN. Jermantown Town.
March 25, 1812. March 13, 1815. 6.8.
To wife Jane Robinson, making her sole Executrix. To grandson John Robinson, when of age.
Witnesses: Samuel Wakeling, Mary Harding.

WHITE, GEORGE.
Aug. 29, 1814. March 21, 1815. 6.9.
Estate to George Alexander, appointing sold Executor.
Witnesses: Daniel Bussier, William Harvey.

SUTOR/SUTTER, ELIZABETH. District of Southwark. Phila. Co. Widow of James Sutor.
March 14, 1808. March 21, 1815. 6.10.
To granddaughter Elizabeth Thackara, daughter of Samuel and Margaret Thackara. To daughter-in-law Mary Sutor, wife of son James Whitton Sutor. To daughter Margaret Thackara, wife of said Samuel.
Execs: Son James Whitton Sutor, son-in-law Samuel Thackara, above named.
Witnesses: John Elliott Cresson, William Andrews/Andreuz.
Codicil: July 8, 1812.
Witnesses: Isaac Elliott, Elliott Cresson.
Letters to surviving Executor, Samuel Thackara.

RAY, ANDREW. District of Southwark. Phila. Co. Tavern Keeper.
March 15, 1815. March 20, 1815. 6.12.
To son Thomas Ray. To son Andrew Ray. To daughter Mary Ray. Sole Exec: Said son Thomas.
Witnesses: David Ray, Thomas McKee, Thomas Hoskin.

MARRIOTT, SARAH. Borough of Wilmington, State of Delaware.
Jan. 14, 1809. March 22, 1815. 6.13.
To Joseph Shipley, Jr. (son of my cousin Joseph Shipley). To cousin Merriman Smith, aunt Grace Smith, deceased. To Mary Newlin (daughter of cousin Sarah Newlin). To William Paxson (son of cousin Joseph Papson). To Fanny Ferris, Mary Canby and Anna Canby, daughters of cousin Martha Canby, Lydia Jones, daughter of late cousin Anna Brown. To cousin Sarah Morris. To Monthly Meeting of Women Friends in Phila. To sister-in-law Mary Marriott (widow of late brother Thomas Marriott). In trust for Executors for use of cousin Israel Paxson and his children. Residue of estate to my cousins, Anna Sysum, Martha Canby, Sarah Morris, Isaac Paxson and Anna Gillam, the three first being children of my uncle Thomas Marriott, and the two last children of my aunt Anna Paxson.
Execs: Cousins Isaac Paxson, Simon Gillam and friend Jonathan Willis.

Witnesses: James Canby, John Shipley, Merrit Canby.
Codicil: March 21, 1809. To cousin Mary Landers (sister of said cousin Isaac Paxson).
Witnesses: Same as to will. William Paxson of Phila., Iron Monger, and Richard Paxson of said city, Iron Monger, affirmed.

PHILLIPS, HENRY. Phila. District Pay Master in the U.S. Army.
March 5, 1815. March 24, 1815. 6.17.
To mother Elinor Phillips. To sister Elizabeth McGonagle. To sister Elinor McHugh. To daughter of deceased brother James. To sister Peggy McCamill. To nephew James McGonagle, Jr. Property in Phila., in Salem Co., New Jersey and in town of Baton Rouge, State of Louisiana.
Execs: Friends Edmund Kinsey, William Smiley.
Witnesses: Anthony Gale, Thomas Ashmead, Thomas Dougherty.

STOCK, PHILIP. Northern Liberties. Phila. Gardener.
March 8, 1815. April 3, 1815. 6.19.
To wife Catharine Stock, and after her death to children of son Frederick Stock, interest of same to said son during life.
Sole Exec: Said wife Catharine.
Witnesses: John Bach, Philip Nagar, Isaac Wampole, Jr.

SPIEGEL, JOHN REMIGIUS. Phila. Co. Combmaker.
Sept. 26, 1811. April 3, 1815. 6.20.
To wife Elizabeth. After death of said wife, to children. John Remigius Spiegel (a minor), the only child mentioned.
Execs: Said wife Elizabeth Spiegel, son-in-law Michael Shaffer.
Witnesses: John A. Cullman, John H. Birnbaum.

HOOD, JOHN. Phila.
Sept. 5, 1807. April 5, 1815. 6.21.
About starting for Kentucky. Father, John Hood, owned property in Harding Co., Kentucky, which is about to be vested in me, his only son. Said property I bequeath to mother, Hannah Hood, appointing her sole Executrix.
Witnesses: Daniel Dupuy, Ann Meredith, John Dupuy, Jr.

LAWRENCE, EDWARD. Phila. Inn Keeper.
March 24, 1815. April 4, 1815. 6.22.
Estate to wife Mary Lawrence and to her heirs. Said wife sole Executrix.
Witnesses: Joseph Klapp, George Yeoward.

HARRIS, JOHN.
April 13, 1809. April 10, 1815. 6.23.
To wife Jane Harris, whom I appoint sole Executrix. After death of said wife, property to John, the son of William Riddle our nephew, he to provide for my adopted child, Alexander Harris Morrison.
Witnesses: Mathew Weaver, William Weir.

DONOVAN, JEREMIAH.
Jan. 1, 1815. April 14, 1815. 6.25.
To Jeremiah, Catharine, Margaret, Daniel and Henry Donovan, children of Daniel and Frances Donovan of Ross Carbury, County Cork, Ireland, and in case of the death of either of the above legatees, the share to two other children of deceased brother Daniel Donovan. To Jeremiah Donovan, son of deceased brother. To Florence Donovan of Phila. (now an apprentice to the Tanning business in Bucks Co.). Catharine Newell, sister of said Jeremiah, having neglected me, I exclude her. To friend Mrs. Marg't. Donovan of Old Court Skibbereer. To sister Mrs. McCarthy of Skibbereer. To be buried in St. Peter's, no announcement of death or burial in newspapers.
Execs: Friend Robert Adams, Daniel W. Coxe.
Prudent Casamajor, Jr. and Daniel W. Coxe, affirmed.

DEPERVAIN, HENRY. Passyunk Township. Phila. Co. Farmer.
March 11, 1815. April 15, 1815. 6.26.
To wife Margaret Depervain. To son Peter Depervain. To Elizabeth Shutt. To Catharine Summers. Executors to dispose of plantation in lower part of Passyunk Township, proceeds to my six children: Peter Depervain, Catharine Young, Margaret Stuart, Sophia Stinger (wife of Frederick Stinger), Mary Westinberger and Susanna Simon.
Execs: Friends Philip Peltz and John Garritt, both of Passyunk.
Witnesses: David Lentz, John Maag.

BIAYS, JOSEPH. Belonging to the Private armed ship, "Young Wasp" of Phila. Lemuel Rawley, Captain.
Dec., 1813. April 17, 1815. 6.28.
Estate to my friend Barnard Payne of Phila., grocer.
Exec: Said Barnard Payne.
Witnesses: Josiah Ward, Peter Love.

KERLIN, SARAH. Burlington, New Jersey. Widow.
Nov. 20, 1811. April 20, 1815. 6.28.
To niece Debby Ann Lynch, daughter of John and Hannah Kerlin, deceased, and to her heirs. To niece Margaretta Lynch, daughter of John and Hannah Lynch. To William Lynch, Jr., and Caroline Lalls Lynch, children of William and Debby Ann Lynch.

Execs: Before mentioned Margaretta Lynch and William Lynch, her uncle.
Witnesses: Nath'l. Coleman, Elizabeth Coleman, Mary Decow.

BONACKER, JACOB. Northern Liberties. Phila. Co. Distiller.
Nov. 4, 1813. April 20, 1815. 6.30.
All estate to Jacob Klazer of same place, yeoman.
Exec: Said Jacob Klazer.
Witnesses: George Mill, Henry Weaver.

BAYNE, ROBERT. Phila. Coach Maker.
March 27, 1815. April 20, 1815. 6.31.
To wife Hester and to son Samuel Plat Bayne, when of age. Nephew John Bayne and his sister, Hester Bayne, children of deceased brother Charles Bayne.
Execs: Friends Heronimus Warner, Thomas Hennesy of Phila.
Thomas Hennesy also to be Guardian of said son.
Witnesses: Jacob Lybrand, Frederick Beates.

HOFFMAN, WOLFGANG. Phila. Combmaker.
Feb. 10, 1815. April 21, 1815. 6.32.
To wife Maria Phillipbina Hoffman and to my eight children: John, Mary, Ann Catharine, William, Samuel, Maria, Sophia and George.
Sole Exec: Said wife Maria Phillipbina Hoffman.
Witnesses: John Mingle, Isaac Wampole

COURTNEY, JOHN. Phila. Co. Mariner.
July 28, 1814. April 24, 1815. 6.34.
All estate to wife Ann Courtney of said county.
Exec: Said wife Ann.
Witnesses: George Colwell, Richard Palmer.

JUGIEZ, MARTIN. Phila. Carver.
July 19, 1814. April 25, 1815. 6.35.
Legacy to nephew Jerome Jugiez. All residue to friend John Bernard and to his heirs.
Exec: Said friend John Bernard.
Codicil: July 19, 1814. Legacy left to Jerome Jugiez to remain in hands of Executor John Bernard until Martin Jugiez, son of Jerome Jugiez shall attain age of 21 years.
Witnesses to Will and Codicil: George Glentworth, Joshua Robinson.

HOWARD, THOMAS. Phila. Lumber Merchant.
April 18, 1815. April 26, 1815. 6.37.

To wife Sarah P. Howard. To son Caleb N. Howard. To daughters Sarah N. Conway, Edith N. Howard and Deborah Howard. To son Charles Howard. To daughters Emma and Eliza Howard.
Execs: Samuel Newbold, my first wife's brother, and Anthony M. Buckley, my present wife's brother.
Witnesses: Benjamin Cooper, Howard Malcom, Peter Thomson.

CONWAY, BERNARD. Phila. Storekeeper.
April 24, 1815. April 27, 1815. 6.39.
To wife Harriet Conway. To mother Catherine Conway of Ireland. To half-brothers, John and Daniel Conway, and half-sister, Catherine Conway of Ireland. To Patrick Conway, son of Daniel Conway. To Timothy Harran. To Bernard Conway, Catherine Conway and Patrick Conway, three children of Niell Conway.
Execs: John McGlinsy of Southwark, Thomas Burke of Phila., Storekeepers.
Witnesses: Nathaniel Burt, John Johnston.

ELMSLIE, JOHN. Phila. Formerly Turner, now not in business.
April 10, 1815. April 28, 1815. 6.40.
To daughters Sarah Burling, Elizabeth Garrigues, wife of Benjamin P. Garrigues, and Hannah Paleske. To my nine granddaughters, five of whom are the children of daughter Sarah Burling, three the children of Elizabeth Garrigues and one the child of Hannah Paleske.
Execs: Friends Joseph Lownes, Joseph S. Lewis, City of Phila.
Witnesses: John Hallowell, William Parker.

ALEXANDER, JOHN B. Phila. Merchant.
July 18, 1811. April 28, 1815. 6.42.
To my housekeeper, Juliana Whittemore. To my adopted child Juliana Alexander. To children of my sister Ann Fisher. To children of my brother James Alexander. To children of brother-in-law Joseph Burden. To mother Lilly Cunningham. To Joseph Burden, Jacob Mitchell and Robert Connell, in trust for use of sister Ann Fisher. Should said Ann again live with her husband John Fisher, the estate left to her shall be given to her children, to the children of brother James Alexander and to the children of brother-in-law Joseph Burden.
Execs: Said Joseph Burden, Jacob Mitchell, Robert Connell.
Witnesses: I. H. Levering, George Walter, Jacob Colladay, John Rigler, Joseph Laning.

KEYSER, JOHN. N. Liberties. Phila. Yeoman.
March 28, 1815. May 1, 1815. 6.44.
Wife, Susanna Keyser, shall have use, income, etc. of all estate. After her death, to my children.

Execs: Wife Susanna Keyser, my friend John Bender/Binder, Sr., storekeeper, Northern Liberties, Jacob Belsterling, innkeeper of Northern Liberties.
Witnesses: I. Henry, Ch. Helmuth, Frederick Daniel Terrier.

MC CULLOCH, ANN. Now of Lower Merion Township, Montgomery Co.
April 14, 1815. May 4, 1815. 6.45.
To Rev'd. Horatio Gates Jones for use of the new Baptist Church in Lower Merion. To Christiana Bickham Neill, daughter of Lewis Neill of Phila., merchant. To Thomas Neill, son of Lewis Neill, aforesaid. Lewis Neill of Phila., merchant, whom I appoint sole Executor, to have residue of estate.
Witnesses: Francis Worley, Charles Thomson, Mary Shoeste.

HEIT, PETER. Northern Liberties, Phila. Co. Victualler.
April 16, 1815. May 5, 1815. 6.46.
To wife Augusta Maria Heit, the property whereon I live on Germantown turnpike, and after her decease to my children, three sons and one daughter. If said wife should marry, said tenement to be under care of my brother-in-law Martin Lauber, until youngest is of age.
Sole Exec: Said Martin Lauber.
Witnesses: Daniel Ley, Abraham H. Poul, Jacob Krider.

SELTZER, HENRY, SR. Northern Liberties. Phila. Yeoman.
May 3, 1815. May 8, 1815. 6.47.
To wife Elizabeth Seltzer. To son Henry. Executors to sell property, proceeds to my children.
Execs: Brother-in-law Casper Schlatter, my son Henry.
Witnesses: Seth Collom, Henry Statzell.

BLAIR, ROBERT. Phila.
April 24, 1815. May 11, 1815. 6.48.
Articles in possession of Ann Church to be delivered to my sister Elizabeth Blair. Annuity to said Ann, so long as she remains single. My gun to John Stewart. All residue to said sister Elizabeth Blair, whom I appoint Executrix.
Witnesses: James Smith, William Williams, James Madison Porter.

BLAKE, JONATHAN. Phila.
Aug. 9, 1814. Nov. 28, 1814. 6.49.
All property to wife Sarah Blake, if she marries to be divided between her and my two children Leven Blake and Sarah Blake, if both children die, their share to son-in-law Joseph Bower and wife.

Witnesses: William Smith, Kime Robinson.
N.B. I have so far altered my Will as to allow my daughter Hannah Bower my cradle and two dollars.

SPECHT, GEORGE. Northern Liberties. Phila. Grocer.
April 27, 1815. May 15, 1815. 6.49.
All estate to wife Elizabeth, she to pay 6 and 1/4 cents of U.S. money to each of my first and second cousins if demanded within two years after my decease.
Execs: Said wife Elizabeth Specht, friend Leonard Stricker of Northern Liberties.
Witnesses: John Miller, Adam Minser.

BODLY, THOMAS. Phila.
Feb. 22, 1815. May 16, 1815. 6.50.
To wife Hagar Bodly, land in the borough of Frankford, granted to me by Philip Thomas and Ann, his wife, of the said borough, also all other property of which I am possessed.
Exec: Said wife Hagar Bodly.
Witnesses: John Lodor, Jane Lodor, Edwin A. Atlee.

STILES, JOHN. Northern Liberties. Phila. Co. Lumber Merchant.
May 4, 1815. May 19, 1815. 6.51.
Wife Nancy. Seven children, Henry, John, Mary Ann, Joseph, James, William and Nancy.
Execs: Friends Jesse Cleaver, William Gregory, Peter Keyser, George Knorr and my said wife, Nancy, and eldest son, Henry.
Witnesses: Thomas Stroud, Isaac Williams, Caleb Carmalt, Jr.

FALCONER, SARAH. Phila. Widow of Nathaniel Falconer, late of said city.
July 31, 1810. May 20, 1815. 6.54.
To friends Joseph Crukshank of said city, printer and stationer, Peter Thomson of said city, conveyancer in trust for relation Susanna Miller (wife of John Miller and daughter of late Hester Hewlings). To three children of Susanna Miller by her former husband: William Preston, John Preston and Hester Preston. To friend Joseph Moulder of Phila. To four nephews: Alexander Pratt, Abraham Pratt, Thomas Pratt and Nathaniel Falconer Pratt (sons of brother Abraham Pratt, late of Long Island, in the West Indies).
Execs: Said Joseph Crukshank, Peter Thomson.
Witnesses: Conrad Gerhard, Charles Thomson.
Codicil: July 30, 1813. To said Executors in trust for Monthly Meeting of Society of Friends and for the First Baptist Church in Phila. To

friend Ann Powell. In case of her death before me, then to her sister Martha Powell.
Witnesses: Conrad Gerhard, Peter Thomson.

OXENER, PETER. Northern Liberties. Phila. Farmer.
Oct. 30, 1781. April 27, 1815. 6.59.
To brothers Isaac Oxener and Frederick Oxener and to sisters Anna Maria, the wife of Christian Kafe, and Magdalen, the wife of Henry Dietz, all of Karscheim on Brem in Zeller Thal in Germany, all said legacies to be paid out of estate in said Karscheim. All residue of estate to wife Barbara Oxener.
Execs: Said wife, Barbara, friends Frederick Shinckl of Phila., merchant, Peter Smith of Northern Liberties, aforesaid, farmer.
Witnesses: Henry Lotz, Christopher Baker, Christian Hubbert, George A. Baker affirmed.
Letters to Barbara Oxener, the surviving Executrix.

WEST, SAMUEL. Phila. Lumber Merchant.
April 6, 1815. May 25, 1815. 6.60.
Estate to wife Anna West, and my seven children: Thomas G. West, Robert L. West, Mary West, Samuel West, Elizabeth West, Sarah West and Anna West.
Execs: Said wife Anna West, Benjamin Rulon.
Witnesses: Preston C. Firth, Jonathan Conard, Charles C. West.
Letters to Benjamin Rulon.

HOUMAN, MARY. Moyamensing Township. Phila. Co. Spinster.
Jan. 12, 1815. May 29, 1815. 6.62.
After death of mother, Mary Houman, all my real estate to be sold, proceeds to sister Barbara Smith and my three nephews: John, George and William Houman, sons of deceased brother Joseph Houman.
Exec: Friend Thomas Parker of Phila., watch and clock maker.
Witnesses: Thomas Hoskin, Michael Schinder.

SNYDER, CATHARINE. Northern Liberties. Phila. Widow.
May 4, 1815. May 30, 1815. 6.63.
To sons William and Lewis all residue of estate including my interest in estate of my father, George Dunnot, deceased. To daughter Catharine and to Elizabeth Norman, Hannah Wynecope, late Norman and John Joseph Norman, children of late daughter Margaret. To son-in-law Joseph Norman for the use of daughter Susan Goodwin. After her death, to her two children, Elizabeth Goodwin and James Goodwin.
Execs: Joseph Norman and his son, John Joseph Norman.
Witnesses: Robert Whitehead, John Jones.

GURNEY, FRANCIS. Phila. Merchant.
May 8, 1815. June 1, 1815. 6.64.
To Francis Gurney Roche, son of Edward and Maria Roche. To
Elizabeth Roche, daughter of said Edward and Maria. To relation Maria
and to her husband, Edward B. Roche. To sister Martha Lelly. To niece
Sarah Lalley. To friend and partner Daniel Smith. To my namesake,
Francis Gurney Smith. To namesake Gurney Smith, son of John S.
Smith. To my wife Mary Gurney, my place on Shippens Lane, called
Cherry Grove. After death of my wife, to be divided amongst my three
children: Jane, Elizabeth and Martha. Daughter Jane, said wife, Mary,
and friends Daniel Smith and George Sheaff, Guardians of children
Elizabeth and Martha.
Execs: Said wife, Mary, son-in-law Charles A. Poulson, friends Daniel
Smith, George Sheaf, James S. Smith.
Witnesses: R. L. Smith, Eliza Smith, Ann Ritchie.
Letters to Charles A. Poulson, Daniel Smith, George Sheaff, James G.
Smith.

STOW, LAZARUS. Phila.
May 30, 1815. June 2, 1815. 6.67.
To sister Mary Stow. After death of said sister, to my two nephews,
Samuel Stow and Isaac Stow.
Sole Exec: Brother Charles Stow.
Witnesses: Lloyd Mifflin, Joseph M. Paul.

BROWN, ELIZABETH. Phila. Widow.
May 23, 1815. May 30, 1815. 6.69.
To son-in-law John Brown, Esq. All residue of estate to Rev. Robert
Blackwell and said John Brown, upon trust for Sophia Huber, widow,
who resides with me and after her decease, for the benefit of Elizabeth
Huber, Sophia Huber, Mary Huber and Isaac Huber, children of said
Sophia Huber, first named. Said Trustees to be Executors.
Witnesses: Hannah Blackwell, James Gibson.

MC ANNAL, WILLIAM.
May 28, 1815. June 5, 1815. 6.70.
To wife Isabel. To eldest son William. To second son John. To grandson
William McAnnal. To nephew William McAnnal. To son James.
Execs: Gabriel Holmes, Carpenter and John S. Furey, Schoolmaster,
both of Phila.
Witnesses: Andrew Bailey, Charles Furey.

PARKER, THOMAS. Southwark. Yeoman.
May 20, 1815. June 6, 1815. 6.71.

To wife Anne Parker, all my property and after her decease, to my
oldest son Thomas, Henry, Mary Jane and Ann's children.
Sole Exec: Wife Anne. William Gibson, Assistant Exec.
Witnesses: John Turnbull, James Gibson.

PFLAUME, FRANCIS. Northern Liberties. Phila. Baker.
June 12, 1813. May 9, 1815. 6.71.
Wife Catharine Pflaume to have use, income, etc. of estate. After death
or intermarriage, to daughter Elizabeth Pflaume.
Execs: Said wife Catharine, friend Abraham Resch of Phila, merchant.
After death or intermarriage of wife, said Abraham Resch to be
Guardian of daughter Elizabeth.
Witnesses: Robert Whitehead, Christian Bethausen, Charles Robinson.
Letters to Catharine Pflaume.

LEGARE, ANN. Phila. Spinster.
June 10, 1815. June 21, 1815. 6.73.
To Jane Ludlam, wife of James Ludlam of Cape May Co., New Jersey,
and to her sister Ann Retchie, all my wearing apparel. To Juliana
Poulson and Charles Smith (children of Daniel Smith of said city,
merchant).
Sole Exec: Friend Daniel Smith.
Witnesses: Sarah Walker, Catharine Hayes.

HUMMEL, DAVID. Northern Liberties. Phila. Yeoman.
May 23, 1815. June 20, 1815. 6.73.
Wife Margaret Hummel to have use, interest, etc. of all estate.
Daughter Agnes Hummel to have a fetter bed, bedding, etc. After
decease of said wife, estate shall be sold and divided between my
children or their heirs.
Execs: Said wife Margaret Hummel, my friend John Rickert, grocer, of
Northern Liberties.
Witnesses: Jacob Belsterling, Anthony Freed.
Exec. affirmed June 20, 1815.

LINDSAY, ELIZABETH. Phila. Widow.
June 20, 1815. June 26, 1815. 6.74.
To sister Hannah McConnell. To sister Susanna Jones. To niece
Margaret Dixon. To nephew Matthew McConnell. To Eliza McConnell,
daughter of nephew Thomas McConnell. To friend Elizabeth Brown.
After decease of said sisters, all residue of estate to four children of
sister Hannah McConnell: Thomas McConnell, Elizabeth McConnell,
Margaret Dixon and Matthew McConnell.
Sole Exec: Said nephew Thomas McConnell.
Witnesses: Ebenezer Betts, Amos Holahan.

STONEMETZ, JACOB. Northern Liberties. Phila. Brickmaker.
April 7, 1807. June 29, 1815. 6.76.
To wife Rachel Stonemetz and my three children, Jacob Stonemetz, Jr., William Stonemetz and Elizabeth Stonemetz, I bequeath property granted to me by William Morris and Sarah, his wife, William Shippen and wife, Thomas Willing and Ann, his wife, David Rose and wife, Jacob Benner and wife, James Chevalier, Everard Bolton and wife, Philip S. Bunting and wife, James Logan by Paul Sturmfels and wife, Benjamin Hooten and wife, Dr. John Kearsley, Jr., Edward Bonsall and wife, Bowyer Brooke and wife, John Hanchman, Jr., and wife, Charles Meckelburgh and wife, Thomas Paul and wife, Jacob Waspe and wife, Thomas Willing and wife, Jacob Coats and wife. Ground released to me from Thomas Robinson and wife, and by release between John Kessler and myself.
Execs: Two sons Jacob and William Stonemetz.
Witnesses: William Tod, Robert Whitehead, Benjamin Brown.
Codicils: March 27, 1810, March 15, 1811, November 13, 1811. Ground laid out for family burying place in Northern Liberties, said lot to remain as a family burial ground.
Witnesses: Robert Whitehead, Thomas Holme, Samuel Volans, Jacob Meitte, Richard Yardley, Joseph Harker.

WILSON, SARAH. Phila. Widow.
June 23, 1815. June 30, 1815. 6.83.
To three grandchildren: Sarah, Louisa and Matilda Saulmier, children of late daughter Mary. In trust for daughter-in-law Mary Wilson, wife of son Joel W. Wilson, with whom I live. After her decease, to heirs of said son, Joel W. Wilson.
Execs: Friends John Milner, Thomas Hart. Said Thomas Hart to be Trustee for purposes before mentioned.
Witnesses: Isaac W. Blanchard, Elisha Smith.

CURRY, CHRISTOPHER. District of Southwark. Co. of Phila. Grocer.
June 22, 1815. July 3, 1815. 6.85.
To wife Eleanor Curry. To son George and to daughter Mary, five dollars each. All residue of estate to my children: John, Thomas, Jane, William and Elizabeth and to my grandson James King Curry, who now lives with me. Sons Thomas and John to be Guardians of the minor children and of said grandson James.
Execs: Said wife Eleanor Curry, son John Curry.
Witnesses: Thomas Mitchell, Samuel Leddon.

CRONEN, ELEANOR. At present of Phila., but formerly of Bristol in the United Kingdom of Great Britain and Ireland.
May 6, 1813. July 20, 1815. 6.86.

All monies to which I am entitled from Father John Cronen, who resided near London, I bequeath to Mary Foulke of Phila., widow, whom I appoint sole Executrix.
Wit: Joseph Pepper, John McGuigan.

TOWELL, JOHN. District of Southwark, State of Pennsylvania.
March 25, 1815. July 18, 1815. S.87.
To wife Jane Towell, daughter Jane Patterson and son William Towell. Execs: Said wife Jane, my friend John Elliott of said District.
Witnesses: Henry Stork, Richard Renshaw. Letters to Jane Towell.

TORR, JOHN. City of Phila.
June 30, 1810. July 21, 1815. 6.88.
To wife Hannah. To daughter Rebecca. To daughter Elizabeth. To sons Joseph, John, Josiah, Jaboel. To granddaughter Hannah Atkinson. To granddaughter Rebecca Evens, daughter of my daughter Elizabeth. Execs: Two sons Joseph and John Torr.
Witnesses: Abraham Lower, Andrew Ashton.

WISTAR, SARAH. Phila. Spinster.
Jan. 23, 1815. July 28, 1815. 6.90.
To nephew Richard Wistar, property devised to me by my father, Caspar Wistar. Should he die during my life, then to his son Richard. To nephew Dr. Caspar Wistar, the property whereon I live. To nephew John Wistar. To nephew Thomas Wistar. To Caspar Wistar, son of said nephew John Wistar, and to the brothers and sisters of said Caspar. To Caspar Wistar and his brothers and sisters, children of said nephew Thomas Wistar. To all my nephews and nieces: Elizabeth Miller, Catharine Bache, Luke W. Morris, Sarah Wistar, wife of Richard Wistar, Caspar W. Morris, Isaac W. Morris, Israel W. Morris, Catharine W. Morris and Catharine Sharpless. To niece Elizabeth Shotwell. To children of niece Sarah Davids. To children of niece Sarah Davids, deceased. To nephew Luke W. Morris and to his son Samuel Morris. To Catharine, Richard and Sarah Wistar, children of said niece Sarah Wistar, wife of said nephew Richard. To nephew Caspar W. Morris. To nephews Isaac W. Morris, Israel W. Morris, nieces Catharine W. Morris, Sarah Pennock, Catharine Sharpless, nephew Reuben Haines. To friend, Rebecca Jones. To John Wistar and Thomas Stewardson in trust for school education and religious instruction under care of Monthly Meeting of Friends in Pennsylvania and New Jersey. To nephew Thomas Wistar and Roberts Vaux in trust. To Catharine Morris and Hannah Lewis for the house of Industry. To Dr. Caspar Wistar for use of Phila. Dispensary. To Catharine W. Morris and Elizabeth Howell. To niece Sarah Wistar, Jr. To Sarah Morris, daughter of Luke Morris. To Caspar Morris, son of Caspar W. Morris,

Caspar Morris, son of Israel W. Morris. To Caspar Pennock and to Caspar Sharpless. All residue to Isaac W. Morris, son of nephew Isaac W. Morris, Hannah Morris, daughter of nephew Israel W. Morris, Sarah Pennock, daughter of niece Sarah Pennock and Elizabeth Morris, Mary Morris, Sarah Morris and Hannah Morris, daughters of nephew Luke W. Morris.
Execs: Luke W. Morris, Isaac W. Morris.
Witnesses: Zachariah Poulson, John Poulson, both of Phila., printers.
Codicil: March 31, 1815. Since publishing my Will, nephew John Wistar has died. Legacy devised to him, I bequeath to Mary Davis, Charlotte Wistar and Hannah Wistar, three of the daughters of said nephew, John Wistar, deceased.
Witnesses: Same as to Will.

MARTIN, JOHN. Phila. Carter.
July 21, 1815. July 29, 1815. 6.95.
To wife Elizabeth Martin and two children Thomas and Mary Ann Martin.
Execs: Friends George Peterman of said city, flour merchant, and Samuel Fox of same place, brick maker.
Witnesses: William Griffith, William Rastor.

GRAY, JOHN. Phila. Taylor.
July 29, 1815. Aug. 1, 1815. 6.97.
To my brother George Gray in the Kingdom of Ireland. To brother William Gray. To sister Nancy Gray and to sister Margaret Brady. To brother William's lawful children, which I believe to be five. To brother William's illigitimate or natural child, Jane Gray. To sister Margaret Brady's three children. To Mrs. Margaret Sproul and her three daughters. Money in the funded debt of Fourth Presbyterian Church to remain in said funds forever. To friend the Rev. George Potts. To friend Hugh Sloan. To friend Alexander Miller's son, David. To brother William's son, John Gray. To friend Charles Hill. To friend Adam Reid. To John Sproule.
Execs: Rev. George Potts, Adam Reid, Charles Hill.
Witnesses: Henry McCully, Andrew Montgomery.

OWEN, PATRICK. Northern Liberties. Phila. Grocer.
Oct. 5, 1811. Aug. 1, 1815. 6.98.
To wife Mary Owen, whom I appoint sole Executrix.
Witnesses: Robert Whitehead, Henry Froust.

HAY, JOHN. Phila. Inn Keeper.
Feb. 23, 1808. Aug. 2, 1815. 6.99.

To son William. To wife Catharine. Late brother Lawrence Herbert, deceased. To Evangelical Lutheran Congregation of St. John's Church in city and vicinity of Phila. To nephew Francis Hay. To Elizabeth and Catharine Cressman, daughters of my wife's sister, Elizabeth Cressman. Land in Berks Co.
Execs: Friends Jacob Chrystler, Isaac Wampole.
Witnesses: John Singer, William Peirsol.

CUNNINGHAM, ROBERT. Phila. Weaver.
June 4, 1814. July 18, 1815. 6.102.
To wife Sarah Cunningham. To Rosewell Graves and Nicholas B. Lyon of city of New York in trust for son Matthew Cunningham and his family.
Execs: Wife Sarah Cunningham, said Rosewell Graves, Nicholas B. Lyon.
Witnesses: Robert Walker, Daniel C. Ellis.

LESHER, CATHRINE. Oxford Township. Phila. Co.
July 3, 1815. Aug. 10, 1815. 6.102.
To sister Rachel Retzer, with whom I live. To sister Elizabeth Dickerson.
Exec: Sister Rachel Retzer.
Witnesses: Jacob Deal, Jacob Harper.

MOFFETT, ROBERT. Phila. Waggoner.
July 18, 1815. Aug. 12, 1815. 6.103.
Property in Phila. to be sold when youngest daughter is of age, monies to daughters Sarah, Rachel and Frances.
Execs: Charles Smith, David Montgomery.
Witnesses: Mary Carpenter, Charles Keyser.

LUGAR, JACOB. Township of Northern Liberties. Phila. Farmer.
July 19, 1815. Aug. 14, 1815. 6.104.
To wife Elizabeth and children Christopher Lugar and John Lugar.
Exec: Elizebeth Lugar.
Witnesses: Christian Hubbert, Jesse T. Hallowell.

WILSON, JOSEPH. Formerly residing in Phila., U.S.A. Now of the city of Dublin. Merchant and American Consul.
Feb. 13, 1809 (Dublin) May 7, 1815. 6.105.
To nephew James Lecky. To Rev. James Horner and Nathaniel Colvill of the city of Dublin, Esq., in trust for children of said nephew James Lecky and for children of niece Catharine Callwell, by her present husband, James Callwell. To James Crawford, Jr., and Samuel Keith, Esq. of Phila., U.S.A. in trust for children of the late Joseph Welsh or

Walsh, of Phila., grocer, being now or late three in number: John H., Elizabeth, Annabella Walsh, their mother, Mrs. Elizabeth Walsh or Welsh, now or lately of Phila., to be their Guardian. To nieces Mrs. Isabella McKenny and Mrs. Maria Callwell. To Mrs Anne Burbon, formerly Anne Wilson. To Mrs. Mary Quinton, wife of Richard Quinton, now or late of Lower Armond Quag. To Sarah Montgomery of Newry, formerly Sarah Moore. To Chichester Bickerstaff and Gay Moore of Newry, merchants, in trust for William Montgomery (a minor), son of said Mrs. Sarah Montgomery. Mrs. Jane Gordon, wife to Alexander Gordon of Dublin, and their son Samuel Gordon. To Miss Esther White now or lately residing in my family. To Miss Jane Haslett, daughter of James Haslett of Malindober, near Colerain. To Rev. James Horner. To wife Elizabeth Wilson. To William Snell Magee and Nathaniel Callwell, Esquires, of Dublin, as Trustees for my children by said wife Elizabeth: Susannah, Lellias, Robert and any child that may be yet born. To Friends Bartholomew Mazier and Nathaniel Callwell, Esquires, of Dublin, in trust for daughter Sarah Wilson and for son Thomas Wilson. Late mother, Mrs. Catherine Wilson. Partner in business, Henry D. Brooke. To John Bradley, bookkeeper and clerk in my office. Wife Elizabeth to be Executrix and Guardian of the Persons of my children by her.
Execs: Friends Bartholomew Maziere, Nathaniel Callwell, Esquires, of Dublin. Son Thomas, if he lives to the age of twenty-five, to be one of the Executors.
Witnesses: Daniel Stewart of Dublin, Barrister-at-Law, William Watson, John Williams.
Codicil: March 13, 1809.
Witnesses: William Watson, John Williams.
Codicil: March 13, 1809.
Witnesses: Robert Lyons, Charles Ryan, Mark Lalon.
Codicil: April 15, 1809.
Witnesses: Thomas Wilson, Henry D. Brooke.

WHARTON, MARY. Phila. Gentlewoman.
Aug. 25, 1787. Aug. 12, 1815. 6.120.
To sister Rachael Crispen, wife of William Crispen, of Phila. To four nieces: Mary Crispen, Sarah Crispen, Hester Crispen, Rachael Crispen, daughters of said sister, Rachael Crispen - lot in Wiccacoa Township, in Phila, willed to me by late aunt Mary Wharton, deceased of said city.
Execs: Brother John Wharton, friend Samuel Caldwell, both of Phila.

DELAVAU, JOHN. District of Southwark. Phila. Co. Shipwright.
March 14, 1815. Aug. 16, 1815. 6.122.
To wife Barbara Delavau and two daughters Hannah and Susan Delavau. Partner in business Robert Burton. To second wife, Barbara,

and friend John Coulter, of Phila., merchant, in trust for use of five
children: Isaac Delavau, Ann Black, Hannah Delavau, Maria Oliver and
Susan Delavau, and the children of deceased daughter, Margaret
Bryant. Friend John Coulter to be Guardian of such of my children
under age.
Execs: Said wife Barbara Delavau, John Coulter.
Witnesses: Benjamin Tilghman, Thomas Singleton.

SIDE, MARGARET. (Margaret Knous), wife of William Side of
Northern Liberties. Phila. Yeoman.
Nov. 14, 1808. Aug. 19, 1815. 6.124.
Property bounded by ground late of Benjamin Knous, deceased, Mary
Dutton and Daniel Barnes. Property to son William Serls, daughter
Mary Thompson, granddaughters Margaret Thompson and Sarah
Thompson, grandson George McGee.
Execs: Friends John Sharp, Esq., Charles Dewees, my son William
Serls.
Witnesses: John Taylor, Jonathan White, John Watts.
Letters to Chas. Dewees and Wm. Serls.

MILLER, JOHN JACOB. Seaman, lately serving on board the U.S.
Frigate, "Constitution," Charles Stewart, Esq., Commander.
Aug. 7, 1815. Aug. 18, 1815. 6.126.
All estate to brother, Philip Miller, of Phila., printer.
Exec: Said Philip Miller.
Witnesses: Conrad Seyfert, John Ormrods.

SCHOLFIELD, ABRAHAM. Township of Lower Dublin, Phila. Co.
Aug. 8, 1815. Aug. 24, 1815. 6.127.
Estate to be sold, proceeds to wife, Frances Scholfield, and two
daughters, Elizabeth and Mary Scholfield.
Execs: Friends Isaac Bolton, James Paul, Jr.
Witnesses: John Robbins, Joseph Yonker.

BROWN, SETH. District of Southwark, Pennsylvania. Mariner.
Sept. 1, 1812. Aug. 24, 1815. 6.127.
All estate to wife Elizabeth Brown, whom I appoint Executrix.
Witnesses: John West, John McLenchy, Richard Renshaw, Esq.,
affirmed.

MILLER, JOHN A. Northern Liberties. Phila. Skin Dresser.
Aug. 15, 1815. Aug. 24, 1815. 6.128.
Legacies to Anthony Z. Brown and Sarah Christine, both minors living
with Anthony Zahrens. To Richard Lee (also a minor), living with me,
in the family of Charles Stricker.

Exec: Friend William Bruner of said Liberties, skin dresser.
Witnesses: Jonathan Carmalt, Jr., Caleb Carmalt, Jr.

MINK, ELIZABETH. Township of Passyunk.
Aug. 7, 1815. Sept. 2, 1815. 6.129.
My place to husband; after his death, to son John, when of age, he to pay annuity to daughter Mary. If said children leave no issue, my place shall belong to Philip Mink, Sr.
Witnesses: Jacob Lusher, Edward Pole, Jr.

MAY, ELIZABETH.
April 8, 1815. Sept. 5, 1815. 6.130.
Former husband Frederick Greiner, deceased. Legacies to friend George Reinboth, son of Frederick Reinboth of Phila. To friend Elizabeth Cook. To friend Elizabeth Sena. To Mary Bower. To my husband, Adam May, whom I appoint Executor.
Witnesses: Adam May, Joseph Simmons, Isaac Wampole.

BRIGGS, MARY. Phila.
Jan. 15, 1815. Aug. 1, 1815. 6.131.
To daughter Hannah Garrigues, to be divided between her children. To son Isaac Briggs. To daughter Elizabeth Lukens, above legacies payable by Isaac Ashton. To said daughter Hannah Garrigues, the remainder of property on condition of her maintaining my sister Elizabeth Ashton.
Execs: Sons William Garrigues, Isaac Briggs, Samuel Lukens.
Witnesses: Israel Maule, John Greaven.
Letters to William Garrigues.

SHARP, RICHARD. Late of the Island of Barbados, now of Phila.
Aug. 10, 1811. April 20, 1815. 6.247.
To sister Mrs. Martha Mason, late of Barbados, now of Phila. (Widow), and for her four children: Mary Jane Mason, Richard S. Mason (her eldest son), George Mason and Henry Michael Mason. To children of my relation Thomas Sharp of the Parish of St. Philip, in the Island of Barbados. To children of relation Michael Hicks Sharp, deceased, brother to above-mentioned Thomas Sharp, formerly of the Parish of Christ Church in Barbados. To Sarah Mason, daughter of William Mason, deceased (Planter and Overseer of Barbados), by his first wife, and to her sister Mihitabel Richardson, formerly Mihitabel Mason, daughter of said William, by first wife, and to their brother William Henry Mason (son of said William, by his first wife), and to his children. To relations: Patience, Sally, Betsey and Samuel Baker, and to Ann, daughter of the above-named Patience of the Parish of St. George in Barbados. To children of Richard S. Baker, late of Barbados, deceased, and brother of above-mentioned Patience, Sally, Betsey and

Samuel. To Elizabeth Frances Pollard, daughter of Armel Henry Pollard and Jane, his wife, and my God-daughter, of Barbados. To friend Mrs. Frances Cragg, relict of William Cragg, Esq., deceased, of Barbados, and to her three sons: George, William and Thomas Cragg. To Ann and Martha, daughters of deceased friend, Arthur Goddard, Esq., of Parish of St. George, of Barbados. To John and Bezin, two sons of friend Bezin King Reese, Esq., Parish of St. Michael, in Barbados. To Julian or Julia, the second daughter of Richard Thomas Atkins Edey, late of Barbados, now of Boston, Massachusetts. To Robert Clinton, Sr., of Phila., merchant. To Jane Olton, late of Barbados, now of Phila., (my housekekeper). To Grace Williams, relict of Hezekiah Williams, merchants of Phila., and to her two daughters, Anna Parry (formerly Anna Williams) and Esther Williams, and to her granddaughter Lydia Williams. Residue of my estate to my relations Sarah Payne and Jane Payne, daughters of my niece Jane Payne, deceased, by her husband Joseph Alleyne Payne, Esq., of Barbados.
Execs: Friends Joseph Alleyne Payne, Bezin King Reese, Esqs., of Barbados, Robert Clinton, Sr., merchant of Phila.
Witnesses: William Pierrepont, William Cheeks, George C. Clinton, William Clinton.
Recorded in Adms. - L, page 247

DOWERS, JOHN. Phila. Sailmaker.
Feb. 3, 1814. Sept. 12, 1815. 6.132.
To my five children: John Dowers, Jane Porter, Mary Meany, Edward Dowers and Kitty Dupuy, wife of William Dupuy.
Execs: Friends Rev. Joseph Turner, Walter Sims, William Sansom, George Simpson, late Cashier of the bank of U.S.
To granddaughter Maria Porter. To Matilda, Mary Ann and John Dowers, the children of said son Edward Dowers. To Mary Thornton Dowers and Elizabeth Catharine Dowers, children of said son John Dowers, and his wife Susan Dowers.
Witnesses: Robert Whitehead, Henry Schell.
Codicil: March 20, 1815. Revokes appointment of Walter Sims as Executor.
Witnesses: Robert Whitehead, Hannah Eyre.
Letters to Rev. Joseph Turner, George Simpson.

TAYLOR, MARIA. Phila. Widow of John Taylor, deceased.
March 23, 1815. May 9, 1815. 6.136.
All estate to my two children.
Executrix: Mother-in-law Jane Taylor, also to be Guardian of said children.
Witnesses: W. W. Woodward, Ann M. Wynkoop.

LOUGHEAD, JAMES. Moyamensing Township. Phila. Co. Carter.
Aug. 16, 1815. Sept. 20, 1815. 6.136.
All real estate to be sold when youngest child is of age and monies to all my children.
Executrix: Wife Eleanor Loughead. If she marries, I appoint cousin William Charlsworth of Morris River in State of New Jersey, sole Executor.
Witnesses: Thomas Hoskins, James Gibson, Moses McIlheny.

ENGLE, JULIAN. Phila. Spinster.
June 1, 1811. Sept. 21, 1815. 6.137.
To brothers James, Joseph and Silas Engle. To sister Mary Benezett, wife of Anthony Benezett. If said sister dies before her husband, her share of estate to said brothers and to James Benezett, son of sister Mary Benezet, when of age.
Exec: Brother James Engle.
Witnesses: Francis Engle, John Watson.

BELSTERLING, JACOB. Township of Northern Liberties. Phila. Co. Inn Keeper and Tax Collector.
Sept. 19, 1815. Sept. 25, 1815. 6.139.
To Mary Belsterling, my wife, her dower according to law. When youngest child is of age, residue of estate to my seven children: Anthony Belsterling, Bellague Catharine Zeisenger, Margaret Montgomery, Jacob Belsterling, Catharine Belsterling, Henry Belsterling and John Foutles Belsterling.
Execs: Frederick Fricke, cabinet maker, Frederick Hoeckly, fringe weaver, both of Northern Liberties, aforesaid.
Witnesses: John Goodman, Anthony Ratzheller, Frederick Haas.

DEAL, JACOB. Kensington. Northern Liberties. Phila. Store Keeper.
Sept. 29, 1808. Sept. 25, 1815. 6.140.
All estate to wife, Elizabeth, she to educate minor children. After her death or marriage, to my seven children: Mary Baker, wife of Joshua Baker, Michael Deal, Charles Deal, John Deal, Simon Peter Deal, Anna Deal and Susanna Deal.
Execs: Said wife, Elizabeth, whilst she remains my widow, friend Charles Albrecht.
Witnesses: Benjamin Brown, Robert Whitehead.

PAINTER, MARGARET. Widow of Niclous Painter. Phila. Co.
Sept. 8, 1815. Oct. 3, 1815. 6.141.
To grandson Jacob Painter, son of Henry Painter. To Elisabeth Painter and Margaret Painter, daughters of Henry Painter, deceased. To Margaret Smith.

Execs: Peter Rambo, William Wallace.
Witnesses: Catharine Brown, Margaret Wallace, Mary McCleery.
Letters to William Wallace.

RACK, JOHN. Boatswain Mate in service of United States.
Oct. 6, 1815. Oct. 9, 1815. 6.142.
Estate to friend Barnard Payne of Phila., Boarding House Keeper.
Exec: Said Barnard Payne.
Witnesses: Robert Smith, Richard Palmer.

THOMAS, SUSANNAH. Township of Northern Liberties. Phila. Co. Widow and sole heir of John Thomas, deceased, who was heir-at-law, and grandson of Thomas Holmes, late Surveyor General of Pennsylvania, deceased.
April 28, 1812. Oct. 9, 1815. 6.143.
To friend, Elijah Hammond of aforesaid Township, shoemaker, whom I appoint Executor.
Witnesses: John Moulder, William Lloyd, Noah Davis.

OURAM, HENRY. Phila. Blacksmith.
May 15, 1815. Oct. 13, 1815. 6.144.
Estate to wife, Nancy, and after her decease, to my four children: Mary, William, Elizabeth and Charlotte.
Executrix: Said wife, Nancy.
Witnesses: Thomas Armstrong, Robert Bishop.

CHILDS, JONATHAN FRIENDS. City and State of New York, Mariner.
Dec. 8, 1813. Oct. 18, 1815. 6.145.
To Louisa Murphy, of Phila., Inn Keeper, whom I appoint Executrix.
Witnesses: Nicholas Diehl, Jr., Stephen Emery.

LUKENS, THOMAS. Germantown. Phila. Co. Cabinet Maker.
Oct. 14, 1815. Oct. 21, 1815. 6.146.
To wife Ann Lukens. After her decease, unto Susanna Fraley, daughter of John Fraley.
Execs: Said wife, Ann Lukens, Henry Fraley, the father of said Ann Lukens.
Witnesses: Stephen Brisburn, Christian Van Lasket, Joseph Rapp.
Letters to Henry Fraley.

STREEPER, JUDITCH. Roxborough Township. Phila. Co. Widow.
Oct. 10, 1815. Oct. 14, 1815. 6.146.

To Jacob Unkle. To my six children: Margeret, John, Sarah Davis, Dennis, Joseph and Mary Streeper, except John Streeper and John Davis, so much as has been paid them.
Exec: George Martin.
Witnesses: Jacob Colp, David Moyer.

SMITH, ABIGAIL. Township of Northern Liberties. Phila. Co.
Dec. 14, 1813. Oct. 25, 1815. 6.147.
To Martha Mervine, Mary Mervine and Jacob Mervine.
Execs: Enoch Wheeler, Thomas Norton, gentlemen.
Witnesses: Charles Albrecht, Michael Deal, Ann F. Wheeler.
Letters to Enoch Wheeler.

SANDWITH, MARY. Phila. Single Woman.
April 3, 1814. Oct. 23, 1815. 6.148.
To nephew Henry S. Drinker. To William Drinker, Jr., son of said Henry S. Drinker. To five children of Jacob Downing, by my niece, his late wife, Sarah Sandwith Downing, deceased. To friends Thomas Stewardson, Samuel W. Fisher, and said nephew Henry S. Drinker, in trust for niece Ann Skyrin, wife of John Skyrin. To niece Mary Rhoads. To Monthly Meeting of Women Friends, Northern District, Phila. All residue of estate to nephew William Drinker, whom I appoint sole Executor.
Witnesses: John Lohra, John C. Lohra, Peter Thomson.

BARNET, MARTHA. Phila.
Oct. 6, 1797. Oct. 30, 1815. 6.150.
To brother Abner Barnet. To daughter Elizabeth Barnet (sometimes called Elizabeth Stedham), now living with Richard and Henrietta Flower at Chester Mill. If said daughter dies under age, to the following: brother Abner Barnet, Elizabeth Barlow and Levina Barlow, daughters of sister Elizabeth, late wife of John Barlow.
Execs: Benjamin Thaw, Raper Hoskins.
Witnesses: Dorothea S. Pennell, William Graham, John G. Hoskins.
Letters to surviving Executor, Benjamin Thaw.

NOBLE, LYDIA. Northern Liberties. Phila. Widow of Samuel Noble, deceased.
Nov. 20, 1793. Oct. 25, 1815. 6.151.
To two sons Richard and Samuel Noble. To son Samuel's wife, Elizabeth Noble. To niece Elizabeth, daughter of said son Samuel. Daughter, Hannah, to have use, etc. of lots in Campentown, said Liberties, and in Town of Campden, New Jersey. To Samuel Jobson and wife.
Execs: Said two sons.

Witnesses: Robert Shoemaker, Ann Easly, Robert Whitehead, Thomas Norton, affirmed. Letters to Sam'l. Noble.

ADAMS, ABIGAIL. City of Phila. Widow.
July 27, 1812. Nov. 2, 1815. 6.152.
To the poor of the Methodist Episcopal Church, called "St. George's."
Execs: David Lake, cordwainer, Alexander McKinley, bricklayer, John McCurdy, Sr., all of Phila.
Witnesses: John McClintock, William Lake, Isaac King.

REINHARD, JOHN. District of Southwark. House Carpenter.
Oct. 8, 1811. Nov. 2, 1815. 6.153.
To son, Jacob Reinhard, and daughter, Elizabeth House. To granddaughter, Catharina Reinhard, daughter of son Martin Reinhard.
Execs: Friends Peter Deal of Kensington, Phila. Co., house carpenter, Joshua Ash of said county, glazier.
Witnesses: Samuel Barclay, Francis Renshaw.

BUSSIER, BARTHOLOMEW. Phila. Co.
Oct. 29, 1815. Nov. 2, 1815. 6.154.
To daughter, Susan Huff. After her death, to her children. To Mary Hesler, wife of William Hesler, carpenter. To son John. To son Bartholomew, Jr. To housekeeper, Mary Lesley.
Execs: Brother Daniel Bussier, brother-in-law Benjamin Morton.
Witnesses: George Schryer, Jacob Harner.

TORENS, PAUL. Township of Northern Liberties. Phila. Co.
Oct. 8, 1812. Nov. 7, 1815. 6.155.
To son Abraham Torens, to be paid from money coming to me in Ireland. To daughters Ann and Ruth Torens. To sons John and William Torens. To Paul Torens, son of son John.
Execs: Son Samuel Torens, my friend William Millikin.
Witnesses: William Reed, John Allison.

WIGGINS, THOMAS.
Oct. 22, 1815. Nov. 8, 1815. 6.156.
To wife Ruth, all estate, she to be sole Executrix.
Witnesses: Daniel Bussier, Andrew McCalla.

TILGHMAN, EDWARD. Phila. Counsellor at Law.
Nov. 19, 1814. Nov. 6, 1815. 6.157.
To wife Elizabeth Tilghman, all my household furniture, etc., both in town and at Providence. Monies due from me as Guardian to Abigail Graham. To son Benjamin. To son Edward. After death of wife, my silver tankard to son Edward, then to his eldest son, and if he has no

son, then to my grandson Edward Tilghman. To daughter Elizabeth, lands in Green County, and my son Benjamin, lands now or lately in Centre County. To daughter Anna Mary, shares in Bank of U. S., in name of Dr. Kuhn, and money secured on my Maryland estate.
Execs: Wife Elizabeth, son Benjamin Tilghman. Wife to be Guardian to daughter Mary, and after her death, my son-in-law William Cooke, Jr.
Witnesses: John Hallowell, Joseph Hopkinson, Horace Binney.

BRICE, JOHN, CAPTAIN. Northern Liberties. Phila. Co. Mariner.
Aug. 9, 1815. Nov. 8, 1815. 6.159.
To son James Brice, All residue to Ann Parish, my housekeeper.
Said Ann Parish, sole Executrix.
Witnesses: Jesse Shelmire, Thomas Mitchell.

MC MACKIN, MICHAEL. City of Phila. Storekeeper.
Nov. 7, 1815. Nov. 13, 1815. 6.159.
To eldest daughter, Eliza, by former wife; after my death, to be placed under controul of my sister, Martha, and her husband, John McClintock. To wife, Margaret, son James, and my daughters Martha, Rebecca and Mary.
Execs: John McClintock, James Donley, both of Phila.
Witnesses: Thomas Sargeant, Jonathan Pounder.

FLAHERTY, DANIEL. City of Phila. Grocer.
Nov. 6, 1815. Nov. 15, 1815. 6.160.
To Executors, in trust for educating one of the sons of my nephew, Michael Maguire, for a Priest of Roman Catholic Church. Should all his sons refuse, then in educating one of the sons of my nephew John Flaherty (if he has any) for same purpose. If they decline, for any one of sons of either of my nephews that reside in Ireland, who may come to this country. To James Wheler. To Catharine Clark. To James Cooney. All my real estate in Pennsylvania to nephews Michael Maguire and John Flaherty. To nieces, Margaret Flaherty and Mary Flaherty of Ireland.
Execs: William O. Leary, John P. Harper of Phila.
Witnesses: Woodbridge Grafton, John Dempsey, Terence Smith.

BOND, PHINEAS, ESQUIRE. His Britannic Majesty's Consul General for the Middle and Southern States of America, now about to embark for England.
June 13, 1811. Jan. 8, 1816. 6.162.
To sister, Rebecca Bond. To nephew, Thomas Cadwallader, Esq., and to his wife. To kinsman, Rev. Thomas Moore, Rector of North Gray and of Foor's Gray in Kent County, England, and to his brother John Moore, chemist to the King. To Simon Temple of Essex Court, London. To

niece, Ann Bond Travis. To sisters, Williamina Cadwalader and
Elizabeth Travis. Said sister, Rebecca Bond, sole Executrix.
Witnesses: Thomas William Moore, James Vaux, Edward S. Lewis.
Codicil: Sept. 25, 1814. David Montagu Erskine, Thomas Erskine,
affirmed.

VILLARD, MARY ANNE, MRS. Native of the place of St. Muzaire in
the Department of Var, residing at Marseilles. Daughter of late Jean
Pierre Villard and Mrs. Agnes Etienne, surviving widow in first
marriage, of Mr. Jean Leron, and in my second marriage, widow of Mr.
Jean Joseph Martin.
Aug. 26, 1814. Nov. 20, 1816. 6.165.
To Jean Baptiste Louis Porte, clerk, in this city, engaged in Military
Escort. To Marie Louise Leron and Marie Anne Leron, my two
daughters by first marriage with said Jean Leron. To Jean Baptiste
Joseph Martin and Marie Catharine Martin, my two children by second
marriage with said Jean Joseph Martin, deceased.
Execs: Francois Clapier, merchant of this city, said Jean Baptiste Louis
Porte, my friends.
Witnesses: Antoine Reguier, Commissioner from Civil Tribunal in this
city, Jean Louis Cyrier, Freeholder, Jean Louis Remusat, Jr., cordial
seller, Augustin Heraud, master mason.

GURNEY, HENRY. Red Spring. Botetourt Co., State of Virginia.
(formerly of Phila.)
Codicil: Jan. 17, 1792. April 17, 1795. 6.167.
Having made my Will March 20, 1790, find it necessary to make a
Codicil. Tract of land on which I live, known as Red Springs, etc. to
Miss Elizabeth Doughty, of Pennsylvania., Spinster (whom I have
brought up through life), appointing her sole Executrix.
Witnesses: William Herbert, Thomas Fife, A. Montgomery.

DU PLESSIS, PETER MARY LE BARBIER. Phila. Conveyancer and
Sworn Interpreter in 59th year.
Jan. 7, 1807. Nov. 15, 1815. 6.169.
To wife, Josephe Genevieve Maurry, widow of late Benjamin Armand,
and to my daughter, Helene.
Executrix: Said wife, Josephe Genevieve Maurry, being convinced that
she will give son, George, all assistance in her power.
Codicil: Sept. 16, 1815. Wife, aforesaid, deceased.
Execs: Said daughter Helene, and John Dubarry, husband of my
daughter Sophia A.
Joseph Barnes, Esq. and Thomas Hennesey, accomptant, both of Phila.
affirmed.

EHRENSTROM, ANDREW FREDERIC. Native of Sweden, at this time citizen of U.S.A. Ship Master.
April 5, 1811. Oct. 18, 1815. 6.171.
To Mrs. Jane Rodgers, widow of my late friend, Capt. John Rodgers, of Phila., Mariner. To Andrew Mickle, son of my friend, Isaac Mickle, Esq., of New Jersey, property in Marcus Hook, Pennsylvania. To my mother Catharina Petrosina Elizabeth Ehrenstrom. After her decease, to my sisters.
Execs: Capt. Norris Stanley of Phila., Isaac Mickle, Esq., of New Jersey. Should they not find it convenient to act, appoint Thomas Harper, merchant of Phila. To Mrs. Sarah Johnston, wife to William Johnston of Phila. After her death, to her children.
Witnesses: Joseph Richards, Samuel F. Saunders.
Letters from said Andrew Frederic Ehrenstrom written from Havana and from Rio Januarie, annexed to Will, in which John, Mary and Rachel Mickle, children of said friend, Isaac Mickle, Esq.
Daniel W. Coxe of Phila., merchant, and John Leamy of Phila., merchant, affirmed.
Letters to Thomas Harper and Isaac Mickle, Esq.

PANCOAST, HANNAH. Phila. Widow.
Nov. 9, 1810. Nov. 23, 1815. 6.175.
Property to son Samuel, daughters Ann Morris and Sarah Byrnes.
Execs: Said son Samuel, son-in-law Luke W. Morris.
Witnesses: Robert Wharton, John Townsend.

MOORE, ANN. District of Southwark. Phila. Co. Widow.
Oct. 11, 1815. Nov. 24, 1815. 6.179.
To friend, John Donaldson, of said District. To David Donaldson, son of said John. To Elen Mary Donaldson, daughter of said John Donaldson, he to be Guardian of property given to his daughter, Elen Mary.
Witnesses: William W. Chambers, Joseph Watson.

YOUNG, PETER. Moyamensing Township. Phila. Co. Farmer.
Aug. 22, 1814. Nov. 24, 1815. 6.180.
To son Peter Young. To wife, Mary. After her decease, to my three children: Sarah Book, Mary Burckhardt and said son Peter Young. To granddaughter, Mary Ann Smith, daughter of my late daughter, Margaret.
Execs: Said wife, Mary, sons-in-law John Book and Daniel Burckhardt.
Witnesses: Isaac Wampole, Jr., Isaac Wampole.

GREINER, SUSANNA. Phila. Widow.
Oct. 30, 1809. Nov. 27, 1815. 6.181.

To son John Greiner. To daughter Euphrosina Grover. After her death, to her children.
Sole Exec: Said son, John Greiner.
Witnesses: Frederick Beates, Jacob Chrystler.

CHAPMAN, MARTHA. Phila. Widow.
June 12, 1813. Nov. 28, 1815. 6.183.
To son John Chapman. To granddaughters: Martha Chapman, Sarah Chapman, Ann Chapman, Mary Roberts. To niece, Martha Johnson Chapman. To grandson, John Chapman. To Elizabeth Thomas.
Sole Exec: Said son, John Chapman.
Witnesses: George W. Gibbons, Abel Satterthwaite.

FLOWER, JOHN. Phila. Mariner.
March 18, 1814. Nov. 30, 1815. 6.184.
To William Williamson of Phila. Late uncle, John Flower. To Caroline Flower of said city, appointing her sole Executrix.
Witnesses: George Hokerspire, Caleb Carmalt, Jr.

BATHO, JOHN. Northern Liberties. Phila. Potter.
May 11, 1812. Dec. 18, 1815. 6.185.
Estate to wife, Martha Batho.
Execs: Said wife, Martha Batho, Joseph Innes, carpenter.
Witnesses: Joseph Innes, Mercy Himer, Rachel Innes.

KNOWS, JOSEPH. Roxborough Township. Phila Co. Yeoman.
Dec. 23, 1812. Dec. 2, 1815. 6.186.
To wife, Margaret, all estate. After her death, to son Jacob. To daughter Margaret's five children. To daughter Catherine and William Heritage.
Execs: Son Jacob Knows, William Heritage.
Witnesses: John Bickings, George Martin.

WEST, HENRY. Lately belonging to U. S. Frigate, "President," now attached to the Flotilla in the Bay and River Delaware. Mariner.
May 14, 1814. Dec. 6, 1815. 6.187.
To friend, Ann Page, of Southwark. Said Ann to be Executrix.
Witnesses: John McLinchey, Henry Engles.

HARRISON, THOMAS. Phila. Taylor, in 75th year.
June 3, 1814. Dec. 6, 1815. 6.188.
Estate to Ruth Harrison, widow of my son, Robert, and her two daughters, Elizabeth Dawson Harrison and Charlotte Harrison. Cousin Leonard Snowden and my friends Joseph Moor and Daniel Thomas, all of Phila., to render counsel to Will, etc.

Said Ruth Harrison, Executrix, and Guardeen of her children.
Witnesses: Samuel Smith, Ebenezer Levick, William Master.

ENGLISH, GEORGE.
June 12, 1814. Dec. 7, 1815. 6.189.
To sister, Elizabeth Bogle, in Ireland.
Exec: Robert Orr of Phila.
Witnesses: Michael Foy, Patrick Creighton.

MC VAUGH, JAMES. Bristol Township, Phila. Co.
Nov. 25, 1815. Dec. 6, 1815. 6.189.
Money received by me from the estate of Peter Taylor. To each of my children: Jane, Elenor, Taylor, James, William and Elizabeth. Residue to wife, Ann.
Executors and Guardians: Said wife, Ann, friend John Deprefontaine.
Witnesses: Edward C. Gouge, Samuel Vanhorn.

BENNER, JOHN. Phila.
Nov. 6, 1815. Dec. 9, 1815. 6.190.
To sister Eleanor Bradley, appointing her Executrix.
Witnesses: Samuel Barclay, Richard Renshaw.

PENROSE, THOMAS. District of Southwark. Phila. Co. Ship Carpenter.
Jan. 15, 1803. Dec. 5, 1815. 6.191.
To wife Ann Penrose. To Thomas Fisher for educating Black People under care of people called Quakers, in Phila. To cousins Bartholomew Mather and Joseph Mather. To Benjamin Mather. To my two sons, William and Charles Penrose.
Execs: Said wife Ann, sons William and Charles.
Witnesses: Caleb Bickham, Thomas Bickham, John Elliott Cresson.

STEWART, THOMAS. Phila. Sailmaker.
July 28, 1815. Dec. 8, 1815. 6.193.
To children: Sarah Yeardsley, Margaret Harch, John Stewart, Hannah Compton and Maria Stewart.
Execs: Son John Stewart, son-in-law James Yeardsley.
Witnesses: George Wall, Robt. Ross.
Letters to John Stewart.

FOULK OR FOULKE, JANE. Germantown. Widow.
Aug. 27, 1814. Dec. 14, 1815. 6.195.
To son Caleb Foulke. To son Charles Foulk. To daughters Lowry Jones, Hannah Foulk and Jane Foulk.
Execs: Sons Caleb and Charles Foulk.

Caleb and Charles Foulke, affirmed.
Letters to Charles Foulke.

ASHMEAD, WILLIAM. Germantown. Phila. Co. Gentleman.
Nov. 13, 1815. Dec. 18, 1815. 6.195.
To daughter Ann Hood. To daughter Mary Ashmead. To sons John and James Ashmead, whom I appoint Executors.
Witnesses: Thomas Armat, Robert Bringhurst.

POINCY, PETER. Phila. Jeweller.
Sept. 12, 1815. Sept. 14, 1815. 6.196.
To wife Rosalie Cecile Montarlet. To children Adolphé, Lucien, Victor, Olympie and Aglaé.
Executrix: Said wife Rosalie Cecile Montarlet.
Witnesses: Joseph Martin, Charles Goodman.

ADAMS, MARTHA. Byberry. Phila. Co.
Nov. 22, 1815. Dec. 19, 1815. 6.197.
To mother Rebeckah Adams. To three brothers Benjamin, Samuel and Ephraim, and to sister Jane Atkinson. To niece Martha Atkinson.
Execs: Brother Benjamin Adams, brother-in-law Benjamin Atkinson.
Witnesses: John Comly, James Walton.

BELL, WILLIAM. Phila. Stone Cutter.
Nov. 25, 1815. Dec. 18, 1815. 6.198.
To my daughter Mary Ann, and her daughter Maria. To son William.
Execs: Samuel Anderson, Thomas Willson.
Witnesses: Thomas Anderson, Christian Brand.

BINDER, GEORGE. Kensington. Northern Liberties. Phila. Co. Mariner.
Nov. 22, 1815. Dec. 27, 1815. 6.199.
To wife Elizabeth Binder. To my five children: Catharine, Susan, Elizabeth, Margaret and Sophia Binder.
Execs: Said wife Elizabeth, my brother William Binder.
Witnesses: John Krouskop, Henry Strackline.

GREEN, PETER. Northern Liberties. Phila. Tanner.
Oct. 11, 1810. Dec. 11, 1815. 6.200.
To my daughter Mary Taylor. To wife Ann Green. To son John Green. To Executors, in trust for grandchildren: Mary, Betsy and Peter Griffin, children of deceased daughter, Elizabeth, during their minority.
Execs: Said daughter Mary Taylor, my friend Frederick Forepaugh of Phila. Co., house carpenter.
Witnesses: Ebenezer McCullock, Isaac Wampole.

Codicil: Nov. 16, 1811. Frederick Forepaugh, deceased. Appoint friend Thomas Norton, Executor.
Witnesses: John Livensetter, Isaac Wampole.
Codicil: Nov. 28, 1815. My first wife's silver spoons, etc., I give to my daughter Mary Taylor and make void the legacy to grandson Peter Green.
Robert Whitehead of Phila., conveyancer, Thomas Norton, Northern Liberties, gentleman, affirmed.

MC BRINE, CHARLES.
May 23, 1814. Jan. 1, 1816. 6.203.
To wife Elizabeth and my three children: ____, George and Sarrah.
Execs: William Fife, William Dougherty.
Witnesses: William Fife, William Dougherty.
Letters to William Dougherty.
(Original Will torn)

HADOCK, HENRY.
Dec. 7, 1815. Jan. 2, 1816. 6.203.
To sons James and John, and to wife Margaret.
Execs: Dynes Gilpin and wife, Margaret Hadock, they also to be Gardeens of sons, John and James.
Witness: James Castles.

LEECH, MAXIMILIAN. Township of Blockley. Phila. Co.
Dec. 23, 1815. Jan. 6, 1816. 6.204.
Property in Kingsessing Township, on Chester Road, etc., to my wife and children [names not given].
Execs: Friend Lewis Jones, son Isaac.
Witnesses: John Frailey, Amos Penegar, William Hoffman.

FREAS, JOSEPH. Hamilton Village. Township of Blockley. Phila. Co. House Carpenter.
Dec. 19, 1815. Jan. 6, 1816. 6.205.
Estate to wife, Sarah Freas, and our four children: Mary Ann, Joseph, Harriett and Rachel.
Execs: Said wife, Sarah, friends David Hoopes and Lewis Jones of Blockley Township.
Witnesses: Ennion Williams, John Child.
Letters to David Hoopes and Lewis Jones.

BLACKWELL, HANNAH. Wife of Robert Blackwell of Phila., Clerk.
Sept. 6, 1784. Jan. 6, 1816. 6.206.
Agreement made by my said husband, myself and Joseph Stamper and Daniel Benezet, Jr., Trustees, that I should dispose of my real estate,

etc. Income to said husband. After his death, the principal to the child wherewith I am now pregnant. To daughter (by former marriage), Maria Benezet.
Execs: Said husband, Robert Blackwell, friend William Lewis, my uncle Joseph Stamper, brother William Bingham.
Witnesses: Mary Obrien, John Morgan, Miers Fisher.
Codicil: Dec. 31, 1801. Husband and Rev. Robert Blackwell. Daughter Maria Willing, late Maria Benezet, departed this life Aug. 10, 1799.
Witnesses: Henry Hawkins, Mary George, John B. Evens.
Letters to Robert Blackwell.

CLARKE, PETER. Mariner, lately belonging to U.S. Private Armed Brig, *Rattlesnake*, Capt. Maffett.
June 22, 1815. Jan. 4, 1816. 6.209.
Estate to friend Barnard Payne of Phila., Boarding house keeper, whom I appoint Executor.
Witnesses: Henry Payne, Henry Engles.

FARTHING, DAVID. Phila.
July 20, 1814. Jan. 18, 1816. 6.209.
To daughters Catharine Downs and Ann Farthing. To son James Farthing, my property in Haverford Township, County of Delaware, adjoining land of David Humphries, Henry Lawrence, Joseph Price, being part of premises which John Cameron, of Phila., and Dorathe, his wife, granted unto me.
Sole Exec: Said son, James.
Witnesses: Augustus W. Biggs, M. F. Truett, Cadwalader Dickinson.

COX, BAINES. Phila. Shopkeeper.
Dec. 23, 1815. Jan. 19, 1816. 6.210.
To Sarah Gorsuch, Lydia Gorsuch and Hannah Gorsuch, sisters of my wife. To bound girl, Esther Stewart. All residue of estate to wife, Rebecca Cox. To daughter Mary Baines Cox, when 21 years of age. To brothers John and Samuel Cox.
Executrix: Said wife Rebecca Cox, also to be Guardian of said daughter.
Witnesses: Joseph Wood, Peter Thomson.

CONSTANTINE, PETER.
July 25, 1815. Jan. 24, 1816. 6.212.
To Elizabeth Crozer, now wife of John Boddy, bookbinder. To Cynthia Lauderback, now wife of Daniel Dykes. To friend James John Maguire, whom I appoint Executor.
Codicil: Nov. 18, 1815. John Coulter and William Montgomery, merchants of Phila, affirmed.

39

TROTTER, REBECCA. Phila.
Oct. 19, 1815. Jan. 25, 1816. 6.213.
To sister Mary Trotter. To brothers Thomas C. and Joseph Trotter. To aunt Abigail Curtis. To brother Nathan Trotter. To nephews Daniel Trotter Haines, Daniel Trotter and Sansom William Trotter. To cousin Margaret Curtis of Mt. Holly. To cousin Sarah Connarroe of Salem, New Jersey. To cousin Elizabeth Trotter.
Exec: Brother Nathan Trotter.
Witnesses: Ephraim Haines, E. D. Cheyney.

BINES, ELIZA. Phila.
Dec. 16, 1815. Jan. 24, 1816.
All estate to sister Anne Miller for benefit of my children: Robert, Gustavus, Caroline and Thomas Bines. To sisters Mary Reilly, said Anne Miller and Sarah Miller.
Execs: Said sister Anne Miller, brother-in-law Thomas Reilly.

NICE, GEORGE. Germantown Township. Phila. Co. Yeoman.
April 1, 1812. Jan. 27, 1816. 6.215.
To wife, Margaret Nice, all estate including property in Township aforesaid, adjoining lands of George Cress, Christ'r. Yeakle and others.
Execs: Said wife Margaret, Daniel Thomas, Jr.
Witnesses: Daniel Snyder, William Streper.
Letters to Daniel Thomas, Jr.

DE HAVEN, PETER. Phila. Gentleman.
Dec. 27, 1806. Jan. 26, 1816. 6.217.
To great granddaughter, Sarah Rawle de Haven, and great grandson, Atlee de Haven (children of grandson Peter de Haven). Residue to only child, Hugh de Haven. After his death, to his daughters, Harriet, Amelia and Emma Maria de Haven.
Execs: Said son Hugh, grandson Peter de Haven.
Witnesses: Peter Browne, Henry Gravel.
Letters to Hugh de Haven.

JONES, JAMES. Phila. Silversmith. Son of Richard Jones, late of Lower Merion Township, Montgomery Co., deceased.
Sept. 10, 1815. Jan. 30, 1816. 6.219.
To Edward Harvey of Phila, hatter, with whom I now dwell. After his decease, unto all the children of said Edward. To Richard Jones Harvey, son of said Edward. To Martha Boyle, late of Phila., said to be of Pittsburg, and to Agnes Deave, formerly my father's housekeeper. To Margaret Harvey, wife of above-named Edward.
Exec: Said Edward Harvey.
Witnesses: R. Whitehead, John W. Smith, John Morris.

CHEVALIER, MARGARET. Northern Liberties. Phila. Widow.
June 11, 1805. Jan. 29, 1816. 6.221.
To my children: Isabella Turner, Susanna M. Francis and William Chevalier, whom I appoint Executors. To granddaughters Maria Turner, Molly M. Francis, Ann R. Chevalier and Ann Mary Chevalier.
Witnesses: Jacob Shoemaker, Nicholas Young, Richard Whitehead.
Letters to surviving Executrixes, Isabella Turner and Susanna M. Francis.

GELEY, PETER. Phila. Jeweller.
Oct. 10, 1815. Dec. 16, 1815. 6.222.
To Abraham H. Cohen of Phila., chemist, whom I appoint sole Executor.
Witnesses: John Benner, Thomas Richardson.
Edmund Kinsey of Phila., sadler, affirmed.

WALLACE, SARAH. Phila.
July 15, 1811. Feb. 1, 1816. 6.222.
To friend Rev. Absalom Jones. To Episcopal African Church of St. Thomas, being a member of said church.
Execs: Friends Joseph Randolph, Jeremiah Hill.
Witnesses: Joseph Lloyd, Richard Howell.

THOMAS, DINAH. Late of Township of Willistown, Chester Co., now in Pennsylvania Hospital, Phila.
Jan. 26, 1816. Feb. 6, 1816. 6.223.
To Joseph Thomas Thompson and to Aaron Thompson, sons of sister Phebe, also to Milton Thompson. To Reuben Thomas. To Lydia Thomas, daughter of brother Francis. Said Joseph Thomas Thompson and Aaron Thompson both minors. To David Thompson and my sister, Phebe, his wife.
Exec: Friend Mordecai Thomas of Willistown.
Witnesses: Israel Yarnall, Jane Sellers.

PREVOST, CATHARINE. Wife of Andrew M. Prevost of Phila., merchant.
April 8, 1815. Jan. 29, 1816. 6.225.
To sister Sarah Bridges, wife of Culpepper Bridges. To said husband, Andrew M. Prevost. Late father William Cliffton, deceased. To brother John Cliffton.
Witnesses: Richard Renshaw, Hannah Cliffton, Lewis M. Prevost, Jr., affirmed.

BEIDEMAN, JACOB. Kensington. Phila. Co. Fisherman.
Feb. 6, 1816. Feb. 13, 1816. 6.226.

To wife Catharine Beideman. After her decease, to my children: John, Henry, William, Samuel, Catharine, Mary, and the two children of son Jacob, Jacob and Eliza.
Exec: Friend John C. Browne.
Witnesses: Robert Whitehead, Jacob Hill.

KNIGHT, MARTHA. Phila. Widow. Late husband, Jonathan Knight.
March 10, 1814. Feb. 21, 1816. 6.227.
To Daniel Knight, one of Executors named in Will of said husband, the articles left in my possession during life. To Elizabeth Naile. To niece Martha Lukens, daughter of David Lukens. To mother, Sarah Tomkins, during life. To sisters, Sarah Lukens, wife of David Lukens, Rachel Hallowell and Esther Fielding, wife of Robert Fielding. To brother Samuel Lloyd. To children of deceased sister, Elizabeth Hallowell. To Robert Fielding, in trust for niece Elizabeth Lloyd, daughter of deceased brother Thomas Lloyd, to be paid to her when 18 years of age.
Execs: Friends Thomas Williams, Philip S. Bunting.
Witnesses: Sharon Carter, Samuel Williams.
Letters to Thomas Williams.

HOCKLEY, ELEANOR. Phila.
Feb. 2, 1816. Feb. 21, 1816. 6.228.
Legacy to Mary Hockley, the wife of deceased brother. Residue to sister Elisabeth Twamley and the children of my brother.
Exec: Friend Thomas Cumpston.
Witnesses: Thoms Cumpston, Elisabeth Twamley.

KEEN, MARY. Township of Oxford, Phila. Co.
Dec. 14, 1815. Feb. 22, 1816. 6.229.
To daughter, Mary Renshaw. To granddaughter, Sarah Ann Keen. To grandsons James Keen and Robert Keen.
Exec: Stepson John Keen.
Witnesses: Adilicia Wilkins, John H. Hill.

MAY, ADAM. Phila. Grocer.
July 21, 1807. Feb. 22, 1816. 6.230.
To wife, Elizabeth May. To my five childen: Elizabeth Stewart, Mary Stevenson, Catharine, Sarah and Harriet May.
Execs: Friends Jacob Edenborn, John Geyer, Jr., of said City. Said Executors to be Guardians of minor children.
Witnesses: Frederick Beates, Philip T. Dunn.

DARRACH, JAMES. Phila. Hatter.
Feb. 16, 1816. Feb. 26, 1816. 6.231.

To wife, Elizabeth Darrach, she to be at expense of educating, etc., all
my children. To each of my sons: Thomas Bradford Darrach, William
Darrach, Samuel Fisher Darrach and James Darrach, when twenty-two
years of age. To my two daughters: Charlotte Darrach and Mary
Darrach, when they are twenty years of age. Wife, Elizabeth, and
brother-in-law Thomas Bradford, Jr., Trustees. To Ellen and Sarah
Darrach, all my interest in property in town of Appoquimimink, New
Castle Co., Delaware, formerly the property of their father.
Execs: Wife Elizabeth, son Thomas B. Darrach, brother-in-law Thomas
Bradford, Jr.
Jacob Ritter, Jr., merchant, William Bradford, bookseller, and Charles
Caldwell, physician, all of Phila., affirmed.

HILLBORN, ELIZABETH. Phila.
Sept. 15, 1812. Feb. 28, 1816. 6.233.
To Hannah Hood, now living with me. To nieces Elizabeth West and
Rachel Roberts. To relation Robert Parrish. To friend Isaac Wampole,
scrivener, whom I appoint Executor.
Witnesses: Frederick Beates, Jacob Sulger, Jr.

WILKINSON, WILLIAM. Township of Northern Liberties. Phila.
Taylor.
Jan. 22, 1816. Feb. 28, 1816. 6.234.
Estate to wife, Mary, whom I appoint Executrix.
Witnesses: Henry Probasco, Jacob Knous.

MC GOWAN, THOMAS. Phila. Co.
Aug. 24, 1815. March 4, 1816. 6.236.
To wife Mary McGowan, whom I appoint sole Executrix.
Witnesses: John Donlevy, John Sweeny.

EMLEN, ANNE. Phila. Widow.
June 27, 1815. Feb. 10, 1816. 6.237.
To daughters Mary Beveridge. To deceased daughter, Ann Mifflin's two
sons, Samuel and Lemuel. To daughter Margaret Howell, and her
children. To Phila. Monthly Meeting of Women Friends. Have left
nothing to my sons' children, because my sons received larger
proportion than my daughters, by their father's Will.
Execs: Grandson Samuel E. Howell, Dr. Samuel Emlen.
Witnesses: Joseph Gibbons, William Wood or Hood.

ENGLE, SUSANNA. Germantown. Phila. Co.
Oct. 4, 1814. March 15, 1816. 6.238.
To children of late brother, Cornelius Engle, and his grandson, John
Engle. To children of late brother, John Engle. To children of late

brother, Jacob Engle. To nephew, Joseph Schreiber, son of late sister
Margaret. To Susanna, Mary, Margaret and Sarah, daughters of
nephew, Frederick Schreiber. To niece Ann Engle, daughter of Charles
Engle. To grandniece, Ann Bensell Billings, to be placed at interest by
nephew Francis Engle, until she is 21 years of age. To children of
nephew, Dr. George Bensell. To Susanna Negus, daughter of James
Engle, and Ann, daughter of Charles Engle. To relations: Mary Rush,
Ann Stoneburner, Margaret Snyder, Sarah Watson, Mary Benezet,
Juliann Engle, Elizabeth, widow of Charles Engle. To children of late
sister, Mary Stoneburner. To children of late sister, Margaret
Schreiber, and grandchildren of late sister, Sarah Bensell.
Execs: Nephew James Engle, of Phila., Esq., Isaac Wampole, scrivener,
of said city.
Witnesses: Charles L. Smith, Isaac Wampole, Jr.
Letters to James Engle.

RILEY, WILLIAM. Phila. Co. Labourer. Late a soldier in 26th
Regiment of United States Infantry, Company Commanded by Capt.
Bezeau.
Feb. 17, 1816. March 19, 1816. 6.240.
To only son Joseph Riley.
Exec: John F. Martin of said county, store keeper. Also, to be Guardian
of said son.
Witnesses: Amos Davies, Giles Yournson.

MC MURDY, ROBERT. Northern Liberties. Phila. Co. Labourer.
April 21, 1814. March 21, 1816. 6.241.
To wife, Susannah McMurdy. To daughter, Elizabeth McGill. To
daughter, Mary Blackwood. To daughter, Ann Chace. To daughter,
Susanna Saunders. To daughter, Margaret Moore. To sons Benjamin
McMurdy and Jonathan McMurdy.
Executrix: Said wife, Susanna.
Signed: McMurday.
Witnesses: Aquilla A. Browne, Mary A. Browne.

CONNELLY, PATRICK. Phila.
April 9, 1814. March 9, 1816. 6.242.
To Elizabeth Coutty, with whom I have lived many years, who has
borne my name and passed with the world as my wife. To Martha
Skees, now Martha Coburn. To Ann Gibson, daughter of friend, James
Gibson of Mayamensing Township, distiller. All residue to only son and
child, John Connelly.
Sole Exec: Said James Gibson
Witnesses: Richard Price, Robert Coburn.

JUNGKURTH, FREDERICK. Germantown Township. Phila. Co. Carpenter.
March 3, 1816. March 21, 1816. 6.244.
To wife, Barbera Jungkurth. To my children: Christopher, Henry, Mary Magdalene, Elisabeth, Rebecca, Ann, Catharine, Frederica and Susana Jungkurth.
Execs: Said wife, Barbara, son Christopher.
Witnesses: Georg Tillman, Walter Campbell.

HELER, CATHARINE.
Dec. 22, 1815. March 25, 1816. 6.244.
To daughter, Catharine Orde. To son, Philip Heler (now absent in U. S. Army).
Sole Executrix: Said daughter, Catharine Ord.
Witnesses: James Burns, Kezia Sweetman, Elisabeth B. Stowers, Mary M. Ealer.

MERDIER, SERAPHIN. Pottsgrove.
March 1, 1816. March 25, 1816. 6.245.
To be buyreid in the place nearest where they will permit to Break the Grounds.
Universal heir and Exec: Simon Chaudron, jeweller and watchmaker, of Phila., he to remit to my brother Louis Merdier and my two sisters Francis and Maria.
Amable Brasier of Phila., watchmaker and jeweller and Charles Villar of said city, crockery merchant, affirmed.

MONTGOMERY, JACOB. Northern Liberties. Phila. Co. Nail Manufacturer.
March 12, 1816. March 27, 1816. 6.247.
To wife, Maria Montgomery. To brother, Robert Montgomery.
Exec: Brother John Montgomery.
Witnesses: Bernard Vanhorn, Elizabeth Cadwallader.
(Nuncupative)

WHARTON, ELIZABETH. Phila. Widow.
Aug. 22, 1808. March 12, 1816. 6.248.
To children of deceased daughter, Mary Humphreys. To son, John Wharton. To Joshua Humphreys of Southwark and Eli Canby of Phila., in trust for son Thomas C. Wharton.
Execs: Said Joshua Humphries, Eli Canby.
Witnesses: Ann Thomas, Daniel Thomas.
Codicil: April 16, 1814. March 3, 1815.

As Joshua Humphreys has removed from Phila., appoint Thomas C.
Wharton Executor and Trustee in his place. Mentions Ann, wife of son,
Thos. C. Wharton (formerly Ann Green), and his children.
Witnesses: Anna Gamble, E. Tilghman, Hariet L. Morey, Benjamin
Tilghman. John Wharton and Thomas C. Wharton, two of the
Executors, affirmed.

BRITTON, JOHN, SR. Northern Liberties. Phila.
March 7, 1816. March 15, 1816. 6.251.
To sons John Britton and William Britton and son-in-law, George Budd,
half of what late daughter, Mary ---, would have been entitled for
benefit of her daughter, Eleanor Dewees. All residue to daughter
Susan Budd, son John Britton, daughter Sarah Forde, son William
Britton, children of son Benjamin, deceased: Margaret, Mary, John and
Maria. To said sons John and William, and son-in-law, George Budd for
benefit of my daughter Eleanor, now wife of William Dewees. To son
Saltar Britton. In trust for son Edward Britton. In trust for daughter
Rebecca Hellings.
Execs: Friend Charles Biddle, said sons, John and William Britton, son-
in-law George Budd.
Witnesses: Job B. Remington, Joseph Whitecar.

KENTON, JOSEPH. Phila. Grocer.
Feb. 21, 1816. March 26, 1816. 6.254.
To wife Anna Barbary. To children, sons Joseph and Thomas,
daughters Mary, Deborah, wife of Edwin Tamerlin (or Tamerlane)
Scott, and Catharine and three children of late daughter, Margaret,
late wife of Thomas Ward, namely Hannah, Mary and Deborah.
Execs: Wife, Ann Barbary, son Joseph Kenton.
Witnesses: John Kensel, Edwin T. Scott.

SMITH, CATHARINE. Northern Liberties. Phila. Widow.
March 26, 1816. April 9, 1816. 6.255.
To friend Mary Stoerger, wife of Martin Stoerger, of Northern
Liberties, all estate, except the tin plate stove, which I give to
Jeremiah Keen.
Executrix: Said Mary Stoerger.
Witnesses: Samuel Saltar, Mary Whitelack.

KIMMEY, WILLIAM. Mariner, lately belonging to the Privateer
Schooner, "Surprise" of Baltimore, now belonging to the Privateer
Schooner, "Whig" of Baltimore.
Oct. 20, 1814. April 5, 1816. 6.256.
To friend Catharine Falconer, of Phila., boarding house keeper, whom I
appoint Executrix.

Witnesses: Samuel Barclay, Henry Engles.

BEATES, BARBARA. Phila. Widow.
Nov. 14, 1815. April 4, 1816. 6.257.
To daughters Barbara, Catharine and Mary.
Execs: Sons Frederick Beates, William Beates.
Witnesses: John Geyer, Andrew Geyer.

LESLEY, PETER. Phila. Co. Cabinet Maker.
Aug. 8, 1815. April 6, 1816. 6.258.
Daughters Mary and Margaret to be charged with amounts advanced to them and their husbands. Income of all estate for use of wife, Catharine, daughter, Ann, and my younger children.
Execs: Wife Catharine, daughter Ann, son Peter Lesley, friend Thomas Latimer.
Witnesses: Abraham Stein, Frederick Beates.

ROBERTS, OWEN. Formerly of Wales, but now of Phila. Co.
July 9, 1813. April 10, 1816. 6.259.
To wife, Margaret, and my three children: Griffith, Margaret and Ann Roberts.
Sole Exec: Wife Margaret.
Witnesses: Peter I. Decker, Daniel Bussier.

SMITH, JOHN. Phila.
April 5, 1816. April 11, 1816. 6.260.
To Isaac Kennedy, all estate for use of Eliza Smith, my daughter, to be paid her when of age.
Exec: Isaac P. Kennedy of Phila, bootmaker.
Witnesses: Thomas Bigelow, James M. Hart.

CLEMENT, ANN. Phila. Widow of James Clement, late of said city, deceased.
Oct. 29, 1813. April 13, 1816. 6.260.
To James Dilworth of said city, ironmonger, and to Ann Dilworth, his daughter. To Mary Quamony (a Black girl formerly apprenticed to me). To nieces Sarah T. Wessels, widow of John Frederick Francis Wessells, late of Baltimore, merchant, and Hannah D. Johns.
Execs: Cousin Thomas Savery, my friend Joseph Lownes of said city, silversmith.
Witnesses: Richard Alexander, William Andrews.
Codicil: Oct. 29, 1813. Revokes legacy to Mary Quamony.
Witnesses: Same as to Will.

FRIEL, JOHN. Now resident in Charlestown in Commonwealth of
Massachusetts and a private mariner in service of U.S.A.
Oct. 11, 1815. April 16, 1816. 6.262.
To Adrian Peters, all my wages, etc., with prize money for capture of
vessels by U. S. Frigate, "Constitution," Charles Stuart, Commander,
appointing said Adrian Peters Executor.
Witnesses: Charles Townsend, John Goodwin, Lewis Stratton.

WHEELER, MARY.
Nov. 11, 1815. April 15, 1816. 6.263.
To sister Elizabeth F. Paul. To sister Sarah Johnson. To sister Ann F.
Wheeler. To sister-in-law Henrietta Maria Wheeler. To niece Mary
Paul. To nephews Samuel W. Paul, Jacob Paul and Joseph W. Paul.
Execs: Brother Enoch Wheeler, brother-in-law Joseph Paul, sister
Elizabeth F. Paul.
Witnesses: Hannah R. Poole, Eliza Hawthorn.

COFFMAN, BARNET. Phila. Co.
March 12, 1816. April 16, 1816. 6.264.
To wife, Margaret Coffman. To grandson Barnet Coffman, son of John
Coffman. To children: Jacob, John, Barnet, Joseph, David, Rachel,
Mary and Margaret.
Execs: Said wife Margaret, oldest son Jacob Coffman.
Witnesses: Daniel Ketcham, Jacob Rifefer, William Ketcham.

FYAN, JOHN. Northern Liberties. Phila. Cordwainer.
July 13, 1815. April 17, 1816. 6.265.
To wife Catherine Fyan, whom I appoint sole Executrix.
Witnesses: Robert Whitehead, Lydia Eyre.

KURTZ, PETER. Phila.
May 20, 1815. April 17, 1816. 6.266.
To wife Sarah Kurtz. To my sone Charles, daughter Margaret, and to
his other daughter, Sally Ann. To wife's granddaughter, Fanny ____.
To daughters Sarah and Ann. To sons William, Jacob and Charles -
"unto my Henry." To children of son Peter: Montgomery, George,
Henry, Margaret and Eleanor.
Said wife Sarah, daughter Sarah, son William administator.
Witnesses: Peter A. Stryker, Elizabeth Middleton.

TUSTIAN, THOMAS. Phila. Perfumer.
Signed: July 4, 1805. Feb. 17, 1816.
Proved: April 25, 1816. 6.267.
All estate to wife, Eunice Tustian, whom I appoint sole Executrix.
Witnesses to first signing: William B. Blake, Charles E. Blake.

Witnesses to second signing: Francis Shallus, James Queen.

CHEVALIER, SAMUEL. Northern Liberties. Phila. Tanner.
March 13, 1816. April 25, 1816. 6.268.
Estate to wife, Susanna, and my four children: Elizabeth, William W., Susan and Samuel Chevalier.
Execs: Said wife, my friend William Wagner, Northern Liberties, house carpenter.
Witnesses: Isaac Davis, George Frank.
Letters to Susanna Chevalier.

CONNOR, PETER. American Prisoner, late belonging to the Yankee Privateer, from Rhode Island, the town of Bristol, in U.S.A., now a patient in the royal Navy Hospital at Plymouth (from his Brittanic Majesty's ship, "President"), being a Prisoner of War.
Nov. 28, 1814. April 27, 1816. 6.268.
To wife Eleanor Connor, in Phila., whom I appoint Executrix.
Witnesses: Ja. Symons, Lieut., R. Beddek, Agent, Abel May, Agent's Clerk. John Burns of Southwark, ship joiner, and Edward Brown of same place, mariner, affirmed.

ADAMS, CATHERINE. Germantown.
Nov. 7, 1810. April 24, 1816. 6.269.
To my beloved John Hammer's eldest daughter, Mary Hammer. To nephew John Homer[?].
Execs: Nephew John Hammer, Klinchen Johnson.
Witnesses: Rosina M. Schlosser, Theodora Elizabeth Schlosser, Lydia Thomson.
Codicil: Dec. 27, 1813. To Jacob Good. Letters to John Hammer.

LEVAN, MARY. Phila. Widow.
Dec. 4, 1815. April 30, 1816. 6.270.
To sister Elizabeth Lightfoot, and my brother James Shoemaker. To daughters of late brother Charles Shoemaker, namely Ann Elizabeth, Margaret and Mary Shoemaker. To sons of late brother Charles Shoemaker. To cousin Susan B. Shober.
Execs: Brother James Shoemaker, sister Elizabeth Lightfoot.
Witnesses: Martha Rose, Catherine Shober, T. W. F. Dillingham.
Letters to James Shoemaker.

PALESKE, CHARLES GOTTFRIED. Born in City of Dantzig, May 22, 1758, now a citizen of Phila.
Sept. 14, 1803. May 3, 1816. 6.271.
To wife Hannah Paleska (daughter of John Elmslie), and our three childen: Lewis, Charles Gottfried and Maria Wilhelmina Paleske.

Execs: Wife Hannah Paleske, friend Joseph S. Lewis, merchant in Phila.
Witnesses: Peter Leohra, John Shields, John Lohra, Jr.

STRICKER, ADAM. Phila. Brushmaker.
April 18, 1816. May 2, 1816. 6.271.
Estate to wife Catharine, she to support son George during minority.
To children of late brother, Daniel.
Executrix: Said wife Catharine.
Witnesses: Thomas Moore, John Goodin.

BROWNE, THOMAS. Northern Liberties. Phila. Ship Joiner.
April 26, 1814. May 4, 1816. 6.272.
All estate to wife, Rebecca Browne. After her death, unto Martha Stocker, daughter-in-law of my said wife, and Rebecca, daughter of her, the said Martha.
Execs: Said Martha Stocker, William Painter, husband of her daughter, the said Rebecca.
Witnesses: Robert Whitehead, Hannah Eyre.
Letters to William Painter.

GEIGER, GEORGE. District of Southwark. Mariner.
May 31, 1809. April 30, 1816. 6.273.
To sister Margaret Flowers, wife of Thomas Flowers of said District.
Executrix: Said sister.
Witnesses: James McLinchey, Rebecca Laferty.
Richard Renshaw affirmed.

EWING, JOHN, Esq. Phila.
Aug. 12, 1815. May 2, 1816. 6.273.
To my wife, ___, legacy to sons John, Joseph and Edward, left them by their aunt, Mary Johnson. To daughters, Sarah and Eleanor, and to the child not yet born of which my wife is now imminent.
Elihu S. Sergeant of Phila., Attorney-at-law, Harrison Hall of said City, book seller, affirmed.
Magdalen Ewing and Samuel Ewing affirmed and sworn May 7, 1816.

SHRONK, BARNABAS. City and County and State of Pennsylvania.[sic]
May 3, 1814. May 8, 1816. 6.274.
To wife, Phebe Shronk.
Execs: Said wife, Phebe, friend George Armitage.
Witnesses: Christian Hawk, Lewis May, George Mire.

ROBERTS, BENJAMIN. Phila. Grocer.
March 11, 1816. May 14, 1816. 6.274.
To my four children: Augustus, Edmund, Caroline, Rachel. Friends Joseph Cake, hatter, and William Sagathey, hatter, to be Executors and to see to educating of said children.
Witnesses: John Hopkins, George Hannold.
Robert Wilson of Phila., tobacconist, affirmed.

MARKER, GODFREY. Southwark. Phila. Co. Yeoman.
July 7, 1812. May 28, 1816. 6.275.
Wife, Mary Marker, to have use, interest, etc. of all estate, she to provide for my children: George, Conrad, Jacob, Maria and Elizabeth Marker, and such other children as may yet be born.
Execs: Friend John Propert, said wife. Said John Propert to be Guardian of children if wife marries.
Witnesses: Robert Whitehead, Hannah Eyre.

ANTHONY, JOHN.
Cape of Delaware: May 9, 1816. May 21, 1816. 6.276.
John Barnes to receive all my wages due from ship "Dorothea," he to pay all debts and to receive from Mrs. Jane Long of Phila., all papers belonging to me.
Witnesses: Jacob Harman, Jr., William Smith.

DAWSON, WILLIAM. Phila. Brewer.
Feb. 26, 1816. May 20, 1816. 6.277.
To wife, Elizabeth Dawson. To contributors to Pennsylvania Hospital. To Joseph S. Lewis, Mordecai Lewis, Samuel N. Lewis, and William Morrison in trust for support of grandson, William Dawson, eldest son of late son, William Dawson. To granddaughter, Anne Dawson, and grandson Mordecai Lewis Dawson, children of said son, William, deceased. To nephews and nieces of the whole and half blood, the children of my brother, Robert Dawson, of John Morrison and Sidney, his wife, and of Josiah L. Coates and Mary, his wife.
Execs: Said wife, Elizabeth Dawson, friends Joseph S. Lewis, Mordecai Lewis, Samuel N. Lewis, William Morrison.
Witnesses: James Wills, Jr., Josiah Thompson.

BRYAN, JESSE. Township of Northern Liberties. Phila. Co. Innkeeper.
May 15, 1816. May 24, 1816. 6.279.
All estate in Bucks Co. to my wife, Phoebe Bryan.
Execs: Brother Joseph Bryan, Abraham Reesor of Springfield Township, Bucks Co.
Witnesses: John Rice, Samuel Macferan.

CLOSS, MARIA MARGARET. Germantown. Phila. Co. Widow.
Feb. 7, 1816. May 27, 1816. 6.280.
To Catherine Birch, who now lives with me.
Execs: Friends Abraham Keyser, Jacob Clement, both of Germantown, aforesaid.
Witnesses: Daniel Castor, George Hargesheimer, Abraham Keyser.

EMERICK, CHARLOTTE. Penn Township. Phila. Co.
Feb. 10, 1815. June 1, 1816. 6.280.
To my son John Kensel. To my daughter Mary Kensel. To poor school for orphan children of Trinity Church. To grandson William Harper Kensler.
Execs: Henry S. Harberger, Sr., John Kinsler, grandson Wm. Harper Kensler.
Witnesses: Christopher Heydrick, Henry Harberger, Jr.

GILLMER, ELIZABETH. Phila.
Oct. 18, 1813. May 30, 1816. 6.281.
To sister, Jane Elliott, now residing in England. To friend Sarah Oxley of Phila. To friend Anna Maria Denman. To friend Nancy Hampton. To friend Jonathan Hampton, Esq., of Phila. To servant boy James Alsop.
Exec: Above-named Jonathan Hampton.
Witnesses: Walter Doyle, Francis Francis.

WILSON, WILLIAM. Phila. Book Seller and Stationer.
April 24, 1813. June 5, 1816. 6.282.
To wife Mary Wilson, formerly wife of Richard Humphreys, dec'd. To wife's sister Susanna Anderson. To Mary Gillmore, my wife's niece. To Hannah Litle, widow of John Litle, deceased, of Washington City, District of Columbia. To Catherine Geary and her sister, Ann Armstrong, both of Borough of Pittsburgh. To Samuel Anderson, my wife's nephew. To sister, Hannah Hopkins, and to former wife's sister, Huldah Mott. To niece Mary James. To niece Elizabeth Hunt. To niece Ann Hopkins. To niece Elizabeth Field. To Hannah Harlan. To Dobel Baker. To friends Thomas Stewardson, Samuel Bettle, Isaac W. Morris, all of this city, my property in Burlington, New Jersey. In trust for use of my daughter, Anna King, wife of Reay King, and her children.
Execs: My friends Thomas Stewardson, Samuel Bettle, Isaac W. Morris, of this city, also to be Guardians of my grandchildren.
Witnesses: John B. Wilson, George Tyson, William Folwell, Jr.

BELL, WILLIAM. Phila. Merchant.
June 28, 1814. June 5, 1816.
To daughter Maria Bell. To son William Bell. To nephew William John Bell, and my friends Joseph Bell and Joseph Watson, and to Lydia

Fisher, daughter of my friend Miers Fisher. Residue to my children: William Bell, Margaret, wife of my nephew William John Bell, Hetty, wife of Alexander John Stewart of New York, Maria Bell.
Execs: Friends Joseph Bell, Joseph Watson, nephew William John Bell.
Witnesses: Andrew Pettit, Redwood Fisher, Miers Fisher, Lewis Nicolas.

LIPPINCOTT, SARAH. Phila.
Feb. 8, 1816. June 10, 1816. 6.287.
To niece Sarah Lippincott, daughter of Thomas Lippincott. To sister Elizabeth Lippincott. To brothers Jehu, Joel, Asa and Thomas Lippincott, and sister Abigail White, and Phebe Lippincott, widow of my brother Benjamin Lippincott. To children of said Abigail White.
Exec: Brother Jehu Lippincott.
Witnesses: Henry M. Zollickhoffer, Zebulon Holmes.

CAMPBELL, HELEN. Phila. Widow of George Campbell, Esq., deceased, of said city.
May 1, 1815. June 8, 1816. 6.288.
To my mother Mary Donnaldson. To my four children: Mary D. Tod, wife of William H. Tod, Esq., Sarah C. Wynkoop, widow, George Campbell and Robert W. Campbell.
Exec: Said son George Campbell.
Witnesses: Hugh Donnaldson, John C. Otto.

PAUL, ABRAHAM. Germantown Township. Phila. Co. Yeoman.
Feb. 10, 1815. June 11, 1816. 6.288.
To wife Belkena and my eight children: Andrew Paul, Susanna Paul, Mary, wife of George Berger, Abraham, Joseph and Benjamin Paul, Elizabeth, wife of Adam Dace, Hannah, wife of John Rudolph.
Execs: Sons Andrew and Abraham Paul.
Witnesses: Jacob Good, John Huston.

CASNER, JOHN. Northern Liberties. Phila. House Carpenter.
June 8, 1816. June 12, 1816. 6.289.
To wife Susanna Casner, whom I appoint sole Executrix.
Witnesses: Reuben Jarmin, Samuel Weasey.

THOMPSON, THOMAS. Chestnut Hill. Phila. Co. Stone Cutter.
Feb. 5, 1816. June 19, 1816. 6.290.
To be interred in ground called Pots burying ground, in Phila., with my first wife. All estate to my present wife, Elizabeth.
Execs: Brother-in-law William Carson, John Bennet, stone cutter.
Witnesses: Samuel Cowden, Andrew Lamon, James Bateson.
Letters to William Carson.

ROBERTS, THOMAS. Bristol Township. Phila. Co. Yeoman.
Jan. 6, 1815. June 15, 1816. 6.291.
To wife Susanna Roberts. To son John Roberts, and my two daughters, Mary Roberts and Sarah Roberts. Deceased son, Thomas Roberts. To deceased brother Jonathan Roberts' grandsons, Robert Roberts (who now lives with me). To niece Elizabeth Jones, daughter of my sister Elizabeth Jones.
Execs: Said son John Roberts, my cousin John Livezey of Roxborough Township, miller.
Witnesses: Jacob Baker, John Felter.

MAYER, NICHOLAS. Northern Liberties. Phila. Dyer and Weaver.
April 17, 1815. June 25, 1816. 6.292.
To wife Catherine Mayer. To Elizabeth McCurdy, the granddaughter of my said wife, Catherine. To Elizabeth Trewillone, late Shingler, who was brought up in my family. To sister Foney, the wife of John Kaysore. To sister Elizabeth Dolp. To sister Christiana. To Elizabeth Aldenderfer, daughter of sister Mary. To John Mayer, son of my brother Jacob. To Daniel Mayer, son of my brother Philip. To Elizabeth Smith, a daughter of my first wife's sister. To Elizabeth Lybrand, the daughter of John Yough. To Nicholas Wilen, son of Conrad Wilen. To Sarah, the daughter of Jacob Markle. To stepson Samuel Walker. To Elizabeth McCurdy, the daughter of said stepdaughter.
Exec: Friend and neighbour, George Gorgas.
Witnesses: Robert Whitehead, Asor L. Gregory.
Codicil: Signed: June 8, 1816. Stepdaughter, Elizabeth McCurdy, deceased. To Maria Hartly, late Yough.
Witnesses: Robert Whitehead, Catherine Dunlop.

SCHLENTZ, GEORGE. Township of Northern Liberties. Phila. Co. Carter.
June 17, 1816. June 21, 1816. 6.294.
All estate to wife Catherine Schlentz.
Exec: Friend John Louder of township aforesaid, grocer.
Witnesses: John Newman, Samuel Macferrane.

ADAMS, JOHN STRONG. Charleston, South Carolina.
May 3, 1809. Dec. 18, 1812. 6.295.
To wife Sarah Adams, property in Village of Randalstown, in County of Antrim, Ireland, bequeathed to me by my father. I hereby give to my mother, Ann Adams, and my sister, Ann Eliza Adams. To Christopher Fitzsimons and John Stoney, in trust for benefit of my mother, Ann Adams, sister Ann Eliza Adams, and my brothers, James and Thomas Adams. To my uncle, William Adams.

Execs: Said Christopher Fitzsimons, John Stoney of this state, and my said uncle, William Adams, Executor thereof, in Ireland.
Witnesses: Thomas Shorthouse, David Hamilton, John Magrath.

LINTENBARIGER, JOHN. Germantown. Phila. Co. Yeoman.
April 11, 1816. April 24, 1816. 6.296.
To wife Permelia Lintenbariger. To daughter Pheby Burns. To eldest son, George Lintenbariger. To son John Lintenbariger's three children. To granddaughter, Margaret Birns.
Execs: Klincken Johnson, John L. Williams, Anthony Williams.
Witnesses: Anthony Johnson, Andrew Trollinger.
Letters to Klineken Johnson.

LEWIS, HANNAH. Phila. Widow of Mordecai Lewis.
Feb. 27, 1816. June 28, 1816. 6.297.
To Monthly Meeting of Women Friends, Phila., Southern District. To granddaughter Hannah Saunders Lewis, daughter of my son Reeve Lewis. To granddaughter Hannah Lewis Moore, daughter of my daughter Mary L. Moore. To my aunt Letitia Tillyer. To sister-in-law Abigail Gordon. To each of my daughters-in-law: Frances Lewis, Rachel Lewis, Elizabeth Lewis, Rebecca C. Lewis. Residue to my children: Hannah Lewis, Rachel Wilson, Joseph S. Lewis, Reeve Lewis, Mordecai Lewis, Samuel N. Lewis, Mary L. Moore. To granddaughter Hannah Lewis Wilson. To sister Rachel Crukshank.
Execs: My sons Joseph S. Lewis, Reeve Lewis, Mordecai Lewis, Samuel N. Lewis.
Witnesses: Israel F. Whitall, Edward Garrigues.
Letters to Joseph S., Mordecai and Samuel N. Lewis.

MC MULLIN, DANIEL. District of Southwark. Phila. Co. Cordwainer.
March 17, 1816. July 3, 1816. 6.298.
All estate to my stepmother Elizabeth McMullin. Late father Michael McMulin.
Witnesses: Ebenezer Ferguson, Robert Adams, Rheudolph Bodey.

MILLER, MARY. Phila.
May 31, 1816. July 3, 1816. 6.299.
To Keturah Temple, wife of Daniel G. Temple, of Phila. To Mira Temple, daughter of said Daniel G. Temple. To Henry Carman, of Phila., for benefit of the poor belonging to the Baptist Churches in Phila. To Eliza Smith, wife of William Smith, of the city of Trenton, in whose family I formerly resided.
Exec: Evan Evans of Trenton.
Witnesses: William Widdifield, Samuel Haydock.

DUNGAN, BENJAMIN. Lower Dublin. Phila. Co.
Aug., 1814. July 5, 1816. 6.299.
To wife Mary. To my son Samuel and his wife. To my daughter
Elizabeth Hilverson, to be kept in trust by William Maghee. To the
heirs of my son Josiah, deceased: Benjamin, Mariah, Joseph and Little.
To my son James Reed Dungan and Matilda Wilte, part of my place
adjoining Jesse Dungan's meadow. To son George.
Execs: Sons James Reed Dungan, George Dungan.
Witnesses: William Maghee, Thomas Holme.

MULLIGAN, PATRICK. Phila. Printer.
June 22, 1816. June 28, 1816. 6.300.
To William Duane and Bernard McMahon of Phila, in trust for use of
my sister Ellen Cunningham, and her children.
Execs: Above-named William Duane, of Phila., printer, and Bernard
McMahon, of said city, gentleman.
Witnesses: William J. Duane, Daniel Brady, Terence Smith.

EMERY, JACOB. Township of Northern Liberties. Phila. Co.
Storekeeper.
June 12, 1816. July 22, 1816. 6.301.
To my wife Elizabeth Emery and my children: Frederick, Ann, Jacob,
Elizabeth, Maria, Susan and John Emery.
Execs: Said wife Elizabeth, son Frederick Emery.
Witnesses: Leonard Striker, Seth Collom, Samuel Macferan.

BOULLAY, ABRAHAM.
July 12, 1816. July 23, 1816. 6.302.
Legitimate son of Joseph Boullay, Jr., merchant at Alencon, and
Elizabeth Méteé, his wife, both deceased; aged 63 years, an inhabitant
of the Island of St. Domingo - Three children, Mary Elizabeth Boullay,
commonly called Zeline, aged 18 years, Joseph Boullay, commonly called
Alcide, aged 14 years and Mary Josephine Boullay, commonly called
Irmer, aged about 7 years, are my lawful heirs. Mary Lacroix, my
deceased wife's, legitimate daughter of Francis Lacroix, deceased.
Francis Barault, now in Phila., Executor of all that belonging to me in
U.S.A., as in Island of St. Domingo. I also appoint him Guardian of my
three minor children.
Witnesses: L. Prudot, I. R. Malenfant.

BENNER, GEORGE. Northern Liberties. Phila. Carter.
July 13, 1816. July 26, 1816. 6.302.
To brother Jacob Benner and my brother-in-law Serick Fox, in trust
for benefit of wife, Mary Benner. To my children: George, John, Jacob,
Ann, Hannah and Mary Benner.

Said Jacob Benner and Serick Fox to be Executors, also Guardians of my nine children.
Witnesses: Robert Whitehead, George Dunton.

OLDEN, JAMES. City and County of Phila. Merchant.
Dec. 1, 1815. July 24, 1816. 6.303.
All estate to wife Deborah, whom I appoint sole Executrix.
Witnesses: Robert Whitehead, Elisha N. English.

STARR, JAMES. Late of Phila., now of Northern Liberties of said city. Cordwainer.
May 27, 1814. July 22, 1816. 6.306.
To wife Lydia Starr. To son Moses Starr. To my eight grandchildren: James Starr, Charles W. Starr, Sarah Starr, Joseph Starr, Samuel Starr, John Starr, Lydia Starr, Ann Starr. To my sister-in-law Deborah Starr, widow of my late brother Alexander Starr, and her daughter, Mary Starr. To friends John Parker and Samuel Harlin of Kennet, Chester Co., in trust for my brother-in-law, William Hammond. To Corporation in Pennsylvania for promoting the abolition of slavery.
Execs: Friend Stephen Maxfield and my two grandsons, James Starr and Charles W. Starr.
Witnesses: Thomas Norton, Jonathan Thomas.
Stephen Maxfield, Charles W. Starr, affirmed.

CARLYLE, ALEXANDER. Phila. Tanner. Born in Castle Bank, about ten miles from Dumfries, in Scotland, which place I left when young and served my time in England to trade of Tanner.
Oct. 21, 1814. July 29, 1816. 6.307.
To my sister, Jane Renew, and her blind daughter Jane. To my housekeeper, Margaret Alexander, of city aforesaid. To nephew, John Carlyle, grandson of William Carlyle and his four children: John, William, Alexander and Rachel Carlyle, and also William Renew. After their decease, to male heirs in a lineal descent of my nephew John Carlyle. To nephew Alexander Carlyle.
Execs: Nephew John Carlyle of the District of Southwark, cordwainer, Thomas Dobson of Phila., bookseller and stationery, Edward Lane of said city, accomptant, also to be Trustees.
Witnesses: John Burkingham, James Alexander, John Allison.

BURNHAM, JAMES. Of State of Connecticut, U.S.A., now in city of Funchal, Island of Madeira.
May 10, 1813. Aug. 6, 1816. 6.309.
To brother Thomas Burnham of said Connecticut, he to dispose of estate that parent, brothers and sister may receive a share.

Sole Executor, friend Robert Adams, now here, but of the U.S.A., a resident merchant in Phila.
Witness: John Oliveira.
James Leander Cathcart, Esq., Consul and Agent of U.S.A. for Island of Madeira, do hereby certify that on 30th of May, 1813, James Burnham of Norwich, Connecticut, U.S.A., departed this life. Elijah Keeler Bangs of Phila., Ship Master, affirmed.

SIMONDS, JONAS. Phila. Colonel of the Sixth Regiment of U.S. Infantry.
May 11, 1815. Aug. 9, 1816. 6.310.
To George W. Hawley. To my natural daughter Elizabeth, commonly called Elizabeth Bender, daughter of Elizabeth Darlard. To grandson Walter S. Franklin. If said daughter and grandson die under age, my estate to children of my elder brother, Nathan Simonds.
Exec: Edward D. Corfield, Esq., of Phila. Co.
Witnesses: Marcus Dennison, Peter Miller.

HOFF, JACOB. Northern Liberties. Phila. Bricklayer.
Oct. 22, 1812. Feb. 9, 1813. 6.311.
To Susanna Wolf, my present housekeeper. To my five children: George, John, Elizabeth, Catherine and Henry Hoff.
Exec: Brother John Hoff, of Charleston, South Carolina.
Witnesses: William Ashton, John Weaver.
John Hoff affirmed, Aug. 15, 1816.

MARSHALL, AMOR. Phila.
May 28, 1813. Aug. 4, 1816. 6.312.
To wife, Mary Marshall. To son, Joseph Yorkson Marshall. To my two daughters, Ann Elizabeth Marshall and Frances Matilda Marshall. Said wife to be Guardian of children.
Execs: Wife Mary Marshall, Samuel Walker, William Haslett.
Witnesses: Daniel Steinmetz, George Heyl, Jr.

MYERS, FREDERICK. Phila. Farmer.
June 20, 1816. Aug. 21, 1816. 6.314.
To wife Mary, son Jacob and daughter, Mary Myers.
Exec: Said wife.
Witnesses: John Christ, Margaret Litzenberg.
(Nuncupative Will)

THOMAS, ROBERT. Germantown. Phila. Co. Cordwainer.
July 26, 1816. Aug. 21, 1816. 6.314.
Estate to wife Elizabeth Thomas for purpose of bringing up my lawful issue: Jane, Jacob, William, Joseph and Robert.

Execs: My father-in-law Jacob Bowman, my friend Abraham Keyser, both of Germantown.
Witnesses: William Meredith, John Green.

DEVINE, KEZIAH. Phila. Widow.
Aug. 15, 1816. Aug. 21, 1816. 6.315.
Executors to sell real estate, monies to nephew, William D. Watson and to my brother Clayton Weaver.
Exec: Friend Abraham Link of Phila, hardware merchant.
Witnesses: William Richardson, Thomas Hoskins.

SEEMAN, JOHN ANDREW. Northern Liberties. Phila. Innkeeper.
July 26, 1816. Aug. 23, 1816. 6.316.
To Eve Kittle, my present housekeeper. To my children, Andrew and Dorothy Seeman, when my daughter arrives at lawful age.
Execs: My friends Frederick Hoeckley, Conrad Wickerly. Also Guardians of my said children.
Witnesses: Robert Whitehead, Frederick Huquencle, John Shultz.

MELTONBERGER, CATHERINE. Phila. Widow.
April 30, 1810. Aug. 26, 1816. 6.317.
To my daughter Elizabeth Miltonberger.
Exec: Frederick Haas.
Witnesses: James Gray, John Ricker.

RINK, MARY. Phila. Widow of John Rink.
Nov. 25, 1815. Aug. 30, 1816. 6.318.
To all my children: Mary Elliot, Sarah Florence, William S. Rink, John Rink and Joseph Rink. Son-in-law David Florence.
Exec: Son William S. Rink.
Witnesses: Margaret Whitehead, Samuel Hanse.
Codicil: Aug. 24, 1816.

DAVIS, CATHERINE. Phila. Widow.
May 30, 1816. Aug. 29, 1816. 6.318.
To Sarah C. Bean, now wife of Robert G. Russel. To my children: Sarah Crosby, Maria McPherson, Eliza Hill, Catherine C. Davis.
Execs: Sons-in-law Robert P. Crosby, Robert G. McPherson, Dr. John H. Hill, my brother-in-law David John.
Witnesses: William Rogers, David John, George H. Wood.
Codicil: July 13, 1816. Sarah C. Russel, formerly Sarah C. Bean, deceased.

PAXSON, ISAAC. Phila. Iron Mongery.
June 22, 1816. Sept. 6, 1816. 6.319.

To my wife, Elizabeth Paxson, in full confidence that she will provide for our son Edward Shoemaker Paxson, during his minority. Trustees and Guardians, my friends George Williams and John C. Evans. To brothers, William, Phineas, Thomas, Malon and Joshua Paxson, and my sisters, Mary Landes, wife of David Landes, and Anna Gillam, wife of Simon Gillam, and the children of my brothers, Joseph Paxson and Israel Paxson, deceased.
Execs: Said wife, Elizabeth, said friends, George Williams and John C. Evans.
Witnesses: Samuel Bittle, John McCollin.
Letters to Elizabeth Paxson.

SHERIDAN, DOMINIC. District of Southwark. Phila. Co.
Aug. 22, 1815. Sept. 7, 1816. 6.320.
To wife, Mary Sheridan. To friend, Caleb Ash, son of Caleb Ash of Southwark, deceased. To friends, Joshua Ash, Joseph Ash, Thomas Ash, Neal McGinnes, Joseph Bird, all of Southwark, and to my friend, Thomas Fletcher, Sr., of the township of Abington, Montgomery Co.
Execs: Friends Thomas Fletcher, of Abington Township, Joseph Bird, of Southwark, grazier.
Witnesses: Joshua Bickham, Davis Marshall.

MC GROTTO, EDWARD. Phila.
Dec. 29, 1815. Sept. 10, 1816. 6.321.
To wife, Margaret McGrotto, and my three children, James, John and Mary McGrotto, last-named, a minor.
Execs: Son James McGrotto, John B. Harper.
Witnesses: Nathan Chapin, Samuel Chapin.
Letters to James McGrotto.

JEFFRIES, EDWARD. Northern Liberties. Phila.
Aug. 3, 1816. Sept. 13, 1816. 6.321.
To wife, Barbarry Jeffries. To my two sons, William and Thomas Jeffries, and to my other four children: Edward, Daniel, Samuel and Mary, now Mary White.
Execs: Son Daniel Jeffries, Charles Yetter.
Witnesses: Thomas Coats, Jr., Michael Bower, Joseph Kingluff, Sr.

PARKINSON, ROBERT. Phila. Gentleman.
July 24, 1816. Sept. 17, 1816. 6.322.
To wife, Esther Parkinson, whom I appoint sole Executrix.
Witnesses: Samuel Wilcocks, Joseph R. Ingersoll.

HOCKLEY, ELEANOR. Phila. Widow.
Sept. 10, 1807. Aug. 23, 1816. 6.322.

To my daughter, Elizabeth Twamly. To my daughter, Eleanor Hockley.
To children of my deceased son, Thomas Hockley.
Execs: Friends Thomas Cumpston, merchant, William Carriagues or
Garrigues, house carpenter, John Cooke, merchant.
Witnesses: Simeon Reynolds, Frederick Beates.
Memorandum: Aug. 30, 1816. Daughter, Eleanor Hockley, now deceased.

MARKS, NICHOLAS. Phila.
July 18, 1816. Sept. 17, 1816. 6.324.
To natural children: Samuel, Mary, Louisa and Gabriel Marks.
Execs: My said son, Samuel, my friend, Rev. Richard Allen.
Said Rev. Richard Allen to be Guardian to my daughter, Louisa, and my son, Gabriel, until of age.
Witnesses: A. A. Browne, Clayton Chapman.

PEART, MARY. Phila.
Oct. 8, 1805. Aug. 26, 1816. 6.325.
To my nephew, Benjamin Peart, son of Bryan Peart, deceased, ground in Byberry Township, Phila. Co. To nephew, Thomas Millard, son of Elizabeth Messer, deceased. To nephew, William Peart, son of Thomas Peart, deceased. To my cousin, Mary Peart Boys, wife of Samuel Boys, daughter of late James Hood. To James A. Hood. To Rachel Hood.
Execs: Cousin Rachel Hood, my nephew Thomas Millard.
Witnesses: Thomas Hood, Field J. Lucas, Jr., John Ashmead.
Codicil: Sept. 10, 1810. Rachel Hood and James A. Hood named in Will, now deceased.
Witnesses: John Ashmead, Thomas Hood, Ann Hood.
Letters to surviving Executor, Thomas Millard.

WOOD, JOHN. Township of Roxborough. Phila. Co. Cordwainer.
Aug. 27, 1816. Sept. 18, 1816. 6.326.
To my wife, Catherine Wood. To daughters, Elizabeth, Mary, Catherine and Ann Wood.
Execs: John G. Longstreth, James Fassitt.
Witnesses: John K. Duy, William Dehaven.

ALBERT, CASPER. Northern Liberties. Phila. Innkeeper.
April 4, 1816. Sept. 17, 1816. 6.329.
To my wife, Eve Albert. To my son John Albert, and the daughters of my said wife, Eve: Hannah, Nancy, Elizabeth and Margaret.
Execs: Said wife, Eve, and her son-in-law John Brooke.
Witnesses: Robert Whitehead, John Young.

61

ODENHEIMER, PHILIP. Phila. Gentleman.
June 21, 1811. Sept. 24, 1816. 6.328.
To wife, Barbara. To son, Jacob W. Odenheimer. To daughter, Catherine Odenheimer. To son George W. Odenheimer. To Jacob W. Odenheimer, Lewis Rush and Jacob Edenborn, in trust for daughters, Mary Sutter and Wilhelmina Lawerswyler, during the lives of their husbands.
Execs: Son Jacob W. Odenheimer, my friends Lewis Rush and Jacob Edenborn, of Phila.

APPLETON, LEWIS. Late of State of Delaware, now of Southwark. Phila. Co.
July 25, 1816. Sept. 26, 1816. 6.330.
To nephew, Isaac Birch, and my niece, Sarah Birch, son and daughter of George Birch, deceased.
Exec: Thomas Welden, of Delaware.
Thomas Welden appointed guardian of said Isaac and Sarah Birch.
Witnesses: Thomas Mercer, William Crusin (?), John Allison.

SHAW, WILLIAM A. At present of Phila. Merchant.
May 5, 1816. Sept. 25, 1816. 6.331.
To wife, Anna M. Shaw.
Execs: Said wife and my friend, John Ridgway, Jr., of Phila., merchant.
Witnesses: Peter Lohra, Garret R. Barry, J. Dobson.
John Ridgway, Jr. renounced.

MC MAHON, BERNARD. Phila. Nursery and Seedman.
March 10, 1816. Sept. 27, 1816. 6.331.
To wife, Ann McMahon. To sons Thomas and James McMahon. Portion of farm in Pennsylvania Township devised to son James, to be used for family burial ground. To William Y. Birch and William S. Duane, for use of my daughter (by a former wife), Mary Ogden, wife of Abraham Ogden, book binder, of Phila. To William F. Thornilly. To Manuel Gotlieb Shew. To Margaret Shew, sister of said Manuel.
Execs: William Y. Birch, William I. Duane, of Phila., my said wife.
Witnesses: William Bell, Edmund Kinsey, Benj'n. Bache.
Codicil: Mentions Thomas T. McMahon.

WETHERILL, SAMUEL. Phila. Druggist.
Aug. 28, 1812. Sept. 27, 1816. 6.333.
To wife, Sarah Wetherill. To sons, Samuel and Mordecai Wetherill. To Martha, wife of said son, Mordecai. To son John Wetherill. To daughter, Sarah Lippincott, and her children. To my sisters Anna and Sarah. To nephews Christopher and George Wetherill, sons of my brother, Isaac Wetherill. To Sybil Dawes and Kitty Trip. To my sister-

in-law Deborah Dawes. To Mordecai McDonald and Rebecca Davis. To
Lydia Crispen. To Catherine Murray. To each of four children in
Massachusetts Bay, New Bedford, who have been named Wetherill, out
of respect to my wife and son, Mordecai Wetherill, one of them the son
of Philip Russel, named Samuel Wetherill Russell, one named Sarah
Wetherill Taber, the child's mother is a daughter of Timothy Davis, one
a son of John Janny, named Mordecai Wetherill Janney, and one a son
of Timothy Davis, named Samuel Wetherill Davis. To Betsey Trip. To
Nancy McIlhenny, who now lives with me.
Exec: Son Samuel Wetherill.
Witnesses: Owen Churchman, William Hy. Gumbee, John H. Hoffman.
Codicils: April 13, 1814. June 23, 1813. Sept. 22, 1816.
To Sybil and Rebecca Dawes, daughters of my sister-in-law Deborah
Dawes, and to Rebecca Gumbes. Revoke legacy to Mary McIlhenny.
Legacy to Margaret Bogs and Sarah McCoy, her sister. To Clarissa
Wilson, daughter of John and Betsey Clayport.
Witnesses: James W. Murray, of Phila., Attorney-at-law, Timothy
Marlack, Esq., of Phila., Tench Coxe, Edmund G. Coxe.

STINE, JACOB. Phila. Flour Merchant.
Jan. 26, 1813. Oct. 3, 1816. 6.339.
Executrix: Wife, Mary Stine, of said city, to whom I leave all estate.
Witnesses: John Donaldson, Robert Ross.

WEATHERBY, JOSEPH. Northern Liberties. Phila. Co.
Sept. 5, 1816. Oct. 14, 1816. 6.339.
Estate to wife, Mary Weatherby, whom I appoint sole Executrix.
Witnesses: John Kesler, Jesse Davis, John Kesler, Jr.

GED, MARGARY. Phila. Widow.
Sept. 8, 1813. Oct. 16, 1816. 6.340.
To nephew, William MacKenzie. To William Miller, Secretary of Phila.
Insurance Co., and Garret Cottringer, two of my Executors.
To Julia Barry, daughter of Francis C. Sarmiento. To Rector,
Vestrymen, etc. for use of United Episcopal Churches of Christ, St.
Peter's and St. James', in Phila. Hospital, Christ Church Hospital and
Society for relief of poor and distressed masters of ships, their widows
and children. To Sarah Morrell Broadhead, daughter of my niece Mary
Broadhead, of Barbadoes. To Mary Ann Thomas, widow of my nephew,
William Thomas, late of Barbadoes. To Ann Craig. To Jane Craig. To
Catherine Sarmiento, wife of Francis C. Sarmiento. To Simmons Edey
and Juliann Edey, daughters of Richard T. A. Edy, late of Barbadoes,
now of Phila. To Elizabeth Shippen. Remainder of estate to said
nephew, William Mackenzie, and niece, Mary Broadhead.

Execs: Friends William Miller, Garret Cottringer, my nephew said William Mackenzie.
Witnesses: James Sawer, Abraham Shoemaker.
Letters to surviving Executors, William Miller and William Mackenzie.

MC ADAMS, MARON.
Feb. 25, 1816. Oct.18, 1816. 6.341.
Deceased brother Robert Andrews. Estate to daughter, Mary, and my sons, William and James McAdams.
Execs: Said daughter Mary, Howell Hopkins, Esq.
Witnesses: Francis S. Beattee, Mary Ann Henson.

SKINNER, ELIZABETH. Phila.
May 18, 1814. Oct. 21, 1816. 6.341.
Estate to Samuel Sellers, son of David Sellers, deceased, in trust for benefit of my sister, Mary Reeves, and her children.
Exec: Friend Samuel Kellers, aforesaid.
Witnesses: M. A. Tilghman, Ann Nox, Edward Tilghman.

CRESSON, CALEB, SR. Phila.
July 20, 1815. Oct. 30, 1816. 6.342.
To son, Caleb Cresson, Jr. To grandchildren: Elliott Cresson, Annabella Cresson, Deborah Cresson, Sarah Emlen Cresson (my silver tankard that her grandmother, Sarah Emlen earned by her needle), Mary, Warder, Caleb, the younger (ground rent issuing out of a lot in Southwark left to me by my aunt, Mary Armitt), Emlen and William Cresson. To Jane Lownes. To brother-in-law, Samuel Elliott's daughters. To my housekeeper, Rachel Ivins. To widow and seven children of my son, John E. Cresson, deceased.
Exec: My son, Caleb Cresson, Jr. As he may make a distant voyage, grandson, Elliott Cresson, to serve in his place.
Witnesses: William Andres, Thomas Barnes.
Codicil: May 7, 1816. As I have not mentioned the names of my son John's children, to whom I have devised residue of my estate, I here name them: Elliot, Warder, Annabella, Deborah, Sarah and Clement, little John having passed away.
Witnesses: Rachel H. Ivins, Lewis Kunits.

HAMON, WILLIAM. Citizen of U.S. by Certificate of Naturalization, April, 1798, delivered at Wilmington, Delaware.
June 1, 1816. Oct. 23, 1816. 6.346.
To wife, Mrs. Hamon. I desire to be buried at Wilmington, Delaware near the grave of my son, William, in the Church Yard of the Anglican Church. To (only kinsman to my knowledge who bears my name) Mr. Louis Hamon, born at St. Domingo, now residing in France. To Mr.

Jordain, President of the Royal Court of Rennes and to the Lady, his wife, my kinswoman. To my cousins, the Misses Lusette and Rose Guichard of Rennes, and after their decease, to their niece, Lusetta Guichard. To the widow Pasquin de St. Germain, born Savoye, my kinswoman, residing at Cancale. To Mrs. Léjeé, now in France or Switzerland, born at St. Domingo. To Mrs. Filette Thomasson, mother of Mrs. Léjeé. To Mrs. Louis Chaurard, born Libault, of Nantes, and to her two children, Mrs. Leon and Miss Eugenia Chaurard. To Mr. and Mrs. Forget and their children. To Monsieuer, the Bishop of Rennes (within whose Diocese Cancale is situated), a legacy for establishment of charity and beneficence where those can be educated whose parents have not the means of paying school masters, also a dispensary room where fresh medicines may be distributed to the poor. Father's and Mother's tombstones to be found near the large gate of the Parish Church of Cancale, to be deposited under monument at extremity of Burying Ground.
Execs: John Keating of Phila, John Juhel of New York, or Messrs. Ls. De Mons Dorbigny and Julius Keating (the son) of Phila.
Witnesses: Peter Nairac, Ls. de Mons d'Orbigny, E. I. Given.

SNOOKE, MARY. Phila.
Dec. 13, 1807. Oct. 21, 1816. 6.352.
Estate to friend, Elizabeth Saltar, wife of John Saltar, Esq., Phila. Co., in trust for children of said Elizabeth.
Execs: John Saltar, Jr., George G. Saltar.
Witnesses: John Lardner, John Carman, William Ashton.
John Saltar, the surviving Executor sworn, Oct. 31, 1816.

PEARSON, SAMUEL. Township of Blockley. Phila. Co. Taylor.
Sept. 28, 1812. Oct. 28, 1816. 6.352.
To wife, Lydia, all my estate, and after her decease, to son Samuel, he to pay to heirs of my son, Charles. To my daughter, Rachel, and to my sons, George, John, Joshua and William.
Exec: Said wife, Lydia.
Witnesses: John Pearson, John B. Pearson, Margaret Pearson.

LOWER, HENRY. Township of Northern Liberties. Phila. Co. Taylor.
Feb. 2, 1816. Nov. 4, 1816. 6.353.
To wife, Anna Margaretta, and my three children: Maria Sophia, intermarried with John Kemp, Henry Ludwick Balzer Lower, George Christian Lower.
Exec: Wife, Anna Margaretta.
Witnesses: I. G. Murtzer, Jacob Beckenbach.

BANTLEON, GEORGE. Penn Township. Phila. Co. Victualler.
Oct. 29, 1816. Nov. 4, 1816. 6.354.
To Elizabeth Hemphill. To John Kreamer, money in hands of John
Hinckle of said township, victualler to be paid to George Pealor when
twenty-one years of age. To sister, Ann Miller, for support of
Christiana Danacker. Remainder of my estate to my five sisters: Ann
Miller, Catherine White, Sarah Bantleon, Rachel Lee and Eliza
Bantleon. Friend John Hinckle to be Guardian of my said two sisters,
Rachel Lee and Eliza Bantleon.
Execs: Sister Ann Miller, Thomas Hennessy.
Witnesses: John Hinckle, Charles White.

MORGAN, WILLIAM. Phila. Labourer.
Oct. 30, 1816. Nov. 5, 1816. 6.355.
Estate to "Orphan Society of Phila."
Exec: My friend, William Shufflebottom, of Phila., merchant.
Witnesses: Francis D. Wait, John Hansell.

BLACK, ROBERT. District of Southwark. Carter.
May 22, 1812. Nov. 4, 1816. 6.355.
All estate to my wife, Mary, to enable her to educate our children.
Execs: Said wife, my sister, Isabella, widow of James Stuart.
Witnesses: Alexander Steel, Isaac Black.

HELT, MARY. Biberry Township. Phila. Co.
Sept. 9, 1816. Nov. 13, 1816. 6.356.
To my daughters, Sarah Bowell, Elizabeth Gifford and Mary Buckelew.
To my granddaughter, Mary Worrell. To my daughter Hannah Worrel,
all the residue.
Exec: John Roads, cordwainer.
Witnesses: Samuel W. Comly, G. H. Bauling.

LAIDLEY, JAMES. Phila. Taylor.
April 15, 1815. Nov. 1 2, 1816. 6.356.
To my housekeeper, Phoebe Champion Smith. Remainder of estate to
my two sons, Robert and James Laidley.
Execs: My friends Abraham Small of Phila., bookseller, and Adam
Remage, of said city, joiner.
Witness: Peter Mackie.
Codicil: April 8, 1816. Am about to marry my said housekeeper,
bequeath to her half my estate.
Witnesses: Peter Mackie, Charles Mackie.

RODRIGUEZ, ISAAC. Phila. Shopkeeper.
Jan. 28, 1812. Nov. 15, 1816. 6.358.

To Catherine Despencer, now living with me, and partner in business. Legacy to Portuguese Synagogue. To my nephew, Moses, and his two sisters, legitimate children of my brother, Jacob Rodriguez, of the island of Curacoa, the remainder of all my estate. I recommend Aimee (a mulatto girl now living in my family) and said nephew and nieces to the said Catherine Despencer, whom I appoint Executrix.
Witnesses: John Miller, Jacob Heyberger, John P. Ripley.

ATKINSON, BENJAMIN. Byberry Township. Phila. Co.
Nov. 11, 1807. Nov. 12, 1816. 6.359.
To wife, Jane. To my children, when of age, the boys to be placed as apprentices at age of 16 years to members of Society of Friends.
Execs: Friend John Lingley, John Comly.
Witnesses: Joshua Gilbert, Robert Parry, Rebecca B. Comly.

POTTER, JOSEPH. Phila. Co. Mariner.
Dec. 14, 1813. Nov. 3, 1816. 6.358.
Estate to wife, Elizabeth Potter, and her heirs.
Exec: Said Elizabeth.
Witnesses: Elizabeth Palmer, Richard Palmer.

BUCKLEY, WILLIAM. Phila. Late Merchant.
Sept. 6, 1816. Nov. 14, 1816. 6.360.
To wife, Sarah Buckley. To grandson, Charles P. Howard. Children: Anthony Morris Buckley, Sarah P. Howard, Samuel B. Morris.
Exec: Son, Anthony M. Buckley, to whom I leave remainder of estate.
Witnesses: Richard Hill Morris, Charles Anderson.

BROWN, MARY. Township of Northern Liberties. Phila. Co. Widow of John Brown, formerly of Brandywine Hundred of New Castle, Delaware.
March 26, 1814. Nov. 15, 1816. 6.360.
To sister's children, that is to say, unto Rebecca Anderson, wife of Charles Anderson, Christiana McCorkle, Mary McKissick, wife of John McKissick, Elizabeth McCorkle, William McCorkle, Deborah Bryant, wife of John Y. Bryant, Jane McCorkle, Amy H. Houston, wife of William Houston and Joseph P. McCorkle. To Liha Davis, a coloured girl brought up by me.
Execs: Friends William McCorkle of Phila., printer, Charles Anderson of Northren Liberties, storekeeper, John Y. Bryant of Phila., apothecary.
Witnesses: Joseph Weatherby, John Smith, John Bender.

MC CONNELL, MATTHEW. Phila.
Dec. 11, 1815. Nov. 20, 1816. 6.361.
To wife Ruth McConnell.
Execs: Said wife, friend James Musgrave.
Witnesses: James Glentworth, Thomas Greeves.

JAMES, DAVID, JR. Township of Deerfield. Cumberland Co., New Jersey.
Nov. 2, 1816. Nov. 15, 1816. 6.362.
To brother Lewis James, making him sole Executor.
Witnesses: Eliza Smith, Isaac Smith, George H. Burgen.

BROWN, JOHN. Phila. Gentleman.
April 7, 1814. Nov. 18, 1816. 6.362.
To wife Isabella Brown. To mother, Mary Brown.
Execs: Friends Thomas Jackson and James Graham, and my wife, Isabella Brown.
Witnesses: John B. White, William Gallaher.
Letters to Isabella Brown. Other Executors declined to serve.

PAUL, WILLIAM. Northern Liberties. Phila. Gentleman.
June, 1815. Nov. 26, 1816. 6.364.
To wife Alice Paul. To son William Paul, Jr. Remainder of estate to my three daughters: Elizabeth Paul, Sarah R. Free, Alice C. Duve.
Execs: Wife, Alice Paul, sons-in-law, William I. Paul and Samuel Duve.
Witnesses: Henry Probasco, Joseph Stouse.

BASAN, JACOB. A resident, when at home, of the Parish of Port Royal, in the Island of Jamaica, but now a sojourner in Phila.
Oct. 30, 1816. Dec. 6, 1816. 6.364.
To my wife, Judith, and my four children: Sarah, Esther, George and Caleb Basan. To eldest son, David Basan.
Execs. in Jamaica: wife Judith Basan, Abraham Vetti or Rietti, of Kingston, Jamaica and Ralph Beandon and sons, merchants of London.
Execs.in United States of America: Friends Samuel Bens Akin and Abraham Elken. To Eve Elkins, wife of said friend, Abraham Elkins. To Portuguese Jews Synagogue of Phila.
Witnesses: Robert Beck Laidly, John Brown, Joseph Alexander.

MILLER, HENRY. Late of Township of Northern Liberties, now of Penn Township. Phila. Co. Taylor.
June 28, 1816. Dec. 10, 1816. 6.366.
Estate to my eight children: Mary Bornmann, wife of John Bornmann, Margaret Lawrence, wife of George Lawrence, Catherine Erwin, wife of Caspar Ervin, Elizabeth Ousterhelt, wife of Frederick Ousterhelt,

Sarah Lutz, wife of Philip Lutz, Ann Warner, wife of John Warner, Michael and Sophia Miller. No division to be made until youngest daughter, Sophia, is of age.
Execs: Friends Frederick Ulrick, William Yager.
Witnesses: Charles Lex, John Biddle.

TRAQUAIR, JAMES. Phila. Marble Mason.
Nov. 7, 1816. Nov. 27, 1816. 6.367.
Estate, which I purchased of my father, I bequeath to my brother, Adam, he to pay principle sum which I gave for same. Household furniture to be the property of my mother, during her life. To Mary Ann Scott, niece of my mother. All remainder of estate to my son, Samuel Henderson Traquair.
Execs: Samuel Henderson, Esq., Davis Henderson, John Henderson, Esq. of Montgomery Co.
Witnesses: John Silver, Jacob Rheem.
Samuel Henderson renounced.

DARBLEY, CATHARINA ELIZABETH. Northern Liberties Township. Now of Phila. Widow.
Sept. 18, 1800. Dec. 18, 1816. 6.367.
To my friends Joseph Bastian of said city, Yeoman, and Elizabeth, his wife, with whom I live. I leave all my estate, making said Joseph and Elizabeth Executors.
Witnesses: Richard Whitehead, Benj'n. Brown, Robert Whitehead.
Letters to Joseph Bastian.

CLARK, JOHN. Mariner, lately belonging to the private armed schooner, "Kemp" of Baltimore, Captain Jacobs.
Aug. 22, 1814. Dec. 16, 1816. 6.368.
Estate to my friend, Barnard Payne, of Phila, whom I appoint Executor.
Witnesses: Samuel Barclay, Jacob Winemore.

INGLISH, THOMAS.
Aug. 2, 1813. Dec. 24, 1816. 6.368.
All estate to wife, Mary Inglish, whom I appoint sole Executrix.
Witnesses: Peter J. Decker, Daniel Bussier.

TILLMAN, JOHN GEORGE. Germantown. Phila. Co. Blacksmith.
Nov. 5, 1816. Dec. 14, 1816. 6.369.
Estate to wife, Ann Magdalene Tillman, and after her decease, to my children.
Execs: Said wife, Ann Magdalene, Godlieb Klever.
Witnesses: Samuel Fleckenstin, Elias Sorber.

WARNER, JOHN. Phila. Lumber Merchant.
Nov. 28, 1816. Dec. 14, 1816. 6.369.
To sister, Lydia Cress. To niece, Eliza Cress. To my nephews: John Cress, Peter Cress, William Cress and Isaac Cress. To my three nieces: Lydia, Mary and Rebecca Warner. Remainder of estate to all the children of my late brother-in-law, Algernon Roberts, being ten in number.
Execs: Nephews, Isaac Roberts, Isaac Cress, my friend Isaac Wampole of Phila., scrivener.
Witnesses: Robert Imlay, Enoch Wheeler, I. Wampole.

SCHUMO, BARNEY. Phila. Turner.
Oct. 7, 1816. Dec. 23, 1816. 6.371.
Estate to my wife and children: Thomas, Susanna, Daniel, Joseph, Sarah P., Lydia and Ann. Boys to be placed at some suitable trade when they arrive at fit age.
Execs: Abraham Lower, Alexander Shaw.
Witnesses: Andrew Ashborn, James Sleeper.

BAKER, GEORGE ADAM. Phila. Conveyancer.
Oct. 26, 1813. Dec. 19, 1816. 6.371.
Executrix: Wife Anna Catharine Baker. All my children settled in life except my daughter, Susanna Louisa, but who is now a young lady. Estate to wife, and at her decease, I appoint my sons John Hilary Baker, John Lewis Baker and George Adam Baker, Executors.
Witnesses: Eliakim Garretson, Samuel Keemlé, Isaac Keemlé.

LUDWICK, JOHN. Penn Township. Phila. Co.
March 13, 1816. Dec. 30, 1816. 6.372.
All estate to wife, Elizabeth Ludwick, whom I appoint Executrix.
Witnesses: Charles Louder, Frederick Haas.

HARLAN, HANNAH. Phila. Spinster.
Nov. 18, 1816. Dec. 24, 1816. 6.373.
To sisters Rebecca Carter and Alice Harlan. To my two nieces, Rebecca and Hannah Harlan, at eighteen years of age, daughters of Elisha Harlan.
Execs: Friends John Elliott, Dobell Baker.
Witnesses: Richard Smith, Joseph Knight.

CAMBRIDGE, SARAH. Phila.
May 9, 1815. Dec. 30, 1816. 6.374.
Legacy to my brothers [sic], Charles Hollick. Remainder of estate to my friend, Henry May, of Phila., hatter, whom I appoint sole Executor.
Witnesses: Frederick Beates, Peter Heyler.

RIEM, ELIZABETH. Phila. Widow.
March 29, 1814. Dec. 18, 1816.
Exec: Friend Peter Stine to whom I leave my estate.

TITTERMARY, JOHN. Moyamensing Township. Phila. Co. Rope Maker and Ship Chandler.
Dec. 27, 1816. Dec. 31, 1816. 6.375.
To wife, Loranah, and after decease, to my children: Eleanor Williamson, John C., Lurana, William W., Margaret, Thomas I. and Robert C. Tittermary.
Execs: Friends Joseph S. Lewis, Joseph Johnson, Samuel Neave Lewis, all of Phila.
Witnesses: Robert Wharton, Thomas Mitchell.

GILLCHRIST, LUCRETIA. Relict of Charles Gilchrist of Phila., Merchant.
Oct. 15, 1816. Nov. 28, 1816. 6.376.
Legacy to my friend, Charlotte Ellis. To my friend, Emanuel Walker of Phila., merchant, I leave remainder of estate.
Exec: Appoint said Emanuel Walker and Thomas Markie of Phila., merchant.
Witnesses: Josiah W. Gibbs, William Birnie, Archibald McLean.

BARNHILL, JOHN REDMAN. Phila. Doctor in Medicine.
Aug. 26, 1815. Dec. 12, 1816. 6.377.
Legacy to Kezia Heritage, to Robert Toland and Thomas C. Rockhill. Elder brother, Robert, long since deceased. To sister, Margaretta. The remainder of my property to sister, Sarah Henry, as she has two small children to educate.
Execs: Silas E. Wier, Esq., and in case of his demise, I appoint Thomas Shewell, Esq.
Witnesses: William Richardson, John Dunphy.

RUTTER, GEORGE. Phila.
Sept. 1, 1814. Dec. 31, 1816. 6.377.
To my wife, Elizabeth, she to maintain, educate, etc. my son, Robert Rutter for three years. Legacy to Executors to be distributed amongst widows and orphan children of men of Phila., who have fallen during present contest with Great Britain. Legacy to Mary M. Hains, mother of said wife. Remainder to said son, Robert Rutter.
Execs: Said wife, George Krips, Frederick Hains, of Phila.
Witnesses: Blathwaite Shober, John Nisbet, Frederick Hains. One of Executors sworn.

71

ROBINSON, JOHN. Phila. Oysterman and Book Cleaner.
Oct. 28, 1816. Nov. 11, 1816. 6.378.
To my son, Jacob Robinson. To my brother, William Robinson. Residue of estate to my four children: Jacob, Henry, Louisa and Robinson.
Execs: William Delany, Richard Peters, Jr., also to be Guardians to my children.
Witnesses: William Tovell, George Wilson.

MC ALLISTER, WILLIAM. Phila. Grocer.
June 24, 1816. Dec. 17, 1816. 6.379.
To my father, Alexander McAllister, of Phila., whom I appoint Executor.
Witnesses: John McAllister, Alexander McAllister, Jr.

BORDLEY, SARAH. Phila. Widow.
July 29, 1813. Dec. 30, 1816. 6.379.
To my grandchildren: Sarah, John, Elizabeth and Charles Mifflin. Having advanced to son, John F. Mifflin, his portion of estate. I now bequeath all residue of my estate to my daughter, Elizabeth Bordley.
Execs: Said daughter Elizabeth, friend Edward Burd.
Witnesses: J. J. Vanderkimp, George Clymer. James Gibson, Esq., of Phila., affirmed.

JACKSON, SAMUEL. Phila. Now in occupation of keeping a Livery Stable.
Dec, 4, 1816. Jan. 4, 1817. 6.381.
All estate to my wife, Anna Jackson. Executors to have care of Mary Moore (a blind girl) to provide for her and John Beswick.
Execs: Said wife, Anna Jackson, Charles Keyser, teacher.
Witnesses: Samuel Allen, Samuel Whitehead.

OAKFORD, CHARLES. Phila. Storekeeper.
Dec. 24, 1816. Jan. 8, 1817. 6.381.
To my children, Grace and Julian Oakford and Rachel, Mary, Charles and Isaac Oakford, when they arrive at 21 years of age. All residue of estate to wife, Elizabeth, daughter, Susanna Averly.
Execs: Said wife, my friend William Hill of Kingsessing Township, Phila. Co., farmer.
Witnesses: Richard Renshaw, John Mercer. Elizabeth Oakford, affirmed.

HEMSLEY, ANNA MARIA. Phila. Widow.
Feb. 13, 1815. Jan. 11, 1817. 6.382.
To brother, William Tilghman. To my niece, Elizabeth Hemsley, wife of Thomas Hemsley, Esq., of Queen Anne's Co., Maryland. To niece,

Elizabeth Margaret Tilghman, daughter of my said brother, William Tilghman. To negro slave, Rachel, wife of William Dobson, residing in Maryland, also absolute freedom to her and all her children, except William, to whom I give freedom at 28 years, and Henry Dobson, whom I have already manumitted. To Executor for education of my grandniece, Maria Lloyd Hemsley, daughter of Philemon Hemsley, Esq., until eighteen years, she to live with my daughter-in-law, Sarah Troup, wife of Dr. John Troup of Queen Anne's Co., aforedsaid. After my decease, all residue of my estate to said grandniece, Maria Lloyd Hemsley, my nephew, Richard Lloyd, nephew James Tilghman, son of deceased brother, James Tilghman, and his sisters, Elizabeth Hemsley, wife of Thomas Hemsley, Esq., Maria Tilghman, Ann Brown, wife of Robert Brown, Esq., and Margaret Tilghman.
Exec: My brother, William Tilghman.
Witnesses: Benjamin Tilghman, Edward Earle.
Codicil: Aug. 17, 1815.
Witnesses: Sophia C. Necklin, Benjamin Chew.

BARTON, SARAH PENNINGTON. Phila.
Sept. 9, 1816. Jan. 14, 1817. 6.385.
Estate to mother, Mary P. Barton, whom I appoint sole Executrix.
Witnesses: Elizabeth Sergeant, Elihu Spencer Sergeant, Thomas P. Barton.

PRAHL, SOPHIA. Northern Liberties. Phila. Widow.
Aug. 19, 1815. Jan. 15, 1817. 6.385.
To my children: Sarah Prahl, Elizabeth Wilson, Samuel Prahl.
Executrix: Said daughter, Sarah.
Witnesses: Jacob Sheble, Jr., Joseph Morehane.

BIRCHALL, CALEB. Phila. Hatter.
Dec. 12, 1816. Jan. 16, 1817. 6.386.
To wife, Sarah Birchall.
Execs: Abraham Patton, William Gerhard.
Witnesses: William Hancock, James Birchall.

BROWN, JAMES. Southwark. Phila. Co.
Nov. 1, 1816. Jan. 17, 1817. 6.386.
To Joseph Hassall, Sr., after decease of my wife.
Exec: Appointing said Joseph.
Witnesses: Samuel Barclay, John Tripp.

ROW, JOHN MARTIN. Phila. Baker.
Jan. 6, 1816. Jan. 21, 1817. 6.387.

Estate to my son, Henry Row, he to give legacies to my son, Frederick Row, now living at Lewestown, Delaware. To son, George Row, and to my granddaughter, Catharine Olliphant.
Execs: Philip Mason, George Rees, the elder.
Witnesses: John Menzies, Enoch Watson. Philip Mason, one of Executors affirmed, Feb. 11, 1817.

ROSS, JAMES. Phila. Tavern Keeper.
March 6, 1810. Jan. 22, 1817. 6.388.
To my wife, Elizabeth Ross, otherwise Lee, appointing her sole Executrix.
Witnesses: Thomas Bennis, Samuel Reed, William Morgan.

DALLAS, ALEXANDER JAMES. District Attorney for Pennsylvania.
Aug. 10, 1804. Jan. 23, 1817. 6.388.
Estate to my wife, Arabella Maria Dallas, and my children: Sophia, Alexander, George, Maria, Matilda, Trevanion. To said George, the portrait of Governor Mifflin, after whom he is named. To said daughter, Matilda, the miniature of my sister, Mrs. Byron.
Executrix: Said wife.
Codicil: Jan. 31, 1806: Daughter Sophia, now married.
Jared Ingersoll, Esq., of Phila. and Robert Egglesfield Griffith, of Phila., merchant, affirmed.

EGER, SARAH. Phila. Widow.
March 17, 1815. Jan. 24, 1817. 6.389.
To Roman Catholic Society of St. Joseph for educating poor children in Phila. To John Ashley, Lewis Ryan and Joseph Snyder, blacksmith, for poor widows of Roman Catholic Church of St. Mary's, Phila.
Execs: Said John Ashley, Lewis Ryan, Joseph Snyder.
Witnesses: John W. Moore, Israel F. Whitehall.
Edward Garrigues, Jr., of Phila., affirmed. Letters to John Ashley.

O'DONNELL, JOHN. Phila. Proprietor of Hack Carriages.
Jan. 23, 1817. Feb. 3, 1817. 6.390.
To wife, Bridget O'Donnell, and to my two children, John and Mary.
Execs. and Guardians of said children: Kernan Fitzgerald, stablekeeper, James Brady, Morocco dresser, both of said city.
Witnesses: Lewis Ryan, Thomas Mitchell.

ALBERT, MARY. Phila. Widow.
Feb. 8, 1816. Feb. 6, 1817. 6.391.
Execs: Son, George Durfor, and my daughter, Ann Catherine Galley.
To my four children: said George Durfor, Catherine Galley, Philip Albert and Henry Albert.

Witnesses: Henry Leech, Frederick Beates.

CANER, CHARLES. Phila. Coach Painter.
Oct. 21, 1808. Feb. 11, 1817. 6.392.
To my nephews, John C. Herman and Charles Caner. To my brother, Michael Caner, and sister, Catherine Herman.
Exec: Said brother, Michael.
Witnesses: Thomas Newborn, Joseph Grimer.

ROYAL, GEORGE. Germantown. Phila. Victualler.
Jan. 15, 1816. Feb. 13, 1817. 6.393.
To wife, Mary, and my four sons: George, William, Jacob and Edward.
Execs: Said wife and four sons.
Witnesses: Alexander Prevost, John DePrefontaine. Letters to Mary Royal and George Royal.

GRAVY, HENRY. Northern Liberties. Phila. Inn Keeper.
Jan. 31, 1817. Feb. 17, 1817. 6.394.
Estate to wife, Elizabeth Gravy, and after her decease, to my natural son, Henry Gravy, who now lives in the country.
Executrix: Said wife, Elizabeth.
Witnesses: Thomas Coates, Jr., Frederick Hoeckley, John Louder.

PARKINSON, MARTIN H. District of Southwark. Phila. Mariner.
Dec. 26, 1816. Feb. 18, 1817. 6.394.
To my wife, Rebecca Parkinson, and my children, Martin H. Parkinson, Sarah Parkinson, my step-daughter, Rachel Wilkey, sister-in-law, Rachel Welsh, and to my daughter, Margaret Ann Norman, late Parkinson.
Executrix: My said wife.
Witnesses: Michael Freytag, Robert S. Loughead.

HINKLE, SUSANNA. Penn Township. Phila. Co.
Dec. 11, 1816. Feb. 20, 1817. 6.395.
To my daughter, Mary Oler. To daughter, Anna Hinkle. To daughter, Barbara. Son, Henry, to take charge of my daughter, Elizabeth, until 18 years, son Jacob until 21 years, daughter Barbara until 18 years.
Execs: Son Henry Hinkle, George Knittle, Mary Riffert.

KENTZINGER, GEORGE. Southwark. Phila. Co. Taylor.
Feb. 18, 1817. Feb. 25, 1817. 6.396.
To grandson, Charles Kentzinger, son of deceased son, Christopher. To daughter Catharine Woelpper. To my son-in-law, George Woelpper, in trust for daughter, Elizabeth Kentzinger. Sons George and William, having been considered, I give them no more.

Exec: Son-in-law, George Woelpper.
Witnesses: Peter Kotz, John Bartholomew.

FORBES, MARY. Germantown.
May 18, 1813. Feb. 26, 1817. 6.397.
To my son's son, commonly called James Forbes, to be held by Thomas Biggs until said James if of age. To my four nieces: Anne Lawler, Isabella Bevan, Tacy Ann Stacy, Anne B. Garrett. To Tacy Pryor, granddaughter of my sister, Tacy Pryor. To Mary Anne Garrett. To niece Anne B. Garrett, but if she should not survive me, then to her children, and the daughter of her brother, Benjamin Pearson, which he named after me. To nephews, Charles, Benjamin, Thomas and Beaven Pearson, the sons of my sister Anne Pearson and Matthew L. Bevan, the son of my brother, Davis Bevan. To Eve Maria Brownhultz.
Execs: Nephews Benjamin Pearson, Matthew L. Bevan.
Witnesses: Thomas Whitesides, Alexander Provest.

STRAYLINE, GEORGE. Penn Township. Phila. Co. Yeoman.
Feb. 11, 1817. March 1, 1817. 6.398.
To wife, Elizabeth Strayline, and my five children: George, Catherine, Charles, Elizabeth and William.
Execs: Said wife, my friend John Adam Coleman.
Witnesses: R. Whitehead, George Yensar, Matthias Zimmar.

MEREDITH, DAVID.
Sept. 12, 1807. March 1, 1817. 6.399.
To my son, David, my silver watch when 18 years. To wife, Sophia, and at her decease, to my three children and grandson, David McGray, when of age.
Execs: Friend Jacob Fry, my brother-in-law, Samuel Lehman.
Witnesses: Benjamin Lehman, John Frank.
George Miller, Germantown, clock & watch maker, affirmed.

HERBERT, MARY. Phila. Widow of Lawrence Herbert, deceased.
Feb. 18, 1814. March 4, 1817. 6.400.
To Mary Shuster, now living with me. To Elizabeth Bausman, wife of John Bausman, and to her daughter, Anna Maria Herbert Bausman, and her sister, Caroline, their father and mother to have use of it. To Mary Witmer, wife of Henry Witmer, and daughter of late Michael Hay, and to her daughter Sarah Witmer. To Eliza Hay, sister of Mrs. Witmer. To Mrs. Hay, wife of my friend, John Hay. To Catharine Debler. To my friend, Mrs. Knerr, wife of Henry Knerr. To friend, Sophia Chrystler. To friend, William Hay, son of John Hay. To friend, Isaac Wampole, I give portrait of Alexander Hamilton, Esq. To Trustees of Evangelical Lutheran Congregation of St. John's Church, of

Phila., and vicinity. To Casper Shaffner, Jr., of Lancaster, for use of German Reformed Church of Lancaster. To Phila. Dispensary.
Exec: Friend, Isaac Wampole, of Phila., scrivener.
Codicil: Sept. 9, 1815: Sarah Witmer, lately deceased. To Charlotte Harman, etc.
Witnesses: Thomas M. Hall, Joseph D. Brown. Isaac Wampole, of Phila., conveyancer, and Jacob Christler, of said city, merchant, affirmed.

KURTZ, HENRY.
Proved: March 4, 1817. 6.402.
To brother, Peter Kurtz's son, William Kurtz, I bequeath the place which I purchased from Christopher Meng and Peter Schneider, in Germantown, on conditions that in case Godfrey Schauwecker's wife should become a widow, to have use of frame house, etc. To wife of my brother's son's Charles, etc. and to each of her children. To each of my brother, Jacob's three children. To wife of my brother's son, Peter, and each of her children. To children of my brother's daughter, Nancy. To my brother's son, Henry. To Lutheran Church in Beggarstown, Union Society in Germantown. To George Kurtz's daughter. To three daughters of my sister, Stolz. To my brother, Peter's widow. If an heir of Christopher Berr, Apothecary in Heidelberg should appear in six years, he to have a legacy. To Hospital in Phila. To William Kurtz's two daughters, Elizabeth and Catharine. To be interred in Lutheran Grave Yard in Beggarstown. To wife of my brother's son, Peter Kurtz, and to each of her children, my clothes to her three sons. To little Catharine Grasbery, who lives with me.
Execs: Brother's son, William Kurtz, John Fry, who resides in my house.
Witnesses: George F. Stuckert, Alexander Armer, William Ulmer. John C. Baker, of Township of Germantown, Minister of the Gospel, affirmed.

BYRNE, JAMES MURPHY. Late of Phila., now of Horsham, Montgomery Co.
June 27, 1815. March 5, 1817. 6.403.
To cousin Elizabeth Ann Byrne. To Roman Catholic Society of St. Joseph. To Sarah Lukens, wife of Seneca Lukins, of Horsham Township, aforesaid, and to his two daughters, Martha B. Lukins and Tabitha Kirk. Remainder of estate to children of Edward Carrell by my late sister, Maria. To sister Eleanor Maria Maher. To sister, Ann Jane Clopper. To brother, Patrick John Byrne.
Execs: Said Patrick, John Byrne, my brother-in-law Francis C. Clopper.
Witnesses: Seneca Lukens, Joseph S. Lukens. Michael Hurley, of Phila., Minister of the Gospel, affirmed.

CROZIER, WILLIAM. Phila. Accomptant.
Jan. 7, 1817. March 6, 1817. 6.404.
To be interred in the burying ground of Fourth Presbyterian Church, in Phila., if practicable. If not, any other burying ground most convenient. To Jane Dalzell. To Mary Potts, wife to the Rev. George C. Potts. To Grace Cochran. To Rev. George C. Potts. To Robert Bruce, my nephew. To William Bruce, my brother-in-law. To Jane Bruce, my sister, and wife to William Bruce.
Execs: Gen'l. John Seele, collector of the customs for Phila., Robert Mercer, Esq., merchant of Phila.
Witnesses: John Crombarger, George C. Potts.
Entitled to military land, according to rank in late Army of U.S., as a Lieutenant in 32nd Regiment, legally discharged, etc.

SMITH, JOHN. Northern Liberties. Phila. Superintendant of the incorporated part of said Liberties.
Jan. 20, 1817. March 7, 1817. 6.405.
Estate to wife, Mary Smith, whom I appoint sole Executrix.
Witnesses: Thos. Timings, Elizabeth Shelmire.

ROBERTS, MARY. Phila. Widow of Thomas Roberts of said city.
Dec. 11, 1816. March 5, 1817. 6.406.
To cousin, Robert Cochran, of North Carolina, and to his children now living. To Thomas Cochran, son of above-named Robert Cochran. To Mariah Delah Cochran, daughter of cousin, Richard Cochran, deceased. Executors to place head stones at graves of father and mother, brothers Benjamin and Richard, my aunt Mary and my own. To friend, Lydia Jones, wife of John M. Jones, of Phila. To Mary Cuthbert, daughter of Mary and Anthony Cuthbert, of Phila. To Jane Preston, wife of Dr. Jonas Preston, to be divided among the family of my late husband. To Lydia Thomas of Downingtown, Pennsylvania, a niece of my late husband. To Thomas Price, nephew of my deceased husband. To cousin, Elizabeth Reese, daughter of Asa Davis. To aunt, Catharine Davis, wife of Jesse Davis of Delaware Co., Pennsylvania. To George Betterton. To Harriot (a coloured woman). To Molly Lloyd. These last three are persons brought up in my father's family. To David Young of Lower Merion, Montgomery Co., Pennsylvania. Household furniture to be sold, proceeds to children of cousins, Richard and Robert Cochran. To cousin, Nancy Lindsay, wife of Samuel Lindsay. All residue to said cousin, Robert.
Execs: Friends James Hunter, Esq., Benjamin Tilghman, Esq., both of Phila.
Witnesses: Robert Patterson, Robert M. Patterson.

SMITH, HENRY. Township of Oxford. Phila. Co. Yeoman.
Feb. 21, 1817. March 8, 1817. 6.407.
To my wife, Catharine Smith, and to my four children: Jacob, Margaret, Mary and Catharine Smith.
Execs: Israel Kenton, Benjamin Shallcross of township aforesaid.
Witnesses: William Cherrington, George Foulkrod, Jacob Weaugh.

FORTUNE, PATRICK. Late of Ireland. At present of Phila. Labourer.
Feb. 20, 1817. March 8, 1817. 6.408.
To Catharine Houlan, widow of Patrick Houlan, late of Phila., all my estate, appointing her sole Executrix.
Witnesses: John P. Harper, Kyran O'Neill.

ASH, RACHEL. Wife of James Ash of Phila., Esq. Mentions marriage agreement, in which the names of Charles Biddle, Esq., and Charles French, merchant, are mentioned.
June 20, 1814. March 8, 1817. 6.408.
To my seven childen: Maria Douglass, Jacob M. Douglass, George Douglass, Morgan Ash, Thomas F. Ash, John Ash, Rachel Ash and such other child as I may have.
Execs: Friends Samuel Wetherill, Jr., John Sergeant, both of Phila.
Witnesses: James C. Biddle, John Henderson.

MC INTIRE, JOHN. Kensington, Northern Liberties. Phila. Yeoman.
May 30, 1815. March 8, 1817. 6.409.
Estate to wife, Sarah, and daughter Catharine McIntire.
Execs: Said wife, Sarah McIntire, friend John Weaver of Northern Liberties, aforesaid.
Witnesses: George Cramp, Jacob Tees, John H. West.
Signed: McEntier.

CARVER, JOHN. Township of Byberry. Phila. Co. Yeoman.
June 3, 1815. March 11, 1817. 6.410.
Property in Townships of Byberry and Bensalem, Bucks Co., to sons, John and Joseph, they to pay my daughters, Martha Carver, Sarah Carver, Mary Worthington, Assemith Townsend, Hannah Carver and Elizabeth Townsend.
Execs: Sons John and Joseph Carver.
Witnesses: James Carter, Jesse Walmsley, Cuthbert Hayhurst.

WEAVER, HENRY. Southwark. Dealer.
Feb. 13, 1816. March 12, 1817. 6.411.
Estate to wife, Margaret Weaver, whom I appoint sole Executrix.
Witnesses: Robert Grant, Shewbart Armitage.

SPROGLE, EDWARD. Township of Moyamensing. Phila. Co.
Jan. 31, 1817. March 20, 1817. 6.411.
To wife, Betsy K. Sprogle, and to my four children: Elizabeth M.
Sprogle, Ann Louisa Sprogle, David M. Sprogle, Edward Croston
Sprogle. Executors to be Guardians of daughters until 18 years and
sons until 21 years.
Execs: Wife, Betsy K. Sprogel, friends Isaac Johnston, Philip Peltz,
Richard Peters, Jr., my sister Charlotte Evans.
Witnesses: William Delany, Franklin Lee, James W. Delany.
Signed: Sprogell.

AUSTIN, MARTHA. Township of Lower Dublin. Phila. Co. Widow.
March 9, 1817. March 22, 1817. 6.413.
To daughter, Mary Austin. To Ann Robinson, daughter of Jonathan
Robinson. To Friends Thomas Webster, of Abington, and Samuel
Leech, Jr., of Cheltenham, in trust for daughter, Mary, aforesaid. To
three children of late William Robinson.
Execs. and Guardians to said daughter, my friends Thomas Webster
and Samuel Leech.
Witnesses: Elizabeth Ward, Anthony Yerkes.

PARKE, JACOB. Phila. Late Iron Monger.
Jan. 8, 1817. March 25, 1817. 6.414.
To niece, Sarah Williams, wife of Samuel Williams and daughter of late
Benjamin Boultney, and my sister Hannah, both deceased. To niece
Anne Biddle, the only surviving daughter of Owen Biddle and my
sister, Sarah, both deceased. To Lydia Thompson, wife of James B.
Thompson and daughter of said Benjamin Poultney, by his late wife.
Remainder of estate to brother, Dr. Thomas Parke, said niece, Sarah
Williams, niece Rebecca Smith, wife of John Smith, and the other
daughter of said Benjamin Poultney, and my sister, Hannah, his wife,
deceased. To all children of late nephew, John Biddle, who was eldest
son of aforesaid Owen Biddle and my sister, Sarah, deceased. Children
of late nephew, Owen Biddle, Jr., deceased, son of said Owen and
Sarah Biddle, deceased. Sarah Biddle Thompson and Hannah
Thompson, children of Peter Thompson and my late niece, Rebecca
Owen Thompson, his wife, deceased, which Rebecca was a daughter of,
aforesaid Owen Biddle and my sister, Sarah, deceased, said Anne
Biddle, nephew Clement Biddle, only surviving son of aforesaid Owen
Biddle and Sarah, deceased.
Execs: Two nephews, James Pemberton Parke and Clement Biddle.
Witnesses: Andrew Underhill, Peter Thompson.

DAVAN, KINGSMILL. Phila.
Aug. 15, 1814. March 29, 1817. 6.415.

To friend, James Maury of Liverpool, late American Consul. To St. Mary's and St. Augustine's Roman Catholick Churches for masses for repose of my soul. To St. Andrew's Parish, Dublin, Ireland, formerly called St. Lazarushill Roman Catholic Church, now Townsend's Church. This was Parish of my birth. Tombstones to be placed over graves of my parents in Church Yard near Dublin. Margaret Davan, daughter of William Stone, who died 1758, and her husband, James Davan, who died 1763, both of College Green. Remainder of property to my nieces and nephews, children of my late sister, Mary Davan, daughter to late Mary Davan who married my late father. My late sister married William Donovan, at Phila., returned to Ireland and settled in Dublin, these children, two boys and five girls, all grown up and if alive, in Dublin. To friend, George Simpson, Esq.
Execs: Said George Simpson of Mr. Gerard's Bank, cashier, and James Maury, late Consul for United States.
Witnesses: Joseph Roberts, William Fawcett. George Simpson sworn same day.

CLARK, HANNAH. Phila. Widow of Samuel Clark.
Signed 1810. April 2, 1817. 6.416.
To sister-in-law, Lydia Bruer. To sister, Rebecca Richardson, and my friend, Rachel Cruckshank for use of poor Friends of Phila. Monthly Meeting, Pennsylvania Hospital. All remainder of estate to my two daughters, Mary Clark and Jane Clark.
Execs: Said daughter, Mary, and said daughter, Jane, when she arrives at lawful age, my brother, Joseph Richardson, my friend, Ellis Yarnel of Phila.
Mary Taylor of Northern Liberties, widow, and Rebecca Richardson, single woman, of Phila., affirmed. Letters to Joseph Richardson and Ellis Yarnel.

RICHARDS, WILLIAM. To Phila. Grocer.
Dec. 20, 1815. April 2, 1817. 6.417.
To wife, Margaret. To granddaughter, Sarah Coryell. To son, Benjamin Richards. To daughter, Elizabeth Boyer. To son, William Richards. To grandson, Charles Richards.
Exec: Said son, Benjamin Richards.
Witnesses: Lewis Taylor, Thomas Pearson.

WHITEALL, HESTOR.
Feb. 7, 1817. April 4, 1817. 6.419.
To sister, Joanna Sanders Whiteall. Money in hands of uncle, John Hastings, to be used for educating my son, Edmund. To Rebecca Chatwood.
Execs: Archibald Binny, John Hastings.

Witnesses: Hannah Lees, Rebecca Hastings, Joanna S. Whiteall, John Wright, John Hastings.
John Hastings, one of Executors, sworn.

WEBSTER, ROBERT. Phila.
June 6, 1809. Nov. 11, 1811. 6.419.
To son, Samuel Webster, and daughter, Ann Kennedy. To son, Thomas Webster. Remainder of estate to daughter, Mary Houtzell, and her children.
Execs: Friends, John Webb, William Blair of said city.
Witnesses: Benjamin Hall, John Webb, James Butler, teacher.
John Webb and William Blair, sworn April 7, 1817.

VIAN, MADELAINE. Late of Port au Prince and Cape Francois, now residing in Phila.
March 22, 1817. April 7, 1817. 6.420.
To be interred in burial ground of Roman Catholic Chapel of St. Trinity, in Phila. To nephew, Louis Joseph Benjamin Vian, Phila., cabinet maker, whom I appoint Executor.
Witnesses: John Wright, L. Prudot, Benjamin Nones, Notary Public.

RAY, AGNES. Southwark. Phila. Widow.
April 2, 1817. April 7, 1817. 6.421.
Estate to my two children, Margaret Ann Ray and John Andrew Ray.
Exec: Brother, David Johnston.
Sister, Mary Johnston, Guardian for said children.
Witnesses: Jesse Burrows, Andrew Mecaskey.

AVERY, JAMES. Mariner, lately belonging to U.S. Sloop of War, *Erie* at Baltimore.
March 16, 1816. April 5, 1817. 6.422.
To friend, John C. Behuche [?], of Phila. Co., boarding house keeper, whom I appoint Executor.
Witnesses: James Chambers, John Propet.

MUSGRAVE, AARON. Phila. Merchant.
Jan. 18, 1817. Feb. 28, 1817. 6.422.
Property in Wayne Co., Pennsylvania, to be sold and invested for benefit of my wife, Abigail, and our two younger children, Esther and Abigail. After decease of said wife, estate to my daughter, Lydia, wife of Benjamin Cox, two grandchildren, Abigail and Jonathan Evans, children of my daughter, Deborah, deceased, and to my said daughters, Esther and Abigail Musgrave.
Exec. and Trustee: My brother-in-law, John Cook.
Witnesses: Daniel Pittman, Mary Wright.

OGLE, WILLIAM. Phila. Mariner.
March 20, 1817. April 10, 1817. 6.423.
To wife, Catherine Ogle. To my sisters, Lucy Ogle and Mary Stuart.
Execs: Said wife, Catherine, my friend Thomas Greeves, of said city, broker.
Witnesses: Benjamin S. Janney, William Andrews.

MITCHELL, BENJAMIN. Phila.
Jan. 22, 1817. April 12, 1817. 6.424.
To my wife, Susanna Mitchel. To sons, James Mitchel and Thomas Mitchel. To said wife and sons, James and Thomas Mitchell, in trust for support of son, Benjamin Mitchell, and his wife, Mary, and family.
Execs: Said wife, sons James and Thomas.
Witnesses: Joseph P. Horner, Peter Thomson.

RICARDS, THOMAS. Phila. Barkeeper of Golden Swan Tavern.
April 15, 1817. April 19, 1817. 6.427.
To father, Peter Ricards, brothers Michael and Peter Ricards, and my sister, Mary Ricards, all in Ireland.
Exec: James Dillon.
Witnesses: Thomas Rikards, James Dillon, Thomas Fitzgerald, Edward Fanell.

WATKINS, JOHN. Phila.
June 1, 1816. April 19, 1817. 6.427.
To my wife, Margaret Watkins, and my children, all my estate, including property in the Parish of Standissiliogogo, County of Cardigan, South Wales, which property my brother, David Watkins, has a life estate in, and which at his demise, descends to me.
Execs: Said wife, Margaret Watkins, my friends John R. Griffith and Josiah Evans.
Witnesses: Timothy Thomas, Sarah Brown, George Shaw.
Letters to Exec.

THACKARA, WILLIAM, the elder. Phila.
Dec. 19, 1816. April 21, 1817. 6.428.
To wife, Eleanor Thackara. To children, James Thackara, William Thackara, Jr., Ann McPherson and Samuel Thackara.
Execs: Friends, John B. Palmer, James Musgrave of said city.
Witnesses: Benjamin Jones, James Robertson.

BUCK, GEORGE. Northern Liberties. Phila. Cedar Cooper.
April 4, 1816. April 14, 1817. 6.429.
To my granddaughter, Sophia Seip. To son, John Buck. To daughter, Sarah Buck, a minor.

Exec: Friend, Frederick Schaumkessel of Phila, baker, and said son, John Buck.
Witnesses: Robert Whitehead, Isaac Tyson.

WADMAN, PEACE. Phila. Mariner.
June 29, 1807. April 19, 1817. 6.430.
To wife, Mary Wadman, and after her decease, to my daughters, Mary, Nancy and Christina Wadman. Son-in-law, Payne ____.
Execs: Friends, Isaac Jones, Capt. William Davis.
Witnesses: Robert Whitehead, Benjamin Brown, Mary Tovins.

SHIPLEY, JOHN. Penn Township. Phila. Co. Farmer.
March 9, 1817. April 23, 1817. 6.431.
To wife, Ann Shipley, and to all my children: William, Joseph, Elizabeth, Jane and Thomas Shipley.
Exec: Brother, Thomas Shipley, of Phila., merchant. Also to be guardian of estates of said children.
Witnesses: Isaac Bartram, Frederick Stall, Nathan R. Potts.

KATZ, CATHERINE. Whitemarsh Township. Montgomery Co. Widow.
May 15, 1799. April 23, 1817. 6.432.
To my two grandchildren, Henry Katz and George Katz, children of my son, Conrad Katz, deceased. To my three daughters, Catharine Haga, Mary Beck, Polly Haga. To son, Henry Katz.
Exec: Son-in-law: William Haga.
Witnesses: Richard Whitehead, Robert Whitehead, Philip C. Kunckel. Frederick Beates, of Phila., conveyancer, affirmed.

CROCK, GEORGE. Penn Township. Phila. Co. Farmer.
Dec, 30, 1816. April 22, 1817. 6.433.
To wife, Susanna Crock, charging her with maintenance of my mother, Mary Crock. After death of my said wife, estate to Samuel Elfree, the son of my present wife, my daughter, Elizabeth Root, wife of John Root, my daughter, Susanna Root, wife of Henry Root, my granddaughter, Catherine Root, a child of my daughter, Catherine Root, my sons Bartholomew Crock and George Crock, and my daughters, Anna Maria Crock, Rebecca Crock and my son, Michael Crock.
Exec: Said wife.
Witnesses: A. A. Browne, George Esher, John Fulmer.

HENRIKEL, JACOB. Phila. Taylor.
March 5, 1807. Dec. 18, 1816. 6.434.
Estate to my daughter, Wilhelmina Weiss, wife of John Weiss, and after her decease, to her children.

Execs: Said daughter, Wilhelmina, my friends, Leonard Jacoby, Daniel Clawges.
Witnesses: William West, John Britton, Jr., Robert Whitehead, Benjamin Brown. Wilhelmina Clawges, late Henrikel, one of Executors, sworn June 10, 1817.

WOODLAND, MARY. Northern Liberties. Phila. Widow.
July 10, 1811. April 28, 1817. 6.435.
To brother, Philip Smith. To nephew, Peter Smith. To Mary Snethens, whom I have bro't up.
Exec: Said Mary Snethens.
Witnesses: Frederick Ulbert, Charles Hart.

CAVALHO, EMANUEL NUNEZ. Phila. Hazan of the Hebrew Congregation, Michva, Israel.
March 16, 1817. April 28, 1817. 6.435.
My watch to my nephew, Solomon, the son of my brother, David.
Residue of estate to my wife, Sarah, whom I appoint sole Executrix.
Witnesses: Jacob S. Solis, A. Myers Cohen.

EVANS, DAVID. Phila.
Feb. 29, 1813. April 29, 1817. 6.436.
To my daughter, Gulielma Evans. To sons Charles Evans and David Evans. To granddaughter, Mary Evans, daughter of said son, David. If she should die without issue, then other child or children of said son, David. To granddaughter, Laetitia Jackson. To Ann Mayberry, daughter of John Mayberry and wife, both deceased, of whom I have had charge. I now leave her in charge of my daughter Gulielma Evans. To said son, Charles Evans, and my nephew, Thomas Williams, cabinet maker, and Reed Williams, merchant, a number of ground rents in trust for granddaughter, Laetitia Jackson, wife of Levin Jackson, and after her decease, to her children. Son-in-law, Richard Moore.
Execs: Daughter, Gulielma, son Charles Evans, my friend, Isaac W. Morris, of Phila.
Codicils: March 9, 1815 and March 21, 1817.
Revoke appointment of my daughter and son as Executors, and appoint my nephew, Jonathan Evans of Phila, Co-Executor with Isaac W. Morris.
Witnesses: Samuel Williams, George Pryor, Joseph Gibbons.

HEISZ, FREDERICK. Phila. Merchant.
Jan. 3, 1816. April 30, 1817. 6.442.
To granddaughter, Emily Markland. To sons-in-law, John Markland and Robert Morrell, in trust for benefit of all the children of son, Henry. To Trustees of Evangelical Lutheran Congregation of St. John's Church,

German Lutheran Congregation and German Reformed Congregation, all in Phila. and vicinity, for use of their schools. Land in Columbia and Schuylkill Counties, part of which is held with John Weidman, in trust for daughter, Elizabeth Morrell and her children.
Execs: Sons-in-law, John Markland and Robert Morrell.
Witnesses: James Morrell, John Smith.

WILLIAMSON, JOSEPH. Southwark. Phila. Glazier.
Jan. 11, 1816. May 7, 1817. 6.443.
To wife, Mary, and to my five children: Rebecca Flickwir, widow of David Flickwir, Sarah Williamson, wife of Jesse Williamson, Ann Williamson, Elizabeth Barnes, wife of John Barnes, John Gardener Williamson. In trust for son, Joseph Williamson.
Execs: Son-in-law, Jesse Williamson, son John G. Williamson, son-in-law, David Williamson.
Wit: Thomas Mitchell, Samuel J. Curtis. Jesse Williamson, John G. Williamson, affirmed.

CROCKER, JOHN. Late of Baltimore City, Maryland. Mariner.
June 11, 1812. May 8, 1817. 6.445.
Father John Crocker, late of County of Baltimore, farmer, deceased. To Mary Inloes, wife of David Inloes, Cassandra Broadfoot, wife of James Broadfoot, Nancy Passey, wife of William Passey, all of City of Baltimore. Wm. Grinnel's (of Phila., planemaker) wife, Elizabeth Grinnell, and Actius Crocker of Richmond, Virginia.
Exec: Said Willliam Grinnell.
Witnesses: William Grinnell, Henry Statzell, John Bowers.

POLLOCK, JOHN. Northern Liberties. Phila. Stone Cutter.
Oct. 4, 1816. May 9, 1817. 6.445.
Legacies to sister, Mary, wife of Charles Chesnut, and to brother, Archibald. Remainder of estate to wife, Esther, and my daughter, Mary.
Execs: Friend John McAllister, Sr., whip maker, Phila. Co., and my wife, Esther.
Witnesses: Adam Traquair, Maria Osmond, Archibald Pollock.
Letters to Esther Pollock.

STEVENSON, WILLIAM, SR. Phila. House Carpenter.
May 8, 1817. May 21, 1817. 6.447.
To Executors, in trust for grandson, William, son of deceased son, William, until 21 years, and for son, Robert. Residue of estate unto my children: Cornelius, Ann Lake, wife of Thomas Lake, Hannah, John, Margaretta, Peter and Susan. To Mary Conrad.

Execs: Son, Cornelius Stevenson, friends, Crooke Stevenson, merchant of said city, William Stevenson, also to be Guardians of minor children.
Witnesses: Isaac Stevenson, Alexander Stewart.
Cornelius Stevenson sworn.

YOUNG, JOHN. Phila. Soap Boiler.
March 18, 1817. May 12, 1817. 6.447.
To reputed daughter, Maria Young, and to my wife, Martha.
Execs: Friends, Daniel Creth, William Humes.
Witnesses: Archibald Humes, George Humes.

THOMAS, ALEXANDER. Phila.
Oct. 12, 1816. May 12, 1817. 6.448.
To Daniel McNeilledge of Greenock. To James McNeilledge of St. Croix. To Isabella McFarland of Port Glascow. To Ann McFarland, wife of Robert McFarland, of Hillnorunnack[?]. To Peter McNeilledge, baker in Paesly. To Mary Clark, wife of John Clark of Port Glascow. To my brother, Peter McNeilledge of Paesly. All remainder of estate to wife, Elinor Thomas, of Phila. To my nephew, Alexander McNeilledge. To Peter Galbraith, watchmaker of Phila. To Peter Haines, Stewart of the ship, "Neptune." To be buried in Scotch Presbyterian burying ground.
Execs: Wife, Elenor Thomas, said Peter Galbraith and Andrew Montgomery, teacher of Phila.
Witnesses: George W. Jones, James Hamilton, James Smith, Robert K. Fisher, William Hawkins.
Lewis Taylor, one of Executors, sworn.

RITTENHOUSE, HENRY. Germantown Township. Phila. Co. Farmer.
April 30, 1817. May 14, 1817. 6.449.
To my wife, Margareth Rittenhouse. To my five children: Jacob, Peter, William, Joseph and Catharine.
Execs: Two sons, Peter and William Rittenhouse.
Witnesses: Joseph Bockins, Jacob Horton, John Beck.

GREW, RACHEL. Phila.
April 21, 1817. May 16, 1817. 6.449.
To my brother's son, Theophilus Collin. Furniture in house of Martha Powell, where I have long lived, to my niece Rachel Kitchin, daughter of my brother, David. Wearing apparel to brother, David's wife and two daughters. To said brother, David's children, Rachel, Theophilus, Sarah and George. To be interred in grave with my father, Theophilus Grew.
Execs: William Meredith and Thomas Parker, Jr.
Witnesses: Ann P. Dawson, Thos. S. Smith.

THOMAS, ELINOR. Southwark. Phila. Co. Widow.
March 8, 1817. May 17, 1817. 6.450.
To my mother, Helen Burn, all my estate, appointing her sole Executrix.
Witnesses: Peter Williamson, Mary Lockton.

REMINGTON, ISAAC. Phila. Co. Mariner.
April 17, 1817. May 19, 1817. 6.451.
To wife, Sarah Renington. After her decease, unto my children: Sarah Ann Renington, Elizabeth Elliot, Emily Renington.
Exec: Said wife, Sarah Renington.
Witnesses: William Beatty, Richard Renshaw.
Norris Stanley of Southwark, Ship Master, affirmed.

CASSAN, LEWIS. Southwark. Grocer.
July 27, 1811. May 19, 1817. 6.452.
Estate to mother, Hannah Cassan, whom I appoint Executrix.
Witnesses: Richard Renshaw, John K. Drummond, Eliza McDougal.

LAWRENCE, ELIZABETH. Southwark. Phila. Co. Widow.
Nov. 27, 1811. May 21, 1817. 6.452.
All estate to son, Jacob Lawrence, whom I appoint sole Executor.
Witnesses: Benjamin C. Burden, Peter Thomson.

LEWIS, GEORGE. Southwark. Mariner.
Oct. 12, 1813. May 21, 1817. 6.453.
All estate to friend, Rachel Piper, of said District, widow, appointing her sole Executrix.
Witnesses: James McLinshey, John D. Maher, Richard Renshaw, Esq., of Southwark, affirmed.

MORRIS, JACOB. Lower Merion Township. Montgomery Co. Yeoman.
Aug. 7, 1815. May 24, 1817. 6.453.
To my wife, Meribah Morris. To Executors, in trust for use of daughter, Mary McClenigan. To my grandchildren: Blair, Morris, Mary, George, Jacob, Ann, Matilda and Charles McClenagan.
Execs: Wife, Meribah, friend Horatio G. Jones, my grandsons, Blair and Morris McClenegan, if of age.
Witnesses: Andrew Anderson, Nathan Lewis.
Letters to Meribah Morris, Horatio G. Jones and Blair McClenegan.

HERMAN, MARY. Southwark. Widow.
May 20, 1817. May 28, 1817. 6.454.
To stepson, William Herman, in trust for James McKeever, when 21 years. To sister-in-law, Catharine Herman, in trust, interest to my

brother, John Seasfield. To Ann Maria Herman and such other children of said William Herman, as may hereafter be born.
Exec: Said William Herman.
Witnesses: Richard Renshaw, Thos. D. Ogilley.

WILKINS, CALEB. Phila. Taylor.
May 1, 1812. May 27, 1817. 6.455.
To wife, Amy Wilkins. To my children: Samuel Wilkins, Sarah Haines Covert and Rachel Draper Wilkins.
Executrix: Said wife, Amy Wilkins.
Witnesses: Rachel Draper Wilkins, Sarah Potts, George Wilkins.

MILLER, GEORGE. Kensington. Northern Liberties. Phila. Teacher.
Dec. 3, 1816. May 31, 1817. 6.456.
To wife, Rosina Miller, she to maintain my four children: Maria Sophia, Hannah, George Godfrey and Sarah Ann, until fit to go to trades.
Executrix: My wife, Rossina.
Witnesses: John Christ, John Johnson.

SMITH, STEPHEN. Late of Phila.
March 7, 1817 - Nashville, Tennessee. June 6, 1817. 6.405.
To aunt, Deborah Oldden. To sister, Ann Paxon. To sister, Phebe Speakman. To sister-in-law, Mary Oldden. To niece, Elizabeth Smith, daughter of Hugh and Rebecca Smith, when 20 years of age. To my nephew, Seneca Smith, son of Hugh and Rebecca Smith, when 21 years. To my four daughters: Mary North Smith, Phebe Ann Smith, Rebeccah Marshall Smith, Catharine Oldden Smith, I bequeath all residue of estate at the age of 20 years.
Execs: My uncle, Samuel Scolfield, my friends, Austin Montgomery and Alexander Elmsley.
Codicil: April 1, 1817. Revoke appointment of Alexander Elmsley as Executor. Appoint my brother, Cyrus N. Smith of Cincinnati, in his place.
Witnesses: Samuel Oldden, Vincent L. Lewis, Washington Perkins, Charles Paxon, Mary Oldden.

HAZARD, EBENEZER.
April 20, 1813. June 17, 1817. 6.458.
To wife, Abigail Hazard. To my children: Samuel, Elizabeth and Erskine Hazard. To Sarah Russeller.
Execs: Said wife, Abigail, my sons, Samuel and Erskine Hazard.
Codicil: Jan. 27, 1817. Robert Ralston, affirmed.

STURGESS, JOSHUA.
Nov. 14, 1816. June 7, 1817. 6.460.

My land in State of Maryland, Winchester Co., bounding on Stephen and Maria Reading, to be enjoyed by my wife, Rachell, and after her death to my three children: Abraham, Esther and Joshua Sturges.
Execs: Said wife, Rachell, my brother, Levin, to settle my affairs.
Witnesses: Richard Allen, Richard Allen, Jr.

HIBBARD, SARAH. Blockley. Phila. Co.
Sept. 5, 1815. June 7, 1817. 6.460.
To Elizabeth Lees, the wife of Joseph Lees. To Sarah Smith, sister of George Smith. To John Smith of Kingsessing. To John Johnston, son of Abraham Johnston of Darby. All residue to George Smith, taylor, of Blockley, aforesaid.
Execs: Friends, John Smith of Kingsessing, Abraham Johnston of Darby.
Witnesses: Samuel Gibson, Evan W. Thomas, Jr., John Gibson.

MONACH, JANE M. District of Southwark. Phila. Co.
May 28, 1817. June 11, 1817. A.461.
To my mother, Mary Monach, all my property in Scotland to be held by her as Guardian to my brothers and sisters: James, Mary W., Margaret T. and Andrew B. Monach.
Sole Executrix: Said mother.
Witnesses: Charles Caldwell, James Sawer.

RAYBOLD OR REYBOLD, MARY. Northern Liberties. Phila.
Dec. 2, 1799. June 28, 1817. 6.461.
To daughter, Mary Hubbard, wife of Anthony Hubbard.
Execs: Said daughter, Mary Hubbard, and her daughter, Mary Hubbard, Jr.
Codicil: May 16, 1803. To children of my late daughter, Sarah Bender.
Witnesses: Richard Whitehead, Robert Whitehead, Benjamin Brown, Benjamin Brown. Isaac Wampole of said city, conveyancer, affirmed.
Letters to Mary Torens, late Mary Hubbard, Jr.

ALEXANDER, JOHN. A private soldier in Capt. Isaac Roach, Jr's.
Comp'y, Corps, U.S. Artillery, now stationed at Fort Mifflin, but late of New York, Clerk.
Aug. 29, 1816 (Fort Mifflin, Pennsylvania). June 23, 1817. 6.462.
Estate to my wife, Sarah, and my three children: Sarah Jane, Margaret Anna and William Daniel.
Witnesses: Thomas Parker, David Barr, John Bringhurst.

ALEXANDER, EZEKIEL. Phila. Storekeeper, late of Larne, County of Antrim, Ireland.
June 14, 1817. June 23, 1817. 6.463.

All estate to brother, William Alexander, and sisters, Elizabeth
Alexander and Esther Alexander.
Exec: My friend and countryman, William Faris, of Phila.
Witnesses: Thomas Jameson, Eliza Sharp.

HEMPHILL, JANE. Phila. Widow.
June 18, 1817. June 27, 1817. 6.464.
To Hudson Carlile of Phila., soap boiler and tallow chandler, all my
estate, appointing him sole Executor.
Witnesses: Thomas Hoskin, John Murphey.

HARRISON, MATTHIAS. Phila. Gentleman.
May 27, 1817. June 26, 1817. 6.465.
To son, Henry Harrison. To my wife, Rebecca Harrison. Property in
Centre Co., Pennsylvania and money due by Samuel Mifflin, to my
brother, George Harrison, in trust for my daughter, Rebecca
McMurtrie.
Execs: My wife, son Henry, my son-in-law, James McMurtrie.

DENNISON, ARCHIBALD. Phila. Mariner.
May 24, 1815. June 25, 1817. 6.466.
All estate to friend Barnard Payne of said city, whom I appoint
Executor.
Witnesses: Phebe Palmer, Richard Palmer.

STANBURY, SARAH.
Jan. 1, 1817. July 1, 1817. 6.467.
To sister, Jemima Zimmerman. After death of said sister, to Deborah
Zimmerman.
Execs: Friends, Benjamin Lehman of Germantown, Benjamin Warner
of Phila.
Witnesses: Mary Reedle, Eliza Henry. Letters to Benj'n. Warner.
Benj'n, Lehman renounced.

MC KEAN, THOMAS. Phila. Passed my 80th year.
Aug. 13, 1814. June 27, 1817. 6.467.
Property in Holmesburgh, etc. to my wife, Sarah. To my son, Joseph
Borden McKean. To my granddaughter, Mary McKean, only child of my
second son, Robert McKean, deceased. To Andrew Pettit, who
intermarried with my daughter, Elizabeth, deceased, and by her had
four sons and four daughters. In trust for my said grandchildren,
property in Beaver Co. To daughter, Laetitia Buchanan, widow of Dr.
Geo. Buchanan, land in Beaver Co., near Logstown, Centre Co. To
Joseph B. McKean, in trust for use of Susanna, Mary, Thomas McKean
and Anne Buchanan, four children of daughter, Anne Buchanan,

91

deceased, property on Ohio River, formerly in County of Alleghany, and in Hanover Township, Co. of Luzerne, near Wilkesbarre. To daughter, Sarah Maria Theresa Marchiones de casa Yrujo, land in township of Ohio, Co. of Alleghany. To son, Thomas McKean, plantation called Chatham, in London Grove Township, Co. of Chester. To daughter, Sophia Dorothea, property in Bald Eagle Township, Co. of Centre. To grandson, Samuel Miles McKean, plantation called Mount Equity in Co. of McKean. Executors to sell property in Phila., not already divised, also in New Castle Co., Delaware. All rest of estate to my grandchildren: Thos. McKean Pettit, McKean Buchanan, Thos. McKean Buchanan, Charles Ferdinand de Yrujo and Henry Pratt McKean.
Execs: Son, Joseph B. McKean, son-in-law, Andrew Pettit, my son Thomas McKean.
Son, Joseph B., Guardian of children of daughter, Anne, deceased, and my daughter Laetitia, Guardian of her children, son-in-law, Andrew Pettit, Guardian of his children, and my son ---, Guardian of his son, Henry Pratt McKean.
Witnesses: Jared Ingersoll, Joseph Reed.

ZIMMERMAN, JEMIMA.
Jan. 1, 1817. July 1, 1817. 6.471.
To my sister, Sarah Stansbury, and after her death, to my daughter-in-law, Deborah Zimmerman.
Execs: Friends, Benjamin Lehman, of Germantown, Benjamin Warner, of Phila.
Witnesses: Mary Reedle, Eliza Henry. Letters to Benjamin Warner. Benj'n. Lehman renounced.

LYCAN, ANDREW. Northern Liberties. Phila. Co. House Carpenter.
June 22, 1817. July 3, 1817. 6.471.
To Margaret Fox. To Catharine White. All rest of my estate unto my sister, Mary Stratton, wife of Allen Stratton, and my brother, George Lycan.
Exec: Friend, Thomas Timings, Northern Liberties and County aforesaid.
Witnesses: Isaac Church, Caleb Carmalt, Jr.

BICKHAM, JOSHUA. Phila. Coach Maker.
June 12, 1817. July 5, 1817. 6.472.
All estate to wife, Elizabeth Bickham, whom I appoint sole Executrix.
Witnesses: Isaac W. Morris, John C. Evans.
George W. Bickham, of Southwark, coach maker, affirmed.

LAREMORE, JANE. Phila. Gentlewoman.
Aug. 9, 1815. July 8, 1817. 6.473.

Legacy to Executors, in trust for Mary McKenzie, widow of Caleb McKensie of Baltimore, and after her death, to all her children, excepting James Laremore McKenzie, hereinafter named. For Ann Jones, wife of Nathan Jones, Jr., and after her death, to her children. For Sarah Laremore of New Jersey, and after her death, to her daughter, Sophia Vantilberg. For Elizabeth Williamson, wife of Benjamin Williamson, and after her death, to her daughter Mary Williamson. For Mary Lawrence, widow of Benjamin Lawrence, and to her son, Samuel, and daughter, Deborah. To friend, Sarah Wright, or her children. To said Executors, in trust for support of Jane Eliza Laremore Smyth, daughter of Peter Smyth, until twenty-one years, then to receive principal. To James Laremore McKenzie, when of age. To Executors for education of Sarah Smyth and Hannah Smyth, daughters of above-named Peter Smith, to receive principal at 21 years. To friends, Ashbel Green and Jacob J. Janeway, Rectors of Presbyterian Congregation. To friend, George Williams, and his wife, Ann Williams. To friend, Ashbel Green, in trust for poor of 2nd Presbyterian Church in Phila. To William W. Woodward, of this city, bookseller. To Trustees of General Assembly of Presbyterian Church in U.S. of A. for supporting "Theological Seminary" - Bible Society of Phila. To James and Jane Taylor, children of John Taylor, Jr., deceased. To Cornelia Smith, widow, and to Elizabeth Larew, who now lives with me. To Ashbel Green, Jr., to Jane McKenzie, daughter of above-named Caleb McKensie. To Rebecca Smyth, wife of said Peter Smyth, Elizabeth Owen and Sarah Patton, sisters of Jane Owen, Mary Harbeson, daughter of late Benjamin Harbeson. To Martha Ralston, in trust for use of Orphan House in this city. To Mary Abeel, widow of Dr. Abeel, late of New York, deceased. To Martha Janeway. Remainder of estate to "The Magdalen Society of Phila."
Execs: Friends, Ashbel Green, George Williams.
Witnesses: Thomas Dobson, Isaac Elliott.
Letters to George Williams.

JONES, ELIZA. Late of Germantown, now visiting relations in Chester Co.
March 8, 1817. July 8, 1817. 6.476.
To following-named children of John and Sarah Johnson of Germantown: Elizabeth, Hannah, Ann, William, Margaret, Charles and Norton. To Thomas Connard, property in Detroit. To children of William and Ellenor Powel, Mary, Elizabeth and their two brothers. To John Roberts, son of Daniel and Sarah Roberts, my lot in Columbia, Lancaster Co. Lot in said county to the Adelphia School. To Jesse Kersey of Chester Co. To Norris, Clement and Ann Jones, children of Joseph and Catharine Jones, of Phila. To Ann F. Wheeler, daughter of Samuel and Elizabeth Wheeler, of Phila. To Elizabeth Paul, daughter

of Jacob and Mary Paul. To Rachel Johnson, daughter of John and Rachel Johnson, of Germantown. To Mary Clement or Clemens, nurse. To Samuel and Martha Jones, in Phila., and their daughter, Elizabeth, and son, Jacob. To Martha Jones, daughter of Gibson Jones. To John Roberts, son of Jehu and cousin, Elizabeth Roberts. To Henrietta Leach, wife of Richard I. Leach, of Harrisburg. To Margaret Rieger, of Lancaster. To Phebe Miller, of Brownsvill. Legacy left me by my uncle, Thomas Roberts, I bequeath to his two children, Mary and Sarah. Residue to Elizabeth Roberts and her daughter, Ann.
Execs: Friends, William Webb, of Lancaster Co., Samuel Paul, of Wissehickon.
Codicil: April 9, 1817. Alters legacies.
Witnesses: Jesse Kersey, Hunt Downing, David Gray, Israel W. Downing. Samuel Paul, of Germantown Township, Phila. Co., miller, affirmed.
Letters to Samuel Paul. Other Executor renounced.

MECHLIN, SAMUEL. Germantown. Phila. Co. Tanner.
May 24, 1817. July 14, 1817. 6.479.
To my relation, Jacob Mechlin, of Phila. All residue to son, Samuel Mechlin.
Execs: Son, Samuel, friend Martin Ludie, Esq., of Phila. Co.
Witnesses: William Dedier, William McCulley, Jr.

HOUCK, CHRISTIAN. Phila. Grocer.
Jan. 14, 1817. July 14, 1817. 6.480.
To my five children: Margaret, Sarah Dorrance, George, Maria and Charles. To my son-in-law, Maskell M. Carll.
Excs: Said Sarah Dorrance, Maskell M. Carll.
Codicil: May 16, 1817. Alters legacies.
Witnesses: Isaac Wampole, Jr., Isaac Wampole, Mary Kneass.

SHUSTER, DAVID. District of Spring Garden. Phila. Co. Victualler.
July 19, 1817. July 21, 1817. 6.481.
Estate to my wife, Margaret, and my three children: Adam, Henry and Thomas Francis Shuster. Said wife to support and educate children during minority.
Execs: Wife, Margaret, my brother-in-law, John David Woelpper.
Witnesses: Lewis Lowry, William Drum.

ARCHER, JAMES. Phila. Cordwainer.
July 7, 1817. July 21, 1817. 6.482.
All estate to sister, Jane Archer, of Galligate, New Castle Apontine, if living at time of my decease, if not, to her daughter, Elizabeth. If both

deceased, to John Archer, hair dresser of Galligate, New Castle, Apontine.
Execs: Friends, Andrew Geyer, Patrick Lyon and Lewis Rush.
Witnesses: Robert Short, Peter Parkinson. Andrew Geyer, Lewis Rush, sworn.

HALFPENNY, JANE. Phila. Single Woman.
Dec. 30, 1816. July 22, 1817. 6.483.
To sister, Rachel Halfpenny, widow of brother, Mark Halfpenny. To my niece, Francis Halfpenny, daughter of said Mark. Also, to nephew, James Halfpenny, brother of said Francis. To Mark Halfpenny, son of my later brother, James, (said Mark resides in the Western Country), also to his sister, Margaret Williams, the wife of Evan Williams (they also live in the Western Country), also to my cousin, John Larcum, and to his brother Thomas Larkum, also to his sister, Margaret Burden, wife of Henry Burden. To my friend, Prudence Marshall. To my friend, Catharine Foulke.
Execs: William Waln, Jacob S. Waln, Jr.
Codicil: July 2, 1817. Alters legacies.
Witnesses: Nicholas Waln, Jr., Ann Mifflin.

DONNALDSON, MARY. Phila. Widow of Hugh Donnaldson.
April 8, 1803. July 23, 1817. 6.483.
To my daughter-in-law, Sarah Donnaldson, wife to my son, John. To son, John. To my grandson-in-law, William H. Tod, in trust for my daughter, Helen Campbell, wife of George Campbell, Esq. All residue to said daughter, Helen Campbell.
Execs: Son-in-law, George Campbell, Esq., my grandson, William H. Tod.
Codicil: April 25, 1816. Daughter, Helen Campbell, deceased. I bequeath to granddaughter, Sarah C. Wynkoop, and to my four grandchildren, children of daughter, Helen Campbell.
Witnesses: James McIlhenny, Isaac Wampole, John C. Otto, Catharine Stipe.

JAGERS, JOHN. Phila.
July 17, 1817. July 25, 1817. 6.485.
To daughter, Phebe. To granddaughter, Zippy. To children of son, John. To son, Daniel. To son, Abraham. To daughter, Hannah Fox. To son, Joseph. All residue to son, Jonathan Jagers, whom I appoint Executor.
Witnesses: Jacob Erringer, William Sagathy, Jacob Trexler.

LACKEY, JAMES.
May 21, 1817. July 25, 1817. 6.485.

To wife, Elizabeth Lackey, all estate, making her sole Executrix.
Witnesses: John Fulmer, Andrew Way.

COLDWELL, JOSEPH. Township of Northern Liberties. Phila. Co. 6.486.
To wife, Susan. To my two daughters, Elizabeth and Sarah. To my mother, Sarah Coldwell.
Execs: Friends, Thomas Anderson, Joseph Barton, both of Northern Liberties, Phila.
Witnesses: George L. Tallman, Charles Hunter.
Signed: Colwell.

MURGATROYD, THOMAS. Trenton, New Jersey.
May 11, 1811. July 29, 1817. 6.487.
All estate to my wife, Sarah Philips Murgatroyd, whom I appoint sole Executrix.
Witnesses: Pearson Hunt, Susan Brittain, Rachel Hunt. Richard Rundle of Blockley, and Thomas F. Leaming, of Phila., merchant, affirmed.

HUDSON, SUSANNA. Phila.
June 20, 1814. July 29, 1817. 6.487.
To Jacob Ridgway, Bond and Mortgage of William and Sarah Morris. To my niece, Rebecca Ridgway. To Robert T. Rawle, ground rent in possession of Hannah Pemberton, etc. To Robert Rawle. To James Carman. To my niece, Susan Parke, ground rent, late in possession of Robert Ewen and Abraham Wilt. To my niece, Ann Parke. To Samuel Carman and his sister, Rachel, ground rent late in possession of William Sheaff. After their death, to their mother, Sarah Carman. To Susan Morris, daughter of Luke Morris, ground rent in possession of Samuel Salter and John Means. To my niece, Susan Ridgway, and to her sister, Ann Ridgway. To Elizabeth Balderston. To Sally Carman, and to her son, William, also to her daughter, Sally Carman, not mentioned in my will. To children of my nephew, Luke Morris. To Mary Fisher. To niece, Jane Parke. To Samuel Langdale. To William Hudson. To Mary Pleasant. To Rebecca Jones. To Lidia Love. To niece Rebecca Ridgway.
Execs: Friend James Smith, Jacob Ridgway, Rebecca Ridgway.
Executors to dispose of my personal estate to Sally Parke and my sister, Molly, only two persons not already mentioned. June 26, 1814.
Codicil: June 26, 1814. Niece, Rebecca Ridgway, deceased. Estate given to her, to her five children: Susanna Rotch, Phebe Ann, Benjamin, Caroline and John Jacob Ridgway.
Witnesses: Richard C. Wood, Wm. Andrews of Phila., conveyancer, Richard C. Wood, of said city, Attorney at Law, affirmed.

JARDEN, SAMUEL. Phila. Plaisterer.
June 10, 1817. July 28, 1817. 6.489.
To my wife, Catharine Jarden. To my sister, Mary Killegan. To sister-in-law, Mary Maag. Residue to sons, Robert, John, Samuel and William, daughter Catherine, son Jacob. To Executors, in trust for daughter, Maria McLaughlen, wife of John McLaughlen. After her death, to her children.
Execs: Wife, Catharine, my friend, John Maag of Passyunk Township. Jacob Ballenger and said John Maag, Guardians of minor children.
Witnesses: Reuben Savidge, Frederick Beates.

WILSON, ARCHIBALD. Bristol Township. Phila. Co. Farmer.
June 18, 1817. July 31, 1817. 6.490.
All estate to wife, Mary Wilson, and after her decease, to my six children: Silas, Rebecca, Sarah, Archibald, Rudolph and William.
Execs: Sons Silas and Archibald Wilson.
Witnesses: George DeBenneville, Jacob Peeky.

DOUGHERTY, ROGER. Phila.
March 10, 1817. Aug. 5, 1817. 6.492.
To Michael Dougherty and Thomas Dougherty, sons of my nephew, Daniel Dougherty of said city, when twenty-one years. Said Daniel Dougherty to be their Guardian. To Mary Dougherty, wife of said Daniel. To Roger Dougherty. To Owen Dougherty, son of Owen Dougherty. To Michael Dougherty and John Dougherty, sons of John Dougherty, when at lawful age. To Bell Duffy.
Exec: Said Daniel Dougherty.
Witnesses: Elihu Wright, John Allison.

MEYER, CATHARINE. Phila. Widow.
Oct. 13, 1816. Aug. 5, 1817. 6.493.
Estate to daughter, Rosanna.
Execs: Friend, Matthias Rouch of Phila., said daughter, Rosanna.
Witnesses: Peter Auner, Frederick Beates.

HEARN, ANTHONY. At present, Penn Township. Phila. Co. Born in Waterford, Ireland. Resided about 30 years in Cadiz, Spain and afterward about 17 years in Goshen, Pennsylvania.
May 16, 1816. May 7, 1817. 6.494.
To be interred in Roman Catholic burying ground of St. Augustine's Church, Phila. Annuity to Roman Catholic Pastor of the Borough of West Chester, Pennsylvania. To my wife, Sarah Jenkins. To Valois, Noble and Co. of Cadiz. To Solier Cabanes & Jugle of Cadiz, Spain. To Guiaza brothers & Co. of Cadiz. To Joseph Belduque. To Philip Walsh of said Cadiz. To French & Hopson of London, in Great Brittain. To

Thomas Walpole & Robert Ellison of London, aforesaid. To B. Burton Forbes & Gregory of said London. To Robert Waters of Whitehaven in said Kingdom. My interest in British funds under care of Sir John Lubbock & Co., of London, also under care of Messrs. Christopher & Rich & Puller of said city of London. Discharge from debt John Sharpless, Rev. Patrick Kenny, Charles Kenny, Esq., of West Chester, Conrad Seybert of Phila., Martin Folk, John Patterson, Newberry Smith, Redmond Byrne. Demand against estate of deceased William Barron of Cadiz, Spain, under direction of William Power of said city.
Execs: Redmond Byrne and John Carrell, merchants, and Joseph Snyder, blacksmith of Phila.
Witnesses: Nathaniel Potts, Ger'ld. Byrne, Redmond I. Taggart.
Codicil: Feb. 26, 1817. After my decease, forward to friend, William Power, Esq., Jr., letter to Rob't. Anth'y. Valois & Co. or Anthony Rob't. Valois & Co. of Cadiz, Spain.

WINTON, MARY. Late of New York, now of Phila. Widow.
Aug. 5, 1817. Aug. 12, 1817. 6.496.
Legacy to the widow, Catharine McDermott, residue of my estate to my brother-in-law, Horatio Boate, whom I appoint Executor.
Witnesses: William Hamilton, Michael Walter.

BURNS, HELEN. Phila. Widow.
July 12, 1817. Aug. 5, 1817. 6.497.
To daughter, Catharine. To sister, Jane Galloway. Residue of my estate to John S. Smith and James Sawer, both of Phila., in trust for use of said daughter, Catharine. After her decease, to my grandson, John Wainwright. To sister, Jane Galloway, or if she be dead, to her child or children. To my husband's sisters, Catharine Burns and Isabella Richardson, if living. If not, then to their children. If said daughter shall die without issue, then I give to my two sons, William and Robert. If they die without children, then to my brother and sister in Scotland.
Execs: Said James Sawer, John S. Smith.
Witnesses: Joseph Allen, James S. Smith.

JONES, EDWARD. Southwark. Sea Captain.
March 29, 1817. Aug. 14, 1817. 6.499.
To wife, Marhon Jones. To mother, Patience Jones, and after her decease, to my brother, Reuben Jones, and my sisters, Sarah Gay, Dille Fuller and Barshe Fuller, and the children of my sister Zilpha Green, deceased, and the children of my brother, John Jones.
Execs: Said wife, my friend Phineas Eldridge of Southwark, aforesaid.
Witnesses: Peter Williamson, Richard Renshaw. Nathaniel Holland affirmed.

REDDINGER, JOHN. Township of Penn Co., of Phila. Farmer.
Jan. 2, 1815. Aug. 15, 1817. 6.500.
To sons, Frederick and John. To daughter, Mary, wife of George Gotwolls, and after her decease, to her children. To daughters Ann and Elizabeth. Annuity to wife, Elizabeth.
Execs: Sons, Frederick and John.
Witnesses: John K. Duy, Walter Sim, Joseph Sorber.

SHEAFF, BARBARA. Phila. Widow.
Aug. 5, 1813. Aug. 18, 1817. 6.501.
To my daughter, Mary, widow of Henry W. Muhlenberg. To my daughter, Catharine, wife of John K. Helmuth. To my son, George Sheaff. To my niece, Sophia Gray, late Sophia Seckel, daughter of Henry Seckel, deceased. To my son, John D. Sheaff. To William Guier of Phila., merchant, and Thomas Ross of Norristown, Montgomery Co., attorney at law, in trust for my daughter, Susanna Zantzinger, and after her decease, to her children.
Execs: Son, George Sheaff, son-in-law, John K. Helmuth.
Witnesses: Henry K. Helmuth, Samuel Baker, Damaris Murphy.

WALTON, HANNAH. Township of Byberry. Phila. Co.
June 27, 1809. Aug. 22, 1817. 6.503.
To Rebecca Warrington. To brother, Benjamin. To Benjamin Peart. To Thomas Peart. To Rebecca Wilson. To Beulah Comfort, Phebe Walton, Rebecca Walmsley and Mary Walton, brother William's daughter. After legacies are paid, all residue of my estate to my daughter, Mary Vermityea, and brother, William Walton.
Exec: Said William Walton.
Witnesses: David Comfort, Beulah Comfort.

JONES, DANIEL H. Phila. Shopkeeper.
July 24, 1817. Aug. 25, 1817. 6.503.
To my natural daughter, Eliza Jones, now living at John Morgan's, at 21 years of age or marriage. My father, Nathan Jones, to be her Guardian. All residue of my estate to my said father, whom I appoint sole Executor.
Witnesses: Thomas Dobson, Nathaniel Holland.

HOE, BARBARA. Phila. Co. Widow.
July 21, 1817. Sept. 1, 1817. 6.504.
To my sons, John Hoe and Jacob Hoe. To children of my late daughter, Mary Borsler, or Bouler. To Joseph Parker Norris, of Phila., and John Hoe of county aforesaid, in trust for use of son, George Hoe. After his death, in trust for his daughter, Eliza Hoe.
Exec: Son, John.

Witnesses: Charles Norris, Adam Beinhard.

GRIFFITTS, HANNAH. Phila.
June 1, 1812. Sept. 1, 1817. 6.505.
Execs: Kinsman, Joseph Parker Norris and Dr. Samuel Powel Griffits, of Phila.
To my cousin, Deborah Logan, wife of Dr. George Logan. To Mary Fisher, wife of Redwood Fisher. To Hannah Jones, granddaughter of Mordecai Moore, deceased, and to her sisters, Martha Jones and Margaret Jones. To Elizabeth Morris, who now resides with me. To Deborah Dawes. To Mary Welch. To my cousin, James Griffitts. To Executors, for single women and widows of worthy character, who are in want. To Rebecca Jones. To the Young Women's Benevolent Society. To Female Benevolent Society. To each of the three Monthly Meetings in said city for poor of said meetings. All residue to said Executors.
Codicil: Nov. 29, 1815. Alters legacy to Hannah Jones.
Witnesses: John Elliot, Jonathan Fell, Jr., Daniel Elliott.

STRICKER, CATHARINE. Northern Liberties. Phila. Co. Widow.
May 22, 1817. Sept. 6, 1817. 6.506.
Estate to son, George Stricker. One of my sittings in Crown Street Church, to be kept for said son. After my death, he to be put to Mrs. Mary Dugan's to board, and when of proper age, to learn a trade. If he should die under age, or without issue, then to my sister, Sarah, for use of my brothers and sisters. Uncle, John Ashmead, to be Guardian of son, George, also to be Executor.
Witnesses: James Nice, Washington Nice.

BOURGEOIS, MARY DINAH.
Feb. 9, 1816. Sept. 12, 1817. 6.507.
To my brother, William Chamberlain, one dollar. To William Priestman, Sr., and to his son, William Priestman, Jr. To Emma Priestman. To Sarah Ann McDonnell, my god-daughter, to be received at 21 years. To St. Joseph Orphan Society. To the dispensary. To Ely Pricket and Mary Collis. To be buried in St. Augustine Church Yard. To Sarah McDonnell, if she wishes to learn a trade, etc.
Execs: Willliam Priestman, Sr. and son.
Witnesses: Thomas Cooper, Joseph Bell.

MARTIN, ROBERT. Northern Liberties. Phila. Co. Late Storekeeper.
Aug. 18, 1817. Sept. 12, 1817. 6.508.
Estate to wife, Catharine, whom I appoint sole Executrix.
Witnesses: Thomas Mitchell, John Fullmer.

EVANS, BARBARA. Germantown Township. Phila. Co. Widow of
Isaiah Evans, late of Phila. Plasterer.
May 29, 1812. Sept. 13, 1817. 6.508.
To son, Anthony Conrad. To daughter, Elizabeth Keyser. To my four
grandchildren, the children of my son, Peter Conrad, deceased: Joseph
Conrad, John Conrad, Mary Conrad, Elizabeth Conrad.
Execs: Son Anthony Conrad, daughter, Elizabeth Keyser, friend John
Livezey of Roxborough Township, miller.
Witnesses: Caspar Follar, Jacob Bannar.

BROWN, ROBERT. Northern Liberties. Phila. Tanner.
July 23, 1817. Sept. 15, 1817. 6.509.
Legacy to sister, Ann, now in Ireland. To sister, Margaret. Remainder
of estate to my brother, William Brown, whom I appoint Executor.
Witnesses: Robert Whitehead, David Ennet.

CRITHER, MARY. Phila. Co.
Sept. 13, 1817. Sept. 17, 1817. 6.509.
To daughter, Sarah, and her husband, Henry Habbick. Legacies to sons
Adam and George Crither, and daughters, Mary Kalehoff and Julian
Rumel.
Execs: Henry Hablick, Samuel Harris.
Witnesses: George Clymer, Samuel Harris.

SMITH, SAMUEL. Phila. Flour Merchant.
April 14, 1814. Sept. 19, 1817. 6.510.
To my wife, Mary Smith. After her death, to Lydia Woolston, wife of
Joshua Woolston of Middletown, Bucks Co., and to her daughter,
Lydia Woolston, Jr. To said Joshua Woolston and his son, Joshua
Woolston, Jr. To nephew, David Smith. To Othniel Alsop, of Phila.,
nephew Thomas Smith's son, John. To niece Rachel Fulton, now
residing in Virginia. To niece, Elizabeth Heston. To niece, Phebe
Smith. To my six nephews: Edmund, Thomas, Joseph, John, Abraham,
Benjamin Smith. To nephew, Samuel Smith of Wrightstown, Bucks Co.
To nephew, Robert Smith of Buckingham, Bucks Co. To my brother-in-
law, Joshua Woolston. To my nieces, Sarah Woolston and Elizabeth
Woolston, daughters of Jonathan Woolston, deceased. To nieces Sarah,
Rachel and Ann Woolston, daughters of said Joshua. To niece, Susanna
Atherton, daughter of Joseph Knight. To friend, Josiah Messer of
London. To friends, Jonathan Willis and William Yardley of Phila, and
my nephew Robert Smith and Stephen Woolston of Bucks Co. To
cousin, John Stapler of Bucks Co. To Stephen Woolston in trust for use
of my niece, his sister, Elizabeth Canby, her husband to have no
control. To each of my wife's nieces, to Boarding School at Weston,
Chester Co, under care of Yearly Meeting of Friends for Pennsylvania,

New Jersey, etc. To Institution near Frankford, established by Friends of Phila., for members of said society, afflicted with insanity.
Execs: Said wife, Mary Smith, friends Jonathan Willis and William Yardley, nephews, Robert Smith and Stephen Woolston.
Codicil: June 21, 1816. To religious Society of Friends in Bucks Co., for Boarding School. To Samuel Smith, son of my nephew, Thomas.
Witnesses: James Smith, Peter Thomson, George Williams.

BARCLAY, MARGARET. Phila. Widow.
Jan. 6, 1813. Sept. 25, 1817. 6.514.
To my sons, John Barclay, Hugh Barclay and Richard Barclay. To my daughters, Mary Barr, Sarah Hufty. To daughter-in-law, Jane Barclay.
Exec: Son, John Barclay.
Witnesses: Sarah Medary, Christiana Lapp.

LENTZ, JOHN. Moyamensing Township. Phila. Co.
Sept. 12, 1817. Sept. 30, 1817. 6.514.
To my wife, Sarah Lentz. To Executors, for use of son, William. To my four children: John, Mary, Rebecca and Sarah Lentz. Legacies given to son, John, and daughters, Mary and Sarah, when married.
Execs: Friend, Philip Peltz, Esq., son, John Lentz, Jr., my son-in-law, Richard Peltz.
Witnesses: John Gerritt, John Graham.

MARSH, EDWARD. Phila. Mariner.
Sept. 13, 1814. Oct. 3, 1817. 6.515.
All estate unto my friend, Barnard Payne, of said city, Boarding House Keeper.
Exec: Said Barnard Payne.
Witnesses: Elizabeth Palmer, Richard Palmer.

CLAPHAMSON, JOHN FISHER. Northern Liberties. Phila. Co. Gentleman.
Feb. 5, 1817. Oct. 6, 1817. 6.516.
To wife, Ann, and my son, Samuel Claphamson, and his wife, Mary Ann. To my sister, Martha.
Execs: Friend, William Adams of Phila., grocer, said son, Samuel.
Witnesses: Thomas Mitchell, William Allen.

LEECH, JANE. Phila. Widow of Duncan Leech, formerly of same place, deceased.
Nov. 3, 1809. Oct. 8, 1817. 6.517.
To my children, Edward Leech and Jane Berry, wife of Peter L. Berry. Granddaughter, Margaret Leech, daughter of John Leech. Grandson, Daniel, son of said Edward. Son, Daniel Leech, deceased.

Execs: Friends, James Stuart and Edward Lane, both of Phila.
Witnesses: John Richards, Jr., Israel Thomas.

MC KENZIE, REBECCA. Phila. Spinster.
Sept. 5, 1817. Oct. 10, 1817. 6.518.
All estate to father, Charles McKenzie, whom I appoint sole Executor.
Witnesses: John W. Hamilton, James Wood.

HUGHES, MARGARET. Phila. Widow.
March 22, 1816. Sept. 11, 1817. 6.518.
Property in Northern Liberties to be sold, proceeds to sons, Samuel, Alexander, Thomas and daughters, Elizabeth, Rebecca and Margaret, and children of late son, James, deceased. To son, Alexander, in trust for daughter, Mary Torr.
Execs: Samuel and Alexander.
Witnesses: Isaac Wampole, Jr., Isaac Wampole.
Letters to Samuel Hughes.

ALLEN, MILLER.
Sept. 22, 1817. Oct. 13, 1817. 6.519.
To my sisters, Lydia Allen and Jane Annel. To mother, Jane Allen.
Father, Thomas Allen, deceased.
Exec: Samuel Allen.
Witnesses: Bela Badger, Mary Pearson, Eliza Tomlinson.

HIBBS, MAHLON. Lower Dublin Township. Phila. Co.
Sept. 13, 1817. Oct. 13, 1817. 6.519.
Estate to son, Mahlon Hibbs, except what Agnes Hibbs brought here. To Agnes Hibbs, for support of my son. If said son dies under age, Executors to pay his estate to John Overderff and Livinah Hibbs, when 21 years.
Execs: Jonathan Thomas, Daniel Knight.
Witnesses: Brian Wilkinson, Thomas Gilbert.

FREYMUTH, WILLIAM. Phila. Yeoman.
Oct. 3, 1817. Oct. 15, 1817. 6.520.
To my friend, Catharine Richardson. To my brother, Benjamin E. Freymuth. To my nephew, William Freymuth. To my nephews and nieces, children of said brother, Benjamin.
Execs: Friends, Henry F. Verchaux, William Richardson of said city.
Witnesses: Evan Jones, Joel Jones.

LATIMER, JANE. Phila. Single woman.
July 3, 1817. Oct. 16, 1817. 6.520.

To sister, Margaret Geddes, wife of Henry Geddes. To Sarah B.
Latimer, widow of my deceased brother, William G. Latimer. To Sarah
Cuthbert, Ann Jane Cuthbert, Susanna Cuthbert. To Sophia Geddes,
daughter of my sister, Margaret Geddes. To Elizabeth Latimer and
Margaret Latimer, daughters of brother, George Latimer. To Sarah
Banning, wife of Freeburn Banning, of Talbot Co., Maryland, and
daughter of my sister, Margaret Geddes. To Sarah R. Latimer and
Mary R. Latimer, daughters of my brother, Henry Latimer. To Sarah
G. Cathcart and Jane L. Cathcart, daughters of my deceased sister,
Susan, to be put in trust to their father, Rev. Robert Cathcart. To
Mary Campbell, who now lives in family of my brother, George
Latimer. To brothers, George and Thomas Latimer, my part of tract of
land in Centre Co., Pennsylvania, belonging to estate of my father. To
sister, Sarah Cuthbert, wife of Thomas Cuthbert.
Sole Exec: Brother, George Latimer.
Codicil: July 3, 1817. Oct. 16, 1817.
Sarah B. Latimer, widow of brother, William G. Latimer, deceased,
legacy given to her, I bequeath to her children: James, William,
Elizabeth, Sarah, George and Henry. To Grace Bayley, formerly a
servant of my father.
Witnesses: Ab'r. Claypoole, Charles Pettit, Peter Field, John Gouge.

WILLIAMS, THOMAS. Moreland Township. Phila. Co. Musician.
Aug. 28, 1816. Oct. 22, 1817. 6.522.
To daughter, Elizabeth Williams. If she dies without issue, then to
James Oram, son of Thomas Oram, an indented servant to Jacob
Sommer.
Execs: Said Elizabeth Williams, John Newell of Moreland Township,
Montgomery Co., farmer.
Witnesses: John B. Kroesen, John Newell.

GRIFFITH, ISAAC. Northern Liberties. Phila. Co. House Carpenter.
Oct. 27, 1817. Oct. 30, 1817. 6.522.
To my wife, Catharine Griffith, property conveyed to me by George
Fox and Mary, his wife, also all other of my estate, appointing said wife
Executrix, and my friend William Hallowell, Jr. of Northern Liberties,
Executor.
Witnesses: Joseph Rakestraw, Thomas Mason, John Simmons.

BEARD, MARY. District of Southwark. Widow.
May 22, 1817. Nov. 3, 1817. 6.523.
To my two nieces, Maria Richardson and Elizabeth Richardson,
daughters of my late sister, Sarah Richardson. To my nephew, James
Greeble, in case he returns within seven years.
Exec: My friend, Benjamin Lyndal, of Phila., cabinet maker.

Witnesses: David Coombs, Joshua Brittingham.
Susanna Brittingham, wife of said Joshua, affirmed.

LAMPATER, CATHARINE. Phila. Widow.
Dec. 27, 1816. Nov. 4, 1817. 6.524.
As my daughter, Elizabeth Speigel, has received her portion of my estate, the remainder to my four daughters: Christina Heimer, Margaret Fogel, Sarah Lawrence and Catharine Price.
Execs: Friend and neighbour, Adam Cullman of District of Spring Garden, my said daughter, Christina.
Witnesses: Jacob Gardner, Fred'k. Beates.

MC LANE, ELIZABETH. Widow of Samuel McLane of Phila.
Proved: Nov. 1, 1817. 6.524.
To my nephew, Vincent Lockerman, and his children. To nephew, Joseph Miller Patten, and his children. Also to his sister, my niece, Ann Patten, and her children. All residue of estate to my brother, Samuel Miller.
Execs: Friend William Flintham, merchant of Phila., my brother, Dr. Samuel Miller.
Witnesses: William Flintham, Susan Flintham.

BOSWELL, WILLIAM. Phila. Trader.
April 5, 1813. Nov. 11, 1817. 6.525.
Estate to my wife, Margaret, and after her death, as follows: John Stephens, Jacob Stephens, William Boswell, George Boswell, Samuel Boswell, John Boswell, Elizabeth Boswell, Susanna Boswell, Mary Weaver and William Firtner.
Exec: Joseph Shoemaker, silversmith.
Witnesses: Joseph Shoemaker, Daniel Walton.

BATTEIGER, VALENTINE. Phila. Merchant.
Oct. 29, 1812. Nov. 12, 1817. 6.525.
Estate to brother, Anthony Batteiger. To my sister, Maria Magdalen Koch. To children of late brother, George Jacob Batteiger, and to children of late sister, Maria Klein.
Execs: Friends, Daniel Sutter, Frederick Gaul, of Phila. If Daniel Sutter should die before estate is settled, appoint friend, Peter Hertzog, of said city, merchant, in his stead. All my residuary legatees reside in Westheim, in Germany.
Witnesses: John Goodman, Isaac Wampole.

MARTI, MARTIN. Nicetown. Phila. Co.
Sept. 27, 1817. Nov. 13, 1817. 6.526.

To my wife, Maria Marti. To my children: oldest daughter, Salome, sons, Jacob and John, daughters, Maria, Barbara and Elizabeth.
Exec: My friend, Anthony Roofner.
Witnesses: John Wulzel, John Jacobi, Casper Wack.

STRATTON, FITHIAN. Late of Cumberland Co., West New Jersey, now a resident of Kensington Co. of Phila. Minister of the Gospel. July 29, 1814. Oct. 31, 1817. 6.526.
To my wife, Sarah. To Daniel Parvin, my nephew, house and lot I bought of William Murphy in Port Elizabeth, New Jersey, until his son, Fithian Stratton Parvin is 21 years. To Ephraim Stratton, son of my nephew, Fithian Stratton, Jr., on conditions that he pay legacy unto each of his three youngest sisters, Juda, Sarah and Ruth, when 18 years. To Samuel Stratton, son of Fithian Stratton, Jr., my nephew, property I purchased of Caleb Kemble and Othniel Comly at a place called Schooner Landing, in Cumberland Co., New Jersey, on conditions that he give legacy to Sarah Stratton, daughter of Joel Stratton, my nephew, when 18 years, also to Lot Stratton, son of my brother, William, (deceased), and who is now in Penns Valley, if he should demand it. To Enoch Heritage, son of my niece, Esther. To Thomas Stratton, my nephew, he to pay legacy unto three youngest daughters of William Stratton (deceased) when 18 years. After decease of my wife, to William Stratton, son of my nephew, William Stratton (deceased). Executors to have Guardianship of said William Stratton. To Samuel Parvin and his sister, Louisa, children of Aaron Parvin, my nephew. To Esther, Elizabeth and Clarity Stratton, daughters of my nephew, William Stratton (deceased). To Rachel Cooper, sister of my wife, Sarah Stratton. To my sister, Phoebe Woodruff. To Abel Whitiker. Residue to my nephews, Fithian, Joel and Thomas Stratton, and Daniel Parvin.
Execs: Nephew, Daniel Parvin, friend, George C. Shively.
Witnesses: Robert Hodgdon, William Cobb, Henry Shanonn.

PHILSON, ALEXANDER. Phila. Co.
Oct. 16, 1817. Nov. 19, 1817. 6.528.
To wife, Jane. To son, Matthew, for his education. After decease of said wife, to my four children: Thomas, Frances E. Patton Philson (now Mrs. Breeder), Robert Alexander Philson, Matthew Philson. B. B. Breedir, husband of said daughter, Frances. To my son, James, one dollar on account of his improper conduct. I leave him in hands of his mother who will do justice to him if he reforms.
Execs: Wife, Jane Philson, son Robert Alexander Philson, James Henderson.
Witnesses: James Rush, John Deims, David C. Hopkins, John Haines.

LORAIN, JOHN, JR. Phila. Merchant.
Signed Feb. 26, 1817. 6.529.
All estate to my wife, Lydia, and after her death to my children by her, except my daughter, Elizabeth Shewell Lorain, for whom her aunt, Elizabeth Shewell, has made ample provision.
Execs: Samuel Archer, James Wilmer, Lawrence Cauffman of Phila, merchant, my wife, Lydia Lorain.
Witnesses: Peter Gaskill, Charles Lehman.
Codicil: Samuel G. Wright, Executor, in addition to those named in Will.

KURTZ, GEORGE. Northern Liberties. Phila. Co. Victualler.
Nov. 14, 1817. Nov. 26, 1817. 6.530.
To my wife, Elizabeth. To my daughter, Elizabeth Barnhold, wife of Frederick Barnhold. To my daughter, Margaret Weaver, wife of Michael Weaver. To my grandson, George Weaver, son of said Michael and Margaret. To grandson, Frederick Barnhold, son of said Frederick and Elizabeth. To Mary Tailor. All residue to my wife and my three daughters: Elizabeth Barnhold, Margaret Weaver, Catharine Fricke.
Exec: My friend, Tobias Beehler of Northern Liberties, Phila., grocer.
Witnesses: Michael Baker, Frederick B. Robeson.

JONES, ELIZABETH. Blockley Township. Phila. Co.
May 8, 1815. Nov. 22, 1817. 6.531.
To my oldest son, William, and to daughter, Sarah Smith, each one dollar. To granddaughter, Elizabeth Jones. To son, Peter Jones, property adjoining that of Peter Rose and others.
Execs: Said son, Peter, my nephew, Joseph Rose.
Witnesses: Thomas I. Paschall, John Gibson, Gustavus A. Cox.
Peter Jones affirmed same day.

CARMALT, CALEB. Phila.
July 22, 1812. Nov. 26, 1817. 6.531.
To my brother, Jonathan Carmalt. To my sisters, Rebecca Carmalt and Mary Howell. To Jonathan Carmalt, Jr. To Caleb Carmalt, Jr., and to his sisters, Susan and Rebecca, also to his sons, Jonathan, Isaac, James and daughter, Mary Ann. To James Howell.
Execs: Brother, Jonathan Carmalt, my sisters, Rebekah Carmalt, Mary Howell.
Witnesses: Joseph Moore, Joseph Crukshank.
Jonathan Carmalt and Mary Howell affirmed.

UHL, JOHN. Phila.
Oct. 12, 1814. Dec. 1, 1817. 6.532.

To wife, Catharine, she to support her mother, Eve Reiser. To my
children: son John, eldest daughter Ann Maria Uhl, daughter Elizabeth
Passey, youngest son William Reinhart Uhl.
Execs: Wife, Catharine, my friend Conrad Wile.
Witnesses: Jacob Mechlin, Samuel Mechlin.
Samuel Keemle, of Phila., attorney at law, affirmed.
Signed: Uhle.

GOURLEY, JOHN. Northern Liberties. Phila. Co.
Nov. 16, 1816. Nov. 26, 1817. 6.533.
Estate to wife, Elizabeth Gourley.
Execs: Said wife, Elizabeth, Samuel Macferan, Esq.
Witnesses: John Sowder, Michael Bowers.

MC MAKEN, SAMUEL. Phila.
Aug., 1817. Nov. 25, 1817. 6.534.
To my wife, Margaret, and after her death, to my children: Mary
Sheble, Margaret M. Golder, Julia Ann McMaken, Susanna McMaken,
Samuel McMaken, Eliza McMaken, William McMaken.
Exec: Son-in-law, Adam Sheble, of Phila. Co.
Witnesses: John Gray, Alexander Miller.

JUSTIS, PEDRO. Southwark. Mariner.
Aug. 31, 1811. Dec. 11, 1817. 6.534.
Estate to my wife, Elizabeth, and her child or children.
Exec: Said wife.
Witnesses: Ebenezer Ferguson, Thomas Lake.

BOOTH, ELIZABETH. Widow of William Booth of Phila.
Dec. 3, 1817. Dec. 26, 1817. 6.535.
All my property to my two children: Rachael, wife of Samuel Cornelius,
and John Booth.
Execs: Friends, Richard Nath, John Maris.
Witnesses: Josiah Randall, Isaac Forsyth.

STRIEPY, MARIA. Phila. Widow.
April 30, 1812. Dec. 17, 1817. 6.535.
Exec: Grandson, William Herman. Estate to son, Adam Striepy, and
said grandson.
Witnesses: Andrew Way, Frederick Beates.

HOWELL, REBECCA. Phila.
July 15, 1807. Nov. 28, 1817. 6.535.
To my daughter, Mary Drinker. To granddaughter, Rebecca Drinker,
and other children of said daughter. To grandson, John Drinker, the

property devised to his sister, Rebecca, if she dies under age, he paying his brother half of valuation.
Witnesses: John Drinker, Joseph Thomas, Nathan Thomas.

HAY, FREDERICK AUGUSTUS. Phila.
April 30, 1817. Dec. 4, 1817. 6.536.
Wearing apparel to brother, Francis. All residue of my estate to my sister, Mary Witmer, she may give to my brother and sisters as she thinks proper.
Execs: Said sister, Mary Witmer, my brother-in-law, Henry Witmer.
Witnesses: Isaac Wampole, John C. Otto.

COLLINS, PETER. Phila.
Nov. 13, 1817. Dec. 10, 1817. 6.536.
To nephews, James Collins and Peter Collins. To my relation, Sarah Markens. To Michael Magrath, to be paid by him to Orphan Asyslum attached to Catholic Congregation of St. Mary's Church, in Phila. To wife, Margaret, and to my brothers, John, Anthony and William Collins, and my sister, Elizabeth Cannan.
Execs: James McGill, of Phila., taylor, and John Kessler, Esq. of Northern Liberties, said city.
Witnesses: John P. Milnor, Frederick Beates.
Letters to James McGill.

CRESS, PETER. Phila. Saddler.
April 3, 1812. Dec. 13, 1817. 6.537.
Unto children of my deceased son, John Cress. Unto daughter, Elizabeth, wife of Henry Graff. Unto daughter, Esther Billmeyer. Unto daughter, Rebecca, wife of Henry Erben. To son, George Cress. To daughter, Juliana Hartley.
Execs: Son, George Cress, my son-in-law, Henry Graff.
Witnesses: Abraham Stein, Frederick Beates.

MC ARTHUR, ELEANOR. Phila. Widow.
Aug. 12, 1817. Dec. 17, 1817. 6.538.
To sister, Sarah B. McArthur, whom I appoint Executrix.
Witnesses: George Wilson, Thomas Latimer.

CLYMER, ROBERT. Phila.
Oct. 9, 1811. Jan. 13, 1817. 6.539.
Estate to Clement Biddle, Thomas Biddle, and my son, Jacob Clymer, in trust for daughter, Barbara Clymer, and her children. After their death, to my children: Christopher, Charles, Jacob, George and Archibald Clymer.
Execs: Said Clement and Thomas Biddle, my son, Jacob.

Witnesses: John B. Orso, James C. Biddle.
John G. Biddle, affirmed.

VINCENT, JOHN. District of Southwark. Phila. Co.
Dec. 19, 1816. Nov. 15, 1817. 6.539.
Property to my wife, Elizabeth, and after her death or intermarriage, to my nephew James Townly, son to my sister, Sarah Townly, alias Vincent. To Elizabeth Morton, my indented girl, daughter to my nephew, John Morton.
Execs: William Nesbitt and William Graham, of Southwark.
Witnesses: John Lawrence, John Clarke, Joseph Keefe.

BACON, REBECCA. Phila. Spinster.
Oct. 22, 1814. Dec. 22, 1817. 6.540.
To brother, Joseph Bacon. To sisters, Hannah Evans and Mary Mount. Exhonerate nephew, Joseph Scattergood, from payment of debt. To nephews: James Olden, Charles Bacon, William Evans, Joseph Evans, Joel Evans, Thomas Evans and Charles Evans. To nieces: Rebecca Ridgway, Sarah Bacon, Mary Bacon, Mary Evans and Hannah Evans, Jr. To Sarah Scattergood, widow of Thomas, and to her daughter, Rebecca Scattergood. To cousin, David Denn, of Alloways Creek, New Jersey, and to his sister, Martha Thompson. To cousin, Dorcas Eldridge. To my sister, Mary's grandson, George Oldden. To brother-in-law, Jonathan Evans, in trust for educating poor young women at Westtown Boarding School. To Rebecca Peirce, daughter of Caleb Peirce. To cousin, Sarah Wright. To Ann Bunting, niece of Thomas Hough, deceased. To Sarah Elfrith, daughter of Jeremiah Elfrith. To brother, Joseph Bacon, and brother-in-law, Jonathan Evans, in trust for Asylum for Insane near Phila. To nieces, Mary Evans and Ann Scattergood, in trust for use of poor.
Execs: Two nephews, Joseph Scattergood and William Evans, to whom I leave residue of estate.
Witnesses: Joseph Gibbons, Isaac Lloyd.

LINEHAN, MARGARETTA. Phila. Spinster.
Nov. 6, 1817. Dec. 19, 1817. 6.541.
To step-brother, John Riley, for his education and maintenance. To my sister, Ellen Linehan, and my brother, Coleman Linehan. To my grandmother, Eleanor Green. To my aunt, Eleanor Wray. To "St. Joseph's Society in City of Phila." To brother, James Linehan. To black girl, Jane Faussett, now living with me. Should said Ellen and Coleman Linehan die under age, then to my three brothers: James Linehan, Maurice Linehan and Dennis Linehan.
Execs: Grandmother, said Eleanor Green, also to be Testamentary Guardian of my step-brother, John Riley.

Witnesses: Lewis Shoemaker, Henry Shoemaker.

MOORE, JOSEPH. Phila.
May 28, 1817. Dec. 29, 1817. 6.542.
To my housekeeper, Elizabeth Tustin. To granddaughter, Sarah Moore. To my four grandchildren: Mary Moore, Elizabeth Harr Maddock, Sarah Moore Maddock, Randal Malin Maddock. To grandson, Joseph Moore Truman, in trust for his sister, Susannah Baker. To Joseph Moore Truman, Jeffrey Truman, Richard Truman, George Truman, Joseph Moore, and Elizabeth Moore.
Execs: Friends, James Truman, Thomas Rogers, both of Phila.
Witnesses: Samuel Hildeburn, James Watson.
Griffith Edwards of Phila., grocer, affirmed.

LUTZ, FREDERICK. Northern Liberties. Phila. Co. Ceeder Cooper.
Oct. 7, 1816. Dec. 29, 1817. 6.543.
To wife, Hannah Lutz, and to children: Henry Lutz, John Lutz, Frederick Lutz, Hannah Lutz, Mary Ann Lutz, and such other child as may be hereafter born. Said wife to be Testamentary Guardian to all my children.
Execs: Wife, Hannah, my friend Jonathan Thomas, living at present on Old York Road.
Witnesses: Jacob Sheble, Jr., John I. Heriges.

FOREPAUGH, GEORGE. Phila.
Sept. 29, 1817. Dec. 30, 1817. 6.544.
Legacies to my eldest son, Andrew, and to my son, George. To Mary Hood, sister to my son-in-law, John Hood. To Margaret Rain, my granddaughter. Residue to my daughter, Margaret, wife of John Ruddach.
Execs: Friends, Ludwick Sharp, of Phila., merchant, Daniel Buckley, Northern Liberties of said city, and Archibald McCrellish of same place.
Witnesses: John Anderson, Adam Trazuair, Charles A. Drosdoof.
Execs. Ludwick Sharp and Archibald McCrelish, sworn.

HEATH, ANDREW. Germantown. Phila. Co.
Dec. 15, 1817. Jan. 3, 1818. 6.545.
To wife, Barbara Heath. Legacies to Charles Mackinet and Mary Mackinet. At wife's decease, unto Samuel Tyson, Mary Tyson, three children of Joshua Tyson: Charlotte, Matilda and Edwin Tyson. To Charles Pastorius. Legacy to Executors for poor people of this neighbourhood.
Sole Exec: Friend, Charles Mackinet.
Witnesses: John Leibert, John Baylie, Charlot Yard.

BUDD, GEORGE. Late of Northern Liberties. Phila. Co. Now residing at the Lazaretto, Delaware Co., Pennsylvania.
Feb. 24, 1816. Jan. 6, 1818. 6.545.
Property in Upper Merrian, Montgomery Co., etc. to my wife, Susannah. Tract of land in State of Ohio, also in Phila., to be sold for benefit of my children, George K. Budd and Susannah Budd, not to be divided until youngest is 21 years of age.
Execs: Said wife, Susannah, my friend, Manuel Eyre, of Phila., merchant.
Witnesses: Matthew Randall, Thomas Bradford, Jr., Esq., of Phila.
Letters to Susannah Budd.

QUINN, CHARLES.
Sept. 16, 1816. Nov. 14, 1817. 6.546.
To John Mulcahy, grocer, Phila., my farm in Delaware, near New Castle, and authorize him to demand cash as if in my own personal demands. Said John Mulcahy, a native of Ballynagard, in county of Lim'k., Ireland.
Witnesses: Edmund Donnell, Edmund Whelan, James Burns.
Jan. 7, 1818: Philip Bussell, of Southwark, tallow chandler, affirmed.

WEAVER, ANNA MARIA. Northern Liberties. Phila. Co. Widow.
Dec. 9, 1817. Dec. 31, 1817. 6.546.
To Anna Maria Stephens, daughter of Samuel Stephens, and my niece, Catharine, his wife. Nephew, Dr. Joseph Stouse, to have charge of education of said Anna Maria Stephens during minority. To Sarah Harman Stephens and Elizabeth Weaver Stephens, sisters of said Anna Maria. To sister, Hester Stouse. To nephew, Dr. Joseph Stouse. To nieces, Ann Maria Chambers and Catharine Stephens, wife of Samuel Stephens. Legacy for educating children of Samuel Stephens, born of the body of his present wife, Catharine Stephens. To Peter Knepley, the unexpired term of service of Magdalen Miller, my servant. Residue to Joseph, Daniel, Mary and Catharine, children of sister, Hester Stouse.
Execs: Nephew, Joseph Stouse, M.D. of N.L., and Peter Knepley, of Phila., merchant.
Witnesses: Andrew Brodie, Frederick Wolbert.

REYNOLDS, PETER. District of Southwark. Phila. Co. Bricklayer.
Dec. 7, 1817. Jan. 8, 1818. 6.548.
To wife, Mary Reynolds, and to my children when of age.
Exec: Said wife.
Witnesses: John Maitland, James Eneu, Jr.

KINSEY, GAYNER. Phila. Widow.
Proved: Jan. 14, 1818. 6.548.
To daughters, Catherine Griffith and Elizabeth Servoss; to grandsons, John K. Gravenstine and Joseph Servoss. To granddaughter, Eliza Kentzing. To grandson, Charles K. Servoss. To Gayner Ashton and Gayner Lukens.
Execs: William Britton, lumber merchant, my grandson, John K. Gravenstine.
Witnesses: Groome Obey, William Grinnell.

PEARSON, JOSHUA. Phila. Stationer.
Jan. 18, 1814. Jan. 14, 1818. 6.549.
To my brother, Isaac L. Pearson, whom I appoint Executor.
Witnesses: Edward Lynch, Jr., William G. Govett.

ROOT, ANDREW. Township of Northern Liberties. Phila. Co. Farmer.
Jan. 14, 1818. Jan. 17, 1818. 6.549.
To wife, Mary Root, and after her death, to my children.
Execs: Friends, John Vanhorn and Conrad Root.
Witnesses: John Ord, John Vanhorn.

HUGHES, THOMAS. Kensington. Phila. Co. Inn Keeper.
Jan. 21, 1817. Jan. 25, 1817. 6.550.
To daughter, Susan Hughes, she to pay to my granddaughter, Rachel Coats, $500 at time of her marriage.
Execs: Daughter Susan, friends Richard Johns & John Saylor, Farmer.
Witnesses: Robert Whitehead, George Eyre, John Eyre.

HELM, ADAM. Northern Liberties. Phila.
Jan. 5, 1818. Jan. 19, 1818. 6.550.
Legacy unto my children and all furniture, which belonged to me before my marriage with my present wife. Residue of estate to my wife, Maria Dorothy Helm, and after her death, to my children and those of my said wife.
Execs: Wife, Maria Dorothy, my friend, Philip Read.
Codicil: Jan., 1818. Legacy to Peter Apple, cordwainer.
Witnesses: Henry Shoemaker, Joseph Abbot, John Pfeil.

BROOM, THOMAS. District of Southwark. Phila. Co. Carwinder.
Signed: ___ 19, 1814. Proved: Jan. 22, 1818. 6.551.
To wife, Letitia Broom, full use of estate for her maintenance and that of her dater Roseta Letitia. Should said wife marry, she to have her thirds and the rest to my two daters, Hanah Broom and Roseta Letitia Broom. $10 to son, Lenord Broom, if he shall come home. Grandson Joseph Millwood Broom and Thomas Broom Smith.

Exec: Wife, Letitia Broom, my daughters, Hanah and Letitia. If they
need assistance to call on Jacob Smith, Surgend Dentis, and Joseph
Hartly, apolsterer. If lawfull heirs of Leonard Broome of Rutlandshire,
in England, should come over here, to give them what was his Donesen
[?] land, and also a legacy.
Witnesses: Zachariah Wood, James Farthing.

STEWERT, MARY. Now of Phila.
Sept. 12, 1817. Jan. 27, 1818. 6.552.
Request to be buried in Doctor Read Church burring ground,
Wilmington. To daughter, Hepzibah Stewart, now of Phila., all my
property in New Castle Co., Delaware, also all my personal property in
Phila. Desire said daughter to give George Glasko his liberty when 30
years of age.
Execs: Friends, Morgan Jones, William Cooch or Cuch, both of New
Castle Co., Delaware.
Witnesses: George W. McClelland, James Andrews.

SMITH, EDWARD. District of Southwark. Mariner.
Dec. 30, 1811. Jan. 28, 1818. 6.552.
Estate to my friend, James Nichol, of said District, mariner, whom I
appoint Executor.
Witnesses: John Summers, Stephen Payras.
John Benton of Phila., store keeper, and George Collison, District of
Southwark, mariner, affirmed.

WOELPPER, FREDERICK. Moyamensing. Phila. Co. Victualler.
Jan. 21, 1818. Jan. 30, 1818. 6.553.
Estate to daughter, Margaret, and such other children as shall be born
unto me, subject to payment of 1/3 income of said estate to my wife,
Rachel.
Execs: Said wife, my brother, George Woelpper, said brother to be
Guardian of daughter, Margaret.
Witnesses: Peter Hotz, Henry H. Miller.

BELIN, LOUIS. Late of Paris, in France, and at present, in Phila.
Silversmith and Chaser.
Jan 14, 1818. Jan. 31, 1818. 6.553.
To father, Nicolas Belin, now residing in Paris.
Execs: John Lavalle, Lewis Howard of Phila.
Witnesses: Aaron B. Nones, James McDonald, J. Bletson [?]

ECKFELDT, JACOB. Phila.
Jan. 13, 1818. Feb. 2, 1818. 6.553.

To youngest daughter, Juliana. To my nieces, Elizabeth and Sarah Baush. Executors to pay to son, George. To my sons, Adam, Michael and John, and daughters, Juliana, Sarah Welsh and Elizabeth Anderson, wife of John Anderson.
Execs: Sons, Adam, Michael and John.
Son, Adam, to be Guardian of daughter, Juliana Eckfelt.
Witnesses: Joseph Cloud, Isaac Wampole.

PRICHETT, THOMAS. Phila.
Jan. 7, 1818. Jan. 29, 1818. 6.555.
Provide for wife, Elizabeth. To my sons, Thomas B. Prichett and William B. Prichett. To Executors, in trust for daughters, Hannah B. Prichett, Sarah Ann Prichett and Elizabeth B. Prichett. Executors provide family burial ground where they may think proper or have vault made in Christ or St. Peter's Church yard.
Execs: Wife, Elizabeth B. Prichett, son, Thomas B. Prichett, my friend, James Paul.
Witnesses: Elizabeth Paul, Rebecca C. Rodman.

GORE, REBECCA. Phila. Widow.
Died about July 1, 1809.
Legacies to Rebecca Hutton. To heirs of George Plumstead. Bonds to Rebecca Gore from John Nixon, Joseph Swift, Henry Drinker, Richard Stevens. From Joseph Swift to Mary Plumstead. From George Plumstead to Rebecca Gore. Other relations in England, names not given.
William Crammond of Phila., merchant, Henry Nixon of said city, merchant, affirmed, May 27, 1817.

ORR, JOHN. District of Southwark. Phila. Co. Dealer.
Jan. 16, 1818. Feb. 6, 1818. 6.557.
Real estate not to be disposed of until youngest children, Catharine and John, shall become of age. To my daughters, Catharine and Ann, and to sons, Robert, Samuel, George and John.
Execs: Friends, William Stern, Joseph George, both of Phila.
Witnesses: Cornelius Innes, William Esler.

OSMON, JOHN. Oxford Township. Phila. Co. Gentleman.
Jan. 26, 1815. Feb. 14, 1818. 6.558.
To wife, Elizabeth, and my children: Maria, William B., Esther, Thomas, Eliza, Charles and Anna.
Execs: Sons, William B. Osmon and Thomas Osmon.
Witnesses: William Hurst, Benjamin Prentice, Jessey Castor.

KEEGAN, THOMAS. Phila. Book Binder.
Jan. 26, 1818. Feb. 3, 1818. 6.559.
Estate to wife, Sarah Keegan, late Sarah Doyle, appointing her sole Executrix.
Witnesses: Joseph B. Doyle, William Doyle, Robert Coane, I. Gauchier, Henry Habermehl, Margaret Bradley.

PEARSON, ISAAC. Phila. Stationer.
Dec. 6, 1817. Feb. 18, 1818. 6.559.
To Executors, in trust for use of sister, Lydia Lewis, and to Mary Bowne of said city, widow. To my three children: Martha Pearson, Isaac L. Pearson, and Anna Pearson.
Execs: My friends, Richard Humphreys and Joseph Price of said city, my said son, Isaac L. Pearson.
Witnesses: Thomas Parker, Jonathan Carmalt.
Letters to Joseph Price and Isaac L. Pearson.

JONES, ABSALOM. Phila. Minister of the Gospel. Rector of St. Thomas's African Episcopal Church in said city.
Signed: 1818. Feb. 17, 1818. 6.560.
To Hannah Jones, widow of my brother, William Jones. To nephews, William Jones, Jr. and George Jones. To Elizabeth Stevens, daughter of my half-brother, Jacob Stevens. To St. Thomas's African Episcopal Church. To friend, Anthony Cain, in trust for use of African Masonic Grand Lodge, No. 1, in this city. To William Jones, son of my nephew, George Jones. To Absalom, son of my cousin Venus Dicher. To Martha Jones, present housekeeper. To Tobias White, now of Wayne Co., Pennsylvania. To Absalom, son of said Tobias White. To Adam James. To William Dickson. To Rev. Richard Allen. To niece, Sarah, wife of George Jones. All residuary estate to the children of my brother, William Jones, my nephews, George Jones and William Jones, Jr., my nieces, Diana Clark, Hannah Johnson, Mary Jones and Martha Jones.
Execs: Friends, Belfast Burton, bleeder, James Johnston, painter and glazier, my nephew, George Jones, oysterman, all of Phila.
Witnesses: Edward Jones, Abraham Shoemaker.

WEISS, GEORGE. Nicetown. Phila. Co. Tavern Keeper.
Feb. 17, 1818. Feb. 25, 1818. 6.561.
To my wife, Sarah Weiss, full possession of all my real and personal property for her own and my son, Charles Weiss's maintenance and education. If son dies, under age, then to the children of my sister, Catharine Hottenstein, and Sarah, my wife.
Execs: Friends, Lewis Rush of Phila., Charles Nice, Jr. of Chesnut Hill, jointly with my wife, Sarah.
Witnesses: Francis G. Deimling, John Warner, Anthony Rufner.

BYRNE, JOHN. District of Southwark. Phila. Co. Grocer.
Jan. 30, 1818. Feb. 25, 1818. 6.561.
Executors to sell all estate and by good and sufficient deeds, to convey to purchasers, their heirs, etc.
Execs: Friends, John Maitland, George Humes, both of Phila., distillers.
Witnesses: Michael Cavenaugh, John Johnson.

MORRIS, SARAH. Phila.
March 1, 1815. Feb. 23, 1818. 6.561.
To my daughter, Mary Eliza. To my sons, Anthony, Jeremiah (having had most of his share), and Warder. To my granddaughter, Sarah Morris. Property on Frankford Rhode, left me by my father, Warder.
Execs: Sons Anthony, Jeremiah and Warder.
Witnesses: Jeremiah Warder, Jr., John H. Warder.
Letters to Jeremiah and Warder Morris.

UNGER, GEORGE. Penn Township. Phila. Co. Blacksmith.
Feb. 18, 1818. March 4, 1818. 6.562.
Legacies to my mother, Mary Quinn, and my sister, Catharine Quinn. All residuary estate to my wife, Elizabeth, having full confidence that she will be a true Guardian to my son, Thomas, who is now a minor.
Execs: Said wife, Elizabeth, my brother-in-law, John Duke.
Witnesses: John Deprefontaine, Samuel Weiss.

JOHNSON, RACHEL. Germantown. Phila. Co. Widow.
April 15, 1814. March 4, 1818. 6.562.
To children: William, Rachel, Samuel and John. To Executors in trust for education of children of my daughter, Mary Dorsey. To my two daughters, Mary Dorsey and Rachel Johnson. To my son, Samuel's son, John.
Execs: Son, William Johnson, daughter, Rachel Johnson.
Codicil: April 9, 1815. Legacies to daughters-in-law, Jennett and Sarah Johnson. George Knorr to be Executor in addition to those named in Will.
Witnesses: Joseph Paul, Samuel Keyser.
William Johnson, George Knorr, Executors, affirmed.

HAILER, CHRISTIANA. Phila. Widow.
Dec. 26, 1817. March 5, 1818. 6.563.
To sons, Jacob Snyder and George A. Snyder. To daughter, Christiana Totheron [?]. To Executors, in trust for daughter, Sarah Walker, during life of her present husband.
Execs: Said sons.
Witnesses: Jas. Wilson, Fred'k. Beates.
Richard Loudenslager, of Phila., taylor, affirmed.

George Snyder, one of Executors, sworn.

STRIEBY, ADAM. Northern Liberties. Phila. Carpenter.
Feb. 9, 1818. March 5, 1818. 6.564.
To wife, Sarah, she to educate and maintain my three minor children: Frances, William and John, until 16 years. After decease or intermarriage of said wife, then unto my children: George, Joseph, Maria, Eliza, Rachel, Frances, William and John.
Execs: Son, Joseph, my friends, John Taylor, lumber merchant, John Uhler.
Witnesses: Robert Whitehead, T. I. Bryant.

WILSON, ROBERT. Phila.
Feb. 5, 1818. March 10, 1818. 6.564.
Estate to my wife, Mary Wilson, daughter, Mary Wilson, son Henry Wilson, said son to have all my nautical instruments, charts, etc. To Victorine Lewis, such of my sea clothes worn on present voyage. I have been appointed Executor in conjunction with Isaac Israel Halstead to the estate of John Johnson, seaman, and sole Executor to estate of Joseph N. Domett, both of whom died on ship, "Bigham," on her present voyage. Executors hereinafter named to act in my place. To friend, Hugh Chambers, my right in a servant boy, named Abraham, whom I brought with me from India. To Jethro Myrick. In event of my death before reaching home, I desire that my body be conveyed to my friends, at Phila., for interment, if practicable. I recommend this charge particularly to my friend, Hugh Chambers.
Execs: Joseph Simons, merchant of Phila., my wife, Mary Wilson.
Witnesses: Hugh Chambers, John White, Isaac Israel Halstead.
Letters to Joseph Simons.

DEFNEY, JACOB. (Sometimes calling myself John Johnson)
Oct. 19, 1817. March 12, 1818. 6.565.
To my father, George Jacob Defney, of London, by trade a baker, all of property of every description. If not living, to my mother. In case of her death, to my nearest relation. If no relations can be found, then to my friend, Isaac Israel Halstead, of Phila., whom I appoint Executor.
Witnesses: John Hays, William Murrey, Joseph N. Domett.

SCOTT, JONATHAN. Germantown. Phila. Co. Cooper.
Dec. 20, 1817. March 19, 1818. 6.566.
To wife, Elizabeth Scott.
Execs: Said wife, Elizabeth, and Casper Guyer.
Witnesses: Ernst Felty, George Berger.

GILBERT, MARY. Lower Dublin Township.
Feb. 13, 1818. March 14, 1818. 6.566.
Ten dollars to Mary Gilbert. All my clear money to my nieces and nephews, except Elizabeth Beech, who is to have $20 out of Beech's children's portion. To John Saul's children. Jonathan Beech's children to have balance of their portion after their mother gets $20 aforesaid. To George Weiss's children. Thomas Gilbert's children to have portion as they come of age. To Sarah Beech, Ann Saul, Ann Weiss, Mary Weiss, Susan Weiss, Sarah Ann Gilbert, Mary Gilbert, Susanna Saul, Elizabeth Beech.
Execs: John Saul, Thomas Gilbert.
Witnesses: Jon'a. Thomas, Brian Wilkinson.

HUBBELL, WILLIAM. Phila. Mariner. Lately belonging to U.S. Sloop of War, "Hornet" - Capt. Lawrence.
Dec. 19, 1812. March 19, 1818. 6.566.
All estate to my friend, Lavinia Hickey, of Phila., whom I appoint Executrix.
Witnesses: John Phenix, Mary Clarke. James Hughs, of Phila., tavern keeper, Richard Renshaw, Esq., of Phila., affirmed.

ROSS, DAVID. Late of New Castle Co., Delaware. Now on board Schooner, "Erect."
April 2, 1810. (Signed: Cape Henlopen) June 10, 1818. 6.567.
All my property to my wife, Marcia G. Ross.
Administratrix: Said Marcia G. Ross.
Witnesses: Constant Hough, mate, Thomas Tarrant, pilot.

KING, JOHN. Phila. Shoemaker.
Feb. 27, 1818. March 9, 1818. 6.568.
Executors to sell estate. My two children, John and Ellen King, to have their share as they come of age.
Execs. and Guardians of said children: My friends, William McCollin, Edward King. Executors to furnish a room for my wife.
Witnesses: George Bickerton, William Wharton.

MARSHALL, ELIZABETH. Phila. Co. Widow.
Dec. 31, 1817. March 23, 1818. 6.568.
Legacies to Martha Webb, Agnes Marshall, Margaretta Bedfield, Bell Jane Powell, Elizabeth Powell, Mary Gifford, Mary Boick. To Corporation of the Presbyterian Church in Pine Street, near 4th, in Phila., where my family are interred. To granddaughter, Elizabeth Shenge, formerly Elizabeth Marshall, daughter of Samuel Marshall, deceased. To Hannah Welcome. To Ann McCullough. My apprentice boy, Andrew Clemens, to choose a trade. To granddaughter, Elizabeth

Marshall Sprogell. Property in Gloucester, New Jersey. To daughter-in-law, Susanna Marshall, widow of son, David Marshall. All remainder of my estate to my daughter, Betsey K. Sprogell, and her four children: Elizabeth M., Ann Louisa C., David M. and Edward C. Sprogell, not to be divided until they are 21 years.
Execs: Daughter, Betsey Kezia Sprogell, Luke W. Morris, of Phila.
Witnesses: Robert Walker, William Barker, John R. Vogdes, Richard Peters, Jr.

ALEXANDER, GEORGE. Phila. Mariner.
June 5, 1802. March 21, 1818. 6.569.
Unto Joseph Marble of said city, shop keeper, all my estate in Passyunk, Phila. Co., and elsewhere.
Exec: Said Joseph Marble.
Witnesses: Thomas Armstrong, Nicholas Diehl, Jr.

DANCE, JOSIAH. Phila. Storekeeper.
Jan. 20, 1818. March 24, 1818. 6.569.
Estate to my wife, Sarah, and after her death, to my daughter, Matilda. Bond payable by David Lukins at my mother's death.
Execs: Said wife, Sarah, Abraham Lower.
Witnesses: James Thomas, Ann Benley, Robert McMinn.

RIHL, JACOB. Northern Liberties.
March 23, 1818. March 27, 1818. 6.570.
Estate to wife, Susan Rihl, and at her death, Executors to sell estate and divide proceeds amongst my four children: James, Elizabeth Maria Sophia, John Wiser Rihl, to Executors, in trust, for son, Henry Rihl.
Execs: Wife, Susan, Son, Henry, my friend, Henry Benner, bricklayer.
Witnesses: Thomas Coats, Jr., George Cragg.
Letters to Henry Rihl and Henry Benner.

STRINGER, ANN.
Proved: March 28, 1818. 6.570
Mrs. Sellers and Mrs. Dorrance to dispose of my effects as follows: To Maria Sausmanhaus. To Sally Moss. To Dr. Heberton. To Mrs. Cloppen. To Mrs. Dorrane. To Miss E. Sellers. To Mrs. Dorrance. To Hannah Fisher. To Hannah Harland. To Emma. To Mrs. Sellers. To Mrs. Clopper.
Witnesses: Sarah Dorrance, Rachel Sellers.

GRANT, ALEXANDER. Mariner.
July 8, 1812. April 1, 1818. 6.570.
All estate to wife, Eleanor Grant, whom I appoint Executrix.
Witnesses: John Armond or Ormrod, Samuel Ewing.

DULLES, JOSEPH. Late of City of Charlestown, South Carolina. Now residing in Phila.
May 27, 1816. April 2, 1818. 6.571.
Estate in South Carolina and in Pennsylvania to my wife, Sophia Dulles, my daughter, Mary Elizabeth Cheves, and my son, Joseph Heatly Dulles.
Execs: Said wife, son and daughter, my son-in-law, Langdon Cheves.
Witnesses: Joseph Tagert, Aaron Denman, Henry Kuhl, Samuel Wilson, Jr., John Connelly, Manuel Eyre, John M. Jackson and Elizabeth Bryan. Letters to Joseph Heatley Dulles.

HICKEY, MARGARET. Phila. Widow of Michael Hickey, late of same city.
March 5, 1818. April 2, 1818. 6.571.
Legacies to my nephews and nieces: Thomas, James, Mary, Margaret and Jane Tierman, children of my deceased sister, Mary. Boys to receive theirs at age 21 years, girls at 18. To Betsey Clark, formerly housekeeper for my father. Rest of estate to my two children, Margaret Hickey and Michael Hickey.
Execs: Friends, Philip Smith, Thomas Maitland of said city.
Witnesses: Rebecca Bravard, Nich's. Dowers. Philip Smith sworn.

KEYSER, PETER. Germantown. Phila. Co. Tanner.
May 15, 1810. April 18, 1818. 6.572.
To my children: William, Derick, Elizabeth, Peter and Sarah. Wife's household goods to be returned to her children: Elizabeth, Samuel and Joseph, also the £100 in hands of Daniel Pastorius.
Execs: Two sons, William and Peter.
Witnesses: Frederick Axe, Jacob Bowman.

ETRIS, MARY. Phila.
Nov. 10, 1814. April 18, 1818. 6.572.
To daughter, Sarah Read. Unto my seven children: John, Joseph, James, Sarah, Elizabeth, Rachel and Catharine, and my four grandchildren: George, David, Marcey and Edmund Harrow, children of daughter, Mary Harrow, deceased. Note payable by my brother, Lawrence Egbird. Deceased brother, John Egbird.
Exec: Son-in-law, Joseph Getchel of Phila., blacksmith.
Witnesses: William Mason, Henry Smith.

CARNEY, HANNAH. Phila.
June 2, 1814. April 18, 1818. 6.572.
To Thomas H. White of said city, merchant, in trust for my daughters, Elizabeth Christmas and Hannah Gibson, free from controul of their husbands.

Exec: Said Thomas H. White.
Witnesses: John Willis, Jno. B. Whitaker.

DONNELL, BENJAMIN L. District of Southwark. Lately shipped on private armed Schooner, "Perry" of Baltimore, now at Phila.
March 24, 1814. April 20, 1818. 6.573.
Estate to my sister, Mary F. Donnell, of said district, whom I appoint Executrix.
Witnesses: Isaac Morton, Theodat Mazeu. Nathaniel Donnell of Southwark, gentleman, and James Cochran Donnel, his son, affirmed.

PRICE, SARAH. Phila. Spinster. Daughter of Edward Price and Susanna Baker.
July 16, 1817. April 24, 1818. 6.573.
All property to my mother, said Susanna Baker.
Execs: Mother and friend, John Rink, of this city.
Witnesses: John Wilson, Joseph Price.

LOUGHERY, JOHN. Phila. Merchant.
April 9, 1818. April 13, 1818. 6.573.
All estate to my wife, Esther Loughery, daughter, Kitty Loughery, and my son, Joseph Loughery. Legacy to my mother, during her life.
Execs: My relatives, Capt. John Cochran, Dr. Isaac Heylin, Robert Adams, Esq.
Guardians for children: Capt. John Cochran, Dr. Isaac Heylin.
Witnesses: William North, Isaac Levis, Thomas C. James.

RUMNER, JOHN. Northern Liberties. Phila. Co. Victualler.
March 2, 1818. April 24, 1818. 6.573.
Legacy unto my sister-in-law, Rhoda Williams, and to sister, Mary Oliver. My house and all rest of my property, real or personal, Executors to dispose of and invest for my children until of age.
Execs: Friends, William Warner, Daniel Hutz, also Guardians of my children.
Witnesses: Thomas Coats, Jr., William Smith.

PRESLOR, GEORGE. Township of Northern Liberties. Phila. Co.
Sept. 12, 1807. April 25, 1818. 6.574.
Estate to my wife, Catharine, and my children: Henry, William and Sarah, and to my daughter, Catharina Brown's children, George and Sarah Brown.
Execs: Jacob Kirk, Casper Heft.
Witnesses: Thomas Fisher, George Wile.

KAMMERER, MARY. Phila. Widow.
Aug. 18, 1817. April 25, 1818. 6.574.
To my niece, Caroline Collins, daughter of Chalkley Collins. To my niece, Mary Collins, daughter of Benjamin Collins. The following five in compliance with wishes of deceased mother: Elizabeth Marshall, daughter of Charles Marshall, Mary Wilmot, Sarah Ann Dilhorn, Elizabeth Collins and Mary Collins. To my Uncle and Aunt Smither. To Isabella Martin. To Patrick Byrne. To Mary Wilmot. To Rachel Wilmot. To Elizabeth Stineford. To Sarah Stineford. To Peter John. To my brothers, Joshua and Benjamin Collins. To nephew, Thomas Collins. To nephew, Joshua Collins, son of Chalkley Collins. Residue to Executors George Vaux and John Bacon, in trust for niece, Caroline Collins. If needed, Executors to take advice of friend, Charles Chauney.
Witnesses: Charles Chauncey, Joseph Beale.

CARRELL, DANIEL. Phila. Gentleman.
March 4, 1818. April 27, 1818. 6.575.
Property in Phila. and Roxborough to be sold, proceeds to be used by Executor for support and education of my three children: Charles, Caroline and Thomas, during minority. John Greiner to be Executor, also Guardian of my children.
Witnesses: James Schott, Maria E. Carrell.

TAYLOR, BENJAMIN. Phila.
Nov. 13, 1815. April 27, 1818. 6.576.
To wife, Zada Taylor. After her decease, to daughters, Eliza Taylor and Amy Taylor and to sons, Robert, Enoch and Jacob Taylor. To daughter, Ann Pratt. To Executors, in trust for daughter-in-law, Esther Taylor, wife of my son, Amos, and for her children by said son, Amos, also in trust for daughter, Lydia Howell and her children, except her son, Peter, (he having been provided for by his grandfather, Peter Howell). Execs: Son, Robert Taylor, my nephew, Charles C. French.
Codicil: April 18, 1818. Son, Robert, deceased. Bequeath to his children and to his widow, Rachel Taylor, during her life.
Executor in place of son, Rob't., my son-in-law, James D. Pratt.
Witnesses: Thos. Mitchell, Jonathan Sleeper, Andrew Ashton.

JONES, REBECCA. Phila. Spinster.
March 9, 1816. April 29, 1818. 6.577.
To kinsman, Nathan Jones, and to kinswoman, Jane Donaldson. To cousin, Daniel Jones's daughters, Rebecca and Sarah Jones. To cousin, Chas. Stow, Taylor. Legacy to friends, William Allen and William Phillips, Printer of London, Great Britain, in trust for three daughters of my friends, James and Deborah Townsend, of said city. Said legacy given me by their late aunt, Lydia Hawkesworth of Bristol, deceased.

To Dr. Isaac Cathrall. To my friend, Rachel Brooks, widow. To my
present handmaid, Elizabeth Chattin. To friends, Rebecca Price, Mary
England, Rachel Bauer, Hannah Chattin, Ann Lippincott, Rebecca
Chattin, Mary Ralph Hoops. To my neighbour, Rose O'Donnald, and
her daughter, Mary O'Donnald. To friend, Hannah Cathrall, widow. To
Ann Warder and Ann Stewartson for the poor under care of Women
Friends of North Meeting. To William Allison, Jr. To Rebecca Allinson,
Samuel Allinson, William Allinson, three children of Bernice Allinson
when 21 years. To George Dillwyn, Samuel Emlen and John Cox, of
Burlington, and Leonard Snowdon and Thomas Stewartson, of this city,
in trust, all my books and papers of every kind. Residue to said Bernice
Allinson, to give legacy there from to her sister, Elizabeth. To Mary
Shar, a dumb woman. To Mary Roberts. To Lucy Clark, a Black
woman. To Elizabeth Allinson, a blind woman. To Rebecca Allison.
Execs: Friends, Leonard Snowdon, Thomas Stewartson, James Smith,
Johns Hopkins of this city.
Witnesses: Charles Thomson, Peter Thomson.

VANDIKE, DAVID.
Dec. 20, 1817. April 30, 1818. 6.578.
Estate to wife, Elizabeth Vandike.
Exec: Friend, James R. Dugan.
Witnesses: Robert C. Green, George Fox.

PEACOCK, RALPH. Phila. Merchant.
April 27, 1818. May 5, 1818. 6.578.
Estate to my six children: Dodsworth, Ralph William, George
Steinmetz, Adaline Maria, Mary and Cornelia Peacock.
Execs: Son, Dodsworth Peacock, step-son, John Bowen.
Witnesses: Mary Peacock, John Hughes, William S. Cleavenger.

JACOBS, JOHN. Phila. Formerly of Boston. Merchant.
May 14, 1818. May 19, 1818. 6.578.
To my friend, David Solomon Aaron, of London. To friend, Levin
Lewin, also of London. To Levy Philips of Phila, for use of Synagogue,
Micheve Israel, in Phila., and for Society Bicherhoulen in Phila. To
widow Hart, with whom I now board. Residue to my brother, Aaron
Jacobs, and to my sister, Judith Jacobs, wife of Lyon Jacobs.
Exec: Levy Phillips, of Phila.
Isaac Wampole and Levy Phillips affirmed.

SULLIVAN, JOSHUA. Phila. Innkeeper.
Aug. 11, 1817. May 19, 1818. 6.579.

Income of estate to wife, Sarah Sullivan, for her own use and that of my daughters, while single, and after decease of wife, to all my children.
Execs: Son, Charles Sullivan (my eldest son, David, living and being likely to live in the Western Country), my son-in-law William Worrell, my friend, Robert Wescot.
Witnesses: Alexander Ramsey, Edward Davies, John Butler.

BENNERS, JACOB. Phila. Mariner.
Dec. 24, 1815. May 20, 1818. 6.579.
To wife, Margaret Benners, income, etc. of all estate, and after her death, to my six children: George, Elizabeth, Henry, Mary Ann, James and William S. Benners.
Execs: Said wife, during widowhood, son, George, my brother-in-law, Peter Bartleson.
Witnesses: Robt. Whitehead, L. W. Eyre.

WORKMAN, SAMUEL. District of Southwark. Phila. Co. Boat Builder.
Oct. 14, 1816. May 22, 1818. 6.580.
Estate to my mother, Rebecca Workman, whom I appoint sole Executrix.
Witnesses: Benjamin Duncan, John H. Nezmos.
John Hoover, District of Southwark, rope maker, affirmed.

SAWYER, LEWDEN. Phila. Ladies Shoemaker.
March 25, 1818. May 21, 1818. 6.580.
To my daughter, Hannah. To Joseph Allen, brother of my late wife. To my three children: Joseph Allen Sawyer, Margaret Sawyer, Jane Allen Sawyer. Residue of personal estate to my wife, Ebby Sawyer, for her own use and to enable her to maintain herself and all my children. Real estate to my children, subject to wife's interest during life.
Execs: Said wife, my friends, Charles Allen, Joseph Allen.
Witnesses: Thomas Mitchell, William Barnes, Jr. Letters to Charles and Joseph Allen. Ebby Sawyer affirmed, March 14, 1827.

GOSNER, GEORGE. Phila.
Jan. 3, 1818. March 2, 1818. 6.581.
To wife, Christiana, and at her death, to my step-son, John Willis, and my son, David Gosner.
Execs: Said wife, step-son, John Willis.
Witnesses: John N. Fisher, Isaac Wampole.
Letters to John Willis, June 3, 1818.

STARR, LYDIA. Northern Liberties. Phila. Widow.
Signed: 1817. May 30, 1818. 6.581.

To friend, Mary Shochall. To nephew, Joseph Pryor's daughter,
Elizabeth Pryor. To granddaughters, Lydia Starr and Ann Starr. To
nephew, Jesse Gilbert's daughter, Lydia. To nephew, Joseph Pryor. To
Lydia Starr Iredill, my niece Hannah Iredill's daughter. To my three
sisters and my daughter-in-law, Mary Starr. To my sister, Hannah
Ellis, and her daughters. Residue to son, Moses Starr.
Execs: Friend, Stephen Maxfield, my grandson, James Starr.
Codicil: 1817. To my adopted daughter, Sarah Croney.
Witnesses: Joseph Thomas, Joshua Stokes.
Codicil: To sister, Mary Tomlinson, and to my sister, Marie's four
daughters: Sarah, Mary, Elizabeth and Hannah. To my
granddaughters, Sarah Lippincott and Lydia Starr. To my daughter-in-
law, Mary Starr, and her three daughters: Sarah, Lydia and Ann. To
Hannah Pryor, sister of my nephew, Joseph. To Ann Pryor, second
daughter of my nephew, Joseph Pryor. To my nurse, Margaret
Thomas, and Margaret Mattan, if living with me at my decease.
Witnesses: Michael Steinauer, John H. Crim.
Letters to James Starr.

STOUT, GEORGE P. Northern Liberties. Phila. Co. Well Digger.
May 11, 1818. June 5, 1818. 6.582.
Estate to remain in hands of Executors until youngest child shall arrive
at twenty-one years, then to all my children: George, John Leonard,
Jacob, Maria, William and Joseph Stout.
Execs: Two sons, George and John Leonard Stout.
Witnesses: John Souder, George Thumbert.

MC WATERS, JOHN. Phila. Trader.
May 23, 1818. June 5, 1818. 6.582.
To my wife, a legacy and all estate to which I became entitled in
consequence of my marriage with her. To my brother, Archibald. To
my sister, Elizabeth, of the County of Antrim, in Ireland, to be applied
by her in bringing my father, mother, brother and sisters, in Ireland, to
this country. If they decline to come, then to be divided amongst them.
Execs: James Harper, Jr., of Phila., brickmaker, Thomas Hutchinson,
of said city, watchmaker.
Witnesses: John Darragh, William Mason.

ASHMEAD, JOHN. Phila.
Oct. 12, 1809. June 10, 1818. 6.583.
Estate to my wife, Mary Ashmead, and to my chidren: Benjamin, Ann
and William Ashmead, Mary Clay, wife of Joseph Clay, Eliza Croskey,
wife of George Croskey. Eldest son, John Ashmead, deceased. Legacy
to each of the children of said son, John.

Execs: Said wife, Mary, son Benjamin Ashmead. Daughter, Ann, to act in case of death of Executors.
Codicil: Nov. 4, 1810. Witnesses to Will, Mary Mifflin, Benjamin Mifflin, Margaret Stark. To Codicil: Paul Cox, Thomas Jackson. Letters to Benj'n. Ashmead, June 12, 1818. Jane Ashmead sworn, May 28, 1847. Benj'n. Ashmead, Executor, deceased.

MARTIN, MARY. Widow.
March 10, 1818. June 9, 1818. 6.583.
To Rev. Dr. William Staughton, in trust to be applied to use of missionaries and their families employed by the Baptist Board of Foreign Missions of U.S. To Elizabeth Brinton, daughter of John Brinton, Esq.
Exec: Said Rev. Dr. William Staughton.
Witnesses: Thomas Bradford, Jr., James W. Simes.

KELTON, DAVID M. Davidson Co., Tennessee.
May 30, 1818. June 18, 1818. 6.583.
Legacies to my sisters, Jane Dalrymple and Elizabeth Pitts. To my brothers, Robert Kelton, Thomas Kelton and James Kelton. To my mother, Easther Kelton. To my father, David Kelton. Residue to my sisters, Polly Kelton and Sally Kelton, and my brother, John Loury Kelton.
Execs: Friends, Joseph Woods, Eli Talbot, of Nashville, Tennessee.
Witnesses: William Schlatter, Joseph Lyon.
Postcript: Thomas H. Flecher of Nashville, to be an Executor. Eli Talbot sworn.

KOBER, MARIA BARBARA. Northern Liberties. Phila. Co. Widow of Paul Kober.
March 23, 1804. June 18, 1818. 6.584.
To my daughters, Esther Dorothea Staus and Anne Maria Weaver.
Execs: Said daughters, son-in-law, John Weaver, my grandson, Joseph Staus.
Witnesses: Godfy Smith, Michael Baker, John Bender. Conrad Hester, of Northern Liberties, grocer, affirmed.
Letters to Joseph Staus.

DE GROFEY, CHARLES. Phila. Gentleman.
June 16, 1818. June 23, 1818. 6.584.
Estate to my sister, Albartine DeGrofey, widow of Jacque Remark DeDamseaux of Vervier in Liege in Europe.
Execs: Friends, John Godfried Wachsmuth, John M. Soullier of said city, gentleman.
Witnesses: Louisa Oellers, George A. Baker.

POTE, MATTHIAS. Kensington. Phila. Co. Labourer.
July 15, 1811. June 20, 1818. 6.584.
Estate to my wife, Fanny, and after her death, to my children.
Daughter, Catherine Cornwell, not to have her share during her husband's life.
Execs: Eldest son, Peter Pote, my son-in-law, Charles Higby.
Witnesses: Isaac I. Kip, John Bakeoven, Martin Cramp.

CARRUTHERS, GEORGE. Phila. Nail Cutter. Son of George Carruthers, late of Harrisburgh, Pennsylvania.
May 15, 1818. May 29, 1818. 6.585.
Estate to my mother, Elizabeth Caruthers.
Exec: Joseph Cornman, of Phila., Keeper of Debtor's Jail.
Witnesses: John King, Margaret Peters.

SHOEMAKER, ABRAHAM. Conveyancer and now an Alderman of Phila.
May 24, 1817. June 4, 1818. 6.585.
Property purchased from father-in-law, Joseph Musgrave, deceased, who purchased same of Administrators of Robert Smith, deceased. Said wife, and my six children: Abraham, Lewis, Francis, Henry, Elizabeth and Mary Ann, now living with me, to be supported out of income of estate for one year after my decease. Estate to my wife and my nine children: Susan, wife of Fishbourn Wharton, Deborah, now widow of Moore Wharton, Abraham, Esther, wife of Lewis C. Vanuxen, Lewis, Francis, Henry, Elizabeth and Mary Ann. Legacy to my sister, Mary, now living with me.
Execs: Wife, Deborah Shoemaker, my three sons, Abraham, Lewis and Francis. Executors to be Guardians of Henry, Elizabeth and Mary Ann.
Witnesses: Joseph P. Musgrave, Bankson Hudell, Robert H. Campbell.
Letters to Abraham, Lewis and Francis Shoemaker.

BRINGHURST, SAMUEL. Germantown. Phila.
March 10, 1817. May 11, 1818. 6.586.
Estate to wife, Susanna Bringhurst. After her decease, to my two daughters, Tacy Ashmead and Mary Lehman.
Execs: Said wife, my two sons-in-law, Samuel Ashmead and William Lehman.
Witnesses: Jacob Butcher, Charles Gilbert.
Alexander Provest, of Germantown, stone mason, affirmed.

BARRETT, TOBIAS. Phila. Accomptant.
Jan., 1815. June 24, 1818. 6.587.

Estate to my wife, Elizabeth Barrett, Mary and Elizabeth each to have a third part in the premises.
Execs: John P. Harper, my wife, Elizabeth.
Witnesses: John E. Molineux, Wm. McAllister. Alexander McAllister, Jr., of Phila., grocer, brother of late William McAllister, affirmed. Executrix Elizabeth Barrett affirmed.

MINTIS, DIANA.
April 2, 1816. Dec.6, 1817. 6.587.
My house and ground in Evesham, New Jersey to Kisiah Newira, Hagah Balled, Levina Mintis and to Kisiah Mintis, daughter of Lovina Mintis, and to Mary Ann Mintis, daughter of Besella and Rebecca Mintis. To Perry Gibson. To Mary White and Harinah Mintis. To Andrew Mintis. "Sugure Box to be given to Candy Oliver," and I wish Charles Mintis to settle my estate.
Witnesses: Joseph Cox, Elizabeth Mintis.

BAKER, RICHARD MACE. Passyunk. Phila. Co. Farmer.
May 12, 1808. June 29, 1818. 6.587.
Estate to wife, Mary Baker, whom I appoint sole Executrix.
Witnesses: Benjamin Brown, Robert Whitehead. Peter Sturgis, of Phila., boot and shoe maker, affirmed.

JACKSON, ELIZABETH. Phila. Widow.
Jan. 31, 1818. July 13, 1818. 6.588.
Estate to my daughter, Eliza Jane Stewart, wife of Samuel M. Stewart.
Exec: Said son-in-law, Samuel M. Stewart.
Witnesses: Elizabeth January, William Andrews.

ENGARD, HENRY. Northern Liberties. Phila. Inn Keeper.
March 29, 1816. May 26, 1818. 6.588.
Estate to wife, Rachel Engard, and after her decease, to my grandchildren: Elizabeth and James Beverige, children of daughter, Mary, deceased, Elizabeth Engard, daughter of my son, James, deceased, and the children of my daughter, Rachel.
Execs: Wife, Rachel Engard, my friend, George Armitage.
Witnesses: Robert Whitehead, James McMahon. Thomas McMahon, of Phila., nursery and seedsman, brother of James McMahon, deceased, affirmed. George Armitage sworn, July 10, 1818.

SELL, HENRY. Township of Northern Liberties. Phila. Co.
June 22, 1818. July 11, 1818. 6.588.
To my wife, Sophia Sell. After her decease, to my eight children: Elizabeth Parmer, formerly Elizabeth Sell, Ann, John, Samuel, Jacob, Thomas, Henry and Sophia Sell.

Execs: Brother, Solomon Sell, my friend, Christian Hubbert, both of Northern Liberties, of Phila.
Witnesses: Christian Heis, Elijah Keaton.

WOODS, HANNAH. Phila. Widow.
May 29, 1816. July 17, 1818. 6.589.
Legacy to my daughter, Sarah Baird, widow of Capt. William Baird, late of Southwark. Residue of estate to my three daughters: Mary Chamberlin, wife of Jacob Chamberlin, Hannah Woods and Margaret Smith, wife of William W. Smith.
Exec: Said daughter, Hannah Woods.
Witnesses: Joseph M. Paul, Peter Thomson.

STEEL, ALEXANDER. District of Southwark. Justice of Peace, formerly House Carpenter.
Jan. 20, 1818. July 21, 1818. 6.589.
Rents, etc. of estate to wife, Kezia, she to provide for our children: William, Mary and James.
Execs: Wife, Kezia, my friends, Archibald McLaren, wheat fan maker, James Stuart, revenue officer, John Cochran, late baker, but now a merchant.
Witnesses: Malcolm McNevan, Isaac Davis, Sarah Ann Crawford. Kezia Steel sworn.

WONDERLY, WILLIAM. Phila. Grazier.
July 21, 1818. July 25, 1818. 6.590.
My estate to my wife, Elizabeth, and my children: John Wonderly, Joseph Wonderly, Juliana, wife of Fred'k. Vogel, Elizabeth, wife of William Fitler. To grandson, William K. Wonderly, son of my son, John, and to my grandson, Charles Vogel.
Execs: Sons, John and Joseph, son-in-law, William Fitler.
Witnesses: Moses Williams, Isaac Wampole.

HEYDELL, LEONARD. Phila.
July 28, 1817. July 29, 1818. 6.590.
To my granddaughter, Mary Lynn, wife of Simon Lynn, or her children, appointing their father, Simon Lynn, Testamentary Guardian and Trustee for said children, until 21 years of age. To my granddaughter, Barbara Herrings, wife of Bennett Herriges. To my grandson, John Miller.
Execs: Simon Lynn, John Miller.
Witnesses: Zalegman Phillips, Daniel Wampler. Lewis Allen, of Phila., dry good merchant, affirmed.

CONNOLLY, JOHN. Late Lieut. Col. in the Provincial Line in North America, formerly resident in late Colony of Virginia, and lately at L'agsomption, but now residing at St. John's in Province of Lower Canada.
July 1, 1811. (Signed at St. John's) July 27, 1818. 6.591.
Property at the Falls of the Ohio to be sold. Annuity to wife, Margaret Connolly. To son, James, Capt. in the 26th Reg't. of Foot. To son, Thomas, Capt. in the 15th Reg't. of Foot. To be buried in the Protestant Burial Ground at Montreal.
Execs: Wife, Margaret, Samuel Mifflin of Phila., merchant, son James Connolly, David David of Montreal, merchant, Francis Badgley, also of Montreal, merchant.
Witnesses: M. H. Zeouman, Jos'h. Richardson, Thomas MacLaren, Tench Coxe, Esq., of Phila., son, John Conolly, in business of the estate of the children of late Turbut Francis, Esq., who were under Guardianship of Mrs. Sarah Francis (born Mifflin, afterwards intermarried with said John Connolly), and of General Thomas Mifflin. Rebecca S. Evans, wife of Edward Evans of Phila., plaisterer, affirmed. Letters to Samuel Mifflin.

BROWN, JOSEPH. Township of Oxford. Phila. Co. Labourer.
July 31, 1818. Aug. 8, 1818. 6.592.
Legacy to Joseph Armstrong, Township of Oxford, Phila. Co. Residue of estate to Col. Samuel Castor of said Township, whom I appoint Executor.
Witnesses: Thomas Duffield, Joseph Rorer, James Dyre.

LYNDALL, BENJAMIN. Phila. Cabinet Maker.
July 16, 1818. Aug. 7, 1818. 6.592.
Rents, issues, etc. of estate to my wife, Susanna Lyndall, for support of herself and my two daughters, Ann and Catharine Lyndall. After decease of wife, estate to my seven children: Joseph W., William, Samuel, Robert, Ann, Catharine and Eliza, now Eliza Molther. Legacy to Moravian Church in Race Street.
Execs: Wife, Susanna, my two sons, Joseph W. and Samuel Lyndall.
Witnesses: David Coombs, Henry Barrington, James Cutbush.

MILLARD, THOMAS. Northern Liberties. Phila. Co. Turner and Spinning Wheel Maker.
June 15, 1818. Aug. 13, 1818. 6.593.
To wife, Sarah Millard, and my six children: Thomas, John, William, Clement, Charles and James, and my three grandchildren, the children of my deceased son, George: George, Andrew and Cecilia Millard.
Execs: Brother-in-law, James Boyer, my son, William Millard, my friend, Caleb Carmalt.

Codicil: July 25, 1818. Appoints friend, John Uhler, Executor in place of son, William Millard.
Witnesses to Will: T. I. Bryant, George Uhler.
Witnesses to Codicil: T. I. Bryant, James Carmalt.

LEVERING, ANTHONY. Township of Roxborough. Phila. Co.
July 7, 1818. Aug. 15, 1818. 6.593.
To wife, Mary, and to my five children: Hester, Silas, Titus, Perry and Hannah. Property not to be divided until daughter, Hannah, is 18 years of age.
Execs: Said wife, son-in-law, Charles Levering, my son, Silas Levering.
Witnesses: Horatio G. Jones, Michael Tibben.

PASCALL, BENJAMIN. Township of Kingsessing. Phila. Co.
July 15, 1818. Aug. 22, 1818. 6.594.
To my nephew, John Paschall, a silver tankard marked with initials of my grandfather, Henry Hodge. To cousin, Benjamin Paschall Howell of New Jersey. To my niece, Ann Paschall. To my niece, by the law, Lydia Rudolph, silver plate given to said Lydia Rudolph to be delivered at her decease unto my nephew, Thomas Paschall. To my niece, Hannah Warner. To my nephews, John and Thomas Paschall, sons of my brother, Henry, all my estate in Kingsessing, aforesaid, after death of Lydia Rudolph. All my residuary estate to my nieces, Margaret Hopkins, Frances Lloyd, Mary Paschall, Ann Paschall, Hannah Warner, Elizabeth Smith, Sarah Adams and Beulah Paschall.
Execs: Lydia Rudolph, Thomas Jacob Paschall.
Witnesses: Morris C. Shallcross, Margaret D. Hopkins.

HOPKINS, SAMUEL.
April 11, 1818. July 11, 1818. 6.595.
Made former Will during wife's life, left in hands of Nathan Harper, now I make a new one.
Estate to my two daughters, Ann and Elizabeth.
Execs: My friends, Abraham Barker, Howell Hopkins, Isaac Morris, all of Phila.
Witnesses: Benjamin Borden, Stephen Heaviland, John C. Borden.
Letters to Howel Hopkins and Abraham Barker.

JOBSON, CHARLES. Phila. Co. 6.595.
Jan. 16, 1818. Aug. 27, 1818. 6.595.
To wife, Rebecca Jobson, and our only surviving child, Joseph Jobson.
Execs: Said wife, her uncle, Ellis Yarnall.
Witnesses: Joseph Rakestraw, Joseph Snowdon.

VAUGHAN, WILLIAM. Kensington. Phila. Co. Grocer.
May 11, 1818. Sept. 1, 1818. 6.595.
To wife, Mary Vaughan, and after her decease, to my daughters, Jane and Rebecca Vaughan. To my son, William, and my daughter, Sarah Daniels, each $15. George Ayre to have buildings by me erected on his premises at appraisement.
Sole Exec: Wife, Mary.
Witnesses: Benjamin R. Van Hook, Thomas Vaughan, William Vaughan.

BLACKWELL, JACOB. Phila.
July 21, 1818. Sept. 1, 1818. 6.595.
To my brother, Robert Blackwell. To stepdaughter, Mary Thackray.
Execs: Said stepdaughter, George Heyl, Esq., Jacob Bond.
Witnesses: Benjamin F. Bryant, Daniel Steinmetz.
Letters to Mary Thackray.

MINTZER, ROSANNA. Northern Liberties. Phila. Co. Widow.
March 10, 1818. Aug. 31, 1818. 6.596.
To sons, John and Adam Mintzer. To friend, Robert Brooke, in trust for daughter, Elizabeth, that her present or any future husband shall have no control. For daughter, Mary, on same conditions.
Execs: Said Robert Brooke, my two sons, John and Adam Mintzer.
Witnesses: Jonathan Carmalt, Jr., James Carmalt, Caleb Carmalt. Last two named, witnesses to Codicils, May 21, 1818, and June 23, 1818.

WEAVER, BARNARD. Phila. Yeoman.
May 30, 1818. Sept. 3, 1818. 6.598.
To wife, Eave Weaver. To youngest daughter, Catharan Butcher. To daughter, Margarett Fox. To son, John Weaver. Executors to pay to Hannah Higgins, etc. as per Deed from Franc's. Higgins, deceased.
Execs: Peter Bennar, George Sees of Phila., also Guardians of children.
Witnesses: Francis Borden, George Bumm, Robert Patterson.
Letters to George Sees.

WORRELL, ISAIAH. Borough of Frankford. Phila. Co.
Jan. 8, 1810. Sept. 3, 1818. 6.598.
To sons: Isaac, Robert, Isaiah, William (should he return within seven years), John H., Jacob, Thomas and Stephen Worrell. To daughter, Rebecca. To children of daughter, Sarah Coates, deceased: Paulina, Hannah, Thomas and William Coates, when of age. To daughter, Mary Knight, wife of Thomas Knight. To Preparative Meeting of Friends at Frankford.
Execs: Sons, Isaac and Thomas Worrell.
Witnesses: Nathan Harper, Watson Atkinson.

Letters to Isaac Worrell.

BEDFORD, LUCY. Phila. Co. Widow.
Aug. 25, 1818. Sept. 4, 1818. 6.599.
Estate to friend, Lydia Morton, wife of Abraham Morton of District of Southwark, and to Samuel Bedford.
Exec: Abraham Morton of Phila. Co.
Codicil: Aug. 25, 1818. Revokes appointment of Abraham Morton as sole Executor and appoints Jacob Tapsico of said county, sole Executor.
Witnesses: Joseph P. Norris, Jr., Jacob Tapsico.

MORY, LEWIS. Phila. Mariner.
Oct. 26, 1810. Sept. 5, 1818. 6.600.
To my wife, Elizabeth Mary, whom I appoint sole Executrix.
Witnesses: Thomas Mitchell, James Sawer.

HUGLER, CHARLES. Northern Liberties. Phila. Gentleman.
May 1, 1818. Sept. 8, 1818. 6.600.
Estate to my wife, Catharine, and my children: George, Benjamin, Elizabeth and Mary, and to my two grandchildren, Catharine and Simon Sweitzer, children of said daughter, Mary, by her former husband, Henry Sweitzer, deceased.
Execs: Said sons, Geo. and Benjamin, said daughter, Elizabeth.
Witnesses: John Brooke, Isaac Wampole.
Letters to George Kugler and Elizabeth Kugler.

POINCY, MARIA ROSALIE CECIL MONTAILLET. Northern Liberties. Phila. Widow.
July 12, 1818. Sept. 7, 1818. 6.600.
Estate to my four children: Adolph, Lucien, Victor and Olimpie Poincy.
To sister, Blance, wife of Victor Blane.
Sole Exec: Brother-in-law, Victor Blane, also to be Guardian of my said four children. At his death, appoint friend, John Labour of Phila., merchant, Executor and Guardian.
Witnesses: John deBrot, Peter Thomson. Letters to Victor Blane.
Signed: Rosalie Poincy.

ARCHDEACON, ANNETTE. Southwark. Phila. Co. Widow.
Sept. 4, 1818. Sept. 12, 1818. 6.601.
To Margaretta Eldridge. To Roman Catholic Society of St. Joseph for educating poor orphan children in Phila.
Exec: Friend, Joseph Snyder of Phila., gilder.
Witnesses: Marmaduke Myers, Joseph Snyder.

MOORE, MARMADUKE. Phila. Stone Cutter.
Jan. 6, 1818. Sept. 14, 1818. 6.601.
To wife and children.
Execs: Lodewyk Sharpe, Stephen Henderson of Phila., also to have management of my children.
Witnesses: Thos. Traquair, Ad. C. Salaignac.

HATTON, JOHN. Phila.
Dec. 25, 1816. Sept. 19, 1818. 6.601.
Execs: Daughter, Sarah, son Thomas Hatton. To said daughter, Sarah, half of my estate under following restrictions. That my wife shall receive yearly from her daughter, Sarah Walton, one-half of the clean Income of my said estate. To son, Benjamin, one dollar. To my daughter, Susanna Hampton, and my two sons, John and Thomas, each $20. After decease of wife, her share to my two sons, John and Thomas Hatton. Said daughter, Sarah Hatton, the right to keep all if she chooses. Friends, William Carrigue and Israel Maul, to assist my children with their advice.
John Dudgson of Phila., cordwainer, and Taft Benjamin, of said city, teacher, affirmed. Letters to Sarah Hatton.

WILSON, SAMUEL L. Phila. Merchant.
Sept. 14, 1818. Sept. 23, 1818. 6.602.
Property to be converted into cash. Income of proceeds to my wife, Catharine Wilson, for support of herself and my daughter, Sarah L. Wilson. Should daughter die and wife marry, my father and mother to have 2/3 of estate during their lives, and at decease of said wife, property to my brother and sisters, except my gold watch, which I give to Dr. G. Uhler.
Exec: Father, John B. Wilson.
Witnesses: Abraham Lower, Silas Yerkes.

MEYERS, GEORGE. District of Spring Garden. Phila. Co. Inn Keeper.
Sept. 8, 1818. Sept. 18, 1818. 6.602.
Income of estate to wife, Hannah. After her decease, to my four children: Elizabeth, George, Samuel and William.
Execs: Said wife, my friends, William Warner of Spring Garden, Isaac Wampole of Phila. Wife to be Guardian of said children during her widowhood.
Witnesses: Frederick Haas, Philip Lowry, Isaac Wampole.
Isaac Wampole discharged, by Orphan Court, from duty of Executor.

MC ELWAINE, FERGUSON. Phila.
June 18, 1818. Sept. 22, 1818. 6.603.
To my housekeeper, Jane Bell. To friend, James Stuart.

Execs: James Stuart, grocer, John Workman, merchant.
Witnesses: John W. Thompson, Will'm. Dalzell.

HAINES, DANIEL. Kensington. Township of Northern Liberties. Phila. Co.
Aug. 26, 1799. Sept. 22, 1818. 6.603.
To wife, Catharina, and after her decease or marriage, to my children: Catharine, wife of George Wilkins, Michael Haines, Elizabeth, wife of Sebastian Hoffman, Sarah, Henry, Daniel, John, Jacob and Peter.
Execs: Friends, Peter Deal, house carpenter, Daniel Deal, blacksmith, of Kensington.
Witnesses: Jacob Smith, Dan'l. Sheets, Charles R. Pryor. Letters to Peter Deal. Henry Earnest of Northern Liberties, feed seller, affirmed.

De BEAUREGARD, SOPHIA PICKEL. Late of Canada. At present, in Phila.
June 16, 1818. Sept. 28, 1818. 6.603.
To be interred in the burial ground of the Roman Catholic Chapel of St. Mary's in Phila., at discretion of my husband, James Charles Lambert DeBeauregard. Legacy to said Roman Catholic Chapel. Estate to said husband, whom I appoint sole Executor.
Witnesses: Aaron B. Nones, Joseph G. Marks, Benjamin Nones, Notary Public, Francis Shallus.

SCHEPPACH, JOHN JACOB. Phila. Baker.
March 11, 1815. Sept. 29, 1818. 6.604.
Estate to stepson, John M. Hartley, and to stepdaughter, Margaret Sulger, and after her decease, to her son, Jacob Sulger, Jr.
Execs: Said John M. Hartley, Jacob Sulger, Jr.
Witnesses: Isaac Wampole, Fred'k. Beates.

RICHARDS, ANN. District of Southwark. Widow.
April 22, 1817. Sept. 7, 1818. 6.604.
To sons, Joseph and James Richards. To daughter-in-law, Rachel Richards, and her two children, William and John Richards, when of age.
Execs: George Harkes of Northern Liberties, baker, Henry Barrington of Phila., chocolate manufactory.
Witnesses: John Kern, John Warner.

SHOCK, ELIZABETH. Borough of Frankford. Phila. Co. Widow.
April 21, 1818. June 10, 1818. 6.605.
To my children: Christiana Whittick, John Whittick, Joseph Whittick, Andrew Schock, Jacob Schock, Catharine Schock, Henry Schock, Rebecca Schock.

Execs: Friends, John Foulkrod, William Singleton.
Witnesses: Isaac Worrell, Robert Worrell.
Letters to William Singleton.

WALLACE, JAMES. Phila. Mariner. Lately belonging to U. S. Frigate, "Essex," Capt. Porter.
Dec. 1, 1812. Oct. 5, 1818. 6.605.
Estate to my friend, Lavinia Hickey, of said city, whom I appoint Executrix.
Witnesses: Patrick McGowen, James W. Linchey. Richard Renshaw, Esq. of Phila. Co., affirmed.

HANSER, JACOB. Phila. Trader.
Aug. 27, 1799. Oct. 5, 1818. 6.605.
Estate to my wife, Barbara, whom I appoint Executrix. Wife's grandchildren, George Hambler and Sarah Hambler, should wife not survive me. Appoint Christian H. Denckla, of Phila., merchant, Executor.
Witnesses: Fred'k. Beates, Philip I. Dunn.
Signed: Jacob Hantzel.
John Greiner, of Phila., merchant affirmed.

BARTHE, DOMINICK. Phila. Merchant.
Dec. 16, 1816. Oct. 5, 1818. 6.606.
Having given to my daughter, Sophia Henrietta Emily, a legacy upon her marriage to Michael W. Ash, of this city, attorney at law, and as she has been ungrateful, I bequeath estate to my brother, Jean, sister Jeane Marie, wife of Jacques Gras, brother Jacques, or their representatives, residing at Tarbes, Capital of Department of the Upper Pyranees or elsewhere in France. After fulfilling above legacies, remainder to my son, Peter Dominick Barthe.
Execs: John Dubarry, Lewis Clapier, Charles Brugiere, of Phila., merchants, also Guardians, said son, Peter Dominick.
Witnesses: James S. Duval, Fournier Rostain.

BLAIR, SAMUEL. Township of Germantown. Phila. Co. D.D.
Dec. 13, 1816. Oct. 7, 1818. 6.606.
Father-in-law, William Shippen, deceased, left property to his son, William Shippen, and to his daughter Susan Blair, part of which, said Susan conveyed to me, feeling sure she will afford to my children all needful aid. I do bequeath to said wife, Susan Blair, all my estate, appointing her sole Executrix.
Witnesses: Charles Macknet, John Knorr, Charles Peirce.

ZAHRENS, ANTHONY. Northern Liberties. Phila. Skin Dresser.
March 22, 1816. Oct. 8, 1818. 6.607.
Legacy to my wife's nephew, Anthony Z. Brown, when twenty-one years. All residue of estate to my wife, Catharine, whom I appoint sole Executrix.
Witnesses: Jacob Gardner, Isaac Wampole.

YOUNG, THOMAS. Town of Kinsinton. Phila. Co.
July 18, 1810. Oct. 10, 1818. 6.607.
To my wife, Prissila Young, all my estate, and after her decease, to my step-son, John Griffin, whom I appoint sole Executor, he to pay unto my too step dougters, Mary Marchall, and Margret Phillips, each $100.
Witnesses: Cadw'r. Roberts, Jr., Nathan Evans.

NICHOLAS, MARY. Phila. Widow.
Sept. 28, 1818. Oct. 10, 1818. 6.607.
Property in Phila., Co. of Westmorland and other counties in western part of Pennsylvania, also farm in Township of Abington, Co. of Montgomery, to which I am entitled at death of Hannah Miller, I bequeath to my three children, Samuel, Charles I. and Mary I. Nicholas.
Execs: Said three children.
Witnesses: Nathan Chapman, Eliza Harmar.
Letters to Samuel Nicholas and Mary I. Nicholas.

MALEY, MICHAEL. Phila. House Carpenter.
Feb. 19, 1816. Oct. 12, 1818. 6.608.
Income of estate to my wife, Catharine, and at her death or marriage, estate to be sold, proceeds to my four children: Mary Burbank, John, Samuel and Peter Maley.
Execs: Wife, Catharine, son John, harness maker, my friend, John Hile of Phila., brush maker.
Witnesses: William Griffith, George Wilson, D. Wilson.
Letters to Catharine and John Maley.

FORDE, ANN. Phila.
June 4, 1818. Oct. 12, 1818. 6.608.
Estate to be sold, proceeds to my four nieces, the daughters of late Standish Forde: Ellen Hansell, Mary Forde, Ann Forde, and Margaret Forde. To Mary Blackburn and Elizabeth Neill.
Execs: Sarah Forde, William S. Hansell.
Witnesses: John Colesberry, John Barr, William H. Colesberry.

KEBLER, MARIA.
April 5, 1810. Oct. 14, 1818. 6.608.

Estate to my daughter, Maria Elizabeth Shinneck, except the $100 which my son, Jacob Lentz, owes me, from which my funeral expenses are to be paid, and the remainder to my children.
Exec: Daughter, Maria Elizabeth Shinneck.
Witnesses: Gottlieb Klett, John Reakert.

CROTHERS, JOHN M. Seaman.
May 9, 1818. Oct. 20, 1818. 6.609.
Estate to my wife, Jane Crothers, whom I appoint sole Executrix.
Witnesses: Thompson Tully, John Thompson.

SHARPLESS, MARY. Phila. Bonnet Maker.
Oct. 10, 1818. Oct. 26, 1818. 6.609.
To niece, Mary D. Sharpless, all my plate. To nieces, Edith Sharpless and Mary D. Sharpless, all my wearing apparel. Residue to my five nieces: Hannah, Ann, Edith and Mary, daughters of my late brother, Isaac, and Mary, the daughter of my brother, Joseph.
Execs: Nieces, Edith and Mary Sharpless.
Witnesses: George Williams, Mary James, Lydia Rockhill.
Letters to Edith Sharpless.

HAYDOCK, EDEN. Phila. Plumber.
Oct. 11, 1818. Oct. 26, 1818. 6.609.
To my wife, Mary Ash Haydock, and my six children: Susanna, Elizabeth W., Mary, Eden, Henry and Martha W. Haydock. Property in Blockley Township and Northern Liberties held in company with brother, Samuel Haydock.
Execs: Brother, Samuel Haydock, my friend, Charles Townsend.
Witnesses: Daniel G. Temple, Peter Thompson.

LINDSEY, WILLIAM. Phila.
June 15, 1818. Oct. 28, 1818. 6.610.
To my three nephews and three nieces in Ireland. To Malty Steel and her brother, Samuel Steel. To Andrew Nelson, Co. of Phila. To Wm. Nelson and Sam'l. Biddle.
Exec: Rev. Ezra Stiles Ely, D.D.
Witnesses: Samuel Biddle, Ezra Stiles Ely.

CHAMBERS, JAMES. Phila. Co. Mariner.
July 13, 1814. Nov. 3, 1818. 6.610.
Estate to my wife, Barbara Chambers, and to my four children: Peter, Adam, Ann Maria and George.
Exec: Wife, Barbara.
Witnesses: Robert Whitehead, Lydia W. Eyre.

ORR, ARTHUR. Phila. Iron Founder.
May 23, 1818. Nov. 3, 1818. 6.610.
$2 to son, Arthur. Estate to wife, Margaret, and after her decease, to Thomas Sargent and James I. Rush, in trust for son, John Orr, and his family.
Execs: Friends, Dr. Thomas Sargent, James I. Rush of said city.
Witnesses: Abel Dicks, John Bannen.

LITHGOW, EDWARD. Phila. House Carpenter.
Estate to wife, Elizabeth Lithgow, whom I appoint sole Executrix.
Witnesses: William King, Margaret King.

LAPP, JOHN. Bristol Township. Phila. Co. Cordwiner.
June 19, 1817. Nov. 7, 1818. 6.611.
To son, Anthony Lapp. To daughters, Mary Lukens, Priscilla Lukens and the children of my son, Joseph Lapp.
Execs: Friends, Isaac Kulb of Bristol Township, John Harvey of Township of Cheltenham.
Witnesses: Thomas Shoemaker, Jacob Kulp.
Letters to Isaac Kulp and John Harvey.

SALTAR, ELIZABETH.
Proved: Nov. 9, 1818. 6.611.
Gold chain and locket for my two daughters, Margaret and Maria, also to my son's wife. To my daughters, Lucy and Frances, who are still single, I give all household furniture, etc., also my share of plantation left me by my father.
Execs: Lucy and Frances Saltar.
Frances Edwards of Phila., widow, and James Robertson of said city, affirmed.

MAXWELL, JAMES. Northern Liberties. Phila. Wharf Builder.
Oct. 21, 1818. Nov. 9, 1818. 6.612.
Estate to wife, Hannah. Legacy to son, John Thomas Maxwell, amount of said legacy due me by David Bolton.
Exec: Friend, John Sexton of Northern Liberties, also to be Guardian of said son.
Witnesses: Lawrence Hoover, Joseph Russell.

SEVERN, BENJAMIN. Phila. Yeoman.
March 27, 1813. Nov. 10, 1818. 6.613.
Use of estate to wife, Elizabeth, she to support my son, John, and after her decease, estate to son, William Severn, daughter, Ann Biegler, wife of late Philip Biegler, deceased, and their daughter, Elizabeth Biegler, each one paying annuity to son, John Severn.

Execs: Wife, Elizabeth Severn, daughter, Ann Biegler.
Witnesses: Fred'k. Beates, Tobias Schoenheit.

GRAVIER, JOSEPH. Phila.
Nov. 9, 1818. Nov. 11, 1818. 6.613.
To son, Napoleon Gravier, all estate, but should he die in minority, then to my three brothers: Jean, Brunaut and Rini Gravier, and my sister, Maria Gravier, femme genoit.
Exec: Charles Brugiere.
Witnesses: Daniel Charpentier, Peter Hurtel, John Hurtel.

AUSTIN, WILLIAM. Charleston, South Carolina.
Jan. 28, 1814. May 10, 1815. 6.614.
To my son, William Austin, $4.26. To Maria Elliott, rent of my ferry in Phila. that Benjamin R. Morgan holds in trust for me, if she remains unmarried. At her death, said ferry to eldest son of Samuel Austin, in state of New Jersey, County of Salem. To Louisa Smith. To friend, David Denoon. To George Elliott.
Exec: Friend, Benjamin R. Morgan, Esq., of Phila.
Witnesses: George G. Denoon, Peter X. Lafare, Samuel W. Miller.

KELLY, JAMES. Borough of York, Pennsylvania. Attorney at Law.
Sept. 26, 1818. Feb. 20, 1819. 6.614.
Wife, Mary, to have use of house in which we live, also an annuity. Desire that one of my five children inherit the house Mr. McClure lives in, in Baltimore. Executor, in Pennsylvania, Chares Barnitz, Esq., son of friend, Jacob Barnitz, he to pay attention to education of my two sons. Friends, John Quarles and John Hillin, of city of Baltimore, my Executors, to see Will executed in Maryland. Legacy to Maria Jackson, daughter of my sister, Rebecca Jackson.
Witnesses: Thomas Latimer, Caleb Taylor, Sarah Clopper.

STRUM, HENRICK. Now resident of Boston, Suffolk Co., State of Massachusetts. Seaman.
Dec. 7, 1814. Dec. 28, 1818. 6.616.
Estate to Thomas Lewis of Boston, merchant, whom I appoint Executor.
Witnesses: Sarah Lewis, Eliza Lewis, Eunice B. Newhall.

OTTO, BODO, JR.
Jan. 18, 1782. Feb. 22, 1782.
Estate in Pennsylvania to my wife, Catharine, and after her death, to my four children: Catharine, John, Jacob and Daniel. Said wife to give children education in her power.
Execs: Wife, Catharine Otto, my friend, John Wilkens, Esq.

Witnesses: Jacob Goodin, Thomas Nevis, Thomas Clark.

WOOD, GEORGE. Phila. House Carpenter.
Dec. 29, 1816. Nov. 12, 1818. 6.617.
Legacy for building a church in District of Southwark, Phila.
Remainder of estate to my two children, Mary Ann Wood and George Wood, when younger arrives at lawful age. Their mother to have her Thirds during life.
Exec: Wife, Ann Wood.
Witnesses: Henry Barrington, Thomas Hoskin.

VANDEREN, SUSANNA. Northern Liberties.
Nov. 22, 1815. Nov. 13, 1818. 6.617.
Legacy to my granddaughter, Susanna Vanderin. To granddaughter Susanna Vanderin Johnson all residue of my estate.
Execs: William Garrigues, Caleb Carmalt.
Witnesses: George G. Meyers, Clement Remington.
Letters to surviving Executor, William Garrigues.

LORT, ISAAC. Phila. Cabinet Maker.
Oct. 31, 1814. Nov. 16, 1818. 6.617.
Estate to my sister, Mary Lort, she to provide for our sister, Ann McNeal, as long as she will live separate from her husband.
Legacy to cousin, Thomas G. Connor.
Exec: Said sister, Mary Lort.
Witnesses: John Chapman, Peter Thomson.

MC COY, ARCHIBALD. Phila.
Feb. 11, 1818. Nov. 17, 1818. 6.618.
To my nieces: Agnes McCoy, Mary McCoy and Catharine McCoy, daughters of my brother, Daniel McCoy, at present in Ireland. To my niece, Mary Woods, daughter of my late sister, Margaret, now in Ireland. Residue of estate to my nephew, John McCoy, of Phila., stone cutter, son of my brother, Daniel McCoy.
Execs: Said nephew, John McCoy, my friend, David Stewart, of Phila.
Witnesses: Samuel Porter, James B. Chapman, Thomas Dougherty.

STEWART, CHARLES. Township of Bristol. Phila. Co.
Oct. 18, 1818. Nov. 18, 1818. 6.618.
To my wife, Elizabeth, and my children: Artemus, Parthenia and Harriet Leech, wife of Joseph Leech.
Execs: Wife, Elizabeth, John Harvey.
Witnesses: Jacob Kulp, Isaac Whenor, Eliazer Fenton.

WIESSENBACH, HENRY. Phila.
Nov. 14, 1818. Nov. 20, 1818. 6.619.
To my wife, Elizabeth Wiessenbach, house now occupied by me. Residue of real estate to be sold, proceeds to friend, William Wiessenbach of Northern Liberties, Phila. Co., combmaker, and Catharine, my wife.
Execs: Friends, John Hahn, Joseph Sittel.
Witnesses: Melchior Larer, John Hartman, Peter Myers.
Letters to John Kern, Joseph Siddell.

APT, MICHAEL. Kensington. Northern Liberties. Phila. Co. House Carpenter.
April 25, 1818. Nov. 20, 1818. 6.619.
Son, Michael, to have my carpenter tools. Residue of estate to my wife, Elizabeth, and at her decease, to my son, Michael, and daughter, Julia Ann Apt.
Exec: Wife, Elizabeth.
Witnesses: Thomas Timmings, Peter Dickus.

CULNAN, CHARLES. District of Southwark. Phila. Co.
Oct. 16, 1818. Nov. 20, 1818. 6.620.
Estate to wife, Margaret Culnan, whom I appoint sole Executrix.
Witnesses: Robert Whitehead, Samuel Mount.

BONNER, JAMES. Moreland Township. Phila. Co.
June 13, 1814. Nov. 23, 1818. 6.620.
To my daughter, Hannah Hurley, widow of Thomas Hurley. To children of late daughter, Mary Sample, deceased: James Sample, Ann Sample and Martha Sample to be paid to them by my son, James Bonner. To daughter-in-law, Ury Bonner. Residue to said son, James Bonner, whom I appoint sole Executor.
Witnesses: James Tomlinson, Thomas Tomlinson.

BROWN, WILLIAM. District of Southwark.
Sept. 10, 1818. Nov. 27, 1818. 6.621.
Estate to wife, Margret Brown, and at her decease to my three children: Eliza Brown, George Brown and fany Ann Brown. To my daughter, Hannah Brown.
Execs: Michael Dennis, my wife, Margret Brown of said district.
Witnesses: Elias Mason, William Prichett.

TOOLE, MARY. Phila.
Nov. 17, 1818. Dec. 1, 1818. 6.621.
To daughter, Mary Toole. To son, Samuel Parke, when twenty-one years. To Mary Grace, who lives with me. To my brother, George

Cobourn, if he shall return to the city. Thos. Graham to be Guardian of my children.
Exec: Friend, Thomas Graham, of Phila., merchant.
Witnesses: Mary Martin, Fred'k. Beates.

ROBERTS, MARTHA. Phila. Spinster.
Dec. 4, 1818. Dec. 16, 1818. 6.621.
To my niece, Elizabeth Baker. To niece, Catharine Maxwell, for her children: John, Mary and Martha. To Ann Sickel and her daughter, Mary. To my sister, Ann McClean.
Execs: Friends, Robert Dawson and his son, Josiah Dawson, of Phila., gentleman.
Witnesses: Mary Ann Bunce, Sarah Shade, John Groves.
Letters to Josiah Dawson.

KANE, CONRAD. In and of the city of Phila. Millstone Maker.
To wife, Elizabeth Kane, and to my children: Andrew, Mary Ann, Harriott, George and the child yet unborn.
Exec: Wife, Elizabeth.
Witnesses: Christian B. Merkel, Jonathan Pounder, John McClintock.

BAXTER, JAMES. Phila. Merchant. Son of Capt. John Baxter, deceased.
May 5, 1807. Dec. 21, 1818. 6.622.
Legacy for support and education of Ann Baxter, daughter of my brother, John Baxter. Residue to poor Roman Catholics of Phila., John Walsh, lumber merchant, Northern Liberties, Mary McCarthy, Elizabeth Steinmetz, daughter of Jacob Steinmetz.
Execs: Joseph Bell, Joseph Carson, merchants of this city.
Witnesses: William Nekervis, Samuel Darch, William I. Bell.
Thomas Smith, of Phila., accountant, affirmed.

APPO, JOHN. Phila.
Dec. 3, 1818. Dec. 31, 1818. 6.623.
Estate to my wife, Ann Appo, and my children: Ellen, Joseph, William and Ann Appo. Wife to have rents, etc. of estate until boys are 21 and girls 18 years. Should wife die during minority of children, appoint as guardians, James Forten and Richard Howell.
Execs: Wife, Ann Appo, daughter Ellen Appo, James Forten, Richard Howell.
Witnesses: William I. Duane, Franklin Bache.
Letters to three first-named Executors.

SMITH, GEORGE. Drayman.
Oct. 15, 1818. Jan. 4, 1819. 6.624.

Estate to my wife, Elizabeth Smith, and my daughter, Rosanna Smith (a minor).
Execs: Brother-in-law, John McNamea, my friend, John Maitland, both of Phila.
Witnesses: Stephen McFaden, Bernerd Daily.

ADAMS, PETER. Mariner. Lately belonging to Beunas Ayrean armed Brig., *Constitution*, Appleton Mech, Commander.
Dec. 24, 1818. Jan. 8, 1818. 6.624.
Estate to my friend, James Hughes, of Phila., grocer, whom I appoint Executor.
Witnesses: Ulrick Wale, James Duncan.

NAPIER, ALEXANDER. Phila. Marble Stone Cutter.
Dec. 1, 1818. Jan. 23, 1819. 6.624.
Estate to wife, Ann Napier, brother William Napier, niece Mary Clark, widow of Joseph Clark, William McClean, children of brother, William Napier (Alexander the only one named).
Execs: Wife, Ann Napier, Stephen Kingston.
Witnesses: Acquila A. Browne, John Cochran.
Letters to Ann Napier, Jan. 12, 1819.
Stephen Kingston, the other Executor, sworn June 13, 1822. Said Ann Napier, deceased.

HARE, MARGARET. Phila. Widow.
Feb. 8, 1812. Dec. 22, 1818. 6.625.
To daughter, Martha Hare. To son, Charles W. Hare, and to Mrs. Charles W. Hare. To granddaughter and namesake, Margaretta Hare. To granddaughter, Sarah E. Hare. To grandsons, Robert Hare, William B. Hare, and George E. Hare. To my son, Robert Hare, and to Mrs. Robert Hare. To my son, John Hare Powell. To my sister, Boyed, miniature pictures of sisters, Frances and Abby, and brother, Richard. To sister, Powell, my brother James's pictures, set in gold, also a breast pin inclosing some of sister, Sterling's Hare. To niece, Mrs. Elizabeth P. Fisher. To niece, Mrs. An Morris. To niece, Mrs. L. Page. To my husband's sister, Miss ____ Hare, the picture of my son, John Hare Powell. Picture of James Hare to my said son, Charles. Pictures of Mrs. Hare and of Mr. Powel to said daughter, Martha ____.
Execs: Sons, Charles W. and Robert Hare, John Hare Powell.
Witnesses: Thomas Cadwalader, Charles I. Nicholas.
Robert Hare sworn Jan. 28, 1819.
John Hare Powell sworn March 5, 1819.

GARDNER, VALENTINE. Penn Township. Phila. Co. Skindresser.
Aug. 6, 1818. Jan. 15, 1819. 6.626.

Estate to my wife, Mary Magdalen, and my children.
Execs: Son, Jacob Gardner, friend, John Trout of Northern Liberties, Phila. Co.
Witnesses: John A. Cullman, Jacob Gardner.

BRADY, JOHN. Phila. Teacher.
Jan. 14, 1819. Jan. 18, 1819. 6.626.
To wife, Margaret Brady, to nephew James Sliney.
Exec: Daniel Guirey of Phila. Co., farmer.
Witnesses: John P. Harper, John Hoffecken, Thomas McClean.

READ, COMFORT. Township of Moyamensing. Phila. Co.
Oct. 26, 1818. Jan. 20, 1819. 6.626.
All my real estate to my neighbours, John Jamison and Martha, his wife. Personal estate to my daughters, Elizabeth Gregors and Mary Bivins, and to John Bivins, Jr.
Exec: Said John Jamison.
Witnesses: John Allison, John Diamond.

CARR, ISABELLA. Southwark. Phila. Co. Widow.
July 26, 1805. Jan. 21, 1819. 6.629.
To my six children: John, Henry and William Carr, Ann Orr, Mary McCully and Isabella Carr.
Exec: Son-in-law, Henry McCully.
Witnesses: Gallant Graham, Francis Dayman. Ann Graham, widow of Gallant Graham, affirmed.

WALMSLEY, WILLIAM. Township of Byberry. Phila. Co. Yeoman.
March 3, 1817. Jan. 22, 1819. 6.628.
To wife, Abigail Walmsley. To my sons, Joseph and Israel, all my lands in Byberry Township, also my woodland in Richlew in Bensalem Township, Bucks Co. To daughters, Sarah Phipps and Mary Stackhouse.
Execs: Sons, Joseph and Israel Walmsley.
Witnesses: David Comfort, Amos Hilborne, Ruth Hillborn.

PEACE, ISAAC. Borough of Bristol. Bucks Co. Gentleman.
Aug. 4, 1812. Jan. 23, 1819. 6.628.
To daughter, Mary Hazard, wife of Rowland Hazard. To son, Joseph Peace. To Samuel Emlen and John Coxe, near city of Burlington, New Jersey, for use of said daughter, Mary Hazard, and my daughter Rebecca, wife of Dr. Nathan William Cole. To sister, Johannah Austin.
Execs: My three children: Joseph Peace, Mary Hazard, Rebecca Cole.
Witnesses: Joshua Byron, William Howell, Jacob Shall.

GRIFFITTS, ELIZABETH. Phila. Daughter of Nathaniel, formerly of said city.
Oct. 11, 1804. May 26, 1812.
To cousins, Sarah Powell Montgomery, Hester Montgomery and Abby Eliza Hamilton Montgomery, each to receive their share at 21 years. To cousin, Dr. Samuel Powel Griffitts or his children. To Mary Griffitts, daughter of said Samuel Powel Griffitts. To Elizabeth Ann Lewis, daughter of Joseph S. Lewis, son of said Joseph S. Lewis, the sum of two hundred pounds. To Sidney Hutchinson, widow of Dr. James Hutchinson. To Rebecca Ashbridge, wife of Joseph Ashbridge. To cousins, Mary Lisle, Margaret Lisle and Elizabeth Lisle, daughters of Henry Lisle of Phila., and to Ann Pemberton, daughter of Joseph Pemberton, formerly of said city, deceased. To Henry Lisle of said city, and to Frances Lewis, wife of Joseph S. Lewis.
Execs: Friends, said Samuel Powel Griffitts, of Phila., physician, and said Joseph S. Lewis of said city, merchant.
Witnesses: Thomas Harrison, Samuel Logan, William Master.
Note: For Codicil, see Will Book No. 4, folio 167.

STRATTON, BENJAMIN. Phila. Block and Pump Maker.
Dec. 29, 1818. Jan. 25, 1819. 6.630.
Legacies to my four children: Henry, Jonathan, Benjamin and Elizabeth to be paid them when of age. Elisha Parker, deceased, grandfather of said children. Residue of estate to wife, Grizelda Stratton, she to maintain said Elizabeth and our two children, James and Mary, during their minority.
Exec: Said wife, Grizelda.
Witnesses: Thomas Mitchell, Sophia Cerah.

LAWRENCE, JACOB. District of Southwark. Phila. Co. Gentleman.
The only son of Elizabeth Lawrence, late of same place, widow, deceased.
March 7, 1818. Jan 26, 1819. 6.630.
To Mary McCulloch, wife of Henry McCulloch, John Philpot Carr, Ann Orr, widow, William Carr, Isabella Campbell, wife of James Campbell. To relation, Dr. Hugh Jones of North Co. To relation, Richard Blackledge Jones, brother of said Dr. Hugh Jones. To friend, Peter Thomson, of Phila., conveyancer. Residue to cousin William Blackledge of Newbern, North Carolina.
Execs: Said William Blackledge, William S. Biddle, Esq., of Phila.
Witnesses: Joseph Allen, Charles W. Thomson.
Letters to William S. Biddle.

GILLICHAN, GEORGE. Phila. Brewer.
Sept. 5, 1818. Jan. 27, 1819. 6.630.

To my wife, Mary Gillichan, and after her death, to Executors to be used for education, etc. of Geo. Jenkins (who now lives with me), son of Enoch Jenkins and Eliza, his wife, to Jacob Connelly, Jr., George Connelly, nephews of said wife, to Mary Robinson, niece of said wife, and to her son, George Robinson.
Execs: James Wills, Jr., grocer, William Morrison, brewer, both of said city.
Witnesses: William Andrews, Isaac Elliott.

WILSON, ALEXANDER. Borough of Harrisburg. Dauphin Co.
May 24, 1816. Jan. 28, 1819. 6.631.
Catharine Wilson, my wife, to have use of estate, and after her decease, to poor of city and county of Phila.
Witnesses: Robert McElwce, Daniel J. Heister. James Graham and Matthew Randal affirmed.

ARNOUS, NICHOLAS. Born at Nantzin, France, now in Phila.
Dec. 28, 1818. Jan. 20, 1819. 6.631.
To be interred according to the forms of the Roman Catholic Religion. Brother-in-law, Mr. Merot, residing at Nantz. Legacy to Madame Andigé, residing in Paris, or to her children, to exclusion of Mr. De Dauzy, her son-in-law, also to wife, Athenais Bellerocke, her niece. To my sister, Justine Arnous, residing in France. To eldest son of my niece, Augustine Michell, now Madame de Colville, of which child I must have been the Godfather. Brother Timothy Arnous.
Exec: James Mathwin Benoit, residing at Burlington, New Jersey. Should any misfortune befall Mr. Benoit, desire John Keating, Sr. to take his place.
Witnesses: F"cis. Da Costa, Gabriel Gareschi.

BRADY, MARGARET. Phila. Widow.
Jan. 23, 1819. Feb. 1, 1819. 6.632.
Legacies to Anne Meade and Mary Elizabeth Meade, daughters of my present nurse, Elizabeth Meade. Property in Queen Ann's Co., State of Maryland, and all my other real estate in trust. Said Executors to sell property and proceeds to the following: John Fitzgibbons, Elizabeth Meade, my present nurse, Mary Thornton, who lately nurse[d] me, and to my friends, Hannah Wigmore, Mary Nolan and Margaret Shannon, sister of said Mary. To Orphan Asylum of Phila.
Execs: Benj'n. Tilghman, Esq., William Rawle, Jr., Esq.
Witnesses: Thomas I. Wharton, John Carter, Joseph Azau.

GARRETSON, LYDIA. Phila.
Sept. 23, 1818. Feb. 2, 1819. 6.633.

Legacies to niece, Lydia Ann Garretson, late of the state of North Carolina. To Thomas Garretson, Hannah Garretson and Adelade Garretson, other children of brother, John Garretson, deceased. Residuary estate to sister, Anne Garretson, whom I appoint trustee of said legacies.
Exec: Said sister, Anne.
Witnesses: John Hart, Townsend Sharpless.

HONEY, GEORGE. Phila. Gentleman.
Oct. 25, 1817. Feb. 3, 1819. 6.633.
Execs: Nephews, George Honey, Jr., and John Wallington. Legacies to said nephew, Geo. Honey, Jr., his wife, Margaret and his daughter, Juliana Honey. To other children of Geo. Honey, Jr.: George C., Louisa Ann, Caroline, Harriet and Marg't. Augusta. To said nephew, John Wallington, and to his two children, Sarah and Geo. Edward Wallington. To niece, Mary Wert.
Witnesses: Abraham Stein, Fred'k. Beates.

ROBARTS, JAMES. District of Southwark. Ship Joiner.
Jan. 22, 1819. Feb. 11, 1819. 6.634.
Estate to wife, Migal Robarts, whom I appoint sole Executrix.
Witnesses: Christopher O'Conner, I. Peace, Seth Roberts, James Robb.

JAMES, MARTHA. Phila.
Sept. 1, 1818. Feb. 15, 1819. 6.634.
To sister, Jane. To John Mortimer Kitchen and to Sandford Hamilton Kitchen, sons of Joseph and Ann Kitchen. To Martha Ann Hall. To friend, John Greiner of Phila., merchant, on condition that he give legacies to my niece, Eliza Welch, Isabella Rowan, Nancy Weed, widow of George Weed, nephew, John Andrews, and to my grandniece, Isabella Bliss.
Execs: Said Joseph Kitchen, John Greiner.
Witnesses: James Lamon, Fred'k. Beates.
Feb. 3, 1819: Revokes appointment of Joseph Kitchen as Executor.

ALMENDINGER, JACOB. Phila. Baker.
Jan. 30, 1819. Feb. 20, 1819. 6.635.
All estate to wife, during life, she to educate and maintain my minor children, William, Charles and Ann, and after her decease, estate to all my children: Jacob, George, William, Charles and Anne.
Exec: Wife, Catharine.
Witnesses: Th. Waterman, Jonathan Pounder, Alexander Cook.

NOBLE, REBECCA. Township of Passyunk. Phila. Co. Now of District of Southwark Co. Widow of Joseph Noble of Passyunk, Innkeeper.

Feb. 16, 1819. Feb. 22, 1819. 6.635.
To John Johnson of said district, gentleman, in trust for use of friend, Sarah Porterfield, widow of Moses Porterfield, of same district, painter.
Exec: Said John Johnson.
Witnesses: Mich'l. Hennesey, Mich'l. Queen, John Johnson.

BUTCHER, JOB. Phila. Grocer.
June 3, 1814. Feb. 22, 1819. G.635.
To daughter, Rebecca Pattan, property in Phila. To daughter, Mary Story, property in Salem, New Jersey. To daughter, Ann Pryor. Joseph Pryor to pay debt owing by him to firm of Job and Amos W. Butcher. Residue to son, Amos W. Butcher, whom I appoint sole Executor.
Witnesses: Robert Whitehead, Henry Schell, Lydia W. Eyre.

MORRISON, MORDECAI. District of Southwark. Phila. Co.
July 4, 1816. Feb. 19, 1819. 6.636.
Estate to my wife, Catharine Morrison, daughter, Christiana Robbarts, the heirs of my daughter, Ann Doughty, deceased, daughter Mary Lawrence, heirs to daughter, Margaret Dewitt, deceased.
Execs: Son-in-law, John Robbarts, mariner, Patrick Galbreath, clock and watch maker, both of District of Southwark.
Witnesses: John Grant, Robert Adams, Duncan McFadyen.

SHARP, JOSEPH. District of Southwark. Cordwainer.
Jan. 12, 1818. Feb. 25, 1819. 6.636.
Estate to my wife, Catharine Sharp, and to my children: Francis, Rosanna, Richard, Charles and Lazarus. Wife to be Guardian of said children. Friend, James Lip, of Phila., schoolmaster, to be Guardian of my sons, Joseph Sharp and William Sharp.
Exec: Said wife, Catharine Sharp.
Witnesses: Richard Renshaw, A. McCalla.

HEWITT, SHAMGAR. Northern Liberties. Phila. Mariner.
Feb. 6, 1819. March 2, 1819. 6.637.
Estate to wife, Elizabeth, during life, she to educate and support daughter, Emaline, during minority. After wife's death, estate to said daughter, Emaline.
Execs: Wife, Elizabeth, father, Shamgar Hewit, my brother, Abijah Hewitt.
Witnesses: Robert Whitehead, Jesse Davis.

BLACK, WILLIAM. District of Southwark. Phila. Co. Yeoman.
Sept. 18, 1818. March 4, 1819. 6.637.
Estate to daughter, Mary Black, and to sons, William and John Black.

Execs: James Graham, Alexander Black, both of Township of Moyamensing.
Witnesses: William Allen, John McFarland.

MILLER, MARY. Spruce St. Phila. Widow.
Feb. 27, 1819. March 9, 1819. 6.638.
Estate to my four children: William Alexander Miller, Susanna Hamilton, Elizabeth Dalgell, Margaret Miller.
Exec: Son, William Alexander Miller.
Witnesses: Ebenezer Osbourn, Joseph Watson.

CROW, GEORGE. Borough of Wilmington, New Castle Co., Delaware. Clock Maker.
April 22, 1780. Feb. 18, 1819. 6.638.
Mother, Mary Crow, to have use of my lot on Walnut St. in said Borough during life. To sisters, Sarah Nash and Mary Crow, all estate, subject to Mother's interest in above-mentioned lot. Trustees to settle with my brother, Thomas Crow.
Exec: Sister, Mary Crow.
Trustees: John McKinley, Esq., Bancroft Woodcock, Jacob Broom.
Witnesses: Richard Denny, Benj'n. Laforge, Jaco. Broom.
William Young, of Phila., paper and woolen manufacturer, Isaac Hendrickson of Borough of Wilmington, affirmed.

SCHAEFFER, GEORGE. Phila. Baker.
Sept. 2, 1794. March 15, 1819. 6.639.
Daughter, Catharine Hagner, to have use of estate, and at her death if she leaves any children, they to have use of said estate. If not, then to the ministers, vestrymen and church wardens of the German Lutheran Congregation in and near Phila., for education of poor of said congregation.
Execs: Said daughter, Catharine, nephew, William Rihle, my brother-in-law, John Ecky.
Witnesses: Jesse Williams, Nicholas Weaver, Richard Whitehead.
Jacob Christler of Phila., merchant, affirmed.

PASCHALL, THOMAS J. Township of Kingsessing. Phila. Co.
Jan. 2, 1819. March 16, 1819. 6.639.
Wife, Ann, to have 1/3 of income of estate, the other 2/3 to be used for education and support of my children during minority. To son, Stephen Paschall, tract of land whereon I now dwell, also my marsh meadows and other lands in township aforesaid, subject to bequest in favour of his mother. To daughter, Mary Paschall, when of age, property in Phila, etc., subject to bequest to her mother. Executors to sell my land

in Township of Treydiffren, in Chester Co. Grandfather, Stephen Paschall, dec'd.
Execs: Father-in-law, Samuel Gibson, my friend, Nathan Sellers. Said Samuel Gibson to be Guardian of children.
Witnesses: John Gibson, Thomas Justis.
Letters to Samuel Gibson.

FISHER, MIERS. Ury. Phila. Co. Counsellor-at-Law.
Aug. 2, 1814. March 19, 1819. 6.640.
Estate to my wife, Sarah Redwood Fisher, and my children: Redwood Fisher, Lydia Fisher, Sarah Redwood Longstreth, Hannah Fisher, Jabez Maud Fisher, deceased. Sons, Samuel R. Fisher, Jr. and Miers Fisher, share in Brandywine Mills Estate sold to nephew, Joshua and Thomas Gilpin.
Execs: Son, Redwood Fisher, son-in-law, Samuel Longstreth, friend, Benjamin Warner, my son, Jabez Maud Fisher, when of lawful age.
Wife to consult with my brother, Samuel R. Fisher, and friends, Samuel W. Fisher and John Hallowell.
William Rawle, Sr., John Hallowell, Esq., of Phila., Attorneys at Law, affirmed.

GUENAT, JOHN B. Phila. Merchant.
April 17, 1817. March 23, 1819. 6.642.
Estate to my wife, Margaret Guenat, whom I appoint sole Executrix.
Witnesses: Peter Lohra, Joseph K. Hillegas, Garrett R. Barry.

DE VIAR, DON JOSE IGNACIO. Native of Bilbas, legitimate son of Don Ignacio Francisco de viar y Elexpuri and Dona Josefa Mendiguren, deceased.
Dec. 14, 1818. Jan. 19, 1819. 6.642.
To be interred in Parish Church of St. Mary's. Natural daughter, called Jane Viar, whom I had baptized in St. Mary's Church of this city. Property in Biscay, which I inherited from my father, also in Lima and in the United States, I bequeath to said daughter.
Execs: Don Luis de mis, His Catholic Magesty's Minister Plenopotentiary in United States and Don Juan Leamy, resident in this city.
Witnesses: Carlos Mulvey, Joaquin Tamorana.
Letters to John Leamy.
Signed: Ignacio de Viar.

RIGWAY, ASA. Phila. Bricklayer.
March, 1815. March 27, 1819. 6.643.

To brother, Isaac Rigway. To nephew, Asa Rigway, son of Jeremiah
Rigway. To niece, Charlot Rigway, daughter of Jeremiah Rigway. To
sister Pheby's two daughters. To brother, Jeremiah Rigway.
Execs: Said brother, Jeremiah Rigway, my friend George Peterman,
flour merchant of Phila.
Witnesses: William Griffith, John Evil, Jacob Peterman.
Letters to Jeremiah Ridgway, George Peterman.

ASHBRIDGE, ELIZABETH. Northern Liberties. Phila. Co.
Nov. 11, 1817. March 30, 1819. 6.644.
To daughter, Tacy Ashbridge. To granddaughter, Mary Ashbridge
Roberts. To son-in-law, James Vener. Residue of estate to said
daughter and granddaughters, Mary Ashbridge Roberts and Mary
Ashbridge.
Execs: Daughter, Tacy Ashbridge, son-in-law, James Vence, he to have
charge of estate of Mary Ashbridge until of age.
Witnesses: Edmund I. Hollingshead, Hannah Fletcher.
Letters to Tacy Ashbridge and James Verree.

DUNLAP, JAMES. Phila. Doctor of Physick.
Nov. 3, 1818. April 7, 1819. 6.644.
Estate to wife, Juliana Dunlap, son Thomas Dunlap, daughters, Anna
Dunlap, Mary Dunlap and Margaretta Perit, wife of John W. Perit of
Phila., merchant. To grandchildren, James D. Taylor, Juliana D. Taylor
and Ellen Taylor, as they become of age. James N. Taylor, now of
Phila., late of Washington City, to be released from debts due me.
Execs: Said wife, son, Thomas Dunlap.
Witnesses: Joseph Parrish, Samuel Keemle.
Letters to Thomas Dunlap.

STINE, PETER. Phila. Malster.
Dec. 25, 1817. April 10, 1819. 6.645.
Estate to wife, Mary Stine, until youngest child is 21 years of age.
Witnesses: Robert Aitkens, Henry Volkmar.

DE LA ROCHE, MARY G.
Jan. 21, 1819. April 7, 1819. 6.645.
Legacies to my daughter, Harriet Browne, wife of Peter A. Browne, to
my son, William Harper and to grandson, George Blight Browne, son of
said Peter and Harriet Browne. Negress, Celia, to be set at liberty.
Residue of estate to my son, David Harper.
Execs: Son, David Harper, Peter A. Browne, Esq.
Witnesses: Jacob Rigler, Enoch Arthur.

153

JOHNSTON, JACOB. Blockley. Phila. Co.
Sept. 29, 1814. April 10, 1819. 6.646.
Wife, ___, to be provided for by my children. Property in Blockley and Haverford to my children: Jonathan, Joseph, Jacob, Closs and Aaron Johnston. Legacies to my daughters, Hannah, Elizabeth, Rebecca Ott, and Ann Johnston.
Execs: Sons, Closs and Aaron Johnston, my friend, Isaac Warner Roberts.
Witnesses: Algernon Roberts, John Thomas, Joseph Garrett.
Letters to Aaron Johnston and Isaac Warner Roberts.

BRITTON, EDWARD. Phila. Now on a tour of military duty.
Oct. 13, 1814. April 13, 1819. 6.646.
Estate to sister, Rebecca Hellings, whom I appoint sole Executrix.
Witnesses: John Thompson, Geo. Nagle, Hugh Maxwell.

BLACKISTON OR BLAKISTON, PRESLEY. Phila.
Feb. 19, 1814. April 13, 1819. 6.647.
Estate to my eight children: Ann, Martha, Elizabeth, Sarah, John, Mary, Rebecca and Rachel.
Execs: Daughter, Ann Wetherill, my son, John Blakiston, my son-in-law, Kenneth Jewell. My friends, Thomas P. Cope, Owen Jones and Timothy Paxson to aid my Executors. Sons-in-law, Isaac Forsyth and John O'Neal.
Witnesses: Isaac Wampole, Jr., Isaac Wampole.
Codicils: May 4, 1818, Feb. 25, 1819. Son John's share to be kept in trust by my daughter, Ann Wetherill, and my son-in-law, Kenneth Jewell, and after his death, to all his children. Revoke appointment of son, John, as Executor. Said Trustees to advise with my sons-in-law, Isaac Forsyth and John O'Neill.
Witnesses: Daniel Smith, James S. Smith.

LAMBETH, CATHARINE. Northern Liberties. Phila. School Mistress.
March 26, 1819. April 19, 1819. 6.648.
To Christina Crawford, wife of Alexander Crawford of said Liberties, taylor, all my wearing apparel. To friend, Susanna Endress, whom I appoint sole Executrix.
Witnesses: Thomas Hoskin, Samuel Lehman.

BAUMAN, JOHN. District of Southwark. Phila. Co. Carpenter.
May 18, 1810, April 20, 1819. 6.648.
Estate to wife, Ann, and after her decease, to my eight children: Jacob, Caspar, John, Isaac, Margaret, Daniel, Nancy and Catharine Bauman.
Execs: Wife, Ann, son Caspar Bauman.
Witnesses: William McCall, William Napier, Charles Erdmann.

SONNTAG, WILLIAM L. Phila. Merchant.
Dec. 29, 1817. Sept. 22, 1818. 6.649.
Wife or next survivor to enquire of Dr. Schaeffer or Mr. Frederic
Dreer, what relates to funeral of a Lutheran Christian. My creditors to
be treated in proportion to recovery of my claim upon the French
Government, etc.
Executrix and heir, my wife, Hannah Wright Sonntag.
Witnesses: J. James, Joel Cooke.

BYRON, JOSHUA. Phila. Co.
March 2, 1819. April 22, 1819. 7.4.
Legacies to brother, George Byron, his wife and his children. To Joshua
Byron, son of my brother, Dr. Benjamin Byron, deceased. To Charlotte
Byron, sister to Joshua aforementioned. To my brother, Christopher
Byron, in trust for the children of brother, Charles Byron, deceased. To
my sister, Elizabeth Ash. To said brother, Christopher. To brother,
Rev. Samuel Byron. To John Byron and Elizabeth Byron, son and
daughter of brother, William, deceased. Said Elizabeth is married, and
her name, I believe is Elizabeth Dickinson. To my present
housekeeper, Elizabeth Meredith. To my former housekeeper,
Catharine Barkenbile. To Joseph Meredith, son to said housekeeper.
To Benjamin Parker and to Joshua Byron Parker, his son. To Orphan
Society of Phila. To The Indigent Widow and Single Women's Society
of Phila. To Vestrymen and Church Wardens of Episcopal Church,
called Saint John's in Northern Liberties, of Phila. Co. To the Female
Hospitable Society in Phila. To the Northern Dispensary. To the
Southern Dispensary.
Execs: Friends, John Harland, Alexander Purves, Richard Milne, all of
Phila.
Witnesses: Joseph Jackson, Peter Smith.
Letters to Alexander Purves and Richard Milne.

JOAD, JOHN. Phila.
April 30, 1818. July 7, 1818. 7.5.
Legacy to my housekeeper, Elizabeth Moore, if she continues to live
with me. All residue to my stepdaughter, Margaret Pease, of
Phila., widow. To Breidenhart Evers and Amelia Evers, when of age,
children of Maria Evers. To Charles Allen of Phila., druggist, in trust
for his children. To friend, Thomas Mitchell, of Phila., conveyancer.
Execs: Said Charles Allen, Thomas Mitchell.
Witnesses: Philip Mason, Henry M. Zollickoffer.
Letters to Thomas Mitchell.

ERVINE, JAMES. Phila. Gentleman.
Nov. 11, 1816. May 1, 1819. 7.6.

To cousins, Robert Bethell, William Bethell and William Ker, in trust for cousin, Frances Irvine Browne, daughter of said Robert Bethel and wife of William I. Browne, and her children. To James Irvine Browne and his brother, Peter Browne, sons of said William I. Browne and Frances, his wife. To said William I. Browne and Frances Irvine, his wife, in trust for their daughter, Sarah Dutton Brown, she to receive principal at 19 years. To Robert Bethell, son of William Bethell and Mary, his wife, a bond from his grandfather, Robert Bethell. Late uncle, William Roush, of Phila., Esq., bequeathed to his son-in-law, Joseph Ker, and his daughter, Sarah, wife of said Joseph Ker, and their children, a lot of ground in Phila, etc. Said Joseph Ker, since deceased. To my cousins, William Ker and Frances Ker. To said Sarah Ker, in trust for her son, Irvine Ker. At his death, to his surviving brothers and sisters. To my cousins, James Irvine Rush, Susannah Rush and her sister, Sarah Rush, children of late Joseph Rush, deceased. Residue to Elizabeth Bethell, wife of said Robert Bethell, and said Frances Irvine Browne.
Execs: Robert Bethell, said Frances Irvine Browne.
Witnesses: Susannah Louisa Baker, George A. Baker, Jr., George A. Baker.
Codicil: Nov. 17, 1818. Adds John Claxton to Trustees, also to be Executor in place of William I. Browne. Revokes legacy to James Ivine Browne and Peter Browne, sons of William I. Browne.
Witnesses: Jacob Wayne, Jacob Trexler, Geo. A. Baker.

DAWSON, ROBERT. Phila. Merchant.
May 7, 1818. May 6, 1819. 7.10.
Execs: Wife, Esther, son, Josiah Dawson.
Estate to said wife, and to my children, Rebecca and Josiah Dawson.
Witnesses: Martin Fisher, Fred'k. Beates.
Letters to Josiah Dawson.

DEAL, DANIEL. Kensington. Phila. Co. Blacksmith.
April 9, 1814. April 13, 1819. 7.11.
Income of estate to wife, Mary, she to educate son, William. After decease of said wife, estate to my children: Anne, Sarah, Mary, Jacob, Daniel, Peter, John and William.
Execs: Said wife, my sons-in-law, Andrew Zeiss and William Sutton.
Witnesses: Robt. Whitehead, Anthony McCoy, Anth'y. Kennedy.
Codicil: March 26, 1819. Received from mother-in-law, Barbara Coe, for son, Jacob, to be kept at interest until of age.
Witnesses: Robert Whitehead, Jacob Pister.

GILLICHAN, MARY. Phila. Widow of George Gillichan, late of same place.

Jan. 26, 1819. May 10, 1819. 7.12.
Estate to my nieces, Anna Maria Connelly, Eliza Connelly and Margaret Connelly, children of my brother, Jacob Connelly.
Execs: Friend, William Morrison, said Jacob Connelly.
Witnesses: William T. Palmer, Mordecai L. Dawson.

FISHER, MARY. Bristol Township. Phila. Co. Single Woman.
Nov. 17, 1818. May 15, 1819. 7.12.
Estate to my mother, Elizabeth Fisher, whom I appoint sole Executrix.
Witnesses: John Deprefontaine, Isaac M. Kulp.

LENNOX, SARAH. Phila. Widow.
Oct. 29, 1816. Nov. 24, 1818. 7.13.
Legacy to my brother, James H. McCulloch, residing in Baltimore, and to his son, my nephew, James McCulloch, Jr., and to my two other nephews, Hugh Birckhead and James Birckhead. To my sister, Jane Birkhead. To Trustees of 2nd Presbyterian Church of Phila. To Mary Lawrence of Phila., widow of Benjamin Lawrence. Legacy to Jane Hutchinson, now or lately residing either in Washington City or Georgetown. To my nephews, Lennox Anderson, Alexander Anderson, Lennox Birckhead, and to my niece, Eveline Anderson. To Ashbel Green, Jr., son of Dr. Ashbel Green, and my late niece Christiana, his wife, when of age. To nieces, Augusta Anderson, Christiana Bond and Sarah Birckhead. To my relation, Ann Holland, wife of Charles Holland. To my friends, George Taylor, Samuel Hodgdon and his wife, Mary Hodgdon, Elizabeth Hodgdon, widow of Capt. Benjamin Hodgdon, Mary Lawrence, and to wife of Mr. Pollard Birckhead.
Execs: Friends, Andrew Bayard, Esq., George Taylor, both of Phila., my niece, Augusta Anderson.
Witnesses: Elizabeth Smith, Mary H. Odden, Peter Thomson.
Codicil: Nov., 1818. To Ashbel Green, Jr. of Princeton, New Jersey, to be under direction of his aunt, Augusta Anderson, of Phila. To Samuel Hodgdon, Sr., and Jane, his wife, both of Phila. To Jane Hutchinson of George Town, District of Columbia. To James H. McCulloch, Sr., his son, James H. McCulloch, Jr., Lennox Birckhead, Alexander M. Anderson, Theodore Anderson, all of Baltimore, Maryland, also to Edward Anderson and Lennox Anderson, both of Phila.
Witnesses: Theo'e. Anderson. Letters to Augusta Anderson.

BRADLEY, JAMES. Phila. Grocer.
Nov. 10, 1813. May 22, 1819. 7.15.
Estate to wife, Mary Bradley, whom I appoint sole Executrix.
Witnesses: Thomas Hoskins, Charles McHarahen.

WAY, GEORGE. Washington City, District of Columbia. At present, in Phila., late Printer. At present, Manufacturer of Glass.
May 17, 1819. June 5, 1819. 7.16.
Legacies to my father, Andrew Way, sisters, Elizabeth, Rachel and Mary Way. To my sister, Margaret Hewitt, father, Andrew Way, and my brother, Andrew Way, Jr., in trust for nieces: Juliana, Margaretta, Louisa, Caroline, Ann and Catharine Hewitt. To brother, Andrew Way, and my nephew, George Way.
Execs: Father, Andrew Way, brother Andrew Way, Jr., friend, James McClery of Washington City.
Witnesses: Isaac Wampole, Jr., Jacob F. Hoeckley, Isaac Wampole.
Letters to Andrew Way and Andrew Way, Jr.

LAWS, CLEMENT. Phila. Merchant.
Feb. 9, 1819. May 26, 1819. 7.17.
Real estate in Kent Co. near Smyrna, and in Sussex Co., in Concord, both in State of Delaware, and in Phila. Co., to be sold. Proceeds to my wife, Mary, and my children, William, John, Melson, Elizabeth, Mary and Lydia Laws.
Execs: Ludowick Laws, Elijah Laws, George Laws, all of Phila.
Witnesses: Israel Maule, Joseph Gibbons.
Codicil: March 3, 1819. Witnesses: Othniel Alsop, Joseph Gibbons.
Letters to Elijah Laws and George Laws.

GORDON, THOMAS.
Dec. 20, 1817. June 4, 1819. 7.19.
I leave my trunk of clothes with Rachall Nordike, with power if I die to receive everything that belongeth to me.
Philip Vores, of Phila., oysterman, Rachel Fleming, wife of Alexander Fleming, of Southwark., mariner, affirmed.

EDENBORN, JACOB. Phila. Currier.
Jan. 29, 1819. June 10, 1819. 7.19.
To my wife, Mary Edenborn, she to educate my younger children. To my children: Catharine, Philip, Mary, Harriett, Peter, Jacob, Samuel, Louisa, Joseph, Margaret, Elizabeth and Benjamin.
Execs: Wife, Mary, my son-in-law, Charles Erdman.
Witnesses: Jacob F. Hoeckley, Isaac Wampole.

CATHRALL, ISAAC. Phila. Practitioner of Physick.
Nov. 26, 1816. March 18, 1819. 7.20.
To my wife, Ann, and to my son, Chas. Edward, and my daughter, Mary Cathrall.
Executors, Guardians and Trustees: Nephews, John Elfreth, Isaac C. Elfreth, cousin, Robt. Waln.

Witnesses: Andrew Underhill, Peter Thomson.

STEINMETZ, ANDREW B. Phila. Mariner.
May 9, 1818. June 3, 1819. 7.22.
Estate to son, Henry Stinemetz, and to my stepson, Ellwood Cline.
Exec: Thomas Taylor, of Phila., taylor.
Witnesses: Sarah Fritez, Edw'd. Corfield.
Thomas Watson, of Phila., teacher, affirmed.

WILLIAMS, OLIVER. Phila.
July 27, 1815. June 4, 1819. 7.22
Estate to my wife, Judith Williams, and after her decease, to my children.
Exec: Wife, Judith.
Witnesses: Richard Howell, Jonathan Trusty.

LYCAN, GEORGE. Northern Liberties. Phila.
March 16, 1819. June 7, 1819. 7.22.
Legacy to Rebecca Young, daughter of Marks Young. To my uncle, John Arrison, his daughter, Sarah Arrison, and to William Oram. Residue to my kinsmen, John Arrison and Shipford Arrison.
Exec: My friend, Simon Shugart, the elder.
Witnesses: Robert Whitehead, Ann Petit.

HAMEL, ROSANNA. Phila. Widow of James Hamel, late of same city.
Feb. 25, 1819. June 9, 1819. 7.23.
Legacies to daughter, Polly, granddaughters, Rosanna Rodderfield and Elizabeth Rodderfield. To son, Littleton W. Hamel, land in Pongoteague, in Accomac Co., Virginia, to which I became entitled by decease of my brother, Henry Trader, and by a deed from my brother, Samuel. To my son, Samuel, land in Phila.
Exec: Said son, Samuel Hamel.
Witnesses: James Castles, John Askin, Thomas Mitchell.

BAILEY, HUGH. District of Southwark. Phila.
May 19, 1819. June 12, 1819. 7.24.
Estate to my wife, Catharine, and to my son, John, after her decease.
Execs: Alexander Black, Samuel Glass.
Witnesses: Jeremiah Osbourn, John Allison.

LOPEZ, ANN. Phila. Widow.
Dec. 31, 1816. May 29, 1819. 7.24.
Estate to my granddaughter, Ann Furze, daughter of James Furze.
Exec: Friend, Joseph Simons of said city, merchant. My gold watch to my son, named Joseph Daymon.

Witnesses: William D. Kennedy. Caleb Carmalt, Jr.

GRAMBO, CHRISTIAN. Phila. Merchant.
Oct. 3, 1818. June 18, 1819. 7.25.
Estate to my wife, Elizabeth, and to my two sons, Henry and Edmond. Executors and Guardians: My wife, Elizabeth, my friend, Jacob Bretz.
Witnesses: John J. Mahany, Henry Weaver, James A. Mahany.

WARE, DAVID. District of Southwark. Phila. Co. Merchant.
Dec. 14, 1818. June 19, 1819. 7.25.
Annuity to my mother, Ann Ware. Residue to my wife, Henrietta Ware, whom I appoint sole Executrix.
Witnesses: James Sawer, Caleb Carmalt, Jr.
Resealed Dec. 14, 1818.
Witnesses: Thomas Mitchell, Andrew D. Cash.

REDMAN, REBECCA. Phila.
May 28, 1819. June 21, 1819. 7.26.
To daughter, Juliana Miller, a legacy in satisfaction of a bond given by Joseph Redman and myself for part of her father's estate, which descended to the said Juliana. To daughter, Maria Nicholas, the house where I now dwell, in Phila. Executors to buy house for daughter, Eliza Ewing, in Phila. To my nephew, Bird Wilson. Executors to purchase house, in Phila., for daughter, Juliana Miller. To my niece, Catherine Bird. To Female Association of Phila. To Orphan Asylum, in Phila. To son-in-law, Sam'l. Nicholas. Residue to said three daughters.
Execs: Nephew, Bird Wilson, my sons-in-law, Samuel Ewing and Samuel Nicholas.
Witnesses: Charles Evans, Thomas H. White.
Codicil: Legacies to granddaughter, Rebecca Nicholas, and to Ellen Ewing. Letters to Samuel Ewing.

LLOYD, SUSANNA. Phila.
May 31, 1814. June 22, 1819.
My estate to my sisters, Mary and Hannah Lloyd, and to my brothers, Thomas and Jonathan, and their children. Legacy to Sarah Crosky.
Execs: Thos., Jonathan and Hannah Lloyd.
Witnesses: Thos. Williams, Thos. R. Williams.
Letters to Thos. Lloyd.

MUNSEES, HENRY. Phila. Plaisterer.
Dec. 7, 1818. June 22, 1819. 7.29.
To my sister, Susannah Murray, wife of James Murray, of Phila., storekeeper, my property in Phila., devised to me by my late father, Dieterick Munses.

Exec: Said sister, Susannah Murray.
Witnesses: Henry Long, Thomas Hoskin.

MALONY, BERRY. Northern Liberties. Phila. Co.
Feb. 5, 1818. June 23, 1819. 7.30.
Estate to my wife, Elizabeth Malony, and at her death, to my son, Joseph Malony, and my two daughters, Hannah Malony and Rebecca Malony.
Execs: Said wife, Elizabeth, son, Joseph.
Witnesses: Ralf Briggs, Charles Webster, Jonathan Conard.

RIGHTER, PETER. Roxborough Township. Phila. Co. Yeoman.
Oct. 2, 1817. June 26, 1819. 7.30.
To my wife, Elizabeth Righter, and after her decease, estate to be sold and proceeds to my nine grandchildren, the children of my son, John Righter, deceased, son, Joseph Righter, granddaughter, Hannah Jones, daughter of my daughter, Mary Jones, deceased, granddaughter, Elizabeth Righter, daughter of son, Anthony Righter, deceased, daughter-in-law, Rebecca Righter, widow of son, Anthony, daughter-in-law, ____, widow of son John Righter.
Exec: Friend, John Livezey of Roxborough Township, Phila. Co., miller.
Witnesses: Joseph Livezey, Thomas Livezey.

CHEW, ELIZABETH.
Feb. 22, 1816. June 28, 1819. 7.32.
3,000 pounds to each of my three unmarried daughters, Henrietta, Maria and Catharine Chew. To son, Benjamin Chew, my estate called, Whitehall, in Moyamensing and Passyunk Townships, Phila. Co.
Married daughters: Margaret Howard, Juliana Nicklin, Sophia Philips and Harriet Carroll.
Execs: Son, Benjamin Chew, son-in-law, John E. Howard, Esq., my friend, William Tilghman, Esq.
Witnesses: William Rawle, Thomas M. Willing.
Letters to Benjamin Chew and Wm. Tilghman.

FLOWERS, GEORGE. Phila. Yeoman.
April 19, 1819. June 29, 1819. 7.33.
Estate to my wife, Hannah, and to my five children: James, John, Elizabeth, Sarah and Emeline. Release son, Geo., from payment of rent due to me.
Execs: Daniel Knight, Abraham Woglom.
Witnesses: John Mingle, Jacob F. Hoeckley.

GEDDEN, HENRY. Penn Township. Phila. Co. Victualler.
Jan. 19, 1819. July 6, 1819. 7.33.

My estate to be for use of my wife, Mary, and children, under age.
Execs: Friend, Robert Chapman, my wife, Mary Gedden.
Witnesses: Charles F. Hansel, Abraham Forst.

MC VEA, HENRY. April 2, 1819. July 6, 1819. 7.34.
Legacies to Bernard McGall, near Arnagh, and to Capt. Pole. Residue to my two sisters, Mary and Margaret.
Exec: Hugh McAnulty.
Witnesses: Patrick McCoy, Hugh McAnulty, Jane McAnulty, affirmed.

PREVOST, HENRY M. Phila.
June 15, 1819. July 6, 1819. 7.35.
Estate to Executors in trust for my wife, Emma, and my children.
Execs: Wife, my brothers, Andrew M. Prevost, Lewis M. Prevost.
Guardians of children: Said wife, brother, Andrew.
Witnesses: John Cliffton, Culpeper Bridges, William P. Mort.
Letters to Andrew M. Prevost and Emma Prevost.

GREEVES, THOMAS. Phila. Stock and Exchange Broker.
May 10, 1819. July 10, 1819. 7.35.
Estate to my wife, Mary Emlen Greeves.
Execs: Friends, John Hallowell, Jeremiah Emlen.
Witnesses: John McAllister, Jr., Charles Bruster.

EYRE, NATHAN. Phila. Merchant, Tailor.
Nov. 7, 1818. July 12, 1819. 7.36.
Estate in Phila. and Camden, New Jersey to be sold, proceeds to wife, Elizabeth, and my children: Ann K. Thompson, Maria, Sarah K., Elizabeth K., Joseph K. and Emma K. Eyre. Legacies bequeathed to daughters, Ann K. Thompson, Maria and Sarah K. Eyre, by their grandfather, Joseph Kay. Wife to be Guardian of minor children and Procurator or Guardian of said daughter, Ann K. Thompson.
Execs: Said wife, brother-in-law, Joseph L. Kay and Thomas Redman, Jr., County of Gloucester, New Jersey.
Witnesses: Hugh Christy, Jacob Clement, John Stroup, Jr.
Codicil: July 3, 1819. John Ashburner, Jr., of Phila., Executor, in addition to those in Will.
Witnesses: Hugh Christy, Thomas H. Roberts, Robert Imlay.

YEAGER, JOHN. Phila. Shoemaker.
March 21, 1819. July 14, 1819. 7.37.
Income of estate to my wife, Kitty, for herself and young children, until 21 years, then to be divided between said wife and my ten children by her, and my grandchild, by my late son, George Yeager. To son,

Micheal Yeager, suit of mourning valued at $40, and $25 in cash, etc.,
hoping that he will be more prudent with this last bequeath. Wife to be
Guardian of minor children.
Exec: Son, Joseph Yeager.
Witnesses: Christopher Wetherill, William Laird.

BURN, CATHARINE. Phila. Single Woman.
March 26, 1819. July 14, 1819. 7.38.
To my Executors, John S. Smith and James Sawer, for erecting a
marble tomb over the grave of my parents in the burial ground of the
First Presbyterian Church in Pine St., Phila, the names of my parents,
my brothers and sisters who are buried near, also my own name to be
engraved thereon. Legacy to said Executors for my nephew, John Burn
Wainwright, when of age. To my mother's sister, Jane Galloway, and
her children. Wearing apparel to Elizabeth Dick. Residue to my
brothers, William Burn and Robert Burn.
Witnesses: James S. Smith, Joseph Allen.
Codicil: June 28, 1819. Legacies to Arminilla Groves, Mrs. Margaret
Watson, cousin, Ellen ---, said cousin's legacy to be sent to my aunt,
Catharine Burns. To Miss Jane Snyder, to be delivered to her father,
Geo. C. Snyder. To Mrs. Phoebe Dickinson. Deceased sister, Ellen
Thomas. To Mrs. McDougal.
Witnesses: Joseph Allen, Charles Allen.

SUMMERL, WILLIAM. Phila. Son of Joseph Summerl, late of said
city, merchant, deceased. Now going on a tour of military duty.
Sept. 6, 1814. July 29, 1819. 7.40.
Estate to my wife, Sarah Summerl, and after her death, to my child or
children. If no issue, then to my wife, forever.
Execs: Said wife, Sarah, my friend, Samuel Richards, of Phila.,
silversmith.
Witnesses: Robert Whitehead, Nathan W. Eyre.

STALL, FREDERICK. Phila. Co. Rope Maker.
May 13, 1819. Aug. 3, 1819. 7.40.
Wife, Catharine Stall, to have use of estate. After her decease, to my
daughter, Eliza Reese, son, George Stall, and my daughter, Catharine
Stall.
Exec: Said wife.
Witnesses: John Adam Bernard, Hannah Pinkees, James Butler.

NEVIES, JOHN. Phila. Merchant.
Dec. 12, 1815. Aug. 4, 1819. 7.41.
Estate to my wife, Maria Teresa Johana Nevies, and to all my children
by said wife, should I have any.

Exec: Said wife.
Witnesses: Thomas Mitchell, John Keefe.

EVANS, OLIVER. Phila.
Feb. 17, 1816. April 22, 1819. Admin. Book M.P. 150, no. 97.
Legacy to daughter, Elizabeth, wife of John Lamley. To sons, George, Cadwalader and Oliver, and to daughters, Ann, wife of James I. Rush, Rachel, wife of Peter I. D. Muhlenberg, and Sarah Evans. Residue to wife, Sarah. After her death, to our children. Property in Phila., in Ridley Township, Delaware Co., Pennsylvania, Pittsburgh, Pennsylvania, and in New York. Should wife die before me, sons George and Cadwalader to be Executors. To heirs of Owen Evans.
Exec: Said wife.
Witnesses: Charles I. Ingersoll, Sam'l. Wilcocks, William D. Hopkins, of Phila., student at law, affirmed.
Codicil: April 15, 1819. Since making Will, Feb. 17, 1816, I have married a second wife. To wife, Hetty, should she survive me, my right, title, interest and property, and all the benefit and advantages thereof, within the State of New York only, of and unto my letters Patent for my improvements in the art of manufacturing flour and meal and in the several machines in the said letters patent.
Witnesses: Edm'd. H. Pendleton, David Rogers, Jr., Valentine Mott. Christian B. Merkel, of Phila., burr mill stone maker, affirmed.
Recorded in Administration Book M, 150, No. 97.

MULCAHEY, JOHN. Phila.
Aug. 5, 1818. Aug. 9, 1819. 7.43.
Legacies to my friend, James Welsh, whom I appoint Executor, and to my sister, Mrs. Dalton's son, Andrew. If no son of that name, to my sister, Mrs. Wall's son, Andrew. If she has no son of that name, to Dennis, the son of Richard and said Mrs. Wall. Executors to collect debt from cousin, John Mulcahey.
Witnesses: William Whelan, Patrick McDonnell.

WORRILL, JONATHAN. Phila. Gentleman.
May 23, 1818. Aug. 14, 1819. 7.42.
Legacies to Catherine Sheperd and her sister, Rebecca Simmons, nieces of my wife. To Margaret Williams, my housekeeper. To Susannah Albright, sister of said Margaret Williams. To Catharine Johnson, wife of Richard Johnson of Lyme [?]. After her death, to the children of her brother, Robert Lloyd. To Susannah Chamberlain, wife of Nathaniel Chamberlain. If she leaves no issue, then to West Town Boarding School, under direction of Yearly Meeting of Friends of Pennsylvania, and to the Contributors to Asylum, near Phila., for the insane. To Lydia Lloyd, wife of Robert Lloyd, son of Levi and Hannah

Lloyd, deceased. To Gabriel Parris, son-in-law of Benjamin Olden. To
nephew, Nathan Yarnall. To Joseph, the son of Charles and Rebecca
Jobson of Northern Liberties. To Rachael Dillworth, widow of Joseph
Dillworth.
Execs: Brother-in-law, Ellis Yarnall, Joseph Warner, Benjamin H.
Yarnall.
Witnesses: Thomas Kennedy, Daniel Niles, William Lawrence.

DEIMLING, FRANCIS G. Phila. Co. Merchant.
Feb. 8, 1814. Aug. 11, 1819. 7.43.
Execs: Wife, Maria Gertrauda Deimling, my friend, Francis Ingraham,
of Phila.
The heirs in Germany to the estate of Frederick Weiss, late of
Strasburg Township, Lancaster Co., deceased, by letter of attorney, did
appoint Frederick Augustus Muhlenberg, Esq., and myself to be their
attornies, etc. Said Frederick Augustus Muhlenberg since deceased, I
do hereby substitute my said Executors to be the lawful attornies of
said heirs in Germany. Estate to my wife. To brother, Wilhelm
Gotfreed Deimling, Burgvogt (Bailiff of the Castle) of Emmendingen
in ---. To brother, Ernst Frederick Deimling, Senator, my sisters,
Henrietta Muller and Christiana Gottreu, all of the City of Denlach [?].
To nephew, Francis Christopher Deimling, of Phila.
Witnesses: George Weiss, Isaac Tustin.

SULLIVAN, JEREMIAH. Phila. Shopkeeper.
Oct. 5, 1809. Aug. 14, 1819. 7.45.
Estate to stepdaughter, Honora Carroll, whom I appoint sole Executrix.
Witnesses: Thomas Dugdale, Jr., Peter Thomson.
Resealed: Sept. 22, 1817.
Witnesses: Peter Smith, Peter Thomson.

FALLAR, CASPAR.
Signed: ____. Proved: Aug. 18, 1819. 7.45.
Estate to wife, ____, and to my children, Betzey and Catharina. If said
daughters die without issue, estate to my wife's children.
Execs: Abraham Deaves, Frederick Smith.
Witnesses: Benjamin Gorgas, Sr., Samuel French.

LEWIS, WILLIAM. Phila. Co. Counsellor at Law.
Aug. 5, 1819. Aug. 18, 1819. 7.46.
Execs: Wife, Frances Lewis, only son, Josiah Lewis, my friend, William
Rawle, Esq., Counsellor at Law.
Estate to said wife, son, Josiah, daughter, Margaret Azard, and her
daughter, Martha, granddaughter, Louisa Azard, grandson, Lewis H.
Conover. To friend, William Rawle, Esq. If grandson, William Lewis,

son of my son, Josiah, shall make the law his profession, I give him my
law library.
Witnesses: Mary Gerraty, Charles Caldwell, Robert Collins.
Codicil: Aug. 7, 1819. Mentions his land in Kentucky.
Witnesses: Mary Gerraty, Edward Rawle, Robert Collins.

HALL, MAHLON. Township of Blockley. Phila. Co.
April 9, 1810. Aug. 21, 1819. 7.48.
To my son, Mahlon Hall's children, each $1.00. To my daughter, Sarah
Heston. To my granddaughter, Matilda Heston. To wife, Jane Hall, the
income of my plantation, and to my son, John Hall, the remainder of
my estate.
Execs: Son, John Hall, my grandson, James Hall.
Witnesses: Nathan Dickinson, William Warner, Edward George of
Blockley Township, farmer, affirmed.

DILCART, JOHN. Northern Liberties. Phila. Inn Keeper.
July 16, 1819. Aug. 26, 1819. 7.49.
Legacies to my daughter, Margaret Eckert, son, Peter Dilcart, and my
daughter, Christiana Dilcart. All residue to my daughters: Betsey
Reybold, Susannah Jones, Catharina Arentrue, Barbara Kebler and
Nancy Pfeil.
Execs: Friends, John Baker and Charles Eckert, both of said Liberties.
Witnesses: Nicholas Armbruster, John Kohlen.

SIMSON, JOHN. Phila. Merchant.
Dec. 17, 1817. Aug. 27, 1819. 7.49.
Legacies to friend, Gilbert Robertson, Esq., of Phila., to William Allen,
also of Phila. All residue of estate, including ground in City of
Washington, District of Columbia, I bequeath to my sister, Clementine
Simson, now or late of Taen Ross-shire in North Britain.
Exec: Gilbert Robertson.
Witnesses: William Meredith, B. D. Crane, William M. Meredith. James
J. Barclay of Phila., Attorney at Law, affirmed.

RIGHTER, MICHAEL. Township of Roxborough. Phila. Co. Farmer.
April 4, 1812. Aug. 3, 1819. 7.50.
Estate to my wife, and to my children: Charles, Catharine, Michael,
Samuel, Ann and Jonathan Righter.
Execs: Sons, Charles and Michael Righter.
Witnesses: John K. Duy, John Smith. Jacob B. Smith, of Roxborough,
Phila. Co., teacher, son of said John Smith, affirmed.

HART, SEYMOUR. Northern Liberties. Phila.
Jan. 12, 1810. Aug. 19, 1819. 7.51.

My property, etc. to my children: Catharine Sheppard, John Hart and Rebecca Simmons, wife of Stephen Simmons. To friends, Thomas Stewardson, Thomas Norton, George Williams, in trust for Institution under care of Yearly Meeting of Friends for Pennsylvania and New Jersey. To Pennsylvania Hospital. To my grandson, John S. Hart, son of said son, John Hart, and my daughters, Catharine Sheppard and Rebecca Simmons.
Witnesses: Nathaniel Richardson, William Andrews.
Codicil: Jan. 1, 1813. Revokes legacy to Pennsylvania Hospital. Legacy to Institution for Insane now forming by consent of Yearly Meeting of Friends held at Philadelphia for Pennsylvania and New Jersey, etc. To Elizabeth Snyder, who served her time with me and now lives with my daughter, Catharine Sheppard.
Witnesses: William Andrews, Isaac Elliott.
Letters to John Hart.

MINTZER, JOHN. Northern Liberties. Phila.
July 7, 1819. Sept. 3, 1819. 7.55.
To wife, Deborah Mintzer, during life, the income of all estate, and after her decease, to my children: Jacob Mintzer, my youngest son, William Mintzer, daughters Rosanna Stimble, wife of George Stimble, Sarah Bruner and Eliza Mintzer.
Exec: Joseph Abbott.
Witnesses: Caleb Carmalt, James Carmalt.

PATTERSON, JOHN. Phila. Merchant.
June 7, 1819. Aug. 31, 1819. 7.55.
To my wife, Rachael Patterson. To Ephraim, Sarah Ann and Margaret Pittman, each $100, as they arrive at 21 years. All residue of estate to all my children.
Execs: Said wife, Rachael, my friends, Samuel J. Robbins, John D. Smith. Testamentary Guardians of all my children, said Samuel J. Robbins and John D. Smith.
Witnesses: Henry Snyder, John Martin.

DUFFUS, ANDREW. Phila. Shoemaker.
Feb. 28, 1815. Sept. 6, 1819. 7.56.
Executors to convert my property into cash, to pay interest to my wife, Janet Duffus. After her decease, to my niece, Janet Thompson, of this city, and to the Associate Church of this city, of which I am a member.
Execs: John McCulloch, John McAllister, of this city.
Witnesses: Robert Milliken, William Wardin.

SHOEMAKER, JOSEPH. Phila.
May 5, 1812. Sept. 3, 1819. 7.56.

Estate to my wife, Abigail Shoemaker, and my three daughters: Ann, Rebecca and Abigail. $10 to son, John J. Shoemaker, he having received his share of estate.
Execs: Said wife, my son-in-law, Jaspar Cope, my kinsman, Charles Shoemaker.
Witnesses: John Bonsall, Isaac Bonsall.

PEMBERTON, PHILADELPHIA. Phila. Widow.
Nov. 22, 1817. Sept. 6, 1819. 7.57.
All my property, etc. to my daughters, Sarah and Philadelphia Pemberton, and my son, Henry.
Execs: Son, Henry, daughter Philadelphia Pemberton.
Witnesses: Robert Whitehead, Lydia W. Eyre.

PAUL, JEREMIAH. Phila. Schoolmaster.
Jan. 29, 1816. Sept. 8, 1819. 7.58.
A Quarto Bible to each of my children: Jeremiah and William Paul, Sarah Smith, Nathan, Elizabeth, Lydia, Josiah, Rebecca, Bettle and Samuel Paul. Three minor sons to learn a trade. All estate I bequeath to my wife, Rebecca Paul.
Execs: Said wife, my kinsman, Jacob Ballinger.
Witnesses: Joseph Esherick, David Esherick, Alexander Shaw of Phila., affirmed.

WILLIAMS, CATHARINE. Phila. Single Woman.
March 15, 1819. Sept. 6, 1819. 7.59.
$25 owing to me from John Williams. Legacies to the fifth and to the second Presbyterian Churches of Phila. and Northern Liberties for their poor members.
Exec: Friend, Geo. Durfor.
Witnesses: William Britton, Edward Sprague.

O'NEILL, HENRY. Phila. Merchant.
Feb. 26, 1816. July 12, 1819. 7.59.
Execs: Joseph Donath, Esq., my Mary A. O'Neill, Charles A. Richardson, all of Phila.
Legacy to my mother, Mary O'Neill, sister, Hannah O'Neill, wife of Henry O'Neill, brother, Arthur J. O'Neill, sisters Mary Hesson and Sarah T. O'Neill. To said niece Mary A. O'Neill, daughter of sister, Hannah O'Neill. To my nephew, John O'Neill, and my niece, Ann O'Neill, children of said sister, Hannah. To nephew, Henry O'Neill, son of my deceased brother, Hugh C. O'Neill. To nephew, Arthur O'Neill, son of my brother, Arthur J. O'Neill. To said niece, Mary A. O'Neill, and her heirs, my pew in St. Mary's Church, Phila. To Rev. Dr.

Matthew Carr. To Chief Pastor for time being of St. Mary's Church aforesaid.
Witnesses: John R. Baker, Frederick Beates, Peter Heyler.
Codicil: June 29, 1819. Chas. Parmentier of Phila., clerk, and Joseph Dickson, of same place, to be Executors in place of Joseph Donath and Charles A. Richardson. Bequeath to my wife Mary A. O'Neill, my gold watch and chain and two seals and one key.
Witnesses: Peter Mather, David Wilfong, C. A. Richardson.
Letters to Mary A. O'Neill, Charles Parmentier.

THOMPSON, JOHN. Phila. Merchant.
Sept. 21, 1818. Sept. 25, 1819. 7.61.
To my wife, Rebecca Thompson, and my children: Jonah, George and Samuel. To all the children (including any posthumous child or children) of my deceased son, James B. Thompson, and to daughter, Rebecca C. Lewis, and her children. If my children leave no issue, then to children of my brother, Thomas Thompson, and of my sisters Mary Westcombe, Sarah Neave, and Ann Roberts.
Execs: Son, Jonah Thompson, son-in-law, Samuel N. Lewis, my son, George Thompson.
Witnesses: Isaac Norris, Thomas Norris, Henry Latimer, Jr.

COPE, JOHN. Township of Moyamensing. Phila. Co.
Sept. 17, 1819. Oct. 1, 1819. 7.63.
Estate to my wife, Mary, and after her decease, to my daughter, Margaret, son Charles, and to the children of my deceased son, Henry Cope.
Execs: Brother, Godfrey G. Cope, my wife, Mary Cope.
Witnesses: Francis Read, John Cope, nephew to the Testator.

JOHNSON, JACOB.
May 20, 1819. Sept. 30, 1819. 7.64.
To my wife, 1/3 of personal and 1/3 income of all real estate for life. Legacies to my sisters, Mary and Elizabeth Johnson, to children of deceased sister, Rebecca Maule, and of brother Joseph Johnson, and sister, Ann Hobson. All residue of estate to my children.
Execs: Brother, Benjamin Johnson, Joseph Warner.
Benjamin Warner, of Phila., book seller, and John B. Ellison, of said city, Accomptant, affirmed.

SCHOOCK, MICHAEL. Northern Liberties. Phila. Yeoman.
Oct. 14, 1814. Sept. 28, 1819. 7.65.
Income of all estate to my wife, Margaret, and after her decease, to my daughter, Catharine, so long as she remains single, and at the decease

or intermarriage of said daughter, I bequeath to my five sons, all my estate.
Execs: Son, George Schoock, friend, Jacob Gilbert, of Phila.
Witnesses: John Rees, Jacob Walter.

MORROW, WILLIAM. Township of Passyunk. Phila. Co.
July 20, 1819. Sept. 29, 1819. 7.63.
Legacy to William Allison, son of my cousin, John Allison. Residue of estate (after debts are paid, to Robert Galbreath and John Williams), to my wife, Rebecca Morrow. After her death or marriage, estate to my two sisters and brother's children, in Ireland.
Execs: Robert Galbreath, John Allison, before mentioned.
Witnesses: John Allison, Moses McIlhiney, John Nickle.

CROWLEY, JOHN. District of Southwark.
Sept. 3, 1819. Oct. 5, 1819. 7.66.
Estate to my aunts, Sarah Young and Rebecca Jarman, and to my uncle, Daniel Jarman.
Exec: Timothy Blake, of Phila.
Witnesses: James McLinchey, Richard Renshaw.

FLUCK, ADAM. Phila. Innkeeper.
Sept. 24, 1819. Oct. 7, 1819. 7.67.
All estate to wife, Catharine Fluck, whom I appoint Executrix.
Witnesses: Abraham Beidleman, Michael Reed.

PRESTON, WILLIAM, JR. Northern Liberties. Phila. Boat Builder.
June 12, 1810. Oct. 7, 1819. 7.67.
Estate to my wife, Catharine Preston. To children, Mary and Abigail Preston.
Execs: Said wife, Jesse Oat, of Phila.
Witnesses: Robert Whitehead, John Clark, Hannah Eyre.
Letters to surviving Exec., Catharine Preston.

STRETCH, THOMAS. Phila.
May 15, 1819. Oct, 18, 1819. 7.68.
Estate to Richard W. Meade, Esq.
Execs: Said Richard W. Meade, John Leamy.
Witnesses: Horace Binney, Henry Toland.

DEALCART, NANCY. Northern Liberties. Phila.
Dec. 12, 1809. Oct. 19, 1819.
Estate bequeathed to me by my sister, Barbara Diamond, I now bequeath to my eight children: Peter, Barbara, Catherine, Elizabeth,

Ann, Christiana, Susanna and Margaret Dealcart. Legacies to the children of my daughter, Barbara, named James and Betsey.
Execs: Said son, Peter, my son-in-law, Philip Reybold. Executors to have charge of daughter Christiana's share (she being not of sound mind).
Witnesses: John Krips, John Smith. Mary Smith, widow of John Smith, and Jacob Krips of Northern Liberties, fancy chair maker, brother of said John, deceased, affirmed.
Copied from original Will.

LAWSON, WILLIAM.
Sept. 12, 1818. Dec. 21, 1818. 7.68.
Estate to my wife, Margaret Lawson, and son, Alexander Lawson. Articles which belong to Mrs. Margaret Lawson, through the medium of her late son, Willliam Lawson, shall remain in her possession.
Execs: Brother, Alexander Lawson, my wife, Margaret.
Witnesses: Thomas Swan, Thomas Johnston, Alexander Lawson.
Letters to Alexander Lawson.

WHITE, HANNAH. Phila. Widow.
June 16, 1819. Oct. 20, 1819. 7.68.
Legacies to friends, George Williams and Elihu Pickering, in trust for my daughters, Elizabeth White, wife of Josiah White, and Hannah Roberts, wife of Charles Roberts, and after decease of said daughters, to their children. Late husband Solomon White bequeathed after my decease, all residue of estate to our said two daughters.
Execs: Daughters Elizabeth White and Hannah Roberts.
Witnesses: Charles W. Thomson, Peter Thomson.

KENNEDY, ELIZABETH. Now of Northern Liberties.
July 28, 1818. Oct. 25, 1820. 7.70.
To my children: Mary, George, Elizabeth, Susan, Robert, Andrew and Eleanor. Son, Robert, to have charge of son, George's share, and that of daughter, Mary, until her son, John Tilly, is of age.
Execs: Son, Robert Kennedy, son-in-law, Michael Leib.
Witnesses: William Mettler, Samuel Mettler.

PHILE, JOHN. Northern Liberties. Phila. Turner. Umbrella and Umbrella Stick Maker.
Sept. 2, 1813. Oct. 26, 1819. 7.71.
Estate to my wife, ____, my mother and my son, Joseph, when 21 years. My Theological works to my sister, Hannah Mathews.
Exec: Dr. John Mathews of Millerstown, Lehigh Co., Pennsylvania.
Witnesses: Adam Lingmuller, William Miller.

James McEwen of Northern Liberties, tavern keeper, and William Shute of said Liberties, turner, affirmed.

DOUGHERTY, GEORGE. Phila. Iron Monger.
Aug. 5, 1819. Nov. 3, 1819. 7.71.
To my wife (not named in original), one-third income of estate and residue to my sister, Catharine Wiseman, and her two daughters, Eleanor Maria and Catharine Maria.
Execs: Friends, Josiah H. Lownes, of Phila., silversmith, Joseph Snyder of Phila Co., blacksmith.
Witnesses: Thos. Clayton, Fred'k. Beates.
Codicil: Oct. 2, 1819. Legacy to Elizabeth Sheed.
Witnesses: James Dempsey, Andrew Robinson.

TUNIS, JEHU R. Phila. Merchant.
Oct. 14, 1819. Nov. 8, 1819. 7.72.
Legacy to my wife, Elizabeth Tunis, to sister, Jane Tunis, and to the four children of late sister, Hannah Ellicott, to be paid to their father, Andrew Ellicott, when they arrive at age, boys 21 and girls 18 years. Legacy to cousin, Richard Tunis. To Alexander Greaves. All real estate to my brother, Thomas R. Tunis. To friends and relations, Andrew Ellicott and John R. Thomas, in trust for said brother, Thomas.
Execs: Friend and partner, James Way, my friend, William W. Fisher.
Witnesses: J. Preston, Fred'k. Beates.

CARTER, REBECCA. Northern Liberties. Phila. Co.
Sept. 20, 1819. Nov. 10, 1819. 7.73.
Household goods, etc. to be sold, proceeds and money from John and Daniel Elliott, I bequeath to my two sons, John and Henry Carter, when of legal age.
Execs: Friends, Joseph Townsend, John Simmons, both of Northern Liberties.
Witnesses: Clayton Stratton, Jonathan P. Smith.

HUSE, ANN. Phila.
Sept. 10, 1819. Nov. 12, 1819. 7.74.
Bequeath to Ephraim D. Whitlock, of the United States Navy, whom I hereby appoint Guardian of daughter, Ann Elizabeth, now known by name of Ann Elizabeth Whitlock, all my personal estate, in trust for education and support of said daughter, until 18 years, when he shall account to her for the balance.
Exec: Said Ephraim D. Whitlock.
Witnesses: Louisa O'Neail, Catharine McHerum.

SERMON, MARY.
Dec. 25, 1816. Nov. 19, 1819. 7.75.
Property where I live to my daughter, Jane Worrall, and at her decease, to my three granddaughters: Mary Sermon Worrall, Jane Caroline Worrall and Matilda Worrall, when of age. To my seven grandsons: Joseph C., Thomas, George, Charles, Richard, Isaac and Horatio Worrall. To my son, George Worrall, my worked pocket book with silver clasp.
Execs: Said daughter, Jane Worrall, her husband, George Worrall. Caleb Pierce, of Phila., ironmonger, and William Rumsey of Northern Liberties, physician, affirmed.

STEWART, THOMAS. Late of United States Ship "Essex." Porter.
Nov. 11, 1817. Nov. 23, 1819. 7.76.
Estate to Margaret Stewart, whom I appoint Executrix.
Witnesses: Thomas Bigelow, Richard C. Aspell.

BOYD, PARKS. Phila. Pewterer.
May 9, 1819. Oct. 28, 1819. 7.76.
To John Cook, of Phila, in trust for my children, Sarah Monkhouse, Maria Boyd and Eliza Boyd, until Jan. 1, 1824.
Exec: Said John Cook.
Witnesses: John Morris, George Worrall.
Codicil: May 9, 1819. Said daughter, Sarah Monkhouse, to have no further benefit from my estate as she has had her full share. Executors to pay $1.00 per week for board of her daughter, Eliza Monkhouse, etc.
Witnesses: Same as to Will.

JOHNSON, JAMES C. Now of Phila., late of Pittsburg.
Nov. 16, 1819. Nov. 29, 1819. 7.77.
Legacies to my mother, Margaret Johnson, widow, of the County of Tyrone, in Ireland, and to my six brothers and two sisters, in Ireland, aforesaid. Residue I bequeath to my brother, Archibald Johnson, now in America.
Execs: Said brother, friend, Nathaniel Holmes, both of Pittsburg.
Witnesses: James Arthur, John Allison.
Letters to Alexander Johnston.

LISTER, JOHN SMITH. District of Southward. Phila. Co. Gentleman.
May 13, 1818. Nov. 25, 1819. 7.78.
Estate to wife, Sarah S. Lister, and at her decease, to my children: Mary Aspin, wife of George Aspin, John S. Lister, Thomas S. Lister, Elizabeth S. Lister.
Exec: Said wife, Sarah S. Lister.
Witnesses: Garret Blackhorn, Richard Palmer.

173

CONYNGHAM, GUSTAVUS. Phila. Mariner.
July 28, 1819. Dec. 1, 1819. 7.78.
Legacies to Gustavus Conyngham Stewart, son of Robert R. Stewart, and to Catharine Ann Colhoun, daughter of my niece, Catharine Colhoun. All residue to my niece, Ann McClure, (now residing with me), daughter of my sister, Prudence McClure.
Exec: Said Ann McClure, also to be Guardian of above-named Catharine Ann Colhoun, during minority.
Witnesses: Thomas Mitchell, Andrew D. Cash, Morgan Carr.
Codicil: Sept. 29, 1819. Friend, John Mark, of Phila., my kinsman Redmond Conyngham of Nescopeck Valley, Luzerne Co., Pennsylvania, to be Execs. with my said niece.

CLEAVER, JESSE. Northern Liberties. Phila. Late Lumber Merchant.
July 22 1817. Dec. 2, 1819. 7.80.
Estate to wife, Elizabeth Cleaver, and son, Isaac Cleaver, whom I appoint Executors.
Witnesses: Jonathan Conard, John Lancaster.

POWELL, WILLIAM. Phila. House Carpenter.
July 21, 1819. Dec. 3, 1819. 7.81.
Estate to my wife, Sarah Powell, and our five children: Elizabeth, Ann, Sarah, Joseph Wetherill and William Mifflin Powell. Executors to sell property in Phila., and in counties of Bedford, Beaver or Butler, or any of the western counties in Pennsylvania.
Execs: Wife, Sarah, my friends, Gilbert Gaw and Daniel Knight, of Phila.
Witnesses: James Truman, Christopher Wetherill.

BENNER, JOHN. Borough of Frankford. Phila. Co. Farmer.
Oct. 1, 1819. Dec. 4, 1819. 7.82.
Estate to my wife, Rachel, and my two daughters, Hannah and Mary Ann.
Execs: Said wife, my brother, Jacob Benner.
Witnesses: Samuel Morrow, Michael Newbold.

MANIGAULT, CHARLOTTE. Charleston. Spinster.
Dec. 28, 1818. Feb. 3, 1820. 7.83.
I leave everything I possess to my mother, during her life, and at her death, to my brother, Gabriel Henry Manigault, to my sisters, Elizabeth and Harriet, and to my brother, Charles Manigault.
Witnesses: Lewis Morris, William E. Morris. Margaret Manigault appointed Administratrix.

ANDAULLE, JOHN B. Phila. Merchant.
April 2, 1819. Nov. 30, 1819. 7.84.
Execs: Friends, Joseph Roberts, of said city, and Louis Crousillat, Jr., of ____ . Interest of estate to my sister, Marice Antoniette Andaulle.
Witnesses: Anth'y. Finley, Edmond I. Crawley.
Letters to Joseph Roberts.

GALLE, FREDERICK. Germantown Township. Phila. Co.
May 26, 1810. Dec. 18, 1819. 7.84.
Estate to my wife, Maria Esther Galle, and after her decease, legacies to my brother, George Nicholas Galle, now or late an inhabitant of Swoll, in bailiwick, of Berkenfield, in Germany. To German Lutheran Congregation in Germantown Township, now under care of Rev. Mr. Shaffer. To Magdalena Kline, now living with us and whom we brought up from her infancy.
Exec: Said wife.
Witnesses: Frederick Smith, David Hoffman.

SHAW, JOHN AULDHAM. Of the United States Army.
July 2, 1816. (Signed at Bustleton) Nov. 1, 1819. 7.85.
All estaate to my brother, Thomas Shaw, Phila. Co., gentleman, whom I appoint Executor.
Witnesses: William Campion, Enoch C. Edwards.
John Dungan, of Phila., tavern keeper, affirmed.

HANSELL, GEORGE. Blockley. Phila. Co.
Aug. 19, 1818. Dec. 29, 1819. 7.85.
Estate to my wife, Deborah Hansell, she to educate my minor children until they are 16 years of age. Legacy to my daughter, Hester Hansell. To my grandchild, Richard Hansell, son of my daughter, Hester Hansell. After decease of my wife, estate to all my children.
Execs: Said wife, Isaac W. Roberts.
Witnesses: Hugh Calahan, Andrew Redolpher.

SHIELDS, THOMAS. Phila. Gentleman.
April 17, 1813. Dec. 30, 1819. 7.86.
Property in Phila., in Wayne Co. or any other county in Pennsylvania, and in Baltimore city, I bequeath to my wife, Hannah, and my four sons: Thomas, Robert, John and David Shields.
Execs: Said four sons.
Witnesses: Abr'm. Shoemaker, Joseph Robinson, Fran's. Shoemaker. Abraham Shoemaker, Esq., of Phila., son of Abraham Shoemaker, deceased, affirmed. Robert, John and David Shields, three of Executors, sworn.

INDEX

-A-

AARON, David Solomon, 123
ABBOT, Joseph, 112
ABBOTT, Joseph, 166
ABEEL, Dr., 92; Mary, 92
ADAMS, Abigail, 30; Ann, 53;
 Ann Eliza, 53; Benjamin, 36;
 Catherine, 48; Ephraim, 36;
 James, 53; Jane, 36; John
 Strong, 53; Martha, 36;
 Peter, 144; Rebeckah, 36;
 Robert, 11, 54, 57, 121,
 149; Samuel, 36; Sarah, 53,
 131; Thomas, 53; William,
 53, 54, 101
AITKENS, Robert, 152
AKIN, Samuel Bens, 67
ALBERT, Casper, 60; Eve, 60;
 Henry, 73; John, 60; Mary,
 73; Philip, 73
ALBRECHT, Charles, 27, 29
ALBRIGHT, Susannah, 163
ALCIDE, Joseph, 55
ALDENDERFER, Elizabeth, 53
ALEXANDER, Elizabeth, 90;
 Esther, 90; Ezekiel, 89;
 George, 9, 119; James, 56;
 John, 89; John B., 13;
 Joseph, 67; Juliana, 13;
 Margaret, 56; Margaret Anna,
 89; Richard, 46; Sarah, 89;
 Sarah Jane, 89; William, 90;
 William Daniel, 89
ALLEN, Charles, 124, 154, 162;
 Jane, 102; Joseph, 97, 124,
 146, 162; Lewis, 129; Lydia,
 102; Miller, 102; Richard,
 8, 60, 89, 115; Samuel, 71,
 102; Thomas, 102; William,
 101, 122, 150, 165
ALLINSON, Bernice, 123;
 Elizabeth, 123; Rebecca,
 123; Samuel, 123; William,
 5, 123
ALLISON, John, 30, 56, 61, 96,
 145, 158, 169, 172; Rebecca,
 123; William, 123, 169
ALMENDINGER, Ann, 148; Anne,
 148; Catharine, 148;
 Charles, 148; George, 148;
 Jacob, 148; William, 148
ALSOP, James, 51; Othniel, 100,
 157
ANDAULLE, John B., 174; Marice
 Antoniette, 174
ANDERSON, Alexander, 156;
 Alexander M., 156; Andrew,
 87; Augusta, 156; Charles,
 66; Edward, 156; Elizabeth,
 114; Eveline, 156; John,
 110, 114; Lennox, 156;
 Rebecca, 66; Samuel, 36, 51;
 Susanna, 51; Theodore, 156;
 Thomas, 36, 95
ANDIGE, Madame, 147
ANDRES, William, 63
ANDREUZ, William, 9
ANDREWS, James, 113; John, 148;
 Robert, 63; William, 5, 9,
 46, 82, 95, 128, 147, 166
ANNEL, Jane, 102
ANTHONY, John, 50
APPLE, Peter, 112
APPLETON, Lewis, 61
APPO, Ann, 143; Ellen, 143;
 John, 143; Joseph, 143;
 William, 143
APT, Elizabeth, 142; Julia Ann,
 142; Michael, 142
ARCHDEACON, Annette, 133
ARCHER, Elizabeth, 93; James,
 93; Jane, 93; John, 94;
 Samuel, 106
ARENTRUE, Catharina, 165
ARMAND, Benjamin, 32
ARMAT, Thomas, 36
ARMBRUSTER, Nicholas, 165
ARMER, Alexander, 76
ARMITAGE, George, 49, 128;
 Shewbart, 78
ARMITT, Mary, 63
ARMOND, John, 119
ARMSTRONG, Ann, 51; Hetty, 6;
 Joseph, 130; Thomas, 28, 119
ARNOUS, Justine, 147; Nicholas,
 147; Timothy, 147
ARRISON, John, 158; Sarah, 158;
 Shipford, 158
ARTHUR, Enoch, 152; James, 172
ASBORN, Eleanor, 3
ASH, Caleb, 59; Elizabeth, 154;
 James, 78; John, 78; Joseph,
 59; Joshua, 30, 59; Michael
 W., 136; Morgan, 78; Rachel,
 78; Sophia Henrietta Emily,
 136; Thomas, 59; Thomas F.,
 78
ASHBORN, Andrew, 69
ASHBRIDGE, Elizabeth, 152;
 Joseph, 146; Mary, 152;
 Rebecca, 146; Tacy, 152
ASHBURNER, John, 161
ASHLEY, John, 73
ASHMEAD, Ann, 36, 125, 126;
 Benjamin, 125, 126; Eliza,
 125; James, 36; Jane, 126;

Isaac, 25; William, 57, 64
ASKIN, John, 158
ASPELL, Richard C., 172
ASPIN, George, 172; Mary, 172
ASTON, George, 1; Peter, 1
ATHERTON, Susanna, 100
ATKINSON, Benjamin, 36, 66; Hannah, 20; Jane, 36, 66; Martha, 36; Watson, 132
ATLEE, Edwin A., 15
AUNER, Peter, 96
AUSTIN, Johannah, 145; Martha, 2, 79; Mary, 2, 79; Samuel, 140; William, 140
AVERLY, Susanna, 71
AVERY, Abner, 3; James, 81
AXE, Frederick, 120
AYRE, George, 132
AZARD, Louis, 164; Margaret, 164; Martha, 164
AZAU, Joseph, 147

-B-
B. BURTON FORBES & GREGORY, 97
BACH, John, 10
BACHE, Benjamin, 61; Catharine, 20; Franklin, 143
BACON, Charles, 109; John, 122; Joseph, 109; Mary, 109; Rebecca, 109; Sarah, 109
BADGER, Bela, 102
BADGLEY, Francis, 130
BAILEY, Andrew, 17; Catharine, 158; Hugh, 158; John, 158
BAIRD, Sarah, 129; William, 129
BAKEOVEN, John, 127
BAKER, Anna Catharine, 69; Betsey, 25; Christopher, 16; Dobel, 51; Dobell, 69; Elizabeth, 143; George A., 16, 126, 155; George Adam, 69; Jacob, 53; John, 165; John C., 76; John Hilary, 69; John Lewis, 69; John R., 168; Joshua, 27; Mary, 27, 128; Michael, 106, 126; Patience, 25; Richard Mace, 128; Richard S., 25; Sally, 25; Samuel, 25, 26, 98; Susanna, 121; Susanna Louisa, 69; Susannah, 110; Susannah Louisa, 155
BALDERSTON, Elizabeth, 95
BALLED, Hagah, 128
BALLENGER, Jacob, 96
BALLINGER, Jacob, 167
BANGS, Elijah Keeler, 57
BANNAR, Jacob, 100
BANNEN, John, 139
BANNING, Freeburn, 103; Sarah, 103

BANTLEON, Eliza, 65; George, 65; Rachel Lee, 65; Sarah, 65
BARAULT, Francis, 55
BARCLAY, Hugh, 101; James J., 165; Jane, 101; John, 101; Margaret, 101; Richard, 101; Samuel, 30, 35, 46, 68, 72
BARKENBILE, Catharine, 154
BARKER, Abraham, 131; William, 119
BARLOW, Elizabeth, 29; John, 29; Levina, 29
BARNES, Daniel, 24; Elizabeth, 85; John, 50, 85; Joseph, 32; Thomas, 63; William, 124
BARNET, Abner, 29; Elizabeth, 29; Martha, 29
BARNHILL, John Redman, 70; Margaretta, 70; Robert, 70
BARNHOLD, Elizabeth, 106; Frederick, 106
BARNITZ, Charles, 140; Jacob, 140
BARR, David, 89; John, 137; Mary, 101
BARRETT, Elizabeth, 128; Mary, 128; Tobias, 127
BARRINGTON, Henry, 130, 135, 141
BARRON, William, 97
BARRY, Garret R., 61; Garrett R., 151; Julia, 62
BARTHE, Dominick, 136; Jacques, 136; Jean, 136; Peter Dominick, 136; Sophia Henrietta Emily, 136
BARTHOLOMEW, John, 75
BARTLESON, Peter, 124
BARTON, Joseph, 95; Mary P., 72; Sarah Pennington, 72; Thomas P., 72
BARTRAM, Isaac, 83
BASAN, Caleb, 67; David, 67; Esther, 67; George, 67; Jacob, 67; Judith, 67; Sarah, 67
BASTIAN, Elizabeth, 68; Joseph, 68
BATESON, James, 52
BATHO, John, 34; Martha, 34
BATTEIGER, Anthony, 104; George Jacob, 104; Valentine, 104
BAUER, Rachel, 123
BAULING, G. H., 65
BAUMAN, Ann, 153; Caspar, 153; Catharine, 153; Daniel, 153; Isaac, 153; Jacob, 153; John, 153; Margaret, 153; Nancy, 153
BAUSH, Elizabeth, 114; Sarah,

114

BAUSMAN, Anna Maria Herbert, 75; Caroline, 75; Elizabeth, 75; John, 75
BAXTER, Ann, 143; James, 143; John, 143
BAYARD, Andrew, 156
BAYLEY, Grace, 103
BAYLIE, John, 110
BAYNE, Charles, 12; Hester, 12; John, 12; Robert, 12; Samuel Plat, 12
BEAD, William, 4
BEALE, Joseph, 122
BEAN, Sarah C., 58
BEANDON, Ralph, 67
BEARD, Mary, 103
BEATES, Barbara, 46; Catharine, 46; Frederick, 6, 12, 34, 41, 42, 46, 60, 69, 74, 83, 96, 104, 107, 108, 116, 135, 136, 140, 143, 148, 155, 168, 171; Mary, 46; William, 46
BEATTEE, Francis S., 63
BEATTY, William, 87
BECK, John, 86; Mary, 83
BECKENBACH, Jacob, 64
BEDDEK, R., 48
BEDFORD, Lucy, 133; Samuel, 133
BEECH, Elizabeth, 118; Jonathan, 118; Sarah, 118
BEEHLER, Tobias, 106
BEHUCHE, John C., 81
BEIDEMAN, Catharine, 41; Eliza, 41; Henry, 41; Jacob, 40, 41; John, 41; Mary, 41; Samuel, 41; William, 41
BEIDLEMAN, Abraham, 169
BEINHARD, Adam, 99
BELDUQUE, Joseph, 97
BELIN, Louis, 113; Nicolas, 113
BELL, Elizabeth, 36; Hetty, 52; Jane, 134; Joseph, 51, 52, 99, 143; Margaret, 52; Maria, 51, 52; Mary Ann, 36; William, 36, 51, 52, 61; William I., 143; William John, 51, 52
BELLEROCKE, Athenais, 147
BELSTERLING, Anthony, 27; Bellague Catharine, 27; Catharine, 27; Henry, 27; Jacob, 14, 18, 27; John Foutles, 27; Margaret, 27; Mary, 27
BENDER, Elizabeth, 57; John, 14, 66, 126; Sarah, 89
BENEZET, Daniel, 37; Maria, 38; Mary, 43
BENEZETT, Anthony, 27; James, 27; Mary, 27
BENFIELD, Margaretta, 118
BENJAMIN, Taft, 134
BENLEY, Ann, 119
BENNAR, Peter, 132
BENNER, Ann, 55; George, 55; Hannah, 55, 173; Henry, 119; Jacob, 19, 55, 56, 173; John, 35, 40, 55, 173; Mary, 55; Mary Ann, 173; Rachel, 173
BENNERS, Elizabeth, 124; George, 124; Henry, 124; Jacob, 124; James, 124; Margaret, 124; Mary Ann, 124; William S., 124
BENNET, John, 52
BENNIS, Thomas, 73
BENOIT, James Mathwin, 147
BENSELL, George, 43; Sarah, 43
BENTON, John, 113
BERGER, George, 52, 117; Mary, 52
BERNARD, John, 12; John Adam, 162
BERR, Christopher, 76
BERRY, Jane, 101; Peter L., 101
BESWICK, John, 71
BETHAUSEN, Christian, 18
BETHEL, Robert, 155
BETHELL, Elizabeth, 155; Mary, 155; Robert, 155
BETTETON, George, 77
BETTLE, Samuel, 51
BETTS, Ebenezer, 18
BEVAN, Davis, 75; Isabella, 75; Matthew L., 75
BEVERIDGE, Mary, 42
BEVERIGE, Elizabeth, 128; James, 128; Mary, 128
BIAYS, Joseph, 11
BICKERSTAFF, Chichester, 23
BICKERTON, George, 118
BICKHAM, Caleb, 35; Elizabeth, 91; George W., 91; Joshua, 59, 91; Thomas, 35
BICKINGS, John, 34
BIDDLE, Anne, 1, 79; Charles, 45, 78; Clement, 79, 108; James C., 78, 109; John, 68, 79; John G., 109; Owen, 79; Samuel, 138; Sarah, 79; Thomas, 108; William S., 146
BIEGLER, Ann, 139, 140; Elizabeth, 139; Philip, 139
BIGELOW, Thomas, 46, 172
BIGGS, Augustus W., 38; Thomas, 75
BILLINGS, Ann Bensell, 43
BILLMYER, Esther, 108
BINDER, Catharine, 36;

Elizabeth, 36; George, 36; John, 14; Margaret, 36; Sophia, 36; Susan, 36; William, 36
BINES, Caroline, 39; Eliza, 39; Gustavus, 39; Robert, 39; Thomas, 39
BINGHAM, William, 38
BINNEY, Horace, 31, 169
BINNY, Archibald, 80
BIRCH, Catherine, 51; George, 61; Isaac, 61; Sarah, 61; William H., 61
BIRCHALL, Caleb, 72; James, 72; Sarah, 72
BIRCKHEAD, Hugh, 156; James, 156; Jane, 156; Lennox, 156; Pollard, 156; Pollard, Mrs., 156; Sarah, 156
BIRD, Catherine, 159; Joseph, 59
BIRNBAUM, John H., 10
BIRNIE, William, 70
BIRNS, Margaret, 54
BISBING, Jacob, 3
BISHOP, Robert, 28
BITTLE, Samuel, 59
BIVINS, John, 145; Mary, 145
BLACK, Alexander, 150, 158; Ann, 24; Isaac, 65; John, 149; Mary, 65, 149; Robert, 65; William, 149
BLACKBURN, Mary, 137
BLACKHORN, Garret, 172
BLACKISTON, Ann, 153; Elizabeth, 153; John, 153; Martha, 153; Mary, 153; Presley, 153; Rachel, 153; Rebecca, 153; Sarah, 153
BLACKLEDGE, William, 146
BLACKWELL, Hannah, 17, 37; Jacob, 132; Robert, 17, 37, 38, 132
BLACKWOOD, Mary, 43
BLAIR, Robert, 14; Samuel, 136; Susan, 136; William, 81
BLAKE, Charles E., 47; Jonathan, 14; Leven, 14; Sarah, 14; Timothy, 169; William B., 47
BLAKISTON, John, 153; Presley, 153
BLANCHARD, Isaac W., 19
BLANE, Blance, 133; Victor, 133
BLETSON, J., 113
BLISS, Isabella, 148
BLUMMER, John Christian, 8
BOATE, Horatio, 97
BOCKINS, Joseph, 86
BODDY, Elizabeth, 38; John, 38
BODEY, Rheudolph, 54

BODLY, Hagar, 15; Thomas, 15
BOGLE, Elizabeth, 35
BOGS, Margaret, 62
BOICK, Mary, 118
BOLTON, David, 139; Everard, 19; Isaac, 24
BONACKER, Jacob, 12
BOND, Christiana, 156; Jacob, 132; Phineas, 31; Rebecca, 31, 32
BONNER, Hannah, 142; James, 142; Mary, 142; Ury, 142
BONSALL, Edward, 19; Isaac, 167; John, 167
BOOK, John, 33; Sarah, 33
BOOTH, Elizabeth, 107; John, 107; Rachel, 107; William, 107
BORDEN, Benjamin, 131; Francis, 132; John C., 131
BORDLEY, Elizabeth, 4; Sarah, 71
BORNMANN, John, 67; Mary, 67
BORSLER, Mary, 98
BOSWELL, Elizabeth, 104; Margaret, 104; Susanna, 104; William, 104
BOULER, Mary, 98
BOULLAY, Abraham, 55; Elizabeth Metee, 55; Joseph, 55; Mary Elizabeth, 55; Mary Josephine, 55
BOULTNEY, Benjamin, 79; Hannah, 79; Sarah, 79
BOURGEOIS, Mary Dinah, 99
BOWELL, Sarah, 65
BOWEN, John, 123
BOWER, Hannah, 15; Joseph, 14; Mary, 25; Michael, 59
BOWERS, John, 5, 85; Michael, 107
BOWMAN, Jacob, 58, 120
BOWNE, Mary, 115
BOYD, Eliza, 172; Maria, 172; Parks, 172
BOYER, Dolly, 1; Elizabeth, 80; James, 1, 2, 130
BOYLE, Martha, 39
BOYS, Mary Peart, 60; Samuel, 60
BRACY, Margaret, 21
BRADFORD, Thomas, 42, 111, 126
BRADLEY, Eleanor, 35; James, 156; John, 23; Margaret, 115; Mary, 156
BRADY, Ann, 5; Daniel, 55; James, 73; John, 145; Margaret, 145, 147
BRAND, Christian, 36
BRASIER, Amable, 44
BRAVARD, Rebecca, 120

BRAZIERE, Catharine, 1; Robert, 1
BREEDER, Frances E. Patton Philson, 105
BREEDIR, B. B., 105
BRETZ, Jacob, 159
BRICE, James, 31; John, 31
BRIDGES, Culpepper, 40; Sarah, 40
BRIGGS, Mary, 25; Ralf, 160
BRINGHURST, John, 89; Mary, 127; Robert, 36; Samuel, 127; Susanna, 127; Tacy, 127
BRINTON, Elizabeth, 126; John, 126
BRISBURN, Stephen, 28
BRITTAIN, Susan, 95
BRITTINGHAM, Joshua, 104; Susanna, 104
BRITTON, Edward, 45, 153; Eleanor, 45; John, 45, 84; Margaret, 45; Maria, 45; Mary ---, 45; Rebecca, 45; Saltar, 45; Sarah, 45; William, 45, 112, 167
BROADFOOT, Cassandra, 85; James, 85
BROADHEAD, Mary, 62; Sarah Morrell, 62
BRODIE, Andrew, 111
BROOKE, Bowyer, 19; Henry D., 23; John, 60, 133; Robert, 132
BROOKS, Rachel, 123
BROOM, Hannah, 112, 113; Jacob, 150; Joseph Milwood, 112; Lenord, 112; Letitia, 112, 113; Roseta Letitia, 112; Thomas, 112
BROOME, Leonard, 113
BROWN, Ann, 72, 100; Anna, 9; Anthony Z., 24, 137; Benjamin, 19, 27, 68, 83, 84, 89, 128; Benneville, 7; Catharina, 7, 121; Catharine, 28; Charlotte, 7; Edward, 48; Eliza, 142; Eliza B., 6; Elizabeth, 17, 18, 24; Esther, 7; Fany Ann, 142; George, 7, 121, 142; Hannah, 142; Isabella, 67; Jacob, 7; James, 72; John, 17, 66, 67; Joseph, 7, 130; Joseph D., 7, 76; Margaret, 100; Margret, 142; Mary, 7, 66, 67; Robert, 72, 100; Sarah, 82, 121; Sarah Dutton, 155; Seth, 24; Susanna, 7; William, 100, 142
BROWNE, A. A., 60, 83; Acquila A., 144; Aquilla A., 43; Frances, 155; Frances Irvine, 155; George Blight, 152; Harriet, 152; James Irvine, 155; John C., 41; Mary A., 43; Peter, 39, 152, 155; Peter A., 152; Rebecca, 49; Thomas, 49; William I., 155
BROWNHULTZ, Eve Maria, 75
BRUCE, Jane, 77; Robert, 77; William, 77
BRUER, Lydia, 80
BRUGIERE, Charles, 136, 140
BRUNER, Sarah, 166; William, 25
BRUSTER, Charles, 161
BRYAN, Elizabeth, 120; Jesse, 50; Joseph, 50; Phoebe, 50
BRYANT, Benjamin F., 132; Deborah, 66; John Y., 66; Margaret, 24; T. I., 117, 131
BUCHANAN, Anne, 90; George, 90; Laetitia, 90; McKean, 91; Thomas McKean, 91
BUCK, George, 82; John, 82, 83; Sarah, 82
BUCKELEW, Mary, 65
BUCKLEY, Anthony M., 13, 66; Anthony Morris, 66; Daniel, 110; Sarah, 66; Sarah P., 66; William, 66
BUDD, George, 45, 111; George K., 111; Susan, 45; Susannah, 111
BUMM, George, 132
BUNCE, Mary Ann, 143
BUNTING, Ann, 109; Nicholas, 8; Philip S., 19, 41
BURBANK, Mary, 137
BURBON, Anne, 23
BURCKHARDT, Daniel, 33; Mary, 33
BURD, Edward, 71; Edward Shippen, 4
BURDEN, Benjamin C., 87; Henry, 94; Joseph, 13; Margaret, 94
BURGEN, George H., 67
BURKE, Thomas, 13
BURKINGHAM, John, 56
BURKLEE, Charlotte, 6; Christian C., 6; Frederick, 6; Mark, 6; Mary, 6; Richard, 6
BURLING, Sarah, 13
BURN, Catharine, 162; Helen, 87; James S., 162; Robert, 162; William, 162
BURNHAM, James, 56, 57; Thomas, 56
BURNS, Catharine, 97, 162;

Helen, 97; James, 44, 111; John, 48; Pheby, 54; Robert, 97; William, 97
BURROWS, Jesse, 81
BURT, Nathaniel, 13
BURTON, Belfast, 115; Robert, 23
BUSSELL, Philip, 111
BUSSIER, Bartholomew, 30; Daniel, 9, 30, 46, 68; John, 30; Susan, 30
BUTCHER, Amos W., 149; Ann, 149; Catharan, 132; Jacob, 127; Job, 149; Mary, 149; Rebecca, 149
BUTLER, James, 81, 162; John, 124
BYRNE, Elizabeth Ann, 76; Gerald, 97; James Murphy, 76; John, 116; Patrick, 122; Patrick John, 76; Redmond, 97
BYRNES, Sarah, 33
BYRON, Benjamin, 154; Charles, 154; Charlotte, 154; Christopher, 154; Elizabeth, 154; George, 154; John, 154; Joshua, 145, 154; Mrs., 73; Samuel, 154; William, 154

-C-

CADWALADER, Thomas, 144; Williamina, 32
CADWALLADER, Elizabeth, 44; Thomas, 31
CAIN, Anthony, 5, 115
CAKE, Joseph, 6, 50
CALAHAN, Hugh, 174
CALDWELL, Charles, 42, 89, 165; Samuel, 23
CALLWELL, Catharine, 22; James, 22; Maria, 23; Nathaniel, 23
CAMBRIDGE, Sarah, 69
CAMERON, Dorathe, 38; John, 38
CAMPBELL, George, 52, 94; Helen, 52, 94; Isabella, 146; James, 146; Mary, 103; Robert H., 127; Robert W., 52; Walter, 44
CAMPION, William, 174
CANBY, Anna, 9; Eli, 44; Elizabeth, 100; James, 10; Martha, 9; Mary, 9; Merrit, 10
CANER, Charles, 74; Michael, 74
CANNAN, Elizabeth, 108
CARLILE, Hudson, 90
CARLL, Maskell M., 93
CARLYLE, Alexander, 56; John, 56; Rachel, 56; William, 56
CARMALT, Caleb, 15, 25, 34, 91, 106, 130, 132, 141, 159, 166; Isaac, 106; James, 106, 131, 132, 166; Jonathan, 25, 106, 115, 132; Mary Ann, 106; Rebecca, 106; Rebekah, 106; Susan, 106
CARMAN, Henry, 54; James, 95; John, 64; Rachel, 95; Sally, 95; Samuel, 95; Sarah, 95; William, 95
CARNEY, Hannah, 120
CARPENTER, Mary, 22
CARR, Ann, 145; Henry, 145; Isabella, 145; John, 145; John Philpot, 146; Mary, 145; Matthew, 168; Morgan, 173; William, 145, 146
CARRELL, Caroline, 122; Charles, 122; Daniel, 122; Edward, 76; John, 97; Maria, 76; Maria E., 122; Thomas, 122
CARRIAGUES, William, 60
CARRIGUE, William, 134
CARROLL, Harriet, 160; Honora, 164
CARRUTHERS, Elizabeth, 127; George, 127
CARSON, Joseph, 143; William, 52
CARTER, Ann, 7; Henry, 171; James, 78; Jasper, 6; John, 7, 147, 171; Joseph, 7; Rebecca, 69, 171; Sharon, 41
CARVER, Assemith, 78; Elizabeth, 78; Franklin, 6; Hannah, 78; Jacob, 6; John, 78; John R., 6; Joseph, 78; Martha, 78; Mary, 78; Sarah, 78
CASAMAJOR, Prudent, 11
CASH, Andrew D., 159, 173
CASNER, John, 52; Susanna, 52
CASSAN, Hannah, 87; Lewis, 87
CASTER, Catharine, 6; Christiana, 6; Elizabeth, 6; George, 6; Hannah, 6; Henry, 6; Isaac, 6; Jacob, 6; John, 6; Mary, 6; Sarah, 6
CASTLES, James, 37, 158
CASTOR, Daniel, 51; Jessey, 114; Samuel, 130
CATHCART, James Leander, 57; Jane L., 103; Robert, 103; Sarah G., 103; Susan, 103
CATHRALL, Ann, 157; Charles, 157; Hannah, 123; Isaac, 123, 157; Mary, 157
CAUFFMAN, Lawrence, 106
CAVALHO, David, 84; Emanuel Nunez, 84; Sarah, 84;

Solomon, 84
CAVENAUGH, Michael, 116
CERAH, Sophia, 146
CHACE, Ann, 43
CHAMBERLAIN, Nathaniel, 163;
  Susannah, 163; William, 99
CHAMBERLIN, Jacob, 129; Mary,
  129
CHAMBERS, Adam, 138; Ann Maria,
  111, 138; Barbara, 138;
  George, 138; Hugh, 117;
  James, 81, 138; Peter, 138;
  William W., 33
CHANDLER, John, 4
CHAPIN, Nathan, 59; Samuel, 59
CHAPMAN, Ann, 34; Clayton, 60;
  James B., 141; John, 34,
  141; Martha, 34; Martha
  Johnson, 34; Nathan, 137;
  Robert, 161; Sarah, 34
CHARLSWORTH, William, 27
CHARPENTIER, Daniel, 140
CHATHAM, 91
CHATTIN, Elizabeth, 123;
  Hannah, 123; Rebecca, 123
CHATWOOD, Rebecca, 80
CHAUDRON, Simon, 44
CHAUNCEY, Charles, 122
CHAUNEY, Charles, 122
CHAURARD, Eugenia, 64; Louis,
  Mrs., 64
CHEEKS, William, 26
CHERRINGTON, William, 78
CHERRY GROVE, 17
CHESNUT, Charles, 85; Mary, 85
CHEVALIER, Ann Mary, 40; Ann
  R., 40; Elizabeth, 48;
  James, 19; Margaret, 40;
  Nicholas, 7; Samuel, 48;
  Susan, 48; Susanna, 48;
  William, 40; William W., 48
CHEVES, Langdon, 120; Mary
  Elizabeth, 120
CHEW, Benjamin, 72, 160;
  Catharine, 160; Elizabeth,
  160; Henrietta, 160; Maria,
  160
CHEYNEY, E. D., 39
CHILD, John, 37
CHILDS, Jonathan Friends, 28
CHRIST, John, 57, 88
CHRISTLER, Jacob, 76, 150
CHRISTMAS, Elizabeth, 120
CHRISTOPHER, Mr., 97
CHRISTY, Hugh, 161
CHRYSTLER, Jacob, 22, 34;
  Sophia, 75
CHURCH, Ann, 14; Elizabeth, 14;
  Isaac, 91
CHURCHMAN, Owen, 62
CLAPHAMSON, Ann, 101; John

181

Fisher, 101; Martha, 101;
  Mary, 101; Samuel, 101
CLAPIER, Francois, 32; Lewis,
  136; Mary, 3
CLARK, Betsey, 120; Catharine,
  31; Diana, 115; Hannah, 80;
  Jane, 80; John, 68, 86, 169;
  Joseph, 144; Lucy, 123;
  Mary, 80, 86, 144; Samuel,
  80; Thomas, 141
CLARKE, John, 109; Mary, 118;
  Peter, 38
CLARKSON, Solomon, 5
CLAWGES, Daniel, 84;
  Wilhelmina, 84
CLAXTON, John, 155
CLAY, Joseph, 125; Mary, 125
CLAYPOOLE, Abraham, 103;
  Abraham G., 3
CLAYPORT, Betsey, 62; John, 62
CLAYTON, Thomas, 171
CLEAVENGER, William S., 123
CLEAVER, Elizabeth, 173; Isaac,
  173; Jesse, 15, 173
CLEMENS, Andrew, 118; Mary, 93
CLEMENT, Ann, 46; Jacob, 51,
  161; James, 46; Mary, 93
CLIFFTON, Hannah, 40; John, 40,
  161; William, 40
CLINE, Ellwood, 158
CLINTON, George C., 26; Robert,
  26; William, 26
CLOPPEN, Mrs., 119
CLOPPER, Ann Jane, 76; Francis
  C., 76; Mrs., 119; Sarah,
  140
CLOSS, Maria Margaret, 51
CLOUD, Joseph, 114
CLOVER, Hager, 5; Plim, 5
CLYMER, Archibald, 108;
  Barbara, 108; Charles, 108;
  Christopher, 108; George,
  71, 100, 108; Jacob, 108;
  Robert, 108
COANE, Robert, 115
COATES, Hannah, 132; Josiah L.,
  50; Mary, 50; Paulina, 132;
  Sarah, 132; Thomas, 74, 132;
  William, 132
COATS, Jacob, 19; Rachel, 112;
  Thomas, 59, 119, 121
COBB, William, 105
COBOURN, George, 143
COCHRAN, Grace, 77; John, 121,
  129, 144; Mariah Delah, 77;
  Richard, 77; Robert, 77;
  Thomas, 77
COE, Barbara, 155
COFFMAN, Barnet, 47; David, 47;
  Jacob, 47; John, 47; Joseph,

47; Margaret, 47; Mary, 47; Rachel, 47
COHEN, A. Myers, 84; Abraham H., 40
COLDWELL, Elizabeth, 95; Joseph, 95; Sarah, 95; Susan, 95
COLE, Nathan William, 145; Rebecca, 145
COLEMAN, Elizabeth, 12; John Adam, 75; Nathaniel, 5, 12
COLESBERRY, John, 137; William H., 137
COLHOUN, Catharine, 173; Catharine Ann, 173
COLLADAY, Jacob, 13
COLLIN, Theophilus, 86
COLLINS, Anthony, 108; Benjamin, 122; Caroline, 122; Cato, 1; Chalkley, 122; Elizabeth, 122; Isabella, 1; James, 108; John, 108; Joshua, 122; Margaret, 108; Mary, 122; Peter, 108; Robert, 165; Thomas, 122; William, 108; Zaccheus, 1
COLLIS, Mary, 99
COLLISON, George, 113
COLLOM, Seth, 14, 55
COLP, Jacob, 29
COLVILL, Nathaniel, 22
COLWELL, George, 12
COMFORT, Beulah, 98; David, 98, 145
COMLY, John, 36, 66; Othniel, 105; Rebecca B., 66; Samuel W., 65
COMPTON, Hannah, 35
CONARD, John, 2; Jonathan, 16, 160, 173
CONE, John Redman, 4
CONNARD, Thomas, 92
CONNARROE, Sarah, 39
CONNELL, Robert, 13
CONNELLY, Anna Maria, 156; Eliza, 156; George, 147; Jacob, 147, 156; John, 43, 120; Margaret, 156; Patrick, 43
CONNOLLY, James, 130; John, 130; Margaret, 130; Thomas, 130
CONNOR, Eleanor, 48; Peter, 48; Thomas G., 141
CONOLLY, John, 130
CONOVER, Lewis H., 164
CONRAD, Anthony, 100; Elijah, 2; Elizabeth, 100; John, 100; Joseph, 100; Mary, 85, 100; Peter, 100
CONSTANTINE, Peter, 38

CONWAY, Bernard, 13; Catherine, 13; Daniel, 13; Harriet, 13; John, 13; Patrick, 13; Sarah N., 13
CONYNGHAM, Gustavus, 173; Redmond, 173
COOCH, William, 113
COOK, Alexander, 148; Elizabeth, 25; John, 81, 172
COOKE, Joel, 154; John, 5, 60; William, 31
COOMBS, David, 104, 130
COONEY, James, 31
COOPER, Benjamin, 13; Mrs., 4; Rachel, 105; Rev., 4; Thomas, 99
COPE, Charles, 168; Godfrey G., 168; Henry, 168; Jaspar, 167; John, 168; Margaret, 168; Mary, 168; Thomas P., 153
CORFIELD, Edward, 158; Edward D., 7, 57
CORNELIUS, Rachael, 107; Samuel, 107
CORNMAN, Joseph, 127
CORNWELL, Catherine, 127
CORRIN, Cato, 5
CORYELL, Sarah, 80
COTTRINGER, Garret, 62, 63
COULTER, John, 24, 38
COURTNEY, Ann, 12; John, 12
COUTTY, Elizabeth, 43
COVERT, Sarah Haines, 88
COWDEN, Samuel, 52
COX, Baines, 38; Benjamin, 81; Gustavus A., 106; John, 38, 123; Joseph, 128; Lydia, 81; Mary Baines, 38; Paul, 126; Rebecca, 38; Samuel, 38
COXE, Daniel W., 11, 33; Edmund G., 62; John, 145; Tench, 62, 130
CRAGG, Frances, 26; George, 26, 119; Thomas, 26; William, 26
CRAIG, Ann, 62; Jane, 62
CRAMMOND, William, 114
CRAMP, George, 78; Martin, 127
CRANE, B. D., 165; William M., 165
CRAWFORD, Alexander, 153; Christina, 153; James, 22; Sarah Ann, 129
CRAWLEY, Edmond I., 174
CREIGHTON, Patrick, 35
CRESS, Eliza, 69; Elizabeth, 108; Esther, 108; George, 39, 108; Isaac, 69; John, 69, 108; Juliana, 108; Lydia, 69; Peter, 69, 108; Rebecca, 108; William, 69

CRESSMAN, Catharine, 22;
    Elizabeth, 22
CRESSON, Annabella, 63; Caleb,
    63; Clement, 63; Deborah,
    63; Elliot, 63; Elliott, 9,
    63; Emlen, 63; John E., 63;
    John Elliott, 9, 35; Mary,
    63; Sarah Emlen, 63; Warder,
    63; William, 63
CRETH, Daniel, 86
CRIM, John H., 125
CRISPEN, Hester, 23; Lydia, 62;
    Mary, 23; Rachael, 23;
    Sarah, 23; William, 23
CRITHER, Adam, 100; George,
    100; Mary, 100; Sarah, 100
CROASDALE, Joseph, 4
CROCK, Anna Maria, 83;
    Bartholomew, 83; Catherine,
    83; Elizabeth, 83; George,
    83; Mary, 83; Michael, 83;
    Rebecca, 83; Susanna, 83
CROCKER, Actius, 85; John, 85
CROMBARGER, John, 77
CRONEN, Eleanor, 19; John, 20
CRONEY, Sarah, 125
CROSBY, Robert P., 58; Sarah,
    58
CROSKEY, Eliza, 125; George,
    125
CROSKY, Sarah, 159
CROTHERS, Jane, 138; John M.,
    138
CROUSILLAT, Louis, 174
CROW, George, 150; Mary, 150;
    Thomas, 150
CROWLEY, John, 169
CROZER, Elizabeth, 38
CROZIER, William, 77
CRUCKSHANK, Rachel, 80
CRUKSHANK, Joseph, 5, 15, 106;
    Rachel, 5, 54
CRUMLEY, Henry, 1
CRUSIN, William, 61
CUCH, William, 113
CULLMAN, Adam, 104; John A.,
    10, 145
CULNAN, Charles, 142; Margaret,
    142
CUMPSTON, Thomas, 41, 60
CUNNINGHAM, Ellen, 55; Lilly,
    13; Matthew, 22; Robert, 22;
    Sarah, 22
CURRY, Christopher, 19;
    Eleanor, 19; Elizabeth, 19;
    George, 19; James, 19; James
    King, 19; Jane, 19; John,
    19; Mary, 19; Thomas, 19;
    William, 19
CURTIS, Abigail, 39; Margaret,
    39; Samuel J., 85

CUTBUSH, James, 130
CUTHBERT, Ann Jane, 103;
    Anthony, 2, 77; Mary, 77;
    Sarah, 103; Susanna, 103;
    Thomas, 103
CYRIER, Jean Louis, 32

–D–
DA COSTA, Francis, 147
DACE, Adam, 52; Elizabeth, 52
DAILY, Bernerd, 144
DALGELL, Elizabeth, 150
DALLAS, Alexander, 73;
    Alexander James, 73;
    Arabella Maria, 73; George,
    73; Maria, 73; Matilda, 73;
    Sophia, 73; Trevanion, 73
DALRYMPLE, Jane, 126
DALTON, Andrew, 163; Mrs., 163
DALZELL, Jane, 77; William, 135
DANACKER, Christiana, 65
DANCE, Josiah, 119; Matilda,
    119; Sarah, 119
DANIELS, Sarah, 132
DARBLEY, Catharina Elizabeth,
    68
DARCH, Samuel, 143
DARLAND, Elizabeth, 57
DARRACH, Charlotte, 42;
    Elizabeth, 42; Ellen, 42;
    James, 41, 42; Mary, 42;
    Samuel Fisher, 42; Sarah,
    42; Thomas B., 42; Thomas
    Bradford, 42; William, 42
DARRAGH, John, 125
DAVAN, James, 80; Kingsmill,
    79; Margaret, 80; Mary, 80
DAVID, David, 130
DAVIDS, Sarah, 20
DAVIES, Amos, 43; Edward, 124
DAVIS, Asa, 77; Catharine, 77;
    Catherine, 58; Catherine C.,
    58; Elizabeth, 77; Isaac,
    48, 129; Jesse, 62, 77, 149;
    John, 29; Liha, 66; Mary,
    21; Noah, 28; Rebecca, 62;
    Samuel Wetherill, 62; Sarah,
    29; Timothy, 62; William, 83
DAWES, Deborah, 62, 99;
    Rebecca, 62; Sybil, 61, 62
DAWSON, Ann P., 86; Anne, 50;
    Elizabeth, 50; Esther, 155;
    Josiah, 143, 155; Mordecai
    L., 156; Mordecai Lewis, 50;
    Rebecca, 155; Robert, 50,
    143, 155; William, 50
DAYMAN, Francis, 145
DAYMON, Joseph, 158
DE COLVILLE, Madame, 147
DE DAUZY, Mr., 147
DE LA ROCHE, Mary G., 152

DE MIS, Don Luis, 151
DE VIAR, Don Ignacio Francisco, 151; Ignacio, 151
DE YRUJO, Charles Ferdinand, 91
DEAL, Anna, 27; Anne, 155; Charles, 27; Daniel, 135, 155; Elizabeth, 27; Jacob, 22, 27, 155; John, 27, 155; Mary, 27, 155; Michael, 27, 29; Peter, 30, 135, 155; Sarah, 155; Simon Peter, 27; Susanna, 27; William, 155
DEALCART, Ann, 170; Barbara, 169; Catherine, 169; Christiana, 170; Elizabeth, 169; Margaret, 170; Nancy, 169; Peter, 169, 170; Susanna, 170
DEAVE, Agnes, 39
DEAVES, Abraham, 164
DEBEAUREGARD, James Charles Lambert, 135; Sophia Pickel, 135
DEBENNEVILLE, George, 96
DEBLER, Catharine, 75
DEBROT, John, 133
DECKART, Hannah, 6; John, 6
DECKER, Peter I., 46; Peter J., 68
DECOW, Mary, 12
DEDAMSEAUX, Albartine, 126; Jacque Remark, 126
DEDIER, William, 93
DEFNEY, George Jacob, 117; Jacob, 117
DEGROFEY, Albartine, 126; Charles, 126
DEHAVEN, Amelia, 39; Atlee, 39; Emma Maria, 39; Harriet, 39; Hugh, 39; Peter, 39; Sarah Rawle, 39; William, 60
DEIMLING, Ernst Frederick, 164; Francis Christopher, 164; Francis G., 115, 164; Maria Gertrauda, 164; Wilhelm Gotfreed, 164
DEIMS, John, 105
DELANY, James W., 79; William, 71, 79
DELAVAU, Ann, 24; Barbara, 23, 24; Hannah, 23, 24; Isaac, 24; John, 23; Margaret, 24; Maria, 24; Susan, 23, 24
DEMPSEY, James, 171; John, 31
DENCKLA, Christian H., 136
DENMAN, Aaron, 120; Anna Maria, 51
DENN, David, 109
DENNIS, Michael, 142
DENNISON, Archibald, 90; Marcus, 57

DENNY, Richard, 150
DENOON, David, 140; George G., 140
DENTIS, Surgend, 113
DEPERVAIN, Catharine, 11; Henry, 11; Margaret, 11; Mary, 11; Peter, 11; Sophia, 11; Susanna, 11
DEPREFONTAINE, John, 74, 6, 35, 116, 156
DESPENCER, Catherine, 66
DEVIAR, Don Jose Ignacio, 151
DEVINE, Keziah, 58
DEWEES, Charles, 24; Eleanor, 45; William, 45
DEWITT, Margaret, 149
DIAMOND, Barbara, 169; John, 145
DICHER, Venus, 115
DICK, Elizabeth, 162
DICKERSON, Elizabeth, 22
DICKINSON, Cadwalader, 38; Elizabeth, 154; Nathan, 165; Phoebe, 162
DICKS, Abel, 139
DICKSON, Joseph, 168; William, 115
DICKUS, Peter, 142
DIEHL, Nicholas, 28, 119
DIETZ, Henry, 16; Magdalen, 16
DIFFIELD, Mary, 3
DILCART, Barbara, 165; Betsey, 165; Catharina, 165; Christiana, 165; John, 165; Margaret, 165; Nancy, 165; Peter, 165; Susannah, 165
DILHORN, Sarah Ann, 122
DILLINGHAM, T. W. F., 48
DILLON, James, 82
DILLWORTH, Joseph, 164; Rachael, 164
DILLWYN, George, 123
DILWORTH, Ann, 46; James, 46
DIXON, Margaret, 18
DOBSON, Henry, 72; J., 61; Rachel, 72; Thomas, 56, 92, 98; William, 72
DOLP, Elizabeth, 53
DOMETT, Joseph N., 117
DONALDSON, David, 33; Elen Mary, 33; Hugh, 52; Jane, 122; John, 33, 62; Mary, 52
DONATH, Joseph, 167, 168
DONLEVY, John, 42
DONLEY, James, 31
DONNAKER, George, 4
DONNALDSON, Hugh, 94; John, 94; Mary, 94; Sarah, 94
DONNELL, Benjamin L., 121; Edmund, 111; James Cochran, 121; Mary F., 121;

Nathaniel, 121
DONOVAN, Catharine, 11; Daniel, 11; Florence, 11; Frances, 11; Henry, 11; Jeremiah, 11; Margaret, 11; William, 80
DORAN, Michael, 5
D'ORBIGNY, Ls. de Mons, 64
DORBIGNY, Ls. DeMons, 64
DORLAND, Isaac, 2
DORRANCE, Mrs., 119; Sarah, 93, 119
DORSEY, Mary, 116
DOUGHERTY, Daniel, 96; George, 171; John, 96; Mary, 96; Michael, 96; Owen, 96; Roger, 96; Thomas, 10, 96, 141; William, 37
DOUGHTY, Ann, 149; Elizabeth, 32
DOUGLASS, Ann, 8; George, 78; Jacob M., 78; Maria, 78
DOWERS, Edward, 26; Elizabeth Catharine, 26; Jane, 26; John, 26; Kitty, 26; Mary, 26; Mary Ann, 26; Mary Thornton, 26; Matilda, 26; Nicholas, 120; Susan, 26
DOWNING, Hunt, 93; Israel W., 93; Jacob, 29; Sarah Sandwith, 29
DOWNS, Catharine, 38
DOYLE, Joseph B., 115; Sarah, 115; Walter, 51; William, 115
DREER, Frederic, 154
DRINKER, Henry, 114; Henry S., 29; John, 107, 108; Mary, 107; Rebecca, 107, 108; William, 29
DROSDOFF, Charles A., 110
DRUM, William, 93
DRUMMOND, John K., 87
DU PLESSIS, Peter Mary Le Barbier, 32
DUANE, William, 55; William I., 61, 143; William J., 55; William S., 61
DUBARRY, John, 32, 136; Sophia A., 32
DUDGSON, John, 134
DUFFIELD, Amos, 3; Elizabeth, 3; Hannah, 3; Jacob, 3; Jesse, 3; John, 3; Tacy, 3; Thomas, 130
DUFFUS, Andrew, 166; Janet, 166
DUFFY, Bell, 96
DUGAN, James R., 123; Mary, 99
DUGDALE, Thomas, 164
DUKE, John, 116
DULLES, Joseph, 120; Joseph Heatley, 120; Joseph Heatly, 120; Mary Elizabeth, 120; Sophia, 120
DUNCAN, Benjamin, 124; Isabelle, 1; James, 144
DUNGAN, Benjamin, 55; Elizabeth, 55; George, 55; James Reed, 55; Jesse, 55; John, 174; Joseph, 55; Josiah, 55; Little, 55; Mariah, 55; Mary, 55; Samuel, 55
DUNLAP, Anna, 152; James, 152; Juliana, 152; Margaretta, 152; Mary, 152; Thomas, 152
DUNLOP, Catherine, 53
DUNN, Philip I., 6, 136; Philip T., 41
DUNNOT, Catharine, 16; George, 16
DUNPHY, John, 70
DUNTON, George, 56
DUPUY, Daniel, 10; John, 10; Kitty, 26; William, 26
DURFOR, George, 73, 167
DUTTON, Mary, 24
DUVAL, James S., 136
DUVE, Alice C., 67; Samuel, 67
DUY, John K., 60, 98, 165
DWARF, Jane, 7
DYKES, Cynthia, 38; Daniel, 38
DYRE, James, 130

-E-

EALER, Mary M., 44
EARLE, Edward, 72
EARNEST, Henry, 135
EASLY, Ann, 30
ECKERT, Charles, 165; Hannah, 3; Margaret, 165; Philip, 3
ECKFELDT, Adam, 8, 114; Elizabeth, 114; George, 114; Jacob, 113; John, 114; Juliana, 114; Michael, 114; Sarah, 114
ECKFELT, Juliana, 114
ECKY, John, 150
EDENBORN, Benjamin, 157; Catharine, 157; Elizabeth, 157; Harriett, 157; Jacob, 41, 61, 157; Joseph, 157; Louisa, 157; Margaret, 157; Mary, 157; Peter, 157; Philip, 157; Samuel, 157
EDEY, Julia, 26; Julian, 26; Juliann, 62; Richard T. A., 62; Richard Thomas Atkins, 26; Simmons, 62
EDWARDS, Enoch C., 174; Frances, 139; Griffith, 110
EGBIRD, John, 120; Lawrence, 120

EGER, Sarah, 73
EHRENSTROM, Andrew Frederic, 33; Catharina Petrosina Eliz., 33
ELDRIDGE, Dorcas, 109; Margaretta, 133; Phineas, 97
ELFREE, Samuel, 83
ELFRETH, Isaac C., 157; John, 157
ELFRITH, Jeremiah, 109; Sarah, 109
ELKEN, Abraham, 67
ELKINS, Abraham, 67; Eve, 67
ELLICOTT, Andrew, 171; Hannah, 171
ELLIOT, Daniel, 99; Elizabeth, 87; John, 99; Mary, 58
ELLIOTT, Daniel, 171; Dianah, 5; George, 140; Isaac, 5, 9, 92, 147, 166; Jane, 51; John, 20, 69, 171; John Mades, 5; Maria, 140; Samuel, 63
ELLIS, Charlotte, 70; Daniel C., 22; Hannah, 125
ELLISON, John B., 168; Robert, 97
ELMSLEY, Alexander, 88
ELMSLIE, Hannah, 13, 48; John, 13, 48; Sarah, 13
ELY, Ezra Stiles, 138
EMERICK, Charlotte, 51
EMERY, Ann, 55; Elizabeth, 55; Frederick, 55; Jacob, 55; John, 55; Maria, 55; Stephen, 28; Susan, 55
EMLEN, Anne, 42; Jeremiah, 161; Samuel, 123, 145; Sarah, 63
EMSLIE, Elizabeth, 13
ENDRESS, Susanna, 153
ENEU, James, 111
ENGARD, Elizabeth, 128; Henry, 128; James, 128; Mary, 128; Rachel, 128
ENGLAND, Mary, 123
ENGLE, Ann, 43; Charles, 43; Cornelius, 42; Elizabeth, 43; Francis, 27; James, 27, 43; John, 42, 43; Joseph, 27; Julian, 27; Juliann, 43; Silas, 27; Susanna, 42
ENGLES, Henry, 34, 38, 46
ENGLISH, Elisha N., 56; George, 35
ENNET, David, 100
ERBEN, Henry, 108; Rebecca, 108
ERDMAN, Charles, 157
ERDMANN, Charles, 153
ERRINGER, Jacob, 94
ERSKINE, David Montagu, 32; Thomas, 32

ERVINE, James, 154
ERWIN, Caspar, 67; Catherine, 67
ESHER, George, 83
ESHERICK, David, 167; Joseph, 167
ESLER, William, 114
ETIENNE, Agnes, 32
ETRIS, Catharine, 120; Elizabeth, 120; James, 120; John, 120; Joseph, 120; Mary, 120; Rachel, 120
ETTING, Fanny, 6
EVANS, Abigail, 81; Ann, 163; Barbara, 100; Cadwalader, 163; Charles, 84, 109, 159; Charlotte, 79; David, 84; Deborah, 81; Edward, 130; Elizabeth, 163; Evan, 54; George, 163; Gulielma, 84; Hannah, 1, 109; Hetty, 163; Isaiah, 100; Joel, 109; John, 1; John C., 59, 91; Jonathan, 81, 84, 109; Joseph, 109; Josiah, 82; Mary, 84, 109; Nathan, 137; Oliver, 163; Owen, 163; Rachel, 163; Rebecca S., 130; Sarah, 163; Thomas, 109; William, 109
EVENS, Elizabeth, 20; John B., 38; Rebecca, 20
EVERS, Amelia, 154; Breidenhart, 154; Maria, 154
EVIL, John, 152
EWEN, Robert, 95
EWING, Edward, 49; Eleanor, 49; Eliza, 159; Ellen, 159; John, 49; Joseph, 49; Magdalen, 49; Samuel, 49, 119, 159; Sarah, 49
EYRE, Ann K., 161; Elizabeth, 161; Elizabeth K., 161; Emma K., 161; George, 112; Hannah, 26, 49, 50, 169; John, 112; Joseph K., 161; L. W., 124; Lydia, 47; Lydia W., 138, 149, 167; Manuel, 111, 120; Maria, 161; Nathan, 161; Nathan W., 162; Sarah K., 161

-F-
FALCONER, Catharine, 45; Nathaniel, 15; Sarah, 15
FALLAR, Betzey, 164; Caspar, 164; Catharina, 164
FANELL, Edward, 82
FARIS, William, 90
FARTHING, Ann, 38; Catharine, 38; David, 38; James, 38,

113
FASOON, Susan, 3
FASSITT, James, 60
FAUSSETT, Jane, 109
FAWCETT, William, 80
FEGUSON, Ebenezer, 54
FELL, Jonathan, 99
FELLOWS, Mr., 4; Mrs., 4
FELTER, John, 53
FELTY, Ernst, 117
FENTON, Eliazer, 141
FERGUSON, Ebenezer, 107
FERRIS, Benjamin, 1; Fanny, 9
FIELD, Elizabeth, 51; Peter, 103
FIELDING, Esther, 41; Robert, 41
FIFE, Thomas, 32; William, 37
FINLEY, Anthony, 174
FIRTH, Preston C., 16
FIRTNER, William, 104
FISHER, Ann, 13; Elizabeth, 156; Elizabeth P., 144; Hannah, 119, 151; Jabaez Maud, 151; James, 13; John, 6, 13; John N., 124; Lydia, 52, 151; Martin, 155; Mary, 95, 99, 156; Miers, 2, 5, 38, 52, 151; Redwood, 52, 99, 151; Robert K., 86; Samuel R., 151; Samuel W., 29, 151; Sarah Redwood, 5, 151; Thomas, 35, 121; William W., 171
FITLER, Elizabeth, 129; William, 129
FITZGERALD, Kernan, 73; Thomas, 82
FITZGIBBONS, John, 147
FITZSIMONS, Christopher, 53, 54
FLAHERTY, Daniel, 31; John, 31; Margaret, 31; Mary, 31
FLECHER, Thomas H., 126
FLECKENSTIN, Samuel, 68
FLEMING, Alexander, 157; Rachel, 157
FLETCHER, Hannah, 152; Thomas, 59
FLICKWIR, David, 85; Rebecca, 85
FLINTHAM, Susan, 104; William, 104
FLORENCE, David, 58; Sarah, 58
FLOWER, Caroline, 34; Henrietta, 29; John, 34; Richard, 29
FLOWERS, Elizabeth, 160; Emeline, 160; George, 160; Hannah, 160; James, 160; John, 160; Margaret, 49; Sarah, 160; Thomas, 49

FLUCK, Adam, 169; Catharine, 169
FOGEL, Margaret, 104
FOLK, Martin, 97
FOLLAR, Caspar, 100
FOLWELL, William, 51
FORBES, James, 75; Mary, 75
FORD, Jacob, 8
FORDE, Ann, 137; Ellen, 137; Margaret, 137; Mary, 137; Sarah, 45, 137; Standish, 137
FOREPAUGH, Andrew, 110; Frederick, 36, 37; George, 110; Margaret, 110
FORGET, Mr., 64; Mrs., 64
FORST, Abraham, 161
FORSYTH, Isaac, 107, 153
FORTEN, James, 143
FORTUNE, Patrick, 78
FOULK, Caleb, 35; Charles, 35; Hannah, 35; Jane, 35
FOULKE, Caleb, 35, 36; Catharine, 94; Charles, 36; Jane, 35; Lowry, 35; Mary, 20
FOULKROD, George, 78; John, 136
FOX, George, 6, 103, 123; Hannah, 94; Margaret, 91; Margarett, 132; Mary, 103; Samuel, 21; Serick, 55, 56; Zerech, 2
FOY, Michael, 35
FRAILEY, John, 37
FRALEY, Henry, 28; John, 28; Susanna, 28
FRANCIS, Francis, 51; Molly M., 40; Sarah, 130; Susanna M., 40; Turbut, 130
FRANK, George, 48; John, 75
FRANKLIN, Walter S., 57
FREAS, Harriett, 37; Joseph, 37; Mary Ann, 37; Rachel, 37; Sarah, 37
FREE, Sarah R., 67
FREED, Anthony, 18
FRENCH, Charles, 78; Charles C., 122; Samuel, 164
FRENCH & HOPSON, 97
FRESHWATER, Argyle, 3
FREYMUTH, William, 102
FREYTAG, Michael, 74
FRICKE, Catharine, 106; Frederick, 27
FRIEL, John, 47
FRITEZ, Sarah, 158
FROUST, Henry, 21
FRY, Jacob, 75; John, 76
FULLER, Barshe, 97; Dille, 97
FULLMER, John, 99
FULMER, John, 83, 95

FULTON, Rachel, 100
FUREY, Carpenter, 17; Charles, 17; John S., 17
FURZE, Ann, 158; James, 158
FYAN, Catherine, 47; John, 47
FYE, Andrew, 3; Elizabeth, 3; Philip, 3; Sophy, 3

-G-
GALBRAITH, Peter, 86
GALBREATH, Patrick, 149; Robert, 169
GALE, Anthony, 10
GALLAHER, William, 67
GALLE, Frederick, 174; George Nicholas, 174; Maria Esther, 174
GALLEY, Ann Catherine, 73; Catherine, 73
GALLOWAY, Jane, 97, 162
GAMBLE, Anna, 45
GARDNER, Jacob, 104, 137, 145; Mary Magdalen, 145; Valentine, 144
GARESCHI, Gabriel, 147
GARRETSON, Adelade, 148; Anne, 148; Eliakim, 69; Hannah, 148; John, 148; Lydia, 147; Lydia Ann, 148; Thomas, 148
GARRETT, Anne B., 75; Joseph, 153; Mary Anne, 75
GARRIGUES, Abraham, 8; Benjamin P., 13; Edward, 54, 73; Elizabeth, 13; Hannah, 25; Isaac, 25; William, 25, 60, 141
GARRITT, John, 11
GASKILL, Peter, 106
GAUCHIER, I., 115
GAUL, Frederick, 104
GAW, Gilbert, 173
GAY, Sarah, 97
GEARY, Catherine, 51
GED, Margary, 62
GEDDEN, Henry, 160; Mary, 161
GEDDES, Henry, 103; Margaret, 103; Sophia, 103
GEIGER, George, 49
GELEY, Peter, 40
GEORGE, Edward, 165; Joseph, 114; Mary, 38
GERHARD, Conrad, 7, 15, 16; Elizabeth, 7; William, 7, 72
GERRATY, Mary, 165
GERRITT, John, 101
GETCHEL, Joseph, 120
GEYER, Andrew, 46, 94; John, 41, 46
GIBBONS, George W., 34; Joseph, 42, 84, 109, 157
GIBBS, Josiah W., 70

GIBSON, Ann, 43; Hannah, 120; James, 4, 17, 18, 27, 43, 71; John, 89, 106, 151; Perry, 128; Samuel, 89, 151; William, 18
GIFFORD, Elizabeth, 65; Mary, 118
GILBERT, Charles, 127; Jacob, 169; Jesse, 125; Joshua, 66; Lydia, 125; Mary, 118; Sarah Ann, 118; Thomas, 102, 118
GILLAM, Anna, 9, 59; Simon, 9, 59
GILLCHRIST, Charles, 70; Lucretia, 70
GILLICHAN, George, 146, 155; Mary, 147, 155
GILLMER, Elizabeth, 51
GILLMORE, Mary, 51
GILPIN, Dynes, 37; Thomas, 151
GIVEN, E. I., 64
GLASKO, George, 113
GLASS, Samuel, 158
GLENTWORTH, George, 12
GLENWORTH, James, 67
GODDARD, Ann, 26; Arthur, 26; Martha, 26
GOLDER, Margaret M., 107
GOOD, Jacob, 48, 52
GOODIN, Jacob, 141; John, 49
GOODMAN, Charles, 36; John, 27, 104
GOODWIN, Elizabeth, 16; James, 16; John, 47; Susan, 16
GORDON, Abigail, 54; Alexander, 23; Jane, 23; Samuel, 23; Thomas, 157
GORE, Rebecca, 114
GORGAS, Benjamin, 164; George, 53
GORSUCH, Hannah, 38; Lydia, 38; Sarah, 38
GOSNER, Christiana, 124; David, 124; George, 124
GOTTREU, Christiana, 164
GOTWOLLS, George, 98; Mary, 98
GOUGE, Edward C., 35; John, 103
GOURLEY, Elizabeth, 107; John, 107
GOVETT, William G., 112
GRACE, Mary, 142
GRAFF, Elizabeth, 108; Henry, 108
GRAFTON, Woodbridge, 31
GRAGIN, Charles, 5
GRAHAM, Abigail, 30; Ann, 145; Gallant, 145; James, 67, 147, 150; John, 101; Thomas, 143; William, 29, 109
GRAMBO, Christian, 159; Edmond, 159; Elizabeth, 159; Henry,

159
GRANT, Alexander, 119; Eleanor, 119; John, 149; Robert, 78
GRAS, Jacques, 136; Jeane Marie, 136
GRASBERY, Catharine, 76
GRATZ, Benjamin, 6; Hyman, 6; Joseph, 6; Rachel, 6; Rebecca, 6; Sarah, 6; Simon, 6
GRAVEL, Henry, 39
GRAVENSTINE, John K., 112
GRAVES, Rosewell, 22
GRAVIER, Brunaut, 140; Jean, 140; Joseph, 140; Maria, 140; Napoleon, 140; Rini, 140
GRAVY, Elizabeth, 74; Henry, 74
GRAY, Christiana, 6; Davis, 93; George, 21; James, 58; Jane, 21; John, 21, 107; Nancy, 21; Sophia, 98; William, 6, 21
GREAVEN, John, 25
GREAVES, Alexander, 171
GREEBLE, James, 103
GREEN, Ann, 36; Ann Wharton, 45; Ashbel, 92, 156; Christiana, 156; Eleanor, 109; John, 36, 58; Mary, 36; Peter, 36, 37; Robert, 8; Robert C., 123; Thomas, 1; Zilpha, 97
GREEVES, Mary Emlen, 161; Thomas, 67, 82, 161
GREGORS, Elizabeth, 145
GREGORY, Asor L., 53; William, 15
GREINER, Euphrosina, 34; Frederick, 25; John, 34, 122, 136, 148; Susanna, 33
GREW, David, 86; George, 86; Rachel, 86; Sarah, 86; Theophilus, 86
GRIFFIN, Betsy, 36; Elizabeth, 36; John, 137; Mary, 36; Peter, 36
GRIFFITH, Catharine, 103; Catherine, 112; Isaac, 103; John R., 82; Robert Egglesfield, 73; William, 21, 137, 152
GRIFFITS, Samuel Powel, 99
GRIFFITTS, Elizabeth, 146; Hannah, 99; James, 99; Mary, 146; Nathaniel, 146; Samuel Powel, 146
GRIMER, Joseph, 74
GRINNEL, Elizabeth, 85; William, 85
GRINNELL, William, 85, 112

GROVER, Euphrosina, 34
GROVES, Arminilla, 162; John, 143
GUENAT, John B., 151; Margaret, 151
GUIAZA BROTHERS AND CO., 97
GUICHARD, Lusetta, 64; Lusette, 64; Rose, 64
GUIER, William, 98
GUIREY, Daniel, 145
GUMBEE, William Hy., 62
GUMBES, Rebecca, 62
GURNEY, Francis, 17; Henry, 32; Mary, 17
GUYER, Casper, 117

-H-
HAAS, Frederick, 27, 58, 69, 134
HABBICK, Henry, 100; Sarah, 100
HABERMEHL, Henry, 115
HADOCK, Henry, 37; James, 37; John, 37; Margaret, 37
HAGA, Catharine, 83; Polly, 83; William, 83
HAGNER, Catharine, 150
HAHN, John, 142
HAILER, Christiana, 8, 116; David, 8; Frederick, 8; George Frederick, 8; Mary, 8
HAINES, Caspar W., 8; Catharina, 135; Catharine, 135; Daniel, 135; Daniel Trotter, 39; Elizabeth, 135; Ephraim, 39; Henry, 135; Jacob, 135; John, 105, 135; Michael, 135; Peter, 86, 135; Reuben, 20; Sarah, 135
HAINS, Frederick, 70; Mary M., 70
HALFPENNY, Francis, 94; James, 94; Jane, 94; Mark, 94; Rachel, 94
HALL, Benjamin, 81; Charles, 6; Harrison, 49; James, 165; Jane, 165; John, 165; Mahlon, 165; Martha Ann, 148; Sarah, 165; Thomas M., 76
HALLOWELL, Elizabeth, 41; Jesse T., 22; John, 13, 31, 151; 161; Rachel, 41; William, 103
HALSTEAD, Isaac Israel, 117
HAMBLER, George, 136; Sarah, 136
HAMEL, James, 158; Littleton W., 158; Polly, 158; Rosanna, 158; Samuel, 158
HAMILTON, Alexander, 75; David, 54; James, 86; John W., 102;

Susanna, 150; William, 4, 97
HAMMER, John, 48; Mary, 48
HAMMOND, Elijah, 28; William, 56
HAMON, Louis, 63; Mrs., 63; William, 63
HAMPTON, Jonathan, 51; Nancy, 51; Susanna, 134
HANCHMAN, John, 19
HANCKEL, Ann Dorothea Maria, 3; Anna Dorethy Henrietta, 2; Anna Dorethy Maria, 2; Christian, 2; John Michael, 2
HANCOCK, William, 72
HANNIS, Andrew, 1
HANNOLD, Georg, 50
HANSE, Samuel, 58
HANSEL, Charles F., 161
HANSELL, Deborah, 174; Ellen, 137; George, 174; Hester, 174; John, 65; Richard, 174; William S., 137
HANSER, Barbara, 136; Jacob, 136
HANTZEL, Jacob, 136
HARBERGER, Henry, 51; Henry S., 51
HARBESON, Benjamin, 92; Mary, 92
HARCH, Margaret, 35
HARDING, Mary, 9
HARE, Charles, 144; Charles W., 144; Charles W., Mrs., 144; George E., 144; James, 144; Margaret, 144; Margaretta, 144; Martha, 144; Miss, 144; Mrs., 144; Robert, 144; Robert, Mrs., 144; Sarah E., 144; William B., 144
HARGESHEIMER, George, 51
HARKER, Joseph, 19
HARKES, George, 135
HARLAN, Alice, 69; Elisha, 69; Hannah, 51, 69; Rebecca, 69
HARLAND, Hannah, 119; John, 154
HARLIN, Samuel, 56
HARMAN, Charlotte, 76; Jacob, 50; Susanna, 3
HARMER, Eliza, 137
HARNER, Jacob, 30
HARPER, David, 152; Jacob, 22; James, 125; John B., 59; John P., 5, 31, 78, 128, 145; Nathan, 131, 132; Thomas, 33; William, 152
HARRAN, Niell, 13; Timothy, 13
HARRIS, Jane, 11; John, 11; Samuel, 100
HARRISON, Charlotte, 34; Elizabeth Dawson, 34;

George, 90; Henry, 90; Matthias, 90; Rebecca, 90; Robert, 34; Ruth, 34, 35; Thomas, 34, 146
HARROW, David, 120; Edmund, 120; George, 120; Marcey, 120; Mary, 120
HART, Catharine, 166; Charles, 84; James M., 46; John, 148, 166; John S., 166; Rebecca, 166; Seymour, 165; Thomas, 19; Widow, 123
HARTLEY, John M., 135; Juliana, 108
HARTLY, Joseph, 113
HARTMAN, John, 142
HARVEY, Edward, 39; John, 139, 141; Margaret, 39; Richard Jones, 39; William, 9
HASLETT, James, 23; Jane, 23; William, 57
HASSALL, Joseph, 72
HASTINGS, John, 80, 81; Rebecca, 81
HATTON, Benjamin, 134; John, 134; Sarah, 134; Susanna, 134; Thomas, 134
HAWK, Christian, 49
HAWKESWORTH, Lydia, 122
HAWKINS, Henry, 38; William, 86
HAWLEY, George W., 57
HAWTHORN, Eliza, 47
HAY, Catharine, 22; Eliza, 75; Francis, 22, 108; Frederick Augustus, 108; John, 21, 75; Lawrence Herbert, 22; Mary, 75; Michael, 75; Mrs., 75; Rickey, 6; William, 22, 75
HAYDOCK, Eden, 138; Elizabeth W., 138; Henry, 138; Martha W., 138; Mary, 138; Mary Ash, 138; Samuel, 54, 138; Susanna, 138
HAYES, Catharine, 18
HAYHURST, Cuthbert, 78
HAYS, John, 117
HAZARD, Abigail, 88; Ebenezer, 88; Elizabeth, 88; Erskine, 88; Mary, 145; Rowland, 145; Samuel, 88
HEARN, Anthony, 96; Sarah Jenkins, 96
HEATH, Andrew, 110; Barbara, 110
HEAVILAND, Stephen, 131
HEBERTON, Dr., 119
HEFT, Casper, 121
HEIMER, Christina, 104
HEIS, Christian, 129
HEISTER, Daniel J., 147
HEISZ, Frederick, 84; Henry, 84

HEIT, Augusta Maria, 14; Peter, 14
HELER, Catharine, 44; Philip, 44
HELLINGS, Rebecca, 45, 153
HELM, Adam, 112; Maria Dorothy, 112
HELMUTH, Catharine, 98; Ch., 14; Henry K., 98; John K., 98
HELT, Mary, 65
HEMPHILL, Elizabeth, 65; Jane, 90
HEMSLEY, Anna Maria, 71; Elizabeth, 71, 72; Maria Lloyd, 72; Philemon, 72; Richard, 72; Thomas, 71, 72
HENDERSON, Davis, 68; James, 105; John, 68, 78; Stephen, 134
HENDRICKSON, Isaac, 150
HENNESEY, Michael, 149; Thomas, 32
HENNESSY, Thomas, 65
HENNESY, Thomas, 12
HENRIKEL, Jacob, 83; Wilhelmina, 83
HENRY, Eliza, 90, 91; I., 14; Sarah, 70
HENSON, Mary Ann, 63
HERAUD, Augustin, 32
HERBERT, Lawrence, 75; Mary, 75; William, 32
HERIGES, John I., 110
HERITAGE, Catherine, 34; Enoch, 105; Esther, 105; Kezia, 70; William, 34
HERMAN, Ann Maria, 88; Catharine, 87; Catherine, 74; John C., 74; Mary, 87; William, 87, 88, 107
HERRIGES, Bennett, 129
HERRINGS, Barbara, 129
HERTZOG, Peter, 104
HESLER, Mary, 30; William, 30
HESSON, Mary, 167
HESTER, Conrad, 126
HESTON, Elizabeth, 100; Matilda, 165; Sarah, 165
HEWIT, Abijah, 149
HEWITT, Ann, 157; Caroline, 157; Catharine, 157; Elizabeth, 149; Emaline, 149; George, 157; Juliana, 157; Louisa, 157; Margaret, 157; Margaretta, 157; Shamgar, 149
HEWLINGS, Hester, 15
HEYBERGER, Jacob, 66
HEYDELL, Leonard, 129
HEYDRICK, Christopher, 51

HEYL, Dorothy, 3; Elizabeth, 3; George, 3, 57, 132; Mary, 3; Susanna, 3; William, 3
HEYLER, Peter, 69, 168
HEYLIN, Isaac, 2, 121
HIBBARD, Sarah, 89
HIBBS, Agnes, 102; Mahlon, 102
HICKEY, Lavinia, 118, 136; Margaret, 120; Michael, 120
HIGBY, Charles, 127
HIGGINS, Fanny, 5; Francis, 132; Hannah, 132
HILBORN, Robert, 4
HILBORNE, Amos, 145
HILDEBURN, Samuel, 110
HILE, John, 137
HILL, Charles, 21; Eliza, 58; Jacob, 41; Jeremiah, 40; John H., 41, 58; William, 71
HILLBORN, Amos, 4; Elizabeth, 42; Robert, 4; Ruth, 145
HILLEGAS, Joseph K., 151
HILLIN, John, 140
HILVERSON, Elizabeth, 55
HIMER, Mercy, 34
HINCKLE, John, 65
HINKLE, Anna, 74; Barbara, 74; Elizabeth, 74; Henry, 74; Jacob, 74; Susanna, 74
HOBSON, Ann, 168
HOCKLEY, Eleanor, 41, 59, 60; Mary, 41; Thomas, 60
HODGDON, Benjamin, 156; Elizabeth, 156; Jane, 156; Mary, 156; Robert, 105; Samuel, 156
HODGE, Henry, 131
HOE, Barbara, 98; Eliza, 98; George, 98; Jacob, 98; John, 98; Mary, 98
HOECKLEY, Frederick, 58, 74; Jacob F., 157, 160
HOECKLY, Frederick, 27
HOFF, Catherine, 57; Elizabeth, 57; George, 57; Henry, 57; Jacob, 57; John, 57
HOFFECKEN, John, 145
HOFFMAN, Ann Catharine, 12; David, 174; Elizabeth, 135; George, 12; John, 12; John H., 62; Maria, 12; Maria Phillipbina, 12; Mary, 12; Samuel, 12; Sebastian, 135; Sophia, 12; William, 12, 37; Wolfgang, 12
HOKERSPIRE, George, 34
HOLAHAN, Amos, 18
HOLLAND, Ann, 156; Charles, 156; Nathaniel, 97, 98
HOLLICK, Charles, 69
HOLLINGSHEAD, Edmund I., 152

HOLME, Thomas, 19, 55
HOLMES, Gabriel, 17; Nathaniel, 172; Thomas, 28; Zebulon, 52
HOMER, John, 48
HONEY, Caroline, 148; George, 148; George C., 148; Harriet, 148; Juliana, 148; Louisa Ann, 148; Margaret, 148; Margaret Augusta, 148
HOOD, Ann, 36, 60; Hannah, 10, 42; James, 60; James A., 60; John, 10, 110; Mary, 110; Rachel, 60; Thomas, 60; William, 42
HOOPES, David, 37
HOOPS, Mary Ralph, 123
HOOTEN, Benjamin, 19
HOOVER, John, 124; Lawrence, 139
HOPKINS, Ann, 51, 131; David C., 105; Elizabeth, 131; Hannah, 51; Howel, 131; Howell, 63, 131; John, 50, 123; Margaret, 131; Margaret D., 131; Samuel, 131; William D., 163
HOPKINSON, Joseph, 31
HORNER, James, 22, 23; Joseph P., 82
HORTON, Jacob, 86
HOSKIN, Thomas, 9, 16, 90, 141, 153, 160
HOSKINS, John G., 29; Raper, 29; Thomas, 27, 58, 156
HOTTENSTEIN, Catharine, 115
HOTZ, Peter, 113
HOUCK, Charles, 93; Christian, 93; George, 93; Margaret, 93; Maria, 93; Sarah, 93
HOUGH, Constant, 118; Thomas, 109
HOULAN, Catharine, 78; Patrick, 78
HOUMAN, George, 16; John, 16; Joseph, 16; Mary, 16; William, 16
HOUSE, Elizabeth, 30
HOUSTON, Amy H., 66; William, 66
HOUTZELL, Mary, 81
HOWARD, Caleb N., 13; Charles, 13; Charles P., 66; Deborah, 13; Edith N., 13; Eliza, 13; Emma, 13; John E., 160; Lewis, 113; Margaret, 160; Sarah N., 13; Sarah P., 13, 66; Thomas, 12
HOWELL, Benjamin Paschall, 131; Elizabeth, 20; James, 106; Lydia, 122; Margaret, 42; Mary, 106; Peter, 122;
Rebecca, 107; Richard, 40, 143, 158; Samuel E., 42; William, 145
HOZEY, Charles, 2; Isaac, 2; James, 2; Jane, 2; Margaret, 2; Mary Shortall, 2; Thomas S., 2
HUBBARD, Anthony, 89; Mary, 89
HUBBELL, William, 118
HUBBERT, Christian, 16, 22, 129
HUBER, Elizabeth, 17; Isaac, 17; Mary, 17; Sophia, 17
HUDELL, Bankson, 127
HUDSON, Susanna, 95; William, 95
HUFF, Susan, 30
HUFTY, Sarah, 101
HUGHES, Alexander, 102; Ann, 7; Elizabeth, 102; James, 102, 144; John, 123; Margaret, 102; Rebecca, 102; Samuel, 102; Susan, 112; Thomas, 102, 112
HUGHS, James, 118
HUGLER, Benjamin, 133; Catharine, 133; Charles, 133; Elizabeth, 133; George, 133; Mary, 133
HUMES, Archibald, 86; George, 86, 116; William, 86
HUMMEL, Agnes, 18; David, 18; Margaret, 18
HUMPHREYS, Joshua, 44, 45; Mary, 44, 51; Richard, 51, 115
HUMPHRIES, David, 38
HUNT, Elizabeth, 51; Pearson, 95; Rachel, 95
HUNTER, Charles, 95; James, 77
HUQUENCLE, Frederick, 58
HURLEY, Hannah, 142; Michael, 76; Thomas, 142
HURST, William, 114
HURTEL, John, 140; Peter, 140
HUSE, Ann, 171; Ann Elizabeth, 171
HUSTON, John, 3, 52
HUTCHINSON, James, 146; Jane, 156; Sidney, 146; Thomas, 125
HUTTON, Rebecca, 114
HUTZ, Daniel, 121

-I-

IMLAY, Robert, 69, 161
INGERSOLL, Charles I., 163; Jared, 73, 91; Joseph R., 59
INGLISH, Mary, 68; Thomas, 68
INGRAHAM, Francis, 164
INLOES, David, 85; Mary, 85
INNES, Cornelius, 114; Joseph,

34; Rachel, 34
IREDILL, Hannah, 125; Lydia Starr, 125
IRMER, Mary Josephine, 55
IRVINE, Frances, 155
ISRAEL, Micheve, 123
IVINS, Rachel, 63; Rachel H., 63

-J-

JACKSON, Anna, 71; Elizabeth, 128; John M., 120; Joseph, 154; Laetitia, 84; Levin, 84; Maria, 140; Rebecca, 140; Samuel, 71; Thomas, 67, 126
JACOBI, John, 105
JACOBS, Aaron, 123; Capt., 68; John, 123; Judith, 123; Lyon, 123
JACOBY, Leonard, 84
JAGERS, Abraham, 94; Daniel, 94; Hannah, 94; John, 94; Jonathan, 94; Joseph, 94; Phebe, 94
JAMES, Adam, 115; David, 67; J., 154; Lewis, 67; Martha, 148; Mary, 51, 138; Thomas C., 121
JAMESON, Thomas, 90
JAMIN, Reuben, 52
JAMISON, John, 145; Martha, 145
JANEWAY, Jacob J., 92; Martha, 92
JANNEY, Benjamin S., 82; Mordecai Wetherill, 62
JANNY, John, 62
JANUARY, Elizabeth, 128
JARDEN, Catharine, 96; Jacob, 96; John, 96; Maria, 96; Robert, 96; Samuel, 96; William, 96
JARMAN, Daniel, 169; Rebecca, 169
JEFFRIES, Barbarry, 59; Daniel, 59; Edward, 59; Mary, 59; Samuel, 59; Thomas, 59; William, 59
JENKINS, Eliza, 147; Enoch, 147; George, 147; Sarah, 96
JEWELL, Kenneth, 153
JOAD, John, 154
JOADE, Margaret, 154
JOBSON, Charles, 131, 164; Joseph, 131, 164; Rebecca, 131, 164; Samuel, 29
JOHN, David, 58; Peter, 122
JOHNS, Hannah D., 46; Richard, 112
JOHNSON, Alexander, 172; Alexander Washington, 6;

193

Alice, 6; Ann, 92; Anthony, 54; Archibald, 172; Benjamin, 168; Catharine, 163; Charles, 92; Elizabeth, 3, 92, 168; Francis, 6; Hannah, 92, 115; Jacob, 168; James, 172; Jeames, 5; Jennett, 116; John, 88, 92, 93, 116, 117, 149; Joseph, 70, 168; Klinchen, 48; Klincken, 54; Margaret, 92, 172; Mary, 49, 168; Mary Erwin, 6; Norton, 92; Rachel, 93, 116; Richard, 163; Samuel, 116; Sarah, 47, 92, 116; Susanna Vanderin, 141; William, 92, 116
JOHNSTON, Aaron, 153; Abraham, 89; Ann, 153; Closs, 153; David, 81; Elizabeth, 153; Hannah, 153; Isaac, 79; Jacob, 153; James, 115; John, 13, 89; Jonathan, 153; Joseph, 153; Mary, 81; Rebecca, 153; Sarah, 33; Thomas, 170; William, 33
JONES, Absalom, 40, 115; Absolom, 5; Ann, 92; Benjamin, 82; Catharine, 92; Clement, 92; Daniel, 98, 122; Edward, 97, 115; Eliza, 92, 98; Elizabeth, 53, 93, 106; Evan, 102; George, 115; George W., 86; Gibson, 93; Hannah, 99, 115, 160; Horatio G., 87, 131; Horatio Gates, 14; Hugh, 146; Isaac, 83; Jacob, 93; James, 39; Jane, 2; Joel, 102; John, 16, 97; John M., 97; Joseph, 92; Lewis, 37; Lowry, 35; Lydia, 9, 77; Margaret, 2, 99; Marhon, 97; Martha, 93, 99, 115; Mary, 115, 160; Mordecai, 99; Morgan, 113; Nathan, 92, 122; Norris, 92; Owen, 153; Patience, 97; Peter, 106; Rebecca, 20, 95, 99, 122; Reuben, 97; Richard, 39; Richard Blackledge, 146; Samuel, 93; Sarah, 115, 122; Susanna, 18; Susannah, 165; William, 106, 115
JORDAIN, Mr., 64
JORDAN, John, 7, 8
JUGIEZ, Jerome, 12; Martin, 12
JUHEL, John, 64
JUNGKURTH, Ann, 44; Barbara, 44; Barbera, 44; Catharine, 44; Christopher, 44;

Elisabeth, 44; Frederica, 44; Frederick, 44; Henry, 44; Mary Magdalene, 44; Rebecca, 44; Susana, 44
JUREMAN, Reuben, 3
JUSTIS, Elizabeth, 107; Pedro, 107; Thomas, 151

-K-

KAFE, Anna Maria, 16; Christian, 16
KALEHOFF, Mary, 100
KAMMERER, Henry, 8; Mary, 122
KANE, Andrew, 143; Conrad, 143; Elizabeth, 143; George, 143; Harriott, 143; Mary Ann, 143
KATZ, Catherine, 83; Conrad, 83; George, 83; Henry, 83
KAY, Joseph, 161; Joseph L., 161
KAYSORE, Foney, 53; John, 53
KEARSLEY, John, 19
KEATING, John, 64, 147; Julius, 64
KEATON, Elijah, 129
KEBLER, Barbara, 165; Maria, 137
KEEFE, John, 163; Joseph, 109
KEEGAN, Sarah, 115; Thomas, 115
KEEL, Catharine, 4; Elias, 4; George, 4
KEEMLE, Isaac, 69; Samuel, 69, 107, 152
KEEN, James, 41; Jeremiah, 45; John, 41; Mary, 41; Robert, 41; Sarah Ann, 41
KEIM, George D. B., 7
KEITH, Samuel, 22
KELLERS, Samuel, 63
KELLY, James, 140; Mary, 140; William, 6
KELSEY, John C., 8
KELTON, David M., 126; Easther, 126; James, 126; John Loury, 126; Polly, 126; Robert, 126; Sally, 126; Thomas, 126
KEMBLE, Caleb, 105
KEMP, John, 64; Maria Sophia, 64
KENNEDY, Andrew, 170; Ann, 81; Anthony, 155; Eleanor, 170; Elizabeth, 170; George, 170; Isaac, 46; Isaac P., 46; Mary, 170; Robert, 170; Susan, 170; Thomas, 164; William D., 159
KENNY, Charles, 97; Patrick, 97
KENSEL, John, 45, 51; Mary, 51
KENSLER, William Harper, 51
KENTON, Anna Barbary, 45; Catharine, 45; Deborah, 45; Israel, 78; Joseph, 45; Margaret, 45; Mary, 45; Thomas, 45
KENTZING, Eliza, 112
KENTZINGER, Catharine, 74; Charles, 74; Christopher, 74; Elizabeth, 74; George, 74; William, 74
KER, Frances, 155; Irvine, 155; Joseph, 155; Sarah, 155; William, 155
KERLIN, Debby Ann, 11; Hannah, 11; John, 11; Sarah, 11
KERN, John, 135, 142
KERSEY, Jesse, 92, 93
KESLER, John, 62
KESSLER, John, 19, 108
KETCHAM, Daniel, 47; William, 47
KEYSER, Abraham, 51, 58; Charles, 22, 71; Derick, 120; Elizabeth, 100, 120; John, 13; Peter, 15, 120; Samuel, 116; Sarah, 120; Susanna, 13, 14; William, 120
KILLEGAN, Mary, 96
KIMMEY, William, 45
KING, Anna, 51; Edward, 118; Ellen, 118; Isaac, 30; John, 118, 127; Margaret, 139; Reay, 51; William, 139
KINGLUFF, Joseph, 59
KINSEY, Edmund, 10, 40, 61; Gayner, 112
KINSLER, John, 51
KIP, Isaac I., 127
KIRK, Jacob, 121; Tabitha, 76
KITCHEN, Ann, 148; Joseph, 148; Mortimer, 148; Sandford Hamilton, 148
KITCHIN, Rachel, 86
KITTLE, Eve, 58
KLAPP, Joseph, 10
KLAZER, Jacob, 12
KLEIN, Maria, 104
KLETT, Gottlieb, 138
KLEVER, Godlieb, 68
KLINE, Magdalena, 174
KNEASS, Mary, 93
KNEPLEY, Peter, 111
KNERR, Henry, 75; Mrs., 75
KNIGHT, Daniel, 41, 102, 160, 173; Jonahan, 41; Joseph, 69, 100; Martha, 41; Mary, 132; Thomas, 132
KNITTLE, George, 74
KNORR, George, 15, 116; John, 136
KNOUS, Benjamin, 24; Jacob, 42; Margaret, 24; Mary, 7

KNOWS, Catherine, 34; Jacob, 34; Joseph, 34; Margaret, 34
KOBER, Maria Barbara, 126; Paul, 126
KOCH, Maria Magdalen, 104
KOHLEN, John, 165
KOTZ, Peter, 75
KREAMER, John, 65
KRIDER, Jacob, 14
KRIPS, George, 70; Jacob, 170; John, 170
KROESEN, John B., 103
KROUSKOP, John, 36
KUGLER, Elizabeth, 133; George, 133
KUHL, Henry, 120
KUHN, Dr., 31
KULB, Isaac, 139
KULP, Isaac, 139; Isaac M., 156; Jacob, 139, 141
KUNCKEL, Philip C., 83
KUNITS, Lewis, 63
KURTZ, Ann, 47; Catharine, 76; Charles, 47, 76; Eleanor, 47; Elizabeth, 76, 106; George, 47, 76, 106; Henry, 47, 76; Jacob, 47, 76; Margaret, 47, 106; Montgomery, 47; Nancy, 76; Peter, 47, 76; Sally Ann, 47; Sarah, 47; William, 47, 76

-L-
LABOUR, John, 133
LACKEY, Elizabeth, 95; James, 94
LACROIX, Francis, 55; Mary, 55
LACROZE, T. T., 7
LAFARE, Peter X., 140
LAFERTY, Rebecca, 49
LAFORGE, Benjamin, 150
LAIDLEY, James, 65; Robert, 65
LAIDLY, Robert Beck, 67
LAIRD, William, 162
LAKE, Ann, 85; David, 30; Thomas, 85, 107; William, 30
LALLEY, Sarah, 17
LALON, Mark, 23
LAMBETH, Catharine, 153
LAMLEY, Elizabeth, 163; John, 163
LAMON, Andrew, 52; James, 148
LAMPATER, Catharine, 104
LANCASTER, John, 173
LANDERS, Mary, 10
LANDES, David, 59; Mary, 59
LANDY, John, 3
LANE, Edward, 56, 102
LANGDALE, Samuel, 95
LANING, Joseph, 13

LAPP, Anthony, 139; Christiana, 101; John, 139; Joseph, 139; Mary, 139; Priscilla, 139
LARCUM, John, 94
LARDNER, John, 64
LAREMORE, Jane, 91; Sarah, 92
LARER, Melchior, 142
LAREW, Elizabeth, 92
LARKUM, Thomas, 94
LATIMER, Elizabeth, 103; George, 103; Henry, 103, 168; James, 103; Jane, 102; Margaret, 103; Mary R., 103; Sarah B., 103; Sarah R., 103; Thomas, 46, 103, 108, 140; William, 103; William G., 103
LAUBER, Martin, 14
LAUDERBACK, Cynthia, 38
LAVALLE, John, 113
LAWERSWYLER, Wilhelmina, 61
LAWLER, Anne, 75
LAWRENCE, Benjamin, 92, 156; Capt., 118; Deborah, 92; Edward, 10; Elizabeth, 87, 146; George, 67; Henry, 38; Jacob, 87, 146; John, 109; Margaret, 67; Mary, 10, 92, 149, 156; Samuel, 92; Sarah, 104; William, 164
LAWS, Clement, 157; Elijah, 157; Elizabeth, 157; George, 157; John, 157; Ludowick, 157; Lydia, 157; Mary, 157; Melson, 157; William, 157
LAWSON, Alexander, 170; Margaret, 170; William, 170
LE BARBIER, Sophia A., 32
LEACH, Henrietta, 93; Richard I., 93
LEAMING, Thomas F., 95
LEAMY, Don Juan, 151; John, 33, 169
LEARY, William O., 31
LEBARBIER, George, 32; Helene, 32; Josephe Genevieve Maurry, 32
LECKY, James, 22
LEDDON, Samuel, 19
LEE, Elizabeth, 73; Franklin, 79; Richard, 24
LEECH, Daniel, 101; Duncan, 101; Edward, 101; Harriet, 141; Henry, 74; Isaac, 37; Jane, 101; John, 101; Joseph, 141; Margaret, 101; Maximilian, 37; Samuel, 2, 79
LEES, Elizabeth, 89; Hannah, 81; Joseph, 89
LEGARE, Ann, 18

LEHMAN, Benjamin, 75, 90, 91; Charles, 106; Mary, 127; Samuel, 75, 153; William, 127
LEIB, Michael, 170
LEIBERT, John, 110
LEINAU, Andrew, 6
LEINEAU, Andrew, 8
LEJEE, Mrs., 64
LELLY, Martha, 17
LENINGTON, I., 3
LENNOX, Sarah, 156
LENTZ, David, 11; Jacob, 138; John, 101; Mary, 101; Rebecca, 101; Sarah, 101; William, 101
LEOHRA, Peter, 49
LEON, Mrs., 64
LERON, Jean, 32; Marie Anne, 32; Marie Louise, 32
LESHER, Cathrine, 22
LESLEY, Ann, 46; Catharine, 46; Margaret, 46; Mary, 30, 46; Peter, 46
LEVAN, Mary, 48
LEVERING, Anthony, 131; Charles, 131; Hannah, 131; Hester, 131; I. H., 13; Mary, 131; Perry, 131; Silas, 131; Titus, 131
LEVICK, Ebenezer, 35
LEVIS, Isaac, 121
LEVY, Aaron, 6; Rachel, 6
LEWIN, Levin, 123
LEWIS, Edward S., 32; Eliza, 140; Elizabeth, 54; Elizabeth Ann, 146; Frances, 54, 146, 164; George, 87; Hannah, 20, 54; Hannah Saunders, 54; Joseph S., 13, 49, 50, 54, 70, 146; Josiah, 164, 165; Lydia, 115; Margaret, 164; Mordecai, 50, 54; Nathan, 87; Rachel, 54; Rebecca C., 54, 168; Reeve, 54; Samuel N., 50, 54, 168; Samuel Neave, 70; Sarah, 140; Thomas, 140; Victorine, 117; Vincent L., 88; William, 38, 164
LEX, Charles, 68
LEY, Daniel, 14
LIBBS, Livinah, 102
LIGHTFOOT, Elizabeth, 48
LINCHEY, James W., 136
LINDSAY, Elizabeth, 18; Nancy, 77; Samuel, 77
LINDSEY, William, 138
LINEHAN, Coleman, 109; Dennis, 109; Ellen, 109; James, 109; Margaretta, 109; Maurice, 109
LINGLEY, John, 66
LINGMULLER, Adam, 170
LINK, Abraham, 58
LINTENBARIGER, George, 54; John, 54; Permelia, 54; Pheby, 54
LIP, James, 149
LIPPINCOTT, Abigail, 52; Ann, 123; Asa, 52; Benjamin, 52; Elizabeth, 52; Jehu, 52; Joel, 52; Phebe, 52; Sarah, 52, 61, 125; Thomas, 52
LISLE, Elizabeth, 146; Henry, 146; Margaret, 146; Mary, 146
LISTER, Elizabeth S., 172; John S., 172; John Smith, 172; Mary, 172; Sarah S., 172; Thomas S., 172
LITHGOW, Edward, 139; Elizabeth, 139
LITLE, Hannah, 51; John, 51
LITZENBERG, Margaret, 57
LIVENSETTER, John, 37
LIVEZEY, John, 53, 100, 160; Joseph, 160; Thomas, 160
LLOYD, Elizabeth, 41; Frances, 131; Hannah, 159, 164; Isaac, 109; Jonathan, 159; Joseph, 40; Levi, 164; Lydia, 163; Mary, 159; Molly, 77; Robert, 163; Samuel, 41; Susanna, 159; Thomas, 41, 159; William, 28
LOCKERMAN, Vincent, 104
LOCKTON, Mary, 87
LODOR, Jane, 15; John, 15
LOGAN, Deborah, 4, 99; Dr., 4; George, 99; James, 19; Samuel, 146
LOHRA, John, 29, 49; John C., 29; Peter, 61, 151
LONG, Henry, 160; Jane, 50
LONGSTRETH, John G., 60; Samuel, 151; Sarah Redwood Fisher, 151
LOPEZ, Ann, 158
LORAIN, Elizabeth Shewell, 106; John, 106; Lydia, 106
LORT, Isaac, 141; Mary, 141
LOTZ, Henry, 16
LOUDENSLAGER, Richard, 116
LOUDER, Charles, 69; John, 53, 74
LOUGHEAD, Eleanor, 27; James, 27; Robert S., 74
LOUGHERY, Esther, 121; John, 121; Joseph, 121; Kitty, 121
LOVE, Lidia, 95; Peter, 11
LOWER, Abraham, 20, 69, 119,

134; Anna Margaretta, 64;
George Christian, 64; Henry,
64; Henry Ludwick Balzer,
64; Maria Sophia, 64
LOWNES, Caleb, 1; Edward, 1;
George, 1; Jane, 63; John,
1; Joseph, 13, 46; Josiah
H., 171; Margaret, 1
LOWRY, Lewis, 93; Philip, 134
LUBBOCK, JOHN & CO., 97
LUCAS, Field J., 60
LUDIE, Martin, 93
LUDLAM, James, 18; Jane, 18
LUDWICK, Elizabeth, 69; John,
69
LUGAR, Christopher, 22;
Elizabeth, 22; Jacob, 22;
John, 22
LUKENS, Ann, 28; David, 41;
Elizabeth, 25; Gayner, 112;
Joseph S., 76; Martha, 41;
Mary, 3, 139; Priscilla,
139; Samuel, 25; Sarah, 41,
76; Seneca, 76; Thomas, 28
LUKINS, David, 119; Martha B.,
76; Seneca, 76; Tabitha, 76
LUSHER, Jacob, 25
LUTZ, Frederick, 110; Hannah,
110; Henry, 110; Jacob, 6;
John, 110; Mary, 6; Mary
Ann, 110; Philip, 68; Sarah,
68
LYBRAND, Elizabeth, 53; Jacob,
12
LYCAN, Andrew, 91; George, 91,
158
LYNCH, Caroline Lalls, 11;
Debby Ann, 11; Edward, 112;
Hannah, 11; John, 11;
Margaretta, 11, 12; William,
11, 12
LYNDAL, Benjamin, 103
LYNDALL, Ann, 130; Benjamin,
130; Catharine, 130; Eliza,
130; Joseph W., 130; Robert,
130; Samuel, 130; Susanna,
130; William, 130
LYNN, Mary, 129; Simon, 129
LYON, Joseph, 126; Nicholas B.,
22; Patrick, 94
LYONS, Robert, 23

-M-

MAAG, John, 11, 96; Mary, 96
MCADAMS, James, 63; Maron, 63;
Mary, 63; William, 63
MCALLISTER, Alexander, 71, 128;
John, 71, 85, 161, 166;
William, 71, 128
MCANNAL, Isabel, 17; James, 17;
John, 17; William, 17

MCANULTY, Hugh, 161; Jane, 161
MCARTHUR, Eleanor, 108; Sarah
B., 108
MCBRINE, Charles, 37;
Elizabeth, 37; George, 37;
Sarrah, 37
MCCALL, Archibald, 4; John C.,
4; William, 153
MCCALLA, A., 149; Andrew, 30
MCCAMILL, Peggy, 10
MCCARTHY, Mary, 143; Mrs., 11
MCCLEAN, Ann, 143; Thomas, 145;
William, 144
MCCLEERY, Mary, 28
MCCLELLAND, George W., 113
MCCLENAGAN, Ann, 87; Blair, 87;
Charles, 87; George, 87;
Jacob, 87; Mary, 87;
Matilda, 87; Morris, 87
MCCLENEGAN, Blair, 87
MCCLENIGAN, Mary, 87
MCCLERY, James, 157
MCCLINTOCK, John, 30, 31, 143;
Martha, 31
MCCLURE, Ann, 173; Mr., 140;
Prudence, 173
MCCOLLIN, John, 59; William,
118
MCCONNELL, Eliza, 18;
Elizabeth, 18; Hannah, 18;
Matthew, 18, 67; Ruth, 67;
Thomas, 18
MCCORKLE, Christiana, 66;
Elizabeth, 66; Jane, 66;
Joseph P., 66; William, 66
MCCOY, Agnes, 141; Anthony,
155; Archibald, 141;
Catharine, 141; Daniel, 141;
John, 141; Mary, 141;
Patrick, 161; Sarah, 62
MCCRELISH, Archibald, 110
MCCRELLISH, Archibald, 110
MCCULLEY, William, 93
MCCULLOCH, Ann, 14; Henry, 146;
James, 156; James H., 156;
John, 166; Mary, 146
MCCULLOCK, Ebenezer, 36
MCCULLOUGH, Ann, 118
MCCULLY, Henry, 21, 145; Mary,
145
MCCURDY, Elizabeth, 53; John,
30
MCDERMOTT, Catharine, 97
MCDONALD, James, 113; Mordecai,
62
MCDONNELL, Patrick, 163; Sarah,
99; Sarah Ann, 99
MCDOUGAL, Eliza, 87; Mrs., 162
MCELWAINE, Ferguson, 134
MCELWCE, Robert, 147
MCEWEN, James, 171

MCFADEN, Stephen, 144
MCFADYEN, Duncan, 149
MCFARLAND, Ann, 86; Isabella, 86; John, 150; Robert, 86; William, 5
MACFERAN, Samuel, 50, 55, 107
MACFERRANE, Samuel, 53
MCGALL, Bernard, 161
MCGEE, George, 24
MCGILL, Elizabeth, 43; James, 108
MCGINNES, Neal, 59
MCGLINSY, John, 13
MCGONAGLE, Elizabeth, 10; James, 10
MCGOWAN, Mary, 42; Thomas, 42
MCGOWEN, Patrick, 136
MCGRAY, David, 75
MCGROTTO, Edward, 59; James, 59; John, 59; Margaret, 59; Mary, 59
MCGUIGAN, John, 20
MCHARAHEN, Charles, 156
MCHERUM, Catharine, 171
MCHUGH, Elinor, 10
MCILHENNY, James, 94; Mary, 62; Nancy, 62
MCILHENY, Moses, 27
MCILHINEY, Moses, 169
MCINTIRE, Catharine, 78; John, 78; Sarah, 78
MCKEAN, Anne, 91; Elizabeth, 90; Henry Pratt, 91; Joseph B., 90, 91; Joseph Borden, 90; Laetitia, 90, 91; Mary, 90; Robert, 90; Samuel Miles, 91; Sarah, 90; Sarah Maria Theresa, 91; Sophia Dorothea, 91; Susanna, 90; Thomas, 90, 91
MCKEE, Thomas, 9
MCKEEVER, James, 87
MCKENNY, Isabella, 23
MCKENSIE, Caleb, 92
MCKENZIE, Charles, 102; James Laremore, 92; Jane, 92; Mary, 92; Rebecca, 102
MACKENZIE, William, 62, 63
MACKIE, Charles, 65; Peter, 65
MACKINET, Charles, 110; Mary, 110
MCKINLEY, Alexander, 30; John, 150
MCKISSICK, John, 66; Mary, 66
MACKNET, Charles, 8, 136
MCLANE, Elizabeth, 104; Samuel, 104
MCLAREN, Archibald, 129
MACLAREN, Thomas, 130
MCLAUGHLEN, John, 96; Maria, 96
MCLEAN, Archibald, 70

MCLENCHY, John, 24
MCLINCHEY, James, 49, 169; John, 34
MCLINSHEY, James, 87
MCMACKIN, Eliza, 31; James, 31; John, 31; Margaret, 31; Martha, 31; Mary, 31; Michael, 31; Rebecca, 31
MCMAHON, Ann, 61; Bernard, 55, 61; James, 61, 128; Thomas, 61, 128; Thomas T., 61
MCMAKEN, Eliza, 107; Julia Ann, 107; Margaret, 107; Margaret M., 107; Mary, 107; Samuel, 107; Susanna, 107; William, 107
MCMINN, Robert, 119
MCMULLIN, Daniel, 54; Elizabeth, 54; Michael, 54
MCMURDAY, Robert, 43
MCMURDY, Ann, 43; Benjamin, 43; Elizabeth, 43; Jonathan, 43; Margaret, 43; Mary, 43; Robert, 43; Susannah, 43
MCMURTRIE, James, 90; Rebecca, 90
MCNAMEA, John, 144
MCNEAL, Ann, 141
MCNEILLEDGE, Daniel, 86; James, 86; Peter, 86
MCNEVAN, Malcolm, 129
MCPHERSON, Ann, 82; Maria, 58; Robert G., 58
MCVAUGH, Ann, 35; Elenor, 35; Elizabeth, 35; James, 35; Jane, 35; Taylor, 35; William, 35
MCVEA, Henry, 161; Margaret, 161; Mary, 161
MCWATERS, Archibald, 125; Elizabeth, 125; John, 125
MADDOCK, Elizabeth Harr, 110; Randal Malin, 110; Sarah Moore, 110
MADEIRA, Catharine, 1; Charles, 1; Esther, 1; George A., 1; Hannah, 1; Jacob, 1; John, 1; Maria, 1; Mary, 1; Sarah, 1; William Jones, 1
MAFFETT, Capt., 38
MAGARGILL, Elizabeth, 6; Jonathan, 6
MAGEE, William Snell, 23
MAGHEE, William, 55
MAGRATH, John, 54; Michael, 108
MAGUIRE, John, 38; Michael, 31; Mrs., 4
MAHANY, James A., 159; John J., 159
MAHER, Eleanor Maria, 76; John D., 87

MAITLAND, John, 111, 116, 144;
  Thomas, 120
MALCOM, Howard, 13
MALENFANT, I. R., 55
MALEY, Catharine, 137; John,
  137; Mary, 137; Michael,
  137; Peter, 137; Samuel, 137
MALONY, Berry, 160; Elizabeth,
  160; Hannah, 160; Joseph,
  160; Rebecca, 160
MANIGAULT, Charles, 173;
  Charlotte, 173; Elizabeth,
  173; Gabriel Henry, 173;
  Harriet, 173; Margaret, 173
MANNING, William, 4
MARACHE, Mary, 1; Solomon, 1
MARBLE, Joseph, 119
MARCHALL, Mary, 137
MARCHIONES, Sarah Maria
  Theresa, 91
MARIS, John, 107
MARJORAM, Rachel, 4
MARK, John, 173
MARKENS, Sarah, 108
MARKER, Conrad, 50; Elizabeth,
  50; George, 50; Godfrey, 50;
  Jacob, 50; Maria, 50; Mary,
  50
MARKIE, Thomas, 70
MARKLAND, Emily, 84; John, 84,
  85
MARKLE, Jacob, 53; Sarah, 53
MARKS, Gabriel, 60; Joseph G.,
  135; Louisa, 60; Mary, 60;
  Nicholas, 60; Samuel, 60
MARLACK, Timothy, 62
MARRIOTT, Mary, 9; Sarah, 9;
  Thomas, 9
MARSH, Edward, 101
MARSHALL, Agnes, 118; Amor, 57;
  Ann Elizabeth, 57; Charles,
  122; David, 119; Davis, 59;
  Elizabeth, 118, 122; Frances
  Matilda, 57; Joseph Yorkson,
  57; Mary, 57; Prudence, 94;
  Samuel, 118; Susanna, 119
MARTI, Barbara, 105; Elizabeth,
  105; Jacob, 105; John, 105;
  Maria, 105; Martin, 104;
  Salome, 105
MARTIN, Catharine, 99;
  Elizabeth, 21; George, 29,
  34; Isabella, 122; Jean
  Baptiste Joseph, 32; Jean
  Joseph, 32; John, 21, 166;
  John F., 43; Joseph, 36;
  Marie Catharine, 32; Mary,
  126, 143; Mary Ann, 21;
  Robert, 99; Thomas, 21
MARTLY, Maria, 53
MASON, Elias, 142; George, 25;

199

Henry Michael, 25; Martha,
  25; Mary Jane, 25;
  Mihitabel, 25; Philip, 73,
  154; Richard S., 25; Sarah,
  25; Thomas, 103; William,
  25, 120, 125; William Henry,
  25
MASTER, William, 35, 146
MATHER, Bartholomew, 35;
  Benjamin, 35; Joseph, 35;
  Peter, 168
MATHEWS, Hannah, 170; John, 170
MATTAN, Margaret, 125
MAUL, Israel, 134
MAULE, Israel, 25, 157;
  Rebecca, 168
MAURRY, Josephe Genevieve, 32
MAURY, James, 80
MAXFIELD, Stephen, 56, 125
MAXWELL, Catharine, 143;
  Hannah, 139; Hugh, 153;
  James, 139; John, 143; John
  Thomas, 139; Martha, 143;
  Mary, 143
MAY, Abel, 48; Adam, 25, 41;
  Catharine, 41; Elizabeth,
  25, 41; Harriet, 41; Henry,
  69; Lewis, 49; Mary, 41;
  Sarah, 41
MAYBERRY, Ann, 84; John, 84
MAYER, Catherine, 53;
  Christiana, 53; Daniel, 53;
  Elizabeth, 53; Foney, 53;
  Jacob, 53; John, 53; Mary,
  53; Nicholas, 53; Philip, 53
MAZEU, Theodat, 121
MAZIER, Bartholomew, 23
MAZIERE, Bartholomew, 23
MEADE, Anne, 147; Elizabeth,
  147; Mary Elizabeth, 147;
  Richard W., 169
MEANS, John, 95
MEANY, Mary, 26
MECASKEY, Andrew, 81
MECH, Appleton, 144
MECHLIN, Jacob, 93, 107;
  Samuel, 93, 107
MECKELBURGH, Charles, 19
MEDARY, Sarah, 101
MEITTE, Jacob, 19
MELTONBERGER, Catherine, 58;
  Elizabeth, 58
MENDIGUREN, Dona Josefa, 151
MENG, Christopher, 76
MENZIES, John, 73
MERCER, John, 71; Robert, 77;
  Thomas, 61
MERDIER, Francis, 44; Louis,
  44; Maria, 44; Seraphin, 44
MEREDITH, Ann, 10; David, 75;
  Elizabeth, 154; Joseph, 154;

Sophia, 75; William, 58, 86, 165
MERKEL, Christian B., 143, 163
MEROT, Mr., 147
MERVINE, Jacob, 29; Martha, 29; Mary, 29
MESSER, Elizabeth, 60; Josiah, 100
METTLER, Samuel, 170; William, 170
MEYER, Catharine, 96; Henry, 3; Jacob, 2; Rosanna, 96
MEYERS, Elizabeth, 134; George, 134; George G., 141; Hannah, 134; Samuel, 134; William, 134
MICHELL, Augustine, 147
MICKLE, Andrew, 33; Isaac, 33; John, 33; Mary, 33; Rachel, 33
MIDDLETON, Elizabeth, 47
MIFFLIN, Ann, 42, 94; Benjamin, 126; Charles, 71; Elizabeth, 71; Governor, 73; John, 71; John F., 71; Lemuel, 42; Lloyd, 17; Mary, 126; Samuel, 42, 90, 130; Sarah, 71, 130; Thomas, 130
MILES, Isabelle, 1; Rebecca, 1
MILL, George, 12
MILLARD, Andrew, 130; Cecilia, 130; Charles, 130; Clement, 130; George, 130; James, 130; John, 130; Sarah, 1, 130; Thomas, 2, 60, 130; William, 2, 130, 131
MILLER, Alexander, 21, 107; Ann, 65, 68; Anne, 39; Catherine, 67; Clement, 2; David, 21; Elizabeth, 20, 67, 150; George, 8, 75, 88; George Godfrey, 88; Hannah, 88, 137; Henry, 67; Henry H., 113; John, 15, 66, 129; John A., 24; John Jacob, 24; Juliana, 159; Margaret, 67, 150; Maria Sophia, 88; Mary, 54, 67, 150; Michael, 68; Peter, 57; Phebe, 93; Philip, 24; Prince, 8; Rachel, 8; Rosina, 88; Rossina, 88; Samuel, 104; Samuel W., 140; Sarah, 39, 68; Sarah Ann, 88; Sophia, 68; Susanna, 15, 150; William, 62, 63, 170; William Alexander, 150
MILLIKEN, Robert, 166
MILLIKIN, William, 30
MILNE, Richard, 154
MILNER, John, 19

MILNOR, George Aston, 1; Isaac, 1; John P., 108
MINGLE, John, 12, 160
MINK, Elizabeth, 25; John, 25; Mary, 25; Philip, 25
MINSER, Adam, 15
MINTIS, Andrew, 128; Besella, 128; Charles, 128; Diana, 128; Elizabeth, 128; Harinah, 128; Kisiah, 128; Levina, 128; Lovina, 128; Mary Ann, 128; Rebecca, 128
MINTZER, Adam, 132; Deborah, 166; Eliza, 166; Elizabeth, 132; Jacob, 166; John, 132, 166; Mary, 132; Rosanna, 132, 166; Sarah, 166; William, 166
MIRE, George, 49
MITCHEL, James, 82; Susanna, 82; Thomas, 82
MITCHELL, Benjamin, 82; Jacob, 13; James, 82; Mary, 82; Thomas, 2, 7, 19, 31, 70, 73, 82, 85, 99, 101, 122, 124, 133, 146, 154, 158, 159, 163, 173
MOFFETT, Frances, 22; Rachel, 22; Robert, 22; Sarah, 22
MOLINEUX, John E., 128
MOLTHER, Eliza, 130
MONACH, Andrew B., 89; James, 89; Jane M., 89; Margaret T., 89; Mary, 89; Mary W., 89
MONKHOUSE, Eliza, 172; Sarah, 172
MONTARLET, Rosalie Cecile, 36
MONTGOMERY, A., 32; Abby Eliza Hamilton, 146; Andrew, 8, 21, 86; Austin, 88; David, 22; Hester, 146; Jacob, 44; John, 44; Margaret, 27; Maria, 44; Robert, 44; Sarah, 23; Sarah Powell, 146; William, 23, 38
MOOR, Joseph, 34
MOORE, Ann, 33; Elizabeth, 110, 154; Gay, 23; Hannah Lewis, 54; John, 31; John W., 73; Joseph, 106, 110; Margaret, 43; Marmaduke, 134; Mary, 71, 110; Mary L., 54; Richard, 84; Sarah, 23, 110; Thomas, 31, 49; Thomas William, 32
MOREHANE, Joseph, 72
MOREY, Hariet L., 45
MORGAN, Benjamin R., 140; John, 38, 98; Nathan, 98; William, 65, 73

MORRELL, Elizabeth, 85; James, 85; Robert, 84, 85
MORRIS, An, 144; Ann, 33; Anthony, 116; Caspar, 20, 21; Caspar W., 20; Catharine, 20; Catharine W., 20; Elizabeth, 21, 99; Hannah, 21; Isaac, 131; Isaac W., 20, 21, 51, 84, 91; Israel W., 20, 21; Jacob, 87; Jeremiah, 116; John, 39, 172; Lewis, 173; Luke, 20, 95; Luke W., 20, 21, 33, 119; Mary, 21, 87; Mary Eliza, 116; Meribah, 87; Richard Hill, 66; Samuel, 20; Samuel B., 66; Sarah, 9, 19, 20, 21, 95, 116; Susan, 95; Warder, 116; William, 19, 95; William E., 173
MORRISON, Alexander Harris, 11; Catharine, 149; Christiana, 149; John, 50; Margaret, 149; Mary, 149; Mordecai, 149; Sidney, 50; William, 50, 147, 156
MORROW, Rebecca, 169; Samuel, 173; William, 169
MORTON, Abraham, 133; Benjamin, 30; Elizabeth, 109; Isaac, 121; John, 109; Lydia, 133
MORY, Elizabeth Mary, 133; Lewis, 133
MOSS, Sally, 119
MOTT, Huldah, 51; Valentine, 163
MOULDER, John, 28; Joseph, 15
MOUNT, Mary, 109; Samuel, 142
MOUNT EQUITY, 91
MOYER, David, 29
MUHLENBERG, Frederick Augustus, 164; Henry W., 98; Mary, 98; Peter I. D., 163; Rachel, 163
MULCAHEY, John, 163
MULCAHY, John, 111
MULLER, Henrietta, 164
MULLIGAN, Patrick, 55
MULVEY, Carlos, 151
MUNSEES, Henry, 159
MUNSES, Dieterick, 159
MURGATROYD, Sarah Philips, 95; Thomas, 95
MURPHEY, John, 90
MURPHY, Damaris, 98; Louisa, 28; William, 105
MURRAY, Catherine, 62; James, 159; James W., 62; Susannah, 159, 160
MURREY, William, 117

MURTZER, I. G., 64
MUSGRAVE, Aaron, 81; Abigail, 81; Deborah, 81; Esther, 81; James, 67, 82; Joseph, 127; Joseph P., 127; Lydia, 81
MYERS, Frederick, 57; Jacob, 57; Marmaduke, 133; Mary, 57; Peter, 142
MYRICK, Jethro, 117

-N-

NAGAR, Philip, 10
NAGLE, George, 153
NAILE, Elizabeth, 41
NAIRAC, Peter, 64
NAPIER, Alexander, 144; Ann, 144; William, 144, 153
NASH, Sarah, 150
NATH, Richard, 107
NEAVE, Sarah, 168
NECKLIN, Sophia C., 72
NEEDHAM, Frederick, 4; Mr., 4; Mrs., 4
NEFF, Rudolph, 8
NEGRO, Celia, 152; Harriot, 77
NEGUS, Susanna, 43
NEILL, Christiana Bickham, 14; Elizabeth, 137; Lewis, 14; Thomas, 14
NEKERVIS, William, 143
NELSON, Andrew, 138; William, 138
NESBITT, William, 109
NEVIES, John, 162; Maria Teresa Johana, 162
NEVIS, Thomas, 141
NEWBOLD, Michael, 173; Samuel, 13
NEWBORN, Thomas, 74
NEWELL, Catharine, 11; John, 103
NEWHALL, Eunice B., 140
NEWIRA, Kisiah, 128
NEWLIN, Mary, 9; Sarah, 9
NEWMAN, John, 53
NEZMOS, John H., 124
NICE, Charles, 115; George, 39; James, 99; Margaret, 39; Washington, 99
NICHOL, James, 113
NICHOLAS, Charles I., 137, 144; Maria, 159; Mary, 137; Mary I., 137; Rebecca, 159; Samuel, 137, 159
NICKLE, John, 169
NICKLIN, Juliana, 160
NICOLAS, Lewis, 52
NILES, Daniel, 164
NISBET, John, 70
NIXON, Henry, 114; John, 114
NOBLE, Elizabeth, 29; Hannah,

29; Joseph, 148; Lydia, 29; Rebecca, 148; Richard, 29; Samuel, 29, 30
NOLAN, Mary, 147
NONES, Aaron B., 113, 135; Benjamin, 81, 135
NORDIKE, Rachall, 157
NORMAN, Elizabeth, 16; John Joseph, 16; Joseph, 16; Margaret Ann, 74; Norman, 16
NORRIS, Charles, 99; Isaac, 168; Joseph P., 133; Joseph Parker, 98, 99; Thomas, 168
NORTH, William, 121
NORTON, Thomas, 29, 30, 37, 56, 166
NOX, Ann, 63

-O-

OAKFORD, Charles, 71; Elizabeth, 71; Grace, 71; Isaac, 71; Julian, 71; Mary, 71; Rachel, 71
OAT, Jesse, 8, 169
OBEY, Groome, 112
OBRIEN, Mary, 38
O'CONNER, Christopher, 148
ODDEN, Mary H., 156
ODENHEIMER, Barbara, 61; Catherine, 61; George W., 61; Jacob W., 61; Philip, 61
O'DONNALD, Mary, 123; Rose, 123
O'DONNELL, Bridget, 73; John, 73; Mary, 73
OELLERS, Louisa, 126
OGDEN, Abraham, 61; Mary, 61
OGILLEY, Thomas D., 88
OGLE, Catherine, 82; Lucy, 82; William, 82
OLDDEN, Deborah, 88; George, 109; Mary, 88; Samuel, 88
OLDEN, Benjamin, 164; Deborah, 56; James, 56, 109
OLER, Mary, 74
OLIVEIRA, John, 57
OLIVER, Candy, 128; Maria, 24; Mary, 121
OLLIPHANT, Catharine, 73
OLTON, Jane, 26
O'NEAIL, Louisa, 171
O'NEAL, John, 153
O'NEILL, Ann, 167; Arthur, 167; Arthur J., 167; Hannah, 167; Henry, 167; Hugh C., 167; John, 153, 167; Kyran, 78; Mary, 167; Mary A., 167, 168; Sarah T., 167
ORAM, James, 103; Thomas, 103; William, 158
ORD, Catharine, 44; John, 112
ORDE, Catharine, 44

ORMROD, John, 119
ORMRODS, John, 24
ORR, Ann, 114, 145, 146; Arthur, 139; Catharine, 114; George, 114; John, 114, 139; Margaret, 139; Robert, 35, 114; Samuel, 114
ORSO, John B., 109
OSBOURN, Ebenezer, 150; Jeremiah, 158
OSMON, Anna, 114; Charles, 114; Eliza, 114; Elizabeth, 114; Esther, 114; John, 114; Maria, 114; Thomas, 114; William B., 114
OSMOND, Maria, 85
OSTAIN, Catharine, 1; Eliza, 1; Francis, 1; John, 1; Maria, 1; Mary, 1; Samuel, 1
OTT, Rebecca, 153
OTTO, Bodo, 140; Catharine, 140; Daniel, 140; Jacob, 140; John, 140; John C., 52, 94, 108
OURAM, Charlotte, 28; Elizabeth, 28; Henry, 28; Mary, 28; Nancy, 28; William, 28
OUSTERHELT, Elizabeth, 67; Frederick, 67
OVERDERFF, John, 102
OWEN, Elizabeth, 92; Jane, 92; Mary, 21; Mrs., 4; Patrick, 21
OXENER, Barbara, 16; Frederick, 16; Isaac, 16; Peter, 16
OXLEY, Sarah, 51

-P-

PAGE, Ann, 34; L., 144
PAINTER, Elisabeth, 27; Henry, 27; Jacob, 27; Margaret, 27; Rebecca, 49; William, 49
PALESKE, Charles Gottfried, 48; Hannah, 13, 48, 49; Lewis, 48; Maria Wilhelmina, 48
PALMER, Elizabeth, 66, 101; John B., 82; Phebe, 90; Richard, 12, 28, 66, 90, 101, 172; William T., 156
PANCOAST, Hannah, 33; Samuel, 33
PAPSON, Joseph, 9
PARISH, Ann, 31
PARKE, Ann, 95; Jacob, 1, 79; James Pemberton, 1; Jane, 95; Sally, 95; Samuel, 142; Susan, 95; Thomas, 79
PARKER, Ann, 18; Anne, 18; Benjamin, 154; Elisha, 146; Henry, 18; James Pemberton,

79; John, 56; Joshua Byron, 154; Mary Jane, 18; Thomas, 16, 17, 18, 86, 89, 115; William, 13
PARKINSON, Esther, 59; Martin, 74; Peter, 94; Rebecca, 74; Robert, 59; Sarah, 74
PARMENTIER, Charles, 168
PARMER, Elizabeth, 128
PARRIS, Gabriel, 164
PARRISH, Joseph, 152; Robert, 42
PARRY, Anna, 26; Robert, 66
PARVIN, Aaron, 105; Daniel, 105; Louisa, 105; Samuel, 105
PASCALL, Benjamin, 131; Henry, 131; John, 131
PASCHALL, Ann, 131, 150; Beulah, 131; Mary, 131, 150; Stephen, 150, 151; Thomas, 131, 150; Thomas I., 106; Thomas Jacob, 131
PASQUIN, Widow, 64
PASSEY, Elizabeth, 107; Nancy, 85; William, 85
PASTORIUS, Charles, 110; Daniel, 8
PATTAN, Rebecca, 149
PATTEN, Ann, 104; Joseph Miller, 104
PATTERSON, Jane, 20; John, 97, 166; Rachael, 166; Robert, 77, 132; Robert M., 77
PATTON, Abraham, 72; Sarah, 92
PAUL, Abraham, 52; Alice, 67; Alice C., 67; Andrew, 52; Belkena, 52; Benjamin, 52; Bettle, 167; Elizabeth, 52, 67, 92, 114, 167; Elizabeth F., 47; Hannah, 52; Jacob, 47, 93; James, 3, 24, 114; Jeremiah, 167; Joseph, 47, 52, 116; Joseph M., 17, 129; Joseph W., 47; Josiah, 167; Lydia, 167; Mary, 47, 52, 93; Nathan, 167; Rebecca, 167; Samuel, 93, 167; Samuel W., 47; Sarah, 167; Sarah R., 67; Susanna, 52; Thomas, 19; William, 67, 167; William I., 67
PAXON, Ann, 88; Charles, 88
PAXSON, Anna, 9; Edward Shoemaker, 59; Elizabeth, 59; Fran's., 174; Isaac, 10, 58; Israel, 9, 59; Joseph, 59; Joshua, 59; Malon, 59; Phineas, 59; Richard, 10; Thomas, 59; Timothy, 153; William, 9, 10, 59

PAYNE, Barnard, 11, 28, 38, 68, 90, 101; Henry, 38; Jane, 26; Joseph Alleyne, 26; Sarah, 26
PAYRAS, Stephen, 113
PEACE, I., 148; Isaac, 145; Joseph, 145; Mary, 145; Rebecca, 145
PEACOCK, Adaline Maria, 123; Cornelia, 123; Dodsworth, 123; George Steinmetz, 123; Mary, 123; Ralph, 123; Ralph William, 123
PEALOR, George, 65
PEARSON, Anna, 115; Anne, 75; Beaven, 75; Benjamin, 75; Charles, 64, 75; George, 64; Isaac, 115; Isaac L., 112, 115; John, 64; John B., 64; Joshua, 64, 112; Lydia, 64; Margaret, 64; Martha, 115; Mary, 102; Rachel, 64; Samuel, 64; Thomas, 75, 80; William, 64
PEART, Benjamin, 60, 98; Bryan, 60; Mary, 60; Thomas, 60, 98; William, 60
PEASE, Margaret, 154
PEEKY, Jacob, 96
PEIRCE, Caleb, 109; Charles, 136; George, 3; Rebecca, 109
PEIRSOL, William, 22
PELTZ, Philip, 1, 11, 79, 101; Richard, 101
PEMBERTON, Ann, 146; Hannah, 95; Henry, 167; Joseph, 146; Philadelphia, 167; Sarah, 167
PENDLETON, Edmund H., 163
PENEGAR, Amos, 37
PENNELL, Dorothea S., 29
PENNOCK, Caspar, 21; Sarah, 20, 21
PENROSE, Ann, 35; Charles, 2, 35; Thomas, 35; William, 35
PEPPER, Joseph, 20
PERIT, John W., 152; Margaretta, 152
PERKINS, Washington, 88
PEROT, Eliston, 1
PETERMAN, George, 21, 152; Jacob, 152
PETERS, Adrian, 47; Margaret, 127; Richard, 71, 79, 119
PETIT, Ann, 158
PETTIT, Andrew, 52, 90, 91; Charles, 103; Elizabeth, 90; Thomas McKean, 91
PFEIL, John, 112; Nancy, 165
PFLAUME, Catharine, 18; Elizabeth, 18; Francis, 18

PHENIX, John, 118
PHILE, John, 170; Joseph, 170
PHILIPS, Levy, 123; Sophia, 160
PHILLIPS, Elinor, 10; Henry, 10; James, 10; Margret, 137; William, 122; Zalegman, 129
PHILSON, Alexander, 105; Frances E. Patton, 105; James, 105; Jane, 105; Matthew, 105; Robert Alexander, 105; Thomas, 105
PHIPPS, Esther, 1; Joshua, 1; Sarah, 145
PICKERING, Elihu, 170
PIERCE, Caleb, 172
PIERREPONT, William, 26
PIKE, Stephen, 5
PINKEES, Hannah, 162
PIPER, Rachel, 87
PISTER, Jacob, 155
PITTMAN, Daniel, 81; Ephraim, 166; Margaret, 166; Sarah Ann, 166
PITTS, Elizabeth, 126
PLEASANT, Mary, 95
PLUMSTEAD, George, 114; Mary, 114
POINCY, Adolph, 133; Adolphe, 36; Aglae, 36; Lucien, 36, 133; Maria Rosalie Cecil Montaillet, 133; Olimpie, 133; Olympie, 36; Peter, 36; Rosalie, 133; Rosalie Cecile Montarlet, 36; Victor, 36, 133
POLE, Capt., 161; Edward, 25
POLLARD, Armel Henry, 26; Elizabeth Frances, 26; Jane, 26
POLLOCK, Archibald, 85; Esther, 85; John, 85; Mary, 85
POLTNEY, Catherine, 5
POOLE, Hannah R., 47
PORTE, Jean Baptiste Louis, 32
PORTER, Capt., 136; Cyrus, 5; James Madison, 14; Jane, 26; Maria, 26; Samuel, 141
PORTERFIELD, Moses, 149; Sarah, 149
POTE, Catherine, 127; Fanny, 127; Matthias, 127; Peter, 127
POTTER, Elizabeth, 66; Joseph, 66
POTTS, George, 21; George C., 77; Mary, 77; Nathan R., 83; Nathaniel, 97; Sarah, 88
POUL, Abraham H., 14
POULSON, Charles A., 17; John, 21; Juliana, 18; Zachariah, 21

POULTNEY, Benjamin, 79; Hannah, 79; Lydia, 79; Rebecca, 79
POUNDER, Jonathan, 31, 143, 148
POWEL, Elizabeth, 92; Ellenor, 92; Mary, 92; Mr., 144; William, 92
POWELL, Ann, 16, 173; Bell Jane, 118; Elizabeth, 118, 173; John Hare, 144; Joseph Wetherill, 173; Martha, 16, 86; Sarah, 173; William, 173; William Mifflin, 173
POWER, William, 97
PRAHL, Samuel, 72; Sarah, 72; Sophia, 72
PRATT, Abraham, 15; Alexander, 15; Ann, 122; James D., 122; Nathaniel Falconer, 15; Thomas, 15
PRENTICE, Benjamin, 114
PRESLOR, Catharina, 121; Catharine, 121; George, 121; Henry, 121; Sarah, 121; William, 121
PRESTON, Abigail, 169; Catharine, 169; Hester, 15; J., 171; Jane, 77; John, 15; Jonas, 77; Mary, 169; Susanna, 15; William, 169
PREVOST, Alexander, 74; Andrew M., 40, 161; Catharine, 40; Emma, 161; Henry M., 161; Lewis M., 40, 161; M., 161
PRICE, Catharine, 104; Edward, 121; Joseph, 38, 115, 121; Rebecca, 123; Richard, 43; Sarah, 121; Susanna, 121; Thomas, 77
PRICHETT, Elizabeth, 114; Elizabeth B., 114; Hannah B., 114; Sarah Ann, 114; Thomas, 114; Thomas B., 114; William, 142; William B., 114
PRICKET, Ely, 99
PRIESTMAN, Emma, 99; William, 99
PROBASCO, Henry, 42, 67
PROPERT, John, 50
PROPET, John, 81
PROVEST, Alexander, 75, 127
PRUDOT, L., 55, 81
PRYOR, Ann, 149; Charles R., 135; Elizabeth, 125; George, 84; Hannah, 125; Joseph, 125, 149; Richard, 2; Tacy, 75
PULLEN, Robert, 7
PULLER, Mr., 97
PURVES, Alexander, 154

-Q-
QUAMONY, Mary, 46
QUARLES, John, 140
QUEEN, James, 48; Michael, 149
QUINN, Barnet, 2; Catharine, 116; Charles, 111; Elizabeth, 116; Mary, 116; Thomas, 116
QUINTON, Mary, 23; Richard, 23

-R-
RACK, John, 28
RAIN, Margaret, 110
RAKESTRAW, Joseph, 103, 131
RALSTON, Martha, 92; Robert, 88
RAMBO [See also Grambo], Peter, 28
RAMSEY, Alexander, 124
RANDAL, Matthew, 147
RANDALL, Josiah, 6, 107; Matthew, 111
RANDOLPH, Joseph, 40
RAPP, Joseph, 28
RASTOR, William, 21
RATZHELLER, Anthony, 27
RAWLE, Edward, 165; Robert, 95; Robert T., 95; William, 147, 151, 160, 164
RAWLEY, Lemuel, 11
RAY, Agnes, 81; Andrew, 9; David, 9; John Andrew, 81; Margaret Ann, 81; Mary, 9; Thomas, 9
RAYBOLD, Mary, 89
READ, Comfort, 145; Dr., 113; Francis, 168; Philip, 112; Sarah, 120
READING, Maria, 89; Stephen, 89
REAKERT, John, 138
RED SPRINGS, 32
REDDINGER, Ann, 98; Elizabeth, 98; Frederick, 98; John, 98; Mary, 98
REDMAN, Joseph, 159; Rebecca, 159; Thomas, 161
REDMOND, Mathew, 5
REDOLPHER, Andrew, 174
REDWOOD, Sarah, 5; William, 5
REED, Joseph, 6, 91; Michael, 169; Samuel, 73; William, 30
REEDLE, Mary, 90, 91
REES, George, 73; John, 169
REESE, Bezin, 26; Bezin King, 26; Elizabeth, 77; Ellen, 162; John, 26
REESOR, Abraham, 50
REEVES, Mary, 63
REGUIER, Antoine, 32
REID, Adam, 21
REILLY, Mary, 39; Thomas, 39
REINBOTH, Frederick, 25; George, 25
REINHARD, Catharina, 30; Elizabeth, 30; John, 30; Martin, 30
REINOLDS, William H., 1
REISER, Eve, 107
REMAGE, Adam, 65
REMINGTON, Clement, 141; Isaac, 87; Job B., 45
REMUSAT, Jean Louis, 32
RENEW, Jane, 56; William, 56
RENINGTON, Elizabeth, 87; Emily, 87; Sarah, 87
RENSHAW, Francis, 30; Mary, 41; Mary Erwin Johnson, 6; Richard, 7, 8, 20, 24, 35, 40, 49, 71, 87, 88, 97, 118, 136, 149, 169
RESCH, Abraham, 18
RETCHIE, Ann, 18
RETZER, Rachel, 22
REYBOLD, Betsey, 165; Mary, 89; Philip, 170
REYNOLDS, Charles, 1; Mary, 1, 111; Peter, 111; Simeon, 60; Simon, 1
RHEEM, Jacob, 68
RHOADS, Mary, 29
RICARDS, Mary, 82; Michael, 82; Peter, 82; Thomas, 82
RICE, John, 50
RICH, Mr., 97
RICHARDS, Ann, 135; Benjamin, 80; Charles, 80; Elizabeth, 80; James, 135; John, 102, 135; Joseph, 33, 135; Margaret, 80; Rachel, 135; Samuel, 162; William, 80, 135
RICHARDSON, Benjamin E., 102; C. A., 168; Catharine, 102; Charles A., 167, 168; Elizabeth, 103; Isabella, 97; Jos'h., 130; Joseph, 80; Maria, 103; Mihitabel, 25; Nathaniel, 166; Rebecca, 80; Sarah, 103; Thomas, 40; William, 58, 70, 102
RICHMOND, Peter, 5
RICKER, John, 58
RICKERT, John, 18
RIDDLE, Edward, 8; James, 8; Johanna, 8; John, 8; William, 8, 11
RIDGWAY, Ann, 95; Benjamin, 95; Caroline, 95; Jacob, 95; John, 61; John Jacob, 95; Phebe Ann, 95; Rebecca, 95, 109; Susan, 95; Susanna, 95
RIEGER, Margaret, 93
RIEM, Elizabeth, 70

RIETTI, Abraham, 67
RIFEFER, Jacob, 47
RIFFERT, Mary, 74
RIGHTER, Ann, 165; Anthony, 160; Catharine, 165; Charles, 165; Elizabeth, 160; John, 160; Jonathan, 165; Joseph, 160; Mary, 160; Michael, 165; Peter, 160; Rebecca, 160; Samuel, 165
RIGLER, Jacob, 152; John, 13
RIGWAY, Asa, 151, 152; Charlot, 152; Isaac, 152; Jeremiah, 152
RIHL, Elizabeth Maria Sophia, 119; Henry, 119; Jacob, 119; James, 119; John Wiser, 119; Susan, 119
RIHLE, William, 150
RIKARDS, Thomas, 82
RILEY, John, 109; Joseph, 43; William, 43
RINK, John, 58, 121; Joseph, 58; Mary, 58; William S., 58
RIPLEY, John P., 66
RITCHIE, Ann, 17
RITTENHOUSE, Abraham, 3; Catharine, 86; Enoch, 3; Henry, 86; Jacob, 3, 86; Joseph, 86; Margareth, 86; Peter, 3, 86; Samuel, 3; William, 86
RITTER, Jacob, 42
ROACH, Isaac, 89
ROADS, John, 65
ROBARTS, James, 148; Migal, 148
ROBB, James, 148
ROBBARTS, Christiana, 149; John, 149
ROBBINS, John, 24; Samuel J., 166
ROBERTS, Algernon, 69, 153; Ann, 46, 93, 168; Augustus, 50; Benjamin, 50; Cadwalader, 137; Caroline, 50; Charles, 170; Daniel, 92; Edmund, 50; Elizabeth, 93; Griffith, 46; Hannah, 170; Isaac, 69; Isaac W., 174; Isaac Warner, 153; Jehu, 93; John, 53, 92, 93; Jonathan, 53; Joseph, 80, 174; Margaret, 46; Martha, 143; Mary, 34, 53, 77, 93, 123; Mary Ashbridge, 152; Owen, 46; Rachel, 42, 50; Robert, 53; Sarah, 53, 92, 93; Seth, 148; Susanna, 53; Thomas, 53, 77, 93; Thomas H., 161
ROBERTSON, Gilbert, 165; James, 82, 139
ROBESON, Elisabeth, 1; Frederick B., 106; Jonathan, 1; Sarah, 1
ROBINSON, Andrew, 171; Ann, 2, 79; Charles, 18; Elizabeth, 2; George, 147; Henry, 71; Jacob, 71; Jane, 9; John, 2, 4, 9, 71; Jonahan, 79; Jonathan, 2; Joseph, 174; Joshua, 12; Kime, 15; Louisa, 71; Mary, 147; Robinson, 71; Thomas, 19; William, 2, 71, 79; William Tennent, 2
ROCHE, Edward, 17; Edward B., 17; Elizabeth, 17; Francis Gurney, 17; Maria, 17
ROCKHILL, Lydia, 138; Thomas C., 70
RODDERFIELD, Elizabeth, 158; Rosanna, 158
RODGERS, Jane, 33; John, 33
RODMAN, Rebecca C., 114
RODRIGUEZ, Isaac, 65; Jacob, 66; Moses, 66
ROGERS, David, 163; Thomas, 110; William, 58
ROMEIS, John, 3
ROOFNER, Anthony, 105
ROOT, Andrew, 112; Catherine, 83; Conrad, 112; Elizabeth, 83; Henry, 83; John, 83; Mary, 112; Susanna, 83
RORER, Joseph, 130
ROSE, David, 19; Joseph, 106; Martha, 48; Peter, 106
ROSS, David, 118; Elizabeth, 73; James, 73; Marcia G., 118; Robert, 35, 62; Thomas, 98
ROSTAIN, Fournier, 136
ROTCH, Susanna, 95
ROUCH, Matthias, 96
ROUSH, John, 6; Matthias, 6; Sarah, 155; William, 155
ROW, Frederick, 73; George, 73; Henry, 73; John Martin, 72
ROWAN, Isabella, 148
ROYAL, Edward, 74; George, 74; Jacob, 74; Mary, 74; William, 74
RUDDACH, John, 110
RUDOLPH, Hannah, 52; John, 52; Lydia, 131
RUFNER, Anthony, 115
RULON, Benjamin, 16
RUMEL, Julian, 100
RUMMEL, Cathrine, 8; Goerge, 8; Mary, 8
RUMNER, John, 121

RUMSEY, William, 172
RUNDLE, Richard, 95
RUSH, James, 105; James I., 139, 163; James Irvine, 155; Joseph, 155; Lewis, 61, 94, 115; Mary, 43; Sarah, 155; Susannah, 155
RUSSEL, Philip, 62; Robert G., 58; Samuel Wetherill, 62; Sarah C., 58
RUSSELL, Joseph, 139
RUSSELLER, Sarah, 88
RUTTER, Elizabeth, 70; George, 70; Robert, 70
RYAN, Charles, 23; Lewis, 73

-S-

SAGATHEY, William, 50
SAGATHY, William, 94
SALAIGNAC, Ad. C., 134
SALTAR, Elizabeth, 64, 139; Frances, 139; George G., 64; John, 64; Lucy, 139; Margaret, 139; Maria, 139; Samuel, 45
SALTER, Samuel, 95
SAMPLE, Ann, 142; James, 142; Martha, 142; Mary, 142
SANDWITH, Mary, 29; Sarah, 29
SANSOM, William, 26
SARGEANT, Thomas, 31
SARGENT, Thomas, 139
SARMIENTO, Catherine, 62; Francis C., 62
SATTERTHWAITE, Abel, 34
SAUL, Ann, 118; John, 118; Susanna, 118
SAULMIER, Louisa, 19; Mary, 19; Matilda, 19; Sarah, 19
SAUNDERS, Samuel F., 33; Susanna, 43
SAUSMANHAUS, Maria, 119
SAVERY, Thomas, 1, 46
SAVIDGE, Reuben, 96
SAWER, James, 63, 89, 97, 133, 159, 162
SAWYER, Ebby, 124; Hannah, 124; Jane Allen, 124; Joseph Allen, 124; Lewden, 124; Margaret, 124
SAYLOR, John, 112
SCATTERGOOD, Ann, 109; Joseph, 109; Rebecca, 109; Sarah, 109; Thomas, 109
SCHAEFFER, Catharine, 150; Dr., 154; George, 150
SCHAUMKESSEL, Frederick, 83
SCHAUWECKER, Godfrey, 76
SCHELL, Henry, 26, 149
SCHEPPACH, John Jacob, 135
SCHINDER, Michael, 16

SCHLATTER, Casper, 14; William, 126
SCHLATTERER, John, 7
SCHLENTZ, Catherine, 53; George, 53
SCHLOSSER, Rosina M., 48; Theodora Elizabeth, 48
SCHNEIDER, Peter, 76
SCHOCK, Andrew, 135; Catharine, 135; Henry, 135; Jacob, 135; Rebecca, 135
SCHOENHEIT, Tobias, 140
SCHOLFIELD, Abraham, 24; Elizabeth, 24; Frances, 24; Mary, 24
SCHOOCK, Catharine, 168; George, 169; Margaret, 168; Michael, 168
SCHOTT, James, 122
SCHREIBER, Frederick, 43; Joseph, 43; Margaret, 43; Mary, 43; Sarah, 43; Susanna, 43
SCHRYER, George, 30
SCHUMO, Ann, 69; Barney, 69; Daniel, 69; Joseph, 69; Lydia, 69; Sarah P., 69; Susanna, 69; Thomas, 69
SCHYDER, Christiana, 8; Sarah, 8
SCOLFIELD, Samuel, 88
SCOTT, Deborah, 45; Edwin T., 45; Edwin Tamerlin/Tamerlane, 45; Elizabeth, 117; Jonathan, 117; Mary Ann, 68
SEASFIELD, John, 88
SECKEL, Henry, 98; Sophia, 98
SEELE, John, 77
SEEMAN, Andrew, 58; Dorothy, 58; John Andrew, 58
SEES, George, 132
SEIP, Sophia, 82
SEITZ, Charlotte, 6
SELL, Ann, 128; Elizabeth, 128; Henry, 128; Jacob, 128; John, 128; Samuel, 128; Solomon, 129; Sophia, 128; Thomas, 128
SELLERS, David, 63; E., 119; Jane, 40; Mrs., 119; Nathan, 5, 151; Rachel, 119; Samuel, 63
SELTZER, Elizabeth, 14; Henry, 14
SENA, Elizabeth, 25
SERGEANT, Elihu S., 49; Elihu Spencer, 72; Elizabeth, 72; John, 78
SERLS, William, 24
SERMON, Mary, 172

SERVOSS, Charles K., 112;
  Elizabeth, 112; Joseph, 112
SEVERN, Ann, 139; Benjamin,
  139; Elizabeth, 139, 140;
  John, 139; William, 139
SEXTON, John, 139
SEYBERT, Conrad, 97
SEYFERT, Conrad, 24
SHADE, Sarah, 143
SHAFFER, Michael, 10; Rev., 174
SHAFFNER, Casper, 76
SHALL, Jacob, 145
SHALLCROSS, Benjamin, 78;
  Morris C., 131
SHALLUS, Francis, 48, 135
SHANNON, Margaret, 147
SHANONN, Henry, 105
SHAR, Mary, 123
SHARP, Catharine, 149; Charles,
  149; Eliza, 90; Francis,
  149; John, 24; Joseph, 149;
  Lazarus, 149; Ludwick, 110;
  Michael Hicks, 25; Richard,
  25, 149; Rosanna, 149;
  Thomas, 25; William, 149
SHARPE, Lodewyk, 134
SHARPLESS, Ann, 138; Caspar,
  21; Catharine, 20; Edith,
  138; Hannah, 138; Isaac,
  138; John, 97; Joseph, 138;
  Mary, 138; Mary D., 138;
  Townsend, 148
SHAW, Alexander, 69, 167; Anna
  M., 61; George, 82; John
  Auldham, 174; Thomas, 174;
  William A., 61
SHEAF, George, 17
SHEAFF, Barbara, 98; Catharine,
  98; George, 17, 98; John D.,
  98; Mary, 98; William, 95
SHEBLE, Adam, 107; Jacob, 72,
  110; Mary, 107
SHEED, Elizabeth, 171
SHEETS, Daniel, 135
SHELMIRE, Elizabeth, 77; Jesse,
  31
SHENGE, Elizabeth, 118
SHEPERD, Catherine, 163
SHEPPARD, Catharine, 166
SHERIDAN, Dominic, 59; Mary, 59
SHEW, Manuel Gotlieb, 61;
  Margaret, 61
SHEWELL, Thomas, 70
SHIELDS, David, 174; Hannah,
  174; John, 49, 174; Robert,
  174; Thomas, 174
SHINCKL, Frederick, 16
SHINGLER, Elizabeth, 53
SHINNECK, Mary Elizabeth, 138
SHIPLEY, Ann, 83; Elizabeth,
  83; Jane, 83; John, 10, 83;
  Joseph, 9, 83; Thomas, 83;
  William, 83
SHIPPEN, Elizabeth, 62; Susan,
  136; William, 19, 136
SHIVELY, George C., 105
SHOBER, Blathwaite, 70;
  Catherine, 48; Susan B., 48
SHOCH, Henry, 6; Sarah, 6
SHOCHALL, Mary, 125
SHOCK, Elizabeth, 135
SHOEMAKER, Abigail, 167;
  Abraham, 63, 115, 127, 174;
  Ann, 167; Ann Elizabeth, 48;
  Charles, 48, 167; Deborah,
  127; Elizabeth, 127; Esther,
  127; Francis, 127, 174;
  Henry, 110, 112, 127; Jacob,
  40; James, 48; John J., 167;
  Joseph, 104, 166; Lewis,
  110, 127; Margaret, 48;
  Mary, 48, 127; Mary Ann,
  127; Rebecca, 167; Robert,
  30; Susan, 127; Thomas, 139
SHOESTE, Mary, 14
SHORT, Robert, 94
SHORTALL, Mary, 2
SHORTHOUSE, Thomas, 54
SHOTWELL, Elizabeth, 20
SHRONK, Barnabas, 49; Phebe, 49
SHUBART, Michael, 8; Widow, 8
SHUFFLEBOTTOM, William, 65
SHUGART, Simon, 158
SHULTE, John, 5
SHULTZ, John, 58
SHUSTER, Adam, 93; David, 93;
  Henry, 93; Margaret, 93;
  Mary, 75; Thomas Francis, 93
SHUTE, Mary, 5; William, 171
SHUTT, Elizabeth, 11
SICKEL, Ann, 143; Mary, 143
SIDDELL, Joseph, 142
SIDE, Margaret, 24; William, 24
SILVER, John, 68
SIM, Walter, 98
SIMES, James W., 126
SIMMONS, John, 103, 171;
  Joseph, 25; Rebecca, 163,
  166; Stephen, 166
SIMON, Susanna, 11
SIMONDS, Elizabeth, 57; Jonas,
  57; Nathan, 57
SIMONS, Joseph, 117, 158
SIMPSON, George, 26, 80
SIMS, Walter, 26
SIMSON, Clementine, 165; John,
  165
SINGER, John, 22
SINGLETON, Thomas, 24; William,
  136
SITTEL, Joseph, 142
SKEES, Martha, 43

SKINNER, Elizabeth, 63
SKYRIN, Ann, 29; John, 29
SLEEPER, James, 69; Jonathan, 122
SLINEY, James, 145
SLOAN, Hugh, 21
SMALL, Abraham, 65
SMILEY, William, 10
SMITH, Abigail, 29; Abraham, 100; Ann, 7; Barbara, 16; Benjamin, 100; Catharine, 5, 45, 78; Catharine Oldden, 88; Charles, 18, 22; Charles L., 3, 43; Cornelia, 92; Cyrus N., 88; Daniel, 2, 17, 18, 153; David, 100; Edmund, 100; Edward, 113; Elisha, 19; Eliza, 17, 46, 54, 67; Elizabeth, 5, 53, 88, 131, 144, 156; Francis Gurney, 17; Frederick, 164, 174; George, 89, 143; Godfy, 126; Grace, 9; Gurney, 17; Henry, 78, 120; Hugh, 88; Isaac, 67; Jacob, 78, 113, 135; Jacob B., 165; James, 14, 86, 95, 101, 123; James G., 17; James S., 17, 153; John, 3, 4, 7, 46, 66, 77, 79, 85, 89, 100, 165, 170; John D., 166; John S., 17, 97, 162; John W., 39; Jonathan P., 171; Joseph, 100; Louisa, 140; Margaret, 27, 33, 78, 129; Mary, 77, 78, 100, 101, 170; Mary Ann, 33; Mary North, 88; Merriman, 9; Mrs., 4; Newberry, 97; Peter, 16, 84, 154, 164; Phebe, 100; Phebe Ann, 88; Philip, 84, 120; Phoebe Champion, 65; R. L., 17; Rebecca, 79, 88; Rebeccah Marshall, 88; Richard, 69; Robert, 28, 100, 101, 127; Rosanna, 144; Samuel, 35, 100, 101; Sarah, 89, 106, 167; Seneca, 88; Stephen, 88; Terence, 31, 55; Thomas, 100, 101, 143; Thomas Broom, 112; Thomas S., 86; William, 5, 15, 50, 54, 121; William W., 129
SMITHER, Aunt, 122; Uncle, 122
SMYTH, Affley, 4; Frederick, 4; Hannah, 92; Jane Eliza Laremore, 92; Miss, 4; Peter, 92; Rebecca, 92; Sarah, 92
SNETHENS, Mary, 84
SNOOKE, Mary, 64

SNOWDEN, Leonard, 34
SNOWDON, Joseph, 131; Leonard, 123
SNYDER, Catharine, 16; Daniel, 39; Elizabeth, 3, 166; George, 117; George A., 116; George C., 162; Henry, 166; Jacob, 116; Jane, 162; Joseph, 2, 73, 97, 133, 171; Lewis, 16; Margaret, 16, 43; William, 16
SOLIER CABANES & JUGLE, 96
SOLIS, Jacob S., 84
SOMMER, Jacob, 3, 103
SONNTAG, Hannah Wright, 154; William L., 154
SORBER, Elias, 68; Joseph, 98
SOUDER, John, 125
SOULLIER, John M., 126
SOWDER, John, 107
SPEAKMAN, Phebe, 88
SPECHT, Elizabeth, 15; George, 15
SPEIGEL, Elizabeth, 104
SPIEGEL, Elizabeth, 10; John Remigius, 10
SPRAGUE, Edward, 167
SPROGELL, Ann Louisa C., 119; Betsey K., 119; Betsey Kezia, 119; David M., 119; Edward C., 119; Elizabeth Ann, 119; Elizabeth Marshall, 119
SPROGLE, Ann Louisa, 79; Betsy K., 79; David M., 79; Edward, 79; Edward Croston, 79; Elizabeth M., 79
SPROUL, Margaret, 21
SPROULE, John, 21
SPRUNCE, Prince, 8
SPRUNEY, John, 8
STACKHOUSE, Mary, 145
STACY, Tacy Ann, 75
STALL, Catharine, 162; Ellen, 162; Frederick, 83, 162; George, 162
STAMPER, Joseph, 37, 38
STANLEY, Norris, 33, 87
STANSBURY, Sarah, 90, 91
STAPLER, John, 100
STARK, Margaret, 126
STARR, Alexander, 56; Ann, 56, 125; Charles W., 56; Deborah, 56; James, 56, 125; John, 56; Joseph, 56; Lydia, 56, 124, 125; Mary, 56, 125; Moses, 56, 125; Samuel, 56; Sarah, 56
STATZELL, Henry, 14, 85
STAUGHTON, William, 126
STAUS, Esther Dorothea, 126;

Joseph, 126
STEDHAM, Elizabeth, 29
STEEL, Alexander, 65, 129;
   James, 129; Kezia, 129;
   Malty, 138; Mary, 129;
   Samuel, 138; William, 129
STEIN, Abraham, 6, 46, 108, 148
STEINAUER, Michael, 7, 125;
   William, 7
STEINMETZ, Andrew B., 158;
   Daniel, 57, 132; Elizabeth,
   143; Henry, 158; Jacob, 143
STEPHENS, Anna Maria, 111;
   Catharine, 111; Elizabeth
   Weaver, 111; Jacob, 104;
   John, 104; Samuel, 111;
   Sarah Harman, 111
STERN, William, 114
STEVENS, Elizabeth, 115; Jacob,
   115; Richard, 114
STEVENSON, Ann, 85; Cornelius,
   85, 86; Crooke, 86; Hannah,
   5, 85; Isaac, 86; John, 85;
   Margaretta, 85; Mary, 41;
   Peter, 5, 85; Robert, 85;
   Susan, 85; William, 5, 85,
   86
STEWARDSON, Thomas, 20, 29, 51,
   166
STEWART, Alexander, 86;
   Alexander John, 52; Artemus,
   141; Charles, 24, 141;
   Daniel, 23; David, 141;
   Eliza Jane, 128; Elizabeth,
   41, 141; Esther, 38;
   Gustavus Conyngham, 173;
   Hannah, 35; Harriet, 141;
   Hepzibah, 113; Hetty, 52;
   John, 14, 35; Margaret, 35,
   172; Maria, 35; Parthenia,
   141; Robert R., 173; Samuel
   M., 128; Sarah, 35; Thomas,
   35, 172
STEWARTSON, Ann, 123; Thomas,
   123
STEWERT, Mary, 113
STILES, Henry, 15; James, 15;
   John, 15; Joseph, 15; Mary
   Ann, 15; Nancy, 15; William,
   15
STIMBLE, George, 166; Rosanna,
   166
STINE, Jacob, 62; Mary, 62,
   152; Peter, 70, 152
STINEFORD, Elizabeth, 122;
   Sarah, 122
STINGER, Frederick, 11; Sophia,
   11
STIPE, Catharine, 94
STOCK, Catharine, 10;
   Frederick, 10; Philip, 10
STOCKER, Martha, 49
STOERGER, Martin, 45; Mary, 45
STOKES, Joshua, 125
STOLZ, Mrs., 76
STONE, Margaret, 80; Mrs., 4;
   Robert, 4; William, 80
STONEBURNER, Ann, 43; Mary, 43
STONEMETZ, Elizabeth, 19;
   Jacob, 19; Rachel, 19;
   William, 19
STONEY, John, 53, 54
STORK, Henry, 20
STORY, Mary, 149
STOUSE, Hester, 111; Joseph,
   67, 111
STOUT, George P., 125; Jacob,
   125; John Leonard, 125;
   Joseph, 125; Maria, 125;
   Mary, 8; William, 125
STOW, Charles, 17, 122; Isaac,
   17; Lazarus, 17; Mary, 17;
   Samuel, 17
STOWERS, Elisabeth B., 44
STRACKLINE, Henry, 36
STRATTON, Allen, 91; Benjamin,
   146; Clarity, 105; Clayton,
   171; Elizabeth, 105, 146;
   Ephraim, 105; Esther, 105;
   Fithian, 105; Grizelda, 146;
   Henry, 146; James, 146;
   Joel, 105; Jonathan, 146;
   Juda, 105; Lewis, 47; Lot,
   105; Mary, 91, 146; Samuel,
   105; Sarah, 105; Thomas,
   105; William, 105
STRAYLINE, Catherine, 75;
   Charles, 75; Elizabeth, 75;
   George, 75; William, 75
STREEPER, Dennis, 29; John, 29;
   Joseph, 29; Juditch, 28;
   Margaret, 29; Mary, 29;
   Sarah, 29
STREET, Griffith, 4
STREPER, William, 39
STRETCH, Thomas, 169
STRICKER, Adam, 49; Catharine,
   49, 99; Charles, 24; Daniel,
   49; George, 49, 99; Leonard,
   15
STRIEBY, Adam, 117; Eliza, 117;
   Frances, 117; George, 117;
   John, 117; Joseph, 117;
   Maria, 117; Rachel, 117;
   Sarah, 117; William, 117
STRIEPY, Adam, 107; Maria, 107
STRIKER, Leonard, 55
STRINGER, Ann, 119
STROUD, Thomas, 15
STROUP, John, 161
STRUM, Henrick, 140

STRYKER, Peter A., 47
STUART, Charles, 47; Isabella, 65; James, 65, 102, 129, 134, 135; Margaret, 11; Mary, 82
STUCKERT, George F., 76
STURGESS, Abraham, 89; Esther, 89; Joshua, 88, 89; Levin, 89; Rachell, 89
STURGIS, Peter, 128
STURMFELS, Paul, 19
SULGER, Jacob, 42, 135; Margaret, 135
SULLIVAN, Charles, 124; David, 124; Jeremiah, 164; Joshua, 123; Sarah, 124
SUMMERL, Joseph, 162; Sarah, 162; William, 162
SUMMERS, Catharine, 11; John, 113
SUTOR, Elizabeth, 9; James, 9; James Whitton, 9; Mary, 9
SUTTER, Daniel, 104; Elizabeth, 9; Mary, 61
SUTTON, William, 155
SWAN, Thomas, 170
SWEAGER, Jane, 4
SWEENY, John, 42
SWEETMAN, Kezia, 44
SWEITZER, Catharine, 133; Henry, 133; Mary, 133; Simon, 133
SWIFT, Joseph, 114
SYMONS, Ja., 48
SYSUM, Anna, 9

-T-

TABER, Sarah Wetherill, 62
TAGERT, Joseph, 120
TAGGART, Redmond I., 97
TAILOR, Mary, 106
TALBOT, Eli, 126
TALLMAN, George L., 95
TAMORANA, Joaquin, 151
TAPSICO, Jacob, 133
TARRANT, Thomas, 118
TATEM, Jeremiah, 2; Mary, 2
TAYLOR, Amos, 4, 122; Amy, 122; Benjamin, 122; Caleb, 140; Eliza, 122; Elizabeth, 4; Ellen, 152; Enoch, 122; Esther, 122; George, 156; Hannah, 4; Jacob, 122; James, 92; James D., 152; Jane, 26, 92; John, 24, 26, 92, 117; John N., 152; Juliana D., 152; Lewis, 80, 86; Maria, 26; Mary, 36, 37, 80; Mercy, 4; Peter, 35; Phany, 4; Rachel, 122; Robert, 122; Sarah, 4;

211

Tacey, 4; Thomas, 158; Zada, 122
TEES, Jacob, 78
TEMPLE, Daniel G., 54, 138; Keturah, 54; Mira, 54; Simon, 31
TERRIER, Frederick Daniel, 14
THACKARA, Ann, 82; Eleanor, 82; Elizabeth, 9; James, 82; Margaret, 9; Samuel, 9, 82; William, 82
THACKRAY, Mary, 132
THAW, Benjamin, 29
THOMAS, Alexander, 86; Ann, 15, 44; Daniel, 34, 39, 44; Dinah, 40; Elenor, 86; Elinor, 86, 87; Elizabeth, 34, 57; Ellen, 162; Evan W., 89; Francis, 40; Israel, 102; Jacob, 125; James, 119; Jane, 57; John, 28, 153; Jonathan, 56, 102, 110, 118; Joseph, 57, 108, 125; Lydia, 40, 77; Margaret, 125; Mary Ann, 62; Mordecai, 40; Nathan, 108; Philip, 15; Reuben, 40; Robert, 57; Susannah, 28; Timothy, 82; William, 57, 62
THOMASSON, Filette, 64
THOMPSON, Aaron, 40; Ann K., 161; Charles W., 170; David, 40; Elizabeth, 52; George, 168; Hannah, 79; James B., 79, 168; Janet, 166; John, 153, 168; John W., 135; Jonah, 168; Joseph Thomas, 40; Josiah, 50; Lydia, 79; Margaret, 24; Martha, 109; Mary, 24; Milton, 40; Peter, 79, 138, 170; Phebe, 40; Rebecca, 168; Rebecca C., 168; Samuel, 168; Sarah, 24; Sarah Biddle, 79; Thomas, 52, 168
THOMSON, Charles, 14, 15, 123; Charles W., 146; Lydia, 48; Peter, 1, 13, 15, 16, 29, 38, 82, 87, 101, 123, 129, 133, 141, 146, 156, 158, 164
THORNILLY, William F., 61
THORNTON, Mary, 147
THUMBERT, George, 125
TIBBEN, Michael, 131
TIERMAN, James, 120; Jane, 120; Margaret, 120; Mary, 120; Thomas, 120
TILBERRY, Elizabeth, 7
TILGHMAN, Anna Mary, 31; Benjamin, 24, 30, 31, 45, 72, 77, 147; E., 45; Edward,

30, 31, 63; Elizabeth, 30, 31; Elizabeth Margaret, 72; James, 72; M. A., 63; Margaret, 72; Maria, 72; Mary, 31; William, 71, 72, 160
TILLMAN, Ann Magdalene, 68; Georg, 44; John George, 68
TILLY, John, 170
TILLYER, Letitia, 54; Sarah, 3
TIMINGS, Thomas, 77, 91
TIMMINGS, Thomas, 142
TITTERMARY, Eleanor, 70; John, 70; John C., 70; Loranah, 70; Lurana, 70; Margaret, 70; Robert C., 70; Thomas I., 70; William W., 70
TOD, Mary D., 52; William, 19; William H., 52, 94
TOLAND, Henry, 169; Robert, 70
TOMKINS, Sarah, 41
TOMLINSON, Eliza, 102; James, 142; Mary, 125; Thomas, 142
TOOLE, Mary, 142
TOPHAM, William, 5
TORENS, Abraham, 30; Ann, 30; John, 30; Mary, 89; Paul, 30; Ruth, 30; Samuel, 30; William, 30
TORR, Elizabeth, 20; Hannah, 20; Jaboel, 20; John, 20; Joseph, 20; Josiah, 20; Mary, 102; Rebecca, 20
TOTHERON, Christiana, 116
TOVELL, William, 71
TOVINS, Mary, 83
TOWELL, Jane, 20; John, 20; William, 20
TOWNLY, James, 109; Sarah, 109
TOWNSEND, Assemith, 78; Charles, 47, 138; Deborah, 122; Elizabeth, 78; Ezra, 4; James, 122; John, 33; Joseph, 171
TRADER, Henry, 158
TRAQUAIR, Adam, 68, 85; James, 68; Samuel Henderson, 68; Thomas, 134
TRAVIS, Ann Bond, 32; Elizabeth, 32
TRAZUAIR, Adam, 110
TREWILLONE, Elizabeth, 53
TREXLER, Jacob, 94, 155
TRIMBLE, George, 4; James, 4; Mary, 4
TRIMMER, Edward, 7; Mary, 7
TRIP, Betsey, 62; Kitty, 61
TRIPP, John, 72
TROLLINGER, Andrew, 54
TROTTER, Ann, 8; Daniel, 8, 39; Elizabeth, 39; Emmeline, 8; Joseph, 8, 39; Margretta C., 8; Mary, 8, 39; Nathan, 39; Rebecca, 8, 39; Sansom William, 8, 39; Thomas C., 39; William, 8
TROUP, John, 72; Sarah, 72
TROUT, John, 145
TRUETT, M. F., 38
TRUMAN, George, 110; James, 110, 173; Jeffrey, 110; Joseph Moore, 110; Richard, 110
TRUNK, John, 2
TRUSTY, Jonathan, 8, 158
TULLY, John, 138; Thompson, 138
TUNIS, Elizabeth, 171; Jane, 171; Jehu R., 171; Richard, 171; Thomas R., 171
TURNBULL, John, 18
TURNER, Isabella, 40; Joseph, 26; Maria, 40
TUSTIAN, Eunice, 47; Thomas, 47
TUSTIN, Elizabeth, 110; Isaac, 164
TWADDELL, James, 2
TWAMLEY, Elisabeth, 41
TWAMLY, Elizabeth, 60
TYSON, Charlotte, 110; Edwin, 110; George, 51; Isaac, 83; Joshua, 110; Mary, 110; Matilda, 110; Samuel, 110

-U-

UHL, Ann Maria, 107; Catharine, 107; Elizabeth, 107; John, 106, 107; William Reinhart, 107
UHLER, G., 134; George, 131; John, 117, 131
ULBERT, Frederick, 84
ULMER, William, 76
ULRICK, Frederick, 68
UNDERHILL, Andrew, 79, 158
UNGER, George, 116
UNKLE, Jacob, 29

-V-

VALOIS NOBLE AND CO., 96
VALOIS, ROBERT ANTHONY & CO., 97
VAN HOOK, Benjamin R., 132
VAN LASKET, Christian, 28
VANDEREN, Susanna, 141
VANDERIN, Susanna, 141
VANDERKIMP, J. J., 71
VANDIKE, David, 123; Elizabeth, 123
VANHORN, Bernard, 44; John, 112; Samuel, 35
VANTILBERG, Sophia, 92
VANUXEN, Esther, 127; Lewis C.,

127
VAUGHAN, Jane, 132; Mary, 132;
  Rebecca, 132; Sarah, 132;
  Thomas, 132; William, 132
VAUX, George, 122; James, 32;
  Roberts, 20
VENCE, James, 152
VENER, James, 152
VERCHAUX, Henry F., 102
VERMITYEA, Mary, 98
VERREE, James, 152
VETTI, Abraham, 67
VIAN, Louis Joseph Benjamin,
  81; Madelaine, 81
VIAR, Jane, 151
VILLAR, Charles, 44
VILLARD, Jean Pierre, 32; Mary
  Anne, 32
VINCENT, Elizabeth, 109; John,
  109; Sarah, 109
VOGDES, John R., 119
VOGEL, Charles, 129; Frederick,
  129; Juliana, 129
VOLANS, Samuel, 19
VOLKMAR, Henry, 152
VORES, Philip, 157

-W-

WACHSMUTH, John Godfried, 126
WACK, Casper, 105
WADMAN, Christina, 83; Mary,
  83; Nancy, 83; Peace, 83
WAGNER, William, 48
WAINWRIGHT, John, 97; John
  Burn, 162
WAIT, Francis D., 65
WAKELING, Samuel, 9
WALE, Ulrick, 144
WALKER, Emanuel, 70; Robert,
  22, 119; Samuel, 53, 57;
  Sarah, 18, 116
WALL, Andrew, 163; Dennis, 163;
  George, 35; Mrs., 163;
  Richard, 163
WALLACE, James, 136; Margaret,
  28; Sarah, 40; William, 28
WALLINGTON, George Edward, 148;
  John, 148; Sarah, 148
WALMSLEY, Abigail, 145; Israel,
  145; Jesse, 78; Joseph, 145;
  Mary, 145; Rebecca, 98;
  Sarah, 145; William, 145
WALN, Jacob S., 94; Nicholas,
  94; Robert, 157; William, 94
WALPOLE, Thomas, 97
WALSH, Annabella, 23;
  Elizabeth, 23; John, 143;
  John H., 23; Joseph, 23;
  Philip, 97
WALTER, George, 13; Jacob, 169;
  Michael, 97

WALTON, Benjamin, 98; Daniel,
  104; Hannah, 98; James, 36;
  Joseph, 5; Mary, 98; Phebe,
  98; Sarah, 134; William, 98
WAMPLER, Daniel, 129
WAMPOLE, I., 69; Isaac, 10, 12,
  22, 25, 33, 36, 37, 42, 43,
  69, 75, 76, 89, 93, 94, 102,
  104, 108, 114, 123, 124,
  129, 133, 134, 135, 137,
  153, 157
WARD, Deborah, 45; Elizabeth,
  79; Hannah, 45; Josiah, 11;
  Margaret, 45; Mary, 45;
  Thomas, 45
WARDER, Ann, 1, 123; Jeremiah,
  1, 116; John H., 116
WARDIN, William, 166
WARE, Ann, 159; David, 2, 159;
  Henrietta, 159
WARNER, Ann, 68; Benjamin, 90,
  91, 151, 168; Hannah, 131;
  Heronimus, 12; John, 68, 69,
  115, 135; Joseph, 164, 168;
  Lydia, 69; Mary, 69;
  Rebecca, 69; William, 121,
  134, 165
WARRINGTON, Rebecca, 98
WASPE, Jacob, 19
WATERMAN, Thomas, 148
WATERS, Robert, 97
WATKINS, David, 82; John, 82;
  Margaret, 82
WATSON, Enoch, 73; James, 110;
  John, 27; Joseph, 33, 51,
  52, 150; Margaret, 162;
  Sarah, 43; Thomas, 158;
  William, 23; William D., 58
WATTS, John, 24
WAY, Andrew, 95, 107, 157;
  Elizabeth, 157; George, 157;
  Hannah, 1; James, 171;
  Joshua, 1; Mary, 157;
  Mathilde, 1; Phebe, 1;
  Rachel, 157
WAYNE, Jacob, 155
WEASEY, Samuel, 52
WEATHERBY, Joseph, 62, 66;
  Mary, 62
WEAUGH, Jacob, 78
WEAVER, Anna Maria, 111; Anne
  Maria, 126; Barnard, 132;
  Catharan, 132; Clayton, 58;
  Eave, 132; George, 106;
  Henry, 12, 78, 159; John,
  57, 78, 126, 132; Margaret,
  78, 106; Margarett, 132;
  Mary, 104; Mathew, 11;
  Michael, 106; Nicholas, 150
WEBB, John, 81; Martha, 118;
  William, 93

WEBSTER, Ann, 81; Charles, 160; Mary, 81; Robert, 81; Samuel, 81; Thomas, 2, 79, 81
WECKERLY, Elizabeth, 6
WEED, George, 148; Nancy, 148
WEIDMAN, John, 85
WEIR, William, 11
WEISS, Ann, 118; Charles, 115; Frederick, 164; George, 115, 118, 164; John, 83; Mary, 118; Samuel, 116; Sarah, 115; Susan, 118; Wilhelmina, 83; Wilhelmina Henrikel, 84
WELCH, Eliza, 148; Mary, 99
WELCOME, Hannah, 118
WELDEN, Thomas, 61
WELSH, Elizabeth, 23; James, 163; Joseph, 22; Rachel, 74; Sarah, 114
WERT, Mary, 148
WESCOT, Robert, 124
WESSELS, John Frederick Francis, 46; Sarah T., 46
WEST, Anna, 16; Charles C., 16; Elizabeth, 16, 42; Henry, 34; John, 24; John H., 78; Mary, 16; Robert L., 16; Samuel, 16; Sarah, 16; Thomas G., 16; Willim, 84
WESTCOMBE, Mary, 168
WESTINBERGER, Mary, 11
WETHERILL, Ann, 153; Anna, 61; Christopher, 61, 162, 173; George, 61; Isaac, 61; John, 61; Martha, 61; Maryanne, 5; Mordecai, 61, 62; Samuel, 61, 62, 78; Sarah, 61
WHARTON, Ann, 45; Elizabeth, 44; Fishbourn, 127; John, 23, 44, 45; Mary, 23; Moore, 127; Robert, 33, 70; Susan, 127; Thomas C., 44, 45; Thomas I., 147; William, 5, 118
WHEELER, Ann F., 29, 47, 92; Elizabeth, 92; Enoch, 29, 47, 69; Henrietta Maria, 47; John, 7; Mary, 47; Samuel, 7, 92
WHELAN, Edmund, 111; William, 163
WHELER, James, 31
WHENOR, Isaac, 141
WHITAKER, John B., 121
WHITALL, Israel F., 54
WHITE, Abigail, 52; Catharine, 3, 91; Catherine, 65; Charles, 65; Elizabeth, 170; Esther, 23; George, 9; Hannah, 170; John, 117; John B., 67; Jonathan, 24; Josiah, 170; Mary, 59, 128; Solomon, 170; Thomas H., 120, 121, 159; Tobias, 115
WHITEALL, Edmund, 80; Hestor, 80; Joanna S., 81; Joanna Sanders, 80
WHITECAR, Joseph, 45
WHITEHALL, 160; Israel F., 73
WHITEHEAD, Margaret, 58; R., 7, 39, 75; Richard, 40, 68, 83, 89, 150; Robert, 6, 8, 16, 18, 19, 21, 26, 27, 30, 37, 41, 47, 49, 50, 53, 56, 58, 60, 68, 83, 84, 89, 100, 112, 117, 124, 128, 138, 142, 149, 155, 158, 162, 167, 169; Samuel, 71
WHITELACK, Mary, 45
WHITESIDES, Thomas, 75
WHITIKER, Abel, 105
WHITLOCK, Ann Elizabeth, 171; Ephraim D., 171
WHITTEMORE, Juliana, 13
WHITTICK, Christiana, 135; John, 135; Joseph, 135
WICKERLY, Conrad, 58
WIDDIFIELD, William, 54
WIER, Silas E., 70
WIESSENBACH, Catharine, 142; Elizabeth, 142; Henry, 142; William, 142
WIGGINS, Ruth, 30; Thomas, 30
WIGMORE, Hannah, 147
WILCOCKS, Samuel, 59, 163
WILE, Conrad, 107; George, 121
WILEN, Conrad, 53; Nicholas, 53
WILFONG, David, 168
WILKENS, John, 140
WILKENSON, Charles, 3; Esther, 3; Jacob, 3; Phebe, 3; Tacy, 3; William, 3
WILKEY, Rachel, 74
WILKINS, Adilicia, 41; Amy, 88; Caleb, 88; Catharine, 135; George, 88, 135; Rachel Draper, 88; Samuel, 88; Sarah, 88
WILKINSON, Brian, 102, 118; Mary, 42; William, 42
WILL, Abraham, 6
WILLARD, Benjamin, 4; James, 4; Joseph, 4; Martha, 4; Rachel, 4; Thomas, 4
WILLIAMS, Ann, 92; Anna, 26; Anthony, 54; Catharine, 167; Elizabeth, 103; Ennion, 37; Esther, 26; Evan, 94; George, 59, 92, 101, 138, 166, 170; Grace, 26; Hezekiah, 26; Isaac, 15;

Jesse, 150; John, 23, 167, 169; John L., 54; Judith, 158; Lydia, 26; Margaret, 94, 163; Moses, 129; Oliver, 158; Reed, 84; Rhoda, 121; Samuel, 41, 79, 84; Sarah, 79; Thomas, 41, 84, 103, 159; Thomas R., 159; William, 14
WILLIAMSON, Ann, 85; Benjamin, 92; David, 85; Eleanor Tittermary, 70; Elizabeth, 85, 92; Jesse, 2, 85; John G., 85; John Gardener, 85; Joseph, 85; Mary, 85, 92; Peter, 87, 97; Rebecca, 85; Samuel, 1, 4; Sarah, 85; William, 34
WILLING, Ann, 19; Maria, 38; Thomas, 19; Thomas M., 160
WILLIS, John, 121, 124; Jonathan, 9, 100, 101
WILLS, James, 50, 147
WILLSON, Thomas, 36
WILMER, James, 106
WILMOT, Mary, 122; Rachel, 122
WILSON, Alexander, 147; Anna, 51; Anne, 23; Archibald, 96; Bird, 159; Catharine, 134, 147; Catherine, 23; Clarissa, 62; D., 137; Elizabeth, 23, 72; George, 71, 108, 137; Hannah Lewis, 54; Henry, 117; James, 116; Joel W., 19; John, 121; John B., 51, 134; Joseph, 22; Lellias, 23; Mary, 19, 51, 96, 117; Rachel, 54; Rebecca, 96, 98; Robert, 23, 50, 117; Rudolph, 96; Samuel, 120; Samuel L., 134; Sarah, 19, 23, 96; Sarah L., 134; Silas, 96; Susannah, 23; Thomas, 23; William, 51, 96
WILT, Abraham, 95
WILTE, Matilda, 55
WINE, George, 7
WINEMORE, Jacob, 68
WINTON, Mary, 97
WISEMAN, Catharine, 171; Catharine Maria, 171; Eleanor Maria, 171
WISTAR, Caspar, 20; Catharine, 20; Charlotte, 21; Hannah, 21; John, 20, 21; Richard, 20; Sarah, 20; Thomas, 8, 20
WITMER, Henry, 75, 108; Mary, 75, 108; Mrs., 75; Sarah, 75, 76
WOELPPER, Catharine, 74; Frederick, 113; George, 74, 75, 113; John David, 93; Margaret, 113; Rachel, 113
WOGLOM, Abraham, 160
WOLBERT, Frederick, 111
WOLF, Susanna, 57
WONDERLY, Elizabeth, 129; John, 129; Joseph, 129; Juliana, 129; William, 129; William K., 129
WOOD, Ann, 60, 141; Catherine, 60; Elizabeth, 60; George, 141; George H., 58; James, 102; John, 60; Joseph, 38; Mary, 60; Mary Ann, 141; Richard C., 95; William, 42; Zachariah, 113
WOODCOCK, Bancroft, 150
WOODLAND, Mary, 84
WOODRUFF, Phoebe, 105
WOODS, Hannah, 129; Joseph, 126; Margaret, 141; Mary, 141
WOODWARD, W. W., 26; William W., 92
WOOLSTON, Ann, 100; Elizabeth, 100; Jonathan, 100; Joshua, 100; Lydia, 100; Rachel, 100; Sarah, 100; Stephen, 100, 101
WORKMAN, John, 135; Rebecca, 124; Samuel, 124
WORLEY, Francis, 14
WORRALL, Charles, 172; George, 172; Horatio, 172; Isaac, 172; Jane, 172; Jane Caroline, 172; Joseph C., 172; Mary Sermon, 172; Matilda, 172; Richard, 172; Thomas, 172
WORREL, Hannah, 65
WORRELL, Isaac, 132, 133, 136; Isaiah, 132; Jacob, 132; John H., 132; Mary, 65, 132; Rebecca, 132; Robert, 132, 136; Sarah, 132; Stephen, 132; Thomas, 132; William, 124, 132
WORRILL, Jonathan, 163
WORTHINGTON, Mary, 78
WRAY, Eleanor, 109
WRIGHT, Elihu, 96; John, 81; Mary, 81; Samuel G., 106; Sarah, 92, 109
WULZEL, John, 105
WYNECOPE, Hannah, 16
WYNKOOP, Ann M., 26; Sarah C., 52, 94

-Y-

YAGER, William, 68

WYNECOPE, Hannah, 16
WYNKOOP, Ann M., 26; Sarah C., 52, 94

-Y-

YAGER, William, 68
YARD, Charlot, 110
YARDLEY, Richard, 19; William, 100, 101
YARNALL, Benjamin H., 164; Ellis, 131, 164; Israel, 40; Nathan, 164
YARNEL, Ellis, 80
YEAGER, George, 161; John, 161; Joseph, 162; Kitty, 161; Micheal, 162
YEAKLE, Christopher, 39
YEARDSLEY, James, 35; Sarah, 35
YENSAR, George, 75
YEOWARD, Joseph, 10
YERKES, Anthony, 79; Silas, 134
YETTER, Charles, 59
YONKER, Joseph, 24
YOUGH, Elizabeth, 53; John, 53; Maria, 53
YOUNG, Catharine, 11; David, 77; John, 60, 86; Margaret, 33; Maria, 86; Marks, 158; Martha, 86; Mary, 33; Nicholas, 40; Peter, 33; Prissila, 137; Rebecca, 158; Sarah, 33, 169; Thomas, 137; William, 150
YOURNSON, Giles, 43

-Z-

ZAHRENS, Anthony, 24, 137; Catharine, 137
ZANTZINGER, Susanna, 98
ZEISENGER, Bellague Catharine, 27
ZEISS, Andrew, 155
ZELINE, Mary Elizabeth, 55
ZEOUMAN, M. H., 130
ZIMMAR, Matthias, 75
ZIMMERMAN, Deborah, 90, 91; Jemima, 90, 91
ZOLLICKHOFFER, Henry M., 52
ZOLLICKOFFER, Henry M., 154

Other books by F. Edward Wright:

Abstracts of Bucks County, Pennsylvania Wills, 1685-1785
Abstracts of Cumberland County, Pennsylvania Wills, 1750-1785
Abstracts of Cumberland County, Pennsylvania Wills, 1785-1825
Abstracts of Philadelphia County Wills, 1726-1747
Abstracts of Philadelphia County Wills, 1748-1763
Abstracts of Philadelphia County Wills, 1763-1784
Abstracts of Philadelphia County Wills, 1777-1790
Abstracts of Philadelphia County Wills, 1790-1802
Abstracts of Philadelphia County Wills, 1802-1809
Abstracts of Philadelphia County Wills, 1810-1815
Abstracts of Philadelphia County Wills, 1815-1819
Abstracts of Philadelphia County Wills, 1820-1825
Abstracts of Philadelphia County, Pennsylvania Wills, 1682-1726
Abstracts of South Central Pennsylvania Newspapers, Volume 1, 1785-1790
Abstracts of South Central Pennsylvania Newspapers, Volume 3, 1796-1800
Abstracts of the Newspapers of Georgetown and the Federal City, 1789-99
Abstracts of York County, Pennsylvania Wills, 1749-1819

Bucks County, Pennsylvania Church Records of the 17th and 18th Centuries Volume 2: Quaker Records: Falls and Middletown Monthly Meetings
Anna Miller Watring and F. Edward Wright

Caroline County, Maryland Marriages, Births and Deaths, 1850-1880
Citizens of the Eastern Shore of Maryland, 1659-1750
Cumberland County, Pennsylvania Church Records of the 18th Century
Delaware Newspaper Abstracts, Volume 1: 1786-1795

Early Charles County, Maryland Settlers, 1658-1745
Marlene Strawser Bates and F. Edward Wright

Early Church Records of Alexandria City and Fairfax County, Virginia
F. Edward Wright and Wesley E. Pippenger

Early Church Records of New Castle County, Delaware, Volume 1, 1701-1800

Frederick County Militia in the War of 1812
Sallie A. Mallick and F. Edward Wright

Inhabitants of Baltimore County, 1692-1763
Land Records of Sussex County, Delaware, 1769-1782

Land Records of Sussex County, Delaware, 1782-1789
Elaine Hastings Mason and F. Edward Wright

Marriage Licenses of Washington, District of Columbia, 1811-1830

Marriages and Deaths from the Newspapers of Allegany and Washington Counties, Maryland, 1820-1830

Marriages and Deaths from The York Recorder, 1821-1830

Marriages and Deaths in the Newspapers of Frederick and Montgomery Counties, Maryland, 1820-1830

Marriages and Deaths in the Newspapers of Lancaster County, Pennsylvania, 1821-1830
Marriages and Deaths in the Newspapers of Lancaster County, Pennsylvania, 1831-1840
Marriages and Deaths of Cumberland County, [Pennsylvania], 1821-1830
Maryland Calendar of Wills Volume 9: 1744-1749
Maryland Calendar of Wills Volume 10: 1748-1753
Maryland Calendar of Wills Volume 11: 1753-1760
Maryland Calendar of Wills Volume 12: 1759-1764
Maryland Calendar of Wills Volume 13: 1764-1767
Maryland Calendar of Wills Volume 14: 1767-1772
Maryland Calendar of Wills Volume 15: 1772-1774
Maryland Calendar of Wills Volume 16: 1774-1777
Maryland Eastern Shore Newspaper Abstracts, Volume 1: 1790-1805
Maryland Eastern Shore Newspaper Abstracts, Volume 2: 1806-1812
Maryland Eastern Shore Newspaper Abstracts, Volume 3: 1813-1818
Maryland Eastern Shore Newspaper Abstracts, Volume 4: 1819-1824
Maryland Eastern Shore Newspaper Abstracts, Volume 5: Northern Counties, 1825-1829
F. Edward Wright and Irma Harper
Maryland Eastern Shore Newspaper Abstracts, Volume 6: Southern Counties, 1825-1829
Maryland Eastern Shore Newspaper Abstracts, Volume 7: Northern Counties, 1830-1834
Irma Harper and F. Edward Wright
Maryland Eastern Shore Newspaper Abstracts, Volume 8: Southern Counties, 1830-1834
Maryland Militia in the Revolutionary War
S. Eugene Clements and F. Edward Wright
Newspaper Abstracts of Allegany and Washington Counties, 1811-1815
Newspaper Abstracts of Cecil and Harford Counties, [Maryland], 1822-1830
Newspaper Abstracts of Frederick County, [Maryland], 1816-1819
Newspaper Abstracts of Frederick County, 1811-1815
Sketches of Maryland Eastern Shoremen
Tax List of Chester County, Pennsylvania 1768
Tax List of York County, Pennsylvania 1779
Washington County Church Records of the 18th Century, 1768-1800
Western Maryland Newspaper Abstracts, Volume 1: 1786-1798
Western Maryland Newspaper Abstracts, Volume 2: 1799-1805
Western Maryland Newspaper Abstracts, Volume 3: 1806-1810
Wills of Chester County, Pennsylvania, 1766-1778

www.ingramcontent.com/pod-product-compliance
Lightning Source LLC
Chambersburg PA
CBHW070657100426
42735CB00039B/2174